New Canadian Readings

A HISTORY OF ONTARIO

SELECTED READINGS

D0631636

Edited by
Michael J. Piva

Copp Clark Pitman Ltd.
A Longman Company
Toronto

ISBN 0-7730-4739-5

Editing: Camilla Jenkins
Design: Kathy Cloutier
Cover Illustration: Susan Coull
Typesetting: Compeer Typographic Services Limited
Printing and Binding: Alger Press Ltd.

Canadian Cataloguing in Publication Data

Main entry under title:
A History of Ontario

(New Canadian Readings)
Bibliography: p.
ISBN 0-7730-4739-5

1. Ontario – History – 1841–1867.* 2. Ontario – History – 1967– .*
I. Piva, Michael J., 1946– . II. Series.

FC3061.H57 1988   971.3   C87-094161-5
F1058.H57 1988

Photo credits: p. 28, Lawrence M. Lande Collection, Public Archives of Canada/PA 112313; p. 162, Provincial Archives of Ontario, Historical Collection, Toronto Board of Education; p. 251, Public Archives of Canada/C26935

Copp Clark Pitman Ltd.
2775 Matheson Blvd. East
Mississauga
Ontario

Associated Companies:
    Longman Group Ltd., London
    Longman Inc., New York
    Longman Cheshire Pty., Melbourne
    Longman Paul Pty., Auckland

Printed and bound in Canada

FOREWORD

New Canadian Readings is an on-going series of inexpensive books intended to bring some of the best recent work by this country's scholars to the attention of students of Canada. Each volume consists of ten or more articles or book sections, carefully selected to present a fully formed thesis about some critical aspect of Canadian development. Where useful, public documents or even private letters and statistical materials may be used as well to convey a different and fresh perspective.

The authors of the readings selected for inclusion in this volume (and all the others in the series) are all first-rank scholars, those who are doing the hard research that is rapidly changing our understanding of this country. Quite deliberately, the references for each selection have been retained, thus making additional research as easy as possible.

Like the authors of the individual articles, the editors of each volume are also scholars of note, completely up-to-date in their areas of specialization and, as the introductions demonstrate, fully aware of the changing nature of the debates within their professions and genres of research. The list of additional readings provided by the editor of each volume will steer readers to materials that could not be included because of space limitations.

This series will continue into the foreseeable future, and the General Editor is pleased to invite suggestions for additional topics.

J.L. Granatstein
General Editor

CONTENTS

Foreword   iii
Introduction _____   1

David P. Gagan, Families and Land: The Mid-Century Crisis   6

Paul Craven and Tom Traves, Canadian Railways as Manufac-   29
turers, 1850–1880

Stephen A. Speisman, Munificent Parsons and Municipal Parsi-   55
mony: Voluntary v. Public Poor Relief in Nineteenth Century
Toronto

Gregory S. Kealey, The Orange Order in Toronto: Religious Riot   71
and the Working Class

Kenneth C. Dewar, Private Electrical Utilities and Municipal   95
Ownership in Ontario, 1891–1900

Craig Heron, The Crisis of the Craftsman: Hamilton's Metal   109
Workers in the Early Twentieth Century

Marilyn Barber, The Women Ontario Welcomed: Immigrant   144
Domestics for Ontario Homes, 1870–1930

Robert M. Stamp, The New Education Movement—Those   161
"Yankee Frills"

Peter Oliver, The Resolution of the Ontario Bilingual Schools   185
Crisis, 1919–1929

John C. Weaver, From Land Assembly to Social Maturity: The   214
Suburban Life of Westdale (Hamilton), Ontario, 1911–1951

Marc J. Gotlieb, George Drew and the Dominion-Provincial   242
Conference on Reconstruction of 1945–6

Peter Oliver, Inner-City Politician   260

Vaughan Lyon, Minority Government in Ontario, 1975–1981: An   284
Assessment

Sylvia B. Bashevkin, Women's Participation in the Ontario Political   301
Parties, 1971–1981

Further Reading _____   316

INTRODUCTION

"**O**ntario, Does it Exist?"[1] When A.R.M. Lower posed the question two decades ago it did not seem as odd as his answer: no. Long before Maurice Careless took the worry out of being parochial, most Canadians understood that theirs was a nation of regions and "limited identities."[2] There was no lack of evidence pointing to strong and potent regional loyalties in the Maritimes, in Quebec and in the West. Ontario, however, was different. No one doubted that Ontario was a region of sorts, yet it seemed to defy description or analysis.

Lower was neither the first nor the last to wonder if Ontario was anything more than "a space on the map, . . . a legal entity administered from Toronto."[3] In the early 1960s, *Ontario History* noted its own preoccupation with pre-Ontario history; only six of seventy-five articles published between 1957 and 1961 were on post-Confederation Ontario.[4] When Peter Oliver, one of only a handful of committed "Ontario" historians, penned a 1975 essay entitled "On Being an Ontarian," he concluded in effect that it remained "Yours to Discover." *Ontario History* had improved its record, yet, as Oliver observed, two-thirds of the articles published between 1971 and 1973 explored pre-Confederation themes.[5] Ontario, he suggested, is "at least so far as written history is concerned, a have-not province."[6]

There have been a number of efforts to correct this situation, including government intervention into scholarly production. In 1971, the provincial government launched the Ontario Historical Studies Series, an ambitious program to produce a "comprehensive history of Ontario." Authors were commissioned, but production has been slow. The first biography, Oliver's *G. Howard Ferguson*, appeared in 1977, followed by J.M.S. Careless's edited collection *The Pre-Conferation Premiers* (1980). *Ontario Since 1867* by Joseph Schull appeared in 1978. The first of the "theme" volumes, Christopher Armstrong's *The Politics of Federalism*, appeared in 1981.

Oliver's 1975 appeal and the appearance of the first volumes of the Ontario Historical Studies Series seemed to portend a renaissance in Ontario scholarship. "Explosion," R.T. Clippingdale suggested in 1977, "is certainly the right word to describe the work now under way."[7] It was an explosion that underwhelmed some scholars. S.F. Wise, for example, begins a 1985 essay on "Ontario's Political Culture" by referring to Lower's question and Oliver's lament.[8]

The lament, however, seems as odd today as Lower's question two decades ago. Wise comments that many of Oliver's colleagues "would resent being called 'Ontario' historians; they, and for that matter most Ontarians, do not perceive the province to be merely a region, but rather a kind of provincial equivalent of Canada as a whole."[9] If not always addressing "regional" issues, Ontario's many historians have, nonetheless, written a great deal about the province. Indeed, there are a number of studies that, although defining their topic in general terms, deal exclusively with the province yet are not readily identified as "regional" history. Gregory Kealey's *Toronto Workers Respond to Industrial Capitalism*, for example, tells us much about life in Ontario, yet was not cited by the Regional History Committee of the Canadian Historical Association. The same could be said for a score of other recent titles.

Certainly enough has been written to make the problem of selection in a collection of this kind difficult. This volume attempts to introduce the reader to the main streams in Ontario history and historiography. It tries to strike a balance between the nineteenth and early twentieth centuries, the interwar and postwar years. Individual articles dealing with more narrowly defined topics together address major political, social, economic, and intellectual trends. They reflect as well diverse methodological and historiographical interests. It is hoped that they will also provoke interest, discussion, and further reading.

Such a collection must begin with Ontarians themselves. At Confederation most lived in the countryside where they tilled the rich soils of the province. In 1872, Oliver Mowat declared that agriculture was "our great source of wealth, upon which our whole population depended."[10] Agriculture, however, was not without its problems. External markets were soft and new land not easy to come by. Ontario's farmers had to adjust; that adjustment is the subject of David Gagan's essay "Families and Land." As he shows, solutions short of subdivision helped maintain the economic health of the agricultural sector, but also promoted high rates of transiency. The "Canadian" inheritance system sent many children packing.

The process of both urbanization and industrialization helped absorb this surplus agricultural population. In the initial stages manufacturing depended upon agriculture. Often, dependence was direct; the province's agrcultural implements industry is an obvious case. The link could also be indirect. As Paul Craven and Tom Traves point out, railways, originally constructed to carry primary products to waiting markets, themselves became major manufacturers in their drive to be cost efficient. Such enterprises were "national" in scope, yet the bulk of the manufacturing development, as Craven and Traves show, was in Ontario. Over the next half-century, manufacturing became increasingly concentrated in Montreal and Ontario. That concentration of secondary manufacturing ensured Ontario's dominant economic position in Canada.

The benefits of economic prosperity generated by rich soils and expanding industries did not always percolate down to the ordinary citizen. Many urban workers, particularly the unskilled, were desperately poor. Their numbers grew, and the state was slow to react to their many problems. Stephen Speisman discusses the factors that promoted private charity but inhibited public welfare during the nineteenth century.

As with private charities, religious and ethnic loyalties divided Ontarians. Protestant-Catholic squabbles, usually over schools, provided grist for the political mill. Industrialization, however, created new social problems and brought new social alignments. Artisans, for example, responded to the new challenges by adapting older pre-industrial traditions and institutions. The tension created when newer class loyalties emerged within the context of older religious loyalties is the topic of Gregory Kealey's "The Orange Order in Toronto."

Industrialization during the last half of the nineteenth century was based primarily upon metal; countries measured their relative industrial might in terms of steel production. In this context, Ontario competed at a disadvantage as many basic raw materials were not available within its borders. At the end of the century, the development of high-tension wires, which allowed the transportation of electricity over great distances, eliminated one of Ontario's major economic liabilities. Not without reason Ontarians referred to hydro-electricity as "white coal." Kenneth Dewar examines the first stage of a decade-long debate over control of this vital resource.

Hydro development was but one factor promoting economic expansion. In addition, a new mining frontier opened in the northern parts of the province, and new markets opened in the west. Together these various factors brought a period of intense industrial growth that transformed both Canada and Ontario. At the heart of this process were technological changes that fundamentally altered the nature of work. Craig Heron analyses this process in his study of Hamilton's metal workers.

Marilyn Barber discusses another aspect of the economic boom. The influx of large numbers of new immigrants promoted economic growth. Many of those immigrants were young single women for whom work was most readily available in domestic service. Indeed, the Canadian elite and the Canadian government undertook programs encouraging the immigration of single women for domestic service. These women, however, often preferred work in factories or in the new and rapidly expanding sales and clerical occupations. These various questions are explored in "The Women Ontario Welcomed."

Rapid industrialization also intensified the process of urbanization, which in turn compounded many social problems such as public health and public welfare. New reform movements emerged to address the problems of drink, juvenile delinquency, infant mortality, slum housing, inefficient civic governments, and a host of other concerns. Such movements sometimes recruited a large following and affected the lives of many people. The reformers who affected the largest numbers revamped Ontario's public education system. Robert M. Stamp discusses the "New Education" introduced into the provincial school system.

The reforms associated with the "new education" aroused fewer passions than the older questions of religion and language. During the 1880s and 1890s, the militant Protestant Protective Association and the Equal Rights Association launched new attacks on the separate school system as a result of exaggerated fears of "papal aggression." The conflict would shift ground around the turn of the century as a result of equally exaggerated fears over language.

Francophones had been moving in increasing numbers into the Ottawa Valley. They often converted local separate schools into separate bilingual schools and, frequently, unilingual French schools. Anglophone fears for the English language combined with Irish Catholic fears over the loss of control of separate school boards to convince the Conservative government in 1912 to act. Regulation 17 denied the Franco-Ontarian community basic linguistic rights. Many scholars have dealt with the crisis itself; Peter Oliver discusses its resolution.

This crisis would be resolved during a decade of prosperity. The automobile had clearly triumphed, and its multifarious impact was becoming manifest. Not the least significant was suburban sprawl. Although we tend to associate the 1950s with the emergence of suburban culture, John Weaver demonstrates that the roots of suburbanization go back several decades before that.

The prosperity of the 1920s ended with the collapse of the American stock market in 1929. An economic catastrophe of the first order, the Depression hit export-led economies like Canada's particularly severely. As governments grappled with unprecedented problems, many observers came to believe that the decentralized nature of Confederation inhibited effective action. Advocates of a more centralized Canada found expression in the studies of the Rowell-Sirois Commission, which submitted its report in 1939. In that year war in Europe helped end the decade-long economic maelstrom; war-time experience, in turn, altered many of the rules of both the economic and the political game.

Under the War Measures Act, the federal government expanded its powers and invaded a number of provincial jurisdictions. Many within the federal government would have liked those changes to become permanent. Many within the Ontario government were equally determined to return to the constitutional status quo ante-bellum. From the days of Oliver Mowat, Ontario had been a loud and consistent voice for the rights of provinces under the British North America Act. As Marc J. Gotlieb shows, it would be no different with George Drew at the first postwar Dominion-Provincial conference in 1945–46.

While challenging the power of the federal government, Drew also helped to establish a Conservative dynasty in the province. During the 1950s the Conservatives governed a dynamic, prosperous, and stable society. By the 1960s, however, a new reform movement emerged to challenge "establishment" parties and politicians. New community-based political forces at the municipal level were at the centre of the political challenge. As Peter Oliver shows, "Unlikely Tories" like Allan Grossman assumed new importance during this more turbulent period, which in turn helped transform the Conservative Party.

Such adaptations allowed the Tories to remain in power. Throughout most of the postwar period, however, the government party fell short — often significantly short — of an electoral majority. By 1975 the three-party system so evident in the popular vote translated itself into a minority government. Although the Conservatives would win a majority in 1981, by 1985 it would be the Liberals' turn to rule as a minority. Vaughan Lyon provides "An Assessment" of Ontario's minority experience between 1975 and 1981 based upon "insider" information provided by politicians and mandarins.

Ontario's minority governments have had to face a number of challenges not the least of which was the emergence of the women's movement during the 1970s. Activist women have helped alter the political agenda in many ways. New issues such as "equal pay for work of equal value" have emerged as old priorities have been reshuffled. Sylvia B. Bashevkin analyses the response of Ontario political parties to women during the 1970s.

This collection of essays cannot be comprehensive. It does, however, touch, as we have seen, some of the more important events and issues that inform our past. The material contained here should do more than instruct; it should stimulate greater interest in ourselves. There are literally dozens of essays and books that I would have liked to include. The bibliography of suggested readings provides a guide for the inquisitive.

Notes

1. A.R.M. Lower, "Ontario — Does It Exist?" *Ontario History* LX (1968): 65–69.
2. J.M.S. Careless, " 'Limited Identities' in Canada," *Canadian Historical Review* L (1969): 1–10.
3. Lower, "Ontario — Does It Exist," 69.
4. Paul Cornell and Kenneth MacKirdy, "An Editorial," *Ontario History* LIV (1962): 225.
5. Peter Oliver, "On Being an Ontarian," in *Public and Private Persons: The Ontario Political Culture, 1914–1934* (Toronto: Clark, Irwin, 1975), 6.
6. Ibid., 10.
7. R.T. Clippingdale, "The Renaissance of Ontario History," *Acadiensis* VIII (1978): 121.
8. S.F. Wise, "Ontario's Political Culture," in *Government and Politics of Ontario*, 3rd. ed., edited by Donald C. MacDonald (Scarborough, Ont.: Nelson, 1985), 160–61.
9. Ibid., 161.
10. *Globe*, 30 November 1872, cited in A. Margaret Evans, "Oliver Mowat: Nineteenth-Century Ontario Liberal," in *Oliver Mowat's Ontario*, edited by D. Swainson (Toronto: Macmillan, 1972), 43.

FAMILIES AND LAND: THE MID-CENTURY CRISIS†

DAVID P. GAGAN

In 1851 the population of Peel County was 24 816. A decade later it had increased by 9.8 percent to 27 240. When the next census was taken in 1871 it revealed that in the preceding decade Peel had lost 5 percent of its 1861 population, in spite of the skyrocketing growth of the county's new town, Brampton, whose population had increased 65 percent in the 1860s. Put another way, the *rural* population of Peel County in 1871 (23 331) was not only significantly smaller, by 10 percent, than it had been a decade earlier, there were actually fewer rural dwellers in the county in 1871 than there had been in 1851 when Peel was still considered a field for immigration, and when there was still vacant land in two of the five townships. Moreover, the population of the county — rural and urban — continued to decline for the remainder of the nineteenth century. In 1890 the total population of Peel was essentially what it had been in 1850.

These are the elementary facts of Peel's demographic history in the middle decades of the nineteenth century. They invite, indeed require, analysis. Why is it that, at a time when Upper Canadians were exercised over the annexation of a new agricultural frontier in the west as an outlet for population, there is striking evidence in Peel and elsewhere in the heartland of Upper Canadian agriculture (see table 1) not of rural overpopulation but rather of demographic decline? What combination of circumstances transformed the frontier of pioneer settlement of the late 1830s and early 1840s in the apparently stagnant community of the 1860s? How did it transpire that an area which was demonstrably underpopulated, in terms of the availability of vacant land, at any time between 1819 and 1855, could move from underpopulation to depopulation in less than two decades? These are questions which might equally be posed in relation to the general pattern of the ebb and flow of population in mid-Victorian Ontario. As table 1 suggests, demographic decline or stagnation was prevalent among the

†David P. Gagan, *Hopeful Travellers: Families, Land, and Social Change in Mid-Victorian Peel County, Canada West* (Toronto, University of Toronto Press, 1981), 40–60.

south-central and eastern lakeshore counties of Canada West in the 1860s, perhaps confirming the gloomy auguries of the politicians. But this trend was clearly offset by a northwestward-moving line of demographic growth which evidently had not run its course by 1870. What factors and processes account for this dichotomy, these paradoxical aspects of growth and stagnation in a rural society in which the oldest communities, in 1860, were barely sexagenarians?

TABLE 1

Net Population Change (%), Selected Ontario Counties, 1850–70

	1850–60	1860–70
Bruce	+869%	+76%
Grey	+193	+57
Essex	+ 49	+30
Kent-Lambton	+ 98	+42
Huron	+171	+27
Middlesex	+ 48	+37
Elgin	+ 26	+ 5
Perth	+145	+22
Oxford	+ 42	+ 4
Norfolk	+ 34	+ 8
Waterloo	+ 46	+ 4
Brant	+ 19	+ 6
Wentworth	+ 12	− 3
Halton	+ 24	− 1
Peel	+ 10	− 5
York	+ 22	nil
Ontario	+ 36	+10
Northhumberland	+ 30	− 2
Hastings	+ 41	+ 8
Prince Edward	+ 10	− 3
Lennox-Addington-Frontenac	+ 31	− 2
Dundas	+ 36	nil
Stormont	+ 24	+ 5
Glengarry	+ 20	− 3

SOURCE: *Census of the Canadas, 1851–2*, vol. I, 311; *Census of the Canadas, 1860–1*, vol. I, 521–7; *Census of Canada, 1870–71*, vol. I, table 1.

At the simplest level of explanation it might appear that, with some anomalies, these demographic trends merely reflect the much-discussed operation of the "frontier" as a force in North American history. Attracted by the opportunities for social and economic improvement represented by undeveloped territory, the theory assumes, populations routinely vacated established communities, moving to new frontiers where the unique social and economic processes inherent in the interaction between men and virgin land were initiated once again. In their wake, these migrant populations left a succession of mature societies in which economic success and social improvement were dependent on techniques of conservation rather than exploitation.[1] No longer attractive to immigrants who equated prosperity with production as opposed, for example, to the greater availability of goods and services in, or the cultural benefits of an established society, these communities attained a state of equilibrium, demographic, social, and economic, and they rested until technological change, industrialization for example, once again altered the nature of opportunity there.

As appealing as this scenario is, it nevertheless fails to account for the anomalies that inevitably arise in real, as opposed to hypothetical historical circumstances. One of those anomalies is self-evident in table 1. Some of the oldest settled rural communities in Canada West continued to add to their rural populations long after they had passed the frontier stage of development and long before either industrialization or urbanization became an important factor there. A more interesting variant is represented by Peel County and, I suspect, other communities in Canada West. Simply put, by the mid-1850s the assimilation of new farm families into the economy of rural Peel County was possible only through the death or displacement of established farmers, or the subdivision of existing farms. Subdivision was unacceptable because it undermined the theory and practice of agrarian capitalism as it had developed under the aegis of the wheat economy. More, not less, land was what the improving farmer thought he required. Thus, established farmers themselves, as much as recently arrived migrants, represented a constant source of pressure on land available for cultivation, land for their own requirements and for their maturing, soon to be independent, children. The upshot of the subsequent mania for land amid unstable economic conditions from 1856 to 1865 was a period of rapid social change as the problem of too many people competing for too little land promoted, equally, a major redistribution of land in Peel County as well as a search for alternative strategies to promote the social and economic security of the farm family as the problem of land availability became more intractable. In effect, the roots of demographic and social change in Peel County from 1850 to 1870 can be traced, in the first instance, to the economic self-interest of the county's improving farm families.

In America, the farmers' frontier lasted until 1890. In parts of Canada, northern Alberta for example, land for homesteading was still available in the late 1960s. In Ontario, the agricultural frontier, if it ever existed as a "frontier" in the classical sense of the term — an area adjacent to a settled region in which a low ratio of population to cheap and abundant land favoured the social and economic objectives of the small agrarian capitalist[2] — came to an end when Bruce County was opened to settlement in 1854. If Peel ever was a frontier in that sense it had moved beyond the frontier stage of its development very quickly. The average price of an acre of Peel's land in the 1840s, $12, was no bargain. Immigrants were taught that they could buy the best farms in developed townships for just $2 an acre more.[3] Nor, as we have seen earlier, was land abundant in Peel in the 1840s. By 1842 nine-tenths of the county's arable acreage was in private hands, however unimproved it might have been. Finally, by 1851 the population per 1000 occupied acres in Peel, 99, was already higher than for some of the earliest settled counties of the province, for example Lennox-Addington and Frontenac (85), and significantly greater than for areas of more recent settlement such as Huron (68), Grey (59), and Perth (67) counties. In short, judged by those measures which define the frontier as a place, Peel had ceased to enjoy that status after twenty years of active settlement.

If, however, we characterize the frontier in terms of the social and economic processes which take place there, there is something to be said for defending Peel's image, even in the 1850s, as a frontier environment. The economics of frontier agriculture consisted in the extensive, rather than intensive, use of land to produce a cash crop for exchange in the marketplace. The crude equation of ample land and labour with productivity and prosperity, and a casual disdain for the scientific farmer's conservationist techniques on the assumption that exhausted soil could always be abandoned for fertile virgin land elsewhere, were the hallmarks of the frontier farmer. In Upper Canada they were called "wheat miners"[4] and the farmers of Peel's till plain were no exceptions. They followed the system of continuous cropping of cereal grains, especially wheat, and were warned as early as 1856 by one of their own, John Lynch of Brampton, who was a recognized authority on agriculture in the province, that "the time will come . . . when the present rich and productive land of Canada will not only fail to produce a heavy crop of wheat . . . but will become incapable of producing wheat at all to any profitable amount."[5] Nevertheless, as late as 1870, when the transition to mixed farming was well under way in Ontario, the single characteristic of agricultural production which set Peel apart from every other county in the province was Peel's significantly higher ratio of cropped to occupied acreage.[6] Thus, throughout the period, land in Peel continued to be evaluated by the pioneer's rule of thumb — "a farm incapable of producing [wheat was] practically valueless"[7] — and was bought and sold on the strength of its natural productivity. For example, in Caledon Township in 1860 reported farm values varied directly and significantly in relation to land capability, that is to soil quality, and bore no significant relationship to any other factor.[8]

This wheat culture, rooted in the extensive cropping of naturally fertile soil by little familial armies of cultivators whose collective labour was at once the motive power and the working capital of the frontier farm, was firmly fixed in place when the wheat boom and the railroad mania of the 1850s conspired to focus the attention of speculators, immigrants, and improving farmers from outside the county on Peel's productive capacity and its new-found agricultural prosperity. Population growth, the appearance of a new commercial town, and the disappearance of the county's remaining vacant lands were all symptomatic of the advent of this new era. So too was the behaviour of Peel's established farm families. Between 1850 and 1860 their ratio of cropped to occupied acreage increased by 22 percent, while the proportion of their cropped acreage devoted to wheat increased by 10 percent. More significantly, they began to expand their farms, enlarging the territory available for cultivation in response to a buoyant market. As table 2 indicates, in 1851 approximately 16 percent of land occupiers in Peel held more than 100 acres. Their acreage represented about 37 percent of all land held. Two decades later, more than 25 percent of Peel's occupiers held at least 101 acres and their lands comprised 54 percent of the county's occupied land. It is clear that these expanding farmers gained at the expense of families who occupied between 11 and 100 acres, many of whom were reduced, apparently, to the level of small-holders. Moreover, it is also clear that this transition was virtually complete by 1861.[9] The result, in any case, was a substantial alteration in the rural landscape. Average farm size increased, in twenty years, by about 40 percent — from 98 to 140 acres. Among the most established group of families, farm size increased by more than 60 percent (see table 8 below). In 1850 Peel County had contained only 56 holdings larger than 200 acres and merely 5 of these exceeded 500 acres. Two decades later, of the 136 farms over 200 acres, 18 encompassed more than 500. Land, lots of land, apparently was still the prescription for economic success and social improvement in this community in spite of the critics who thought that "one of the great banes of the Canadian farmer consists in the occupancy of too much land."[10]

TABLE 2

Distribution of Families by Percentage of Total Land Occupied, Peel County, 1851, 1871

	1851		1871	
	Pop'n (%)	Land (%)	Pop'n (%)	Land (%)
10 acres or less	10.4	0.7	13.8	0.8
11–50 acres	21.3	8.0	15.2	5.0
51–100 acres	52.4	54.0	45.4	40.2
101–200 acres	13.7	29.0	20.7	37.0
Over 200 acres	2.7	8.0	4.7	17.0
Total	100.0	100.0	100.0	100.0

There remained a still more profound reason for the expansion of farm territory in the 1850s, a reason also related to the exigencies of land extensive, labour intensive pioneer agriculture. In the 1840s and 1850s the motive power of the family farm was the farm family, especially its children. Their contribution to the social and economic improvement of the cash-poor immigrant family in a period of chronic labour shortages was universally praised by nineteenth-century commentators. Satisfying children's, especially sons', legitimate expectations of future compensation commensurate with their contribution to the economy of the family was an equally compelling reason to assemble additional property. Indeed (if the memoirs of immigrants are trustworthy reflections of parental motivation) Canadian parents seem to have been anxious to promote the independence and security of their children as a reward for their long subordination to the family's common goal, improvement. Patrick Shirreff, who toured the province in the 1830s, marvelled at the tenacity of a man who systematically acquired 1000 acres, having started with a hundred, so that his nine sons might share his own sense of independence.[11] A hundred acres for each son was a patrimony more readily acquired in the 1830s than in the 1850s or 1860s when the press of population, native-born as well as immigrant, was rapidly eroding the province's frontier of uncultivated land. But such a patrimony was the historical promise of the Canadian backwoods; and the culture of the Canadian farm family, symbolized ultimately by the transmission of property from one generation to the next, bound it to the values and expectations of successive generations of farm children nourished on the promise of security and improvement through the possession of landed property.[12]

TABLE 3

Summary Data for Male Population, Peel County, 1851–71 *

	1851	1861	1871
No. of males over 15 years	7285	8252	6735
Males 15–30 years as percentage of all males	54	52	54
Males 15–30 years per 1000 males 40–60 years	2433	2741	2203
Males 15–30 years per 1000 acres available land†	29	41	29

*From published aggregates.
†'Available land' is calculated as the sum of uncultivated land held by occupiers, all land freed through mortality (20/1000 among males 30–70 years), and land freed through outmigration of occupiers (5 percent of total annually).

In the middle decades of the nineteenth century, half the male population over the age of fifteen consisted of men not yet thirty (see table 3). These were the youths whose labour fuelled the farm economy in the late forties and early fifties and who stood ready, in the late fifties and early sixties, to launch their own enterprises. And like the "boomies" of the 1950s who appeared, like a demographic aneurism, in the arteries of education, employment, and social security in the 1960s and 1970s, this rising generation made its presence felt in the 1850s, especially in terms of the ability of Peel's rural economy to fulfil their social aspirations. Between 1851 and 1861 the number of males aged fifteen to thirty for every 1000 acres of available land in Peel increased by more than 40 percent. Their numbers, in relation to the size of the next oldest cohort (their fathers), increased 13 percent. Few alternatives were available to satisfy this generation's desire for land. Eighty miles to the north, in the "Queen's Bush," land was still plentiful and cheap, and in 1861 the census takers noted that some of Peel's young men were clearing farms in Grey and Bruce counties. Another possibility was to subdivide existing farms into smaller economic units; but the marketplace and his own goal of improvement through extensive cropping clearly led the Canadian farmer to reject this European custom. Instead, some of Peel's farmers chose to compete with their neighbours, with speculators, new immigrants, and, in some cases undoubtedly, their own sons, for new territory which would increase their productivity in the short term and, in the end, perhaps provide patrimonies for more than one of their children. Others, unwilling or unable to compete with what became a rapidly escalating battle for land, turned to the laws of inheritance to resolve the problem of too many men competing for too little land in an economy that favoured the opposite principle. In either case, this problem was essentially homegrown, and it could be resolved only by the application of home remedies.

FIGURE 1

Trend Line and Three-Year Moving Averages for Cost of Land per Acre, Peel County, 1840–70

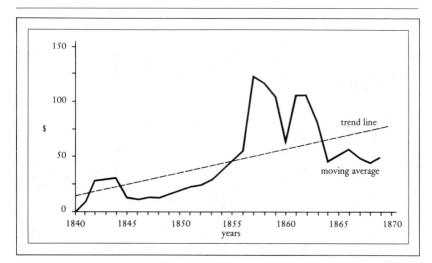

The effects of the economic and demographic pressures on Peel's finite supply of rural land are graphically illustrated in figure 1, which describes both the long-range trend (trend line) and the short-term fluctuations (moving averages) of land prices in Peel between 1840 and 1870.[13] As the trend line predicts, land worth less than $15 an acre in 1840 would more than quadruple in value by 1870. Inflation, devaluation, and variable conversion rates from sterling to decimal currency during the period may account for some of this startling appreciation. Nevertheless, the trend of prices adequately reflects the ever increasing pressure on land in the community as a result of the two most important factors, supply and demand. The situation benefitted established owners in the long run, just as it was detrimental to tenant farmers whose rents were tied to the market value of land (2–4 percent of current value) and to aspiring farmers lacking capital or credit. But the behaviour of land prices in the long term was scarcely cause for alarm. Men of property invested a good deal of faith, after all, in the predictability of rising land prices. It was the unpredictability of the market from year to year, its short-term behaviour, which severely tested the average farmer's faith in land as good security for himself and for his children.

By 1853, at the height of the wheat boom, the mania for land at any price was clearly in full flight, driving the cost of an acre to astronomical levels in just four years. Neither the collapse of the railroad bubble nor the commercial depression of 1857 to 1860 had sustained effects on the price of land. Not until the mid-sixties, after a decade of inflation punctured only by a brief plunge in 1859–60, was some semblance of rationality restored to property values. That development coincided, not surprisingly, with a sudden fall in wheat prices — from $1.40 per bushel in 1859 to $1.15 in 1861, then to 95¢ and 96¢ in 1863 and 1864 respectively — and with the first of a succession of poor harvests as wheat rust and midge increasingly plagued Peel's crops. Farmers were clearly unwilling to risk additional capital at a time when it was more prudent to tighten their belts. Moreover, farmers were speculators too, nothwithstanding the fact that they worked their investments, and many of them had already taken a beating in the scramble for land.[14] The value of property acquired at the height of the expansionist movement plummetted 60 percent in just two years. Its owners would not recover their investment quickly, and in the meantime they had the added burden of repaying the expensive borrowed capital with which many of them had financed their transactions.

TABLE 4

Mortgaged Indebtedness, Peel County, 1850–70

	1851	1861	1871
Percentage of total acreage mortgaged	11.3	38.0	16.2
Value of mortgages ($)	228 708	1 915 029	812 271
Mean debt per mortgaged acre ($)	27.38	64.87	49.54
Debt per acre of county land ($)	1.00	7.00	3.00
Per capita debt, total population ($)	9.00	70.00	30.00
Average interest rate last 10 years (%)	7	8.3	7.4
Average term (years)	4	5	5

In 1850, about 11 percent of the county's acreage was mortgaged, representing a communal debt of approximately $1 per acre or $9 per capita (see table 4). Ten years later, the proportion of indentured acreage had more than tripled and the community's level of indebtedness stood at $70 for each man, woman, and child. Furthermore, the decennial average rate of interest cited in table 4, 8 percent, obscures the more important fact that during the years of highest land prices (1857–61) the effective mortgage interest rate was 11 percent, while rates of 15, 18, and even 20 percent were not uncommon.[15] In short, the costs of more favourable family/land ratios, for whatever purpose, included an unprecedented level of mortgaged indebtedness in a community of farmers who historically had shunned indentures against real property as a means of financing improvements and additions.[16] The farmers of Peel were not unique in this regard. Commenting in 1871 on the land craze of the fifties and its subsequent repercussions, the editor of the *Canadian Farmer* wondered at the otherwise "sober and sedate" people who "spent all their ready cash . . . nay even mortgaged the homestead" with "often fatal" results because they "thought of nothing but additional land."[17] He was also convinced that this phenomenon had been particularly acute in the rural districts west of Toronto. At any rate, as table 6 implies, the Peel farmer who mortgaged his future in the fifties redeemed his notes in the sixties under much altered economic circumstances which had a demonstrably sobering effect on both real estate and mortgage markets throughout the decade.

Who, then, indulged in this costly enterprise? By observing changes over time in the landholding patterns of Peel's rural proprietors it is possible to distinguish those who expanded their holdings from those who did not, and to compare their characteristics. Because of the difficulties of creating continuous data for the entire county from incomplete records, however, a sample is employed here representing those *permanent* families who resided in Chinguacousy Township from before 1850 until after 1870 and for whom continuous data exist. The sample is small but revealing. One-third of the permanent families of Chinguacousy increased their territory, two-thirds did not. The expansionist families added, on the average, 95 acres to their original holdings which in turn had averaged about 95 acres compared to the slightly larger farms (averaging 115 acres) of those families who did not enter the land market for additional acreage. What is of particular importance, at any rate, is that half of the "improving" families added the equivalent of at least one farm (i.e., 100 acres) to their holdings between 1850 and 1870. Moreover, with a single exception all of those struck by the land fever were farmers. Only one apparent "speculator," a merchant, was among them.

More to the point, as table 5 indicates, men who were between the ages of twenty-five and thirty-four in 1852 were significantly overrepresented among the heads of the expansionist families, just as men on the verge of retirement in 1852, that is, aged fifty-five to sixty-four, were particularly visible among those whose farms did not increase in size. In short, additional land seems to have become especially important to men whose families, from the vantage-point of 1852, would predictably increase and grow to maturity in the next twenty years. This conclusion is borne out by the data for family size in relation to farm expansion (table 6). The improving families were represented by a disproportionately large number of men with no children in their households, while men whose families were substantially completed (four to six children living at home) by 1852 were overrepresented among those who were content with the status quo. Put another way, in a community in which five or six children of the eight or nine normally produced by a marriage survived to maturity, nearly half (47 percent) of the families requiring more land in the 1850s and 1860s were still quite small in 1852. From this perspective, farm expansion anticipated the needs of growing families both for a rising standard of living and for land for their sons.

TABLE 5

Distribution of Heads of Family by Age Cohort, 1852, and Farm Extension, Chinguacousy Township, 1850–70

Age of Head of Family, 1852 (years)	Farm Size Increased 1850–70 (%)	Farm Size Did Not Increase 1850–70 (%)	Total Pop'n (%)
15–24	4.7	4.6	4.6
25–34	27.9	19.5	22.3
35–44	37.2	37.9	37.7
45–54	25.6	27.6	26.9
55–65	4.6	9.2	7.7
65 and over	0	1.2	0.8
Total	100.0	100.0	100.0

$N = 130$ $x^2 = 11.4620$ DF $= 5$ Sig. $= 0.05$

TABLE 6

Distribution of Heads of Family by Number of Children at Home, 1852, and Farm Expansion, Chinguacousy Township, 1850–70

Number of Children at Home 1852	Farm Size Increased 1850–70 (%)	Farm Size Did Not Increase 1850–70 (%)	Total Pop'n (%)
0	16.3	2.3	6.7
1–3	30.2	27.6	28.5
4–6	27.9	45.9	40.0
7 or more	25.6	24.2	24.6
Total	100.0	100.0	100.0

$N = 130$ $x^2 = 10.5615$ DF = 3 Sig. = 0.02

Michael Perdue and Thomas Holtby were typical of the men who felt in need of more land during this critical period. Perdue was a tenant farmer on 100 acres worth $300 when he bought it in 1845. At the time he had one son and another was on the way. By 1861 his family of five children, four of them sons, was complete, and in the meantime Perdue had acquired an additional 150 acres at a cost of $42 an acre, twelve times the cost of his original farm. Holtby was also a tenant farmer who worked 100 acres in 1852 to support his wife and three daughters. By 1860 his family had grown to eight, and there were two more additions in the seventies. In 1856 Holtby bought for $4000 the 100 acres he had rented, then paid an equal sum for 50 acres more at the height of the land boom. He evidently had second thoughts about his investment, however, because he divested himself of 50 acres, at a loss, in the mid-sixties. John Snell's situation was not quite so common. In 1852 he was forty-one. Eight of his eventual family of eleven children were living at home, all of them under the age of fourteen. The Snell farm consisted of 100 acres acquired between 1838 and 1845 at a cost of $1300. In 1854, and again in 1863, Snell added 100 acres to his farm. This new land cost an average of $60 an acre. With an additional 125 acres which Snell rented during the wheat boom, his land must have provided the standard of living that so large a family demanded; yet Snell's land promised security, in the long term, for only two of his four sons.

The evidence, then, suggests a regime in which the need to compete for arable land did not affect all families equally. Demographic pressures emanating from within the families of the generation of men who established their households at mid-century and whose families grew in size and maturity over the next twenty years created the most visible group of expansionists. They were part of a distinct minority among the farmers of Peel, but a minority large enough to have exacerbated the increasingly critical shortage of land in the county. This crisis abated only after it became apparent that there were real limits to demographic and economic continuity premised on a finite resource in an overpopulated society dependent on a staple economy. In this respect, the actions of those farm families who either would not or could not indulge in this costly competition are equally central to an understanding of the processes by which this little universe of social activity was transformed.

Even under the most favourable circumstances — cheap land and the absence of demographic pressure — few farmers could afford to satisfy the desire of all their sons to be "their own servants," in David Long's words, by providing them with land. In this sense, the economic and demographic constraints which restricted the availability of land in Peel County and in the region at mid-century simply brought into sharp relief a problem historically common to North American farmers since the beginning of settlement. In response to the competing claims of so many young men, Peel's newest families, those with the freedom to anticipate the expectations of their children in the 1860s and to amortize the costs of meeting those expectations, adopted the strategy of entering the land market to acquire additional land in the 1850s. But it is apparent that not all of the farm families in the community were willing to hazard their new fortunes, and that among the least willing were men whose families were already completed (tables 4 and 5), men faced with making an immediate choice between the equally legitimate expectations of several mature children and the old age security represented by an unencumbered, improved, productive farm. Their strategy, in short, was dictated by their need to balance conflicting and even contradictory objectives[18] represented by the contentment and well-being of deserving children on the one hand, and on the other by a historical attachment to a favourable man/land ratio and to the standard of living associated with it, a cultural bias that militated against the alternative to farm expansion — subdivision. Dividing the indivisible, in short, was the dilemma of those proprietors who were unable or unwilling to risk the rewards of their own labour to satisfy their obligations to their children.

"It is certain," Susanna Moodie complained in the 1850s, "that death is looked upon by many Canadians more as a matter of . . . a change of property into other hands than as a real domestic calamity."[19] But the vocational aspirations of sons (an average of four in families completed before 1870), the legal rights of wives, the social expectations of daughters, and even the sentimental attachments that informed and motivated familial relationships were inevitably linked to the possession of property, its rights, its obligations and, in a society where landed property was a finite resource, its limitations. Mrs. Moodie might have reflected, more accurately, that under such circumstances death and the subsequent transmission of property into other hands created the potential for domestic calamity. Choices had to be made. Justice had to be seen to be done. Calamity had to be avoided if possible. This was the problem facing the rural landholders of Peel who turned, in the 1850s, to the laws of inheritance to resolve their dilemma of dividing the indivisible among all those who perhaps deserved, but could no longer expect, to be men of property. The immediate effects of their strategy included varying degrees of "domestic calamity." In the long run, it produced a permanent alteration in the culture of the farm family.

There are as many ways to devise estates as there are minds to devise them; but in terms of first principles, at least, testators who are survived by more than one dependent face essentially two choices — a single heir or multiple heirs. In a single heir, or impartible, system of inheritance all real and personal property of consequence is assigned to one survivor to the exclusion of all other claims on the estate. The rule of primogeniture (abolished in Canada by law in 1856) simply defined that principal heir as the eldest male heir in order to guarantee the historical continuity of landed property, its perquisites, and obligations. But any number of inheritance systems can promote the same objective.[20] Conversely, multiple heir systems tend toward more or less perfect partibility, that is, the equal distribution of wealth among all of the legitimate claimants. As table 7 indicates, both systems — and a third — were employed by the farmers of Peel County throughout the nineteenth century. More to the point, the third system, the "Canadian" system of inheritance, in one decade became the most common vehicle for transmitting property from one generation to the next.[21]

TABLE 7

Percentage Distribution of Estates Devised by Farmers by Inheritance System Employed and Year Will Written, Peel County, 1845–99

System	1845–55	1856–65	1866–73	1874–90	All Estates
Impartible	32.1	17.3	11.9	18.2	17.1
Partible	28.6	11.5	8.4	6.5	8.7
"Canadian"	39.3	71.2	79.7	75.3	74.2
Total	100.0	100.0	100.0	100.0	100.0

$N = 515^*$ $x^2 = 49.9088$ DF = 6   Sig. = 0.001

*These cases represent estates which were not probated as intestate and in which the testator had to choose between at least two possible heirs in devising his estate.

TABLE 8

Principal Probated Assets of Deceased Farmers, Peel County, 1840–90

	1840s	1850s	1860s	1870s	1880s
Mean acreage	105	112	163	217	150
Average personalty	—	$2000	$2500	$2500	$2600

The "English-Canadian" system of inheritance was a hybrid, a preferential system which deliberately attempted to combine the economic conservatism of the impartible system with the social and sentimental egalitarianism of the partible. (The Canadian social historian A.R.M. Lower employed the term "English-Canadian" in contrast to French-Canadian practice, although preferential systems are, in fact, universal.) It involved devising the estate upon a single heir, usually a son, who in return for his patrimony was obligated to provide, out of his own resources, more or less equitably for all of the residual heirs and legatees as they would have been provided for had the estate been settled in a perfectly partible fashion. In this way land, as much land as one man needed to secure his future could be passed on, undivided; its proven productive capacity, in turn, would bear the costs of compensating the legitimate heirs who had been denied their birthright. Clearly, the system was advantageous to the farmer whose substance, increasingly after 1850, took the form of a single asset — land (table 8).

Thus, for example, a farmer who died in 1867 leaving his farm and a mere $54 in personal property instructed that his son, James, was to inherit the 100-acre farm, its crops, stock, and implements, providing that:

1st He shall find and furnish all the Flour, Pork and Butter and milk,
potatoes and other vegetables with plenty of good firewood ready for use
and . . . keep 1 horse [and buggy] . . . the above shall be found and supplied
during . . . the life of . . . his mother.

2nd He shall pay . . . annually . . . the sum of $100 as part of [her] subsistence
which payments shall be continued until the end of [her] natural [life].

3rd He shall pay . . . to his brother William . . . the sum of $1200 . . . I
give and bequeath to my daughter Jane . . . the sum of $200 which sum her
brother James above mentioned shall pay . . . I give and bequeath to the [5]
children of my late daughter Rachel . . . the sum of $200 . . . which sum
shall be paid . . . by the said James . . . in equal sums when they severally
attain their 20th year. And further the said James . . . shall pay all debts due
by us . . . and defray all our funeral expenses.[22]

The minimum cost to James of inheriting his farm, assuming that his mother
lived for another ten years, was $3400, half the market value of the farm. Obvi-
ously, this farmer counted heavily on his son's willingness to accept these obligations, on his family's willingness to become James's dependants, and on the land's
continued ability to provide adequately for James so that he, in turn, might
provide security for his mother and brother.

This farmer's actions, wittingly or not, conformed to the attitudes of the vast
majority of his peers who drew up their wills after 1855. Whether they acted
independently, sought advice from their neighbours, or had professional counsel
(few did), the result was the definition of a common solution to a common problem. As the correlations in table 9 suggest, partibility, equity, was the traditional
objective of testators. Impartibility was the resort of men with small estates and
small families. But as it became more difficult to acquire land, men with land and
large families conspired to protect their investment and still honour their legal,
moral, and sentimental obligations to all those who survived them. Most stopped
short of entailing their estates to provide livings for all of their heirs; but they
effectively achieved the same goal by making their land and its new masters
contractually responsible for the continued well-being of all their surviving
dependants.

Thus, the generation of young farmers whose farms were the spoils of the land
mania of the late fifties and sixties was the first to bear the new burdens of
inheritance in an overpopulated rural society. In return for their land, approximately half of these farmers became responsible for fulfilling bequests to an average of four surviving legatees and providing an annuity to at least one other; a
further 25 percent were obligated only to pay annuities to a minimum of two
relatives. The remainder, though freed from monetary obligations other than
debts and funeral expenses, normally were entrusted with the direct care or support of the deceased's family. The average total value of direct bequests was
$1600, but half those responsible for these gifts paid more. Annuities averaged
$160 per annum. What these figures meant to the principal heirs is more readily
comprehended from their perspective. An average annuity represented the annual
wages and board of a farm labourer in the 1850s.[23] The total average cost of
direct bequests to a principal heir represented 1200 bushels of wheat, the produce of 66 acres in the best of times, at the 1871 price for fall wheat delivered in

Toronto.[24] It is probably not too wide of the mark to suggest that the real costs of inheritance under this system represented, on the average, the equivalent of at least three years' cash income from a hundred-acre farm. Whatever the actual costs, they were often more, in any case, than the now land-poor second generation could afford out of its own meagre assets. An analysis of all the mortgages against farm property in Toronto Gore Township from 1860 until 1890 reveals that 5 percent of all indentures, and 4 percent of the total debt represented by those indentures, were incurred as the direct result of inheriting property.[25] Indeed, farmers sometimes gave mortgages to principal heirs who took over the farm before their parents' death. These mortgages effectively replaced a will in so far as they stipulated similar contractual obligations, but in addition bound the heir to provide old age security for both the surviving parents. Thus, the cost of inheritance ultimately depended on how long one or both parents survived.[26]

TABLE 9

Correlation of Selected Variables with Inheritance System Preferred by Testators Choosing Between at Least Two Possible Heirs, Peel County, 1845–90

Variable	Canadian	Impartible	Partible
Will written before 1845	no	no	no
Will written 1846–55	yes (−)	no	yes (+)
Will written 1856–65	no	no	no
Will written 1866–72	no	no	no
Will written 1874–90	no	no	no
Farmers	yes (+)	no	yes (−)
Manufacturers	no	no	no
Construction	no	no	no
Labour (unskilled)	no	no	no
Commerce	no	no	no
Transportation	no	no	no
Professional	no	no	no
Retired	no	no	no
Value of personal property	yes (+)	yes (−)	no
Amount of land owned	yes (+)	no	no
Total no. of surviving children	yes (+)	yes (−)	no

NOTE: This table excludes intestates. Significance levels reported are for r_c at 0.01 or better where t_c is for a two-tailed test. Coefficients are derived from the regression matrix.

The residual heirs, three out of every four survivors mentioned in these wills, evidently were compensated according to a complicated formula, part tradition, part legal and sentimental considerations, and, clearly, part impulse to promote continuity in the domestic arrangements of the family at the time of the head of household's death. Thus, sons who did not inherit land were most frequently rewarded with cash bequests, rarely less than a year's income, sometimes a substantial down payment on a farm of their own, more usually $450. Fathers who recorded their aspirations for these secondary male heirs seldom envisaged farming as a possibility. One son was enjoined to learn a trade before receiving his legacy which would buy him a set of tools; another was simply admonished to "betake himself to work as a man should," and a third was expressly instructed to use his $600 to pursue "some honourable profession."[27] Moreover, it seems certain that many parents had attempted to assist some of their sons, especially elder sons, during their lifetime and therefore did not feel compelled to treat them equitably as heirs. As one man explained, "having previously . . . assisted [four of his five sons] by sums of $ and settlements to such an extent as I could afford" they could not expect to share equally with his five daughters and his youngest son.[28]

The succession of one son as head of the household almost certainly meant the exodus from the household of his brothers, who were rarely conceded further claims, including rights of domicile, on the farm. Not so wives and daughters whose domestic arrangements were usually carefully, sometimes elaborately spelled out, for obvious reasons. By law, wives held dower rights (a one-third interest) in their husband's real property, rights which had to be conveyed to the new owner in return for adequate compensation. Thus, testators took care, at the very least, to see that dower rights were formally discharged by their principal heirs in a combination of cash payments, goods, and housing provided for widows. Most husbands' generosity did not end there; but dower rights commuted to goods and services ensured a minimum standard of old age security for widows whose husbands could not leave them cash incomes. How that security was to be delivered by the principal heir was always a matter of careful deliberation, then, for legal as well as sentimental reasons. Unmarried daughters, too, were the objects of special attention. Their only security lay in the extent to which the new head of household acted, or was required to act, *in loco parentis* until they established households of their own.

How actively deceased fathers expected their direct heirs to fulfil this role may be judged by the nature of the strictures under which some of them were empowered to act. Thus, "if any of my three daughters do contract any immoral or vicious habits or be disobedient to their mother," read one testament, "my executors may divide [her legacy] . . . between the other two daughters."[29] More commonly, daughters' choice of husbands had to be acceptable to their brother-parents. In return for this obedience they continued to be housed, fed, clothed, and, eventually, provided with a dowry. It consisted of the same goods their mothers had brought to their husbands: a feather bed and bedding, a cow, clothing, and a sum of money ($100 to $500 was the usual range). In this way, life for surviving daughters continued as before, in a familiar setting, but in the same condition of dependence which had characterized their relationship to their fathers, awaiting the opportunity to begin their own families.

For wives, the death of a husband ended a partnership and signalled the advent of a new stage of life; but in less than a quarter of the "Canadian"-style wills, compared to the vast majority of the partibly or impartibly devised estates, were wives recognized as mistresses of their own futures. They became the dependants of their sons, grandsons, sons-in-law or their husbands' executors, their standard of living and even their future conduct prescribed or proscribed literally from the grave. Thus, more than 20 percent of the deceased husbands who devised their estates according to the "Canadian system" explicitly forbade their wives to remarry or cohabit as a condition of inheritance. The penalties ranged from loss of income and/or rights of domicile to losing guardianship over her own children.[30] Most husbands were not so explicitly restrictive; yet the very nature of the settlements they made for their wives nevertheless had the same effect. "As long as she behaves herself prudently and remains my widow"[31] — one man's expectation — seems to have been the universal hope of husbands contemplating death.

The source of this concern, in part, was sentiment. Few men willingly accept the possibility that they can be replaced in their wives' affections by another after a long and successful partnership. It was also a question of practicality. Once his wife's future security became the contractual obligation of a third party, her only guarantee of security was to continue in the circumstances which required her son, grandson, or son-in-law to fulfil those obligations, particularly the requirement — normal in these cases — to house, feed, convey, and minister to the physical and spiritual needs of surviving widows within a familiar domestic environment. In some instances, principal heirs were instructed to build a small house on the farm where the widowed mother and a female companion could live privately. But in the great majority of cases, the new householder was enjoined to set aside specific rooms and furniture within the family's home, to provide prescribed amounts and types of food, heat, and transportation, and to guarantee the widow continued access to the family garden and to the barn if she wished to keep a cow. These arrangements clearly ensured that the widow's annual income from her trust or annuity, considerably less than if she had received dower rights as either capital or land which could be converted to capital, enabled her to provide herself with amenities over and above her basic requirements of food, shelter, and domestic services. In short, a modest private income nevertheless insufficient to afford independence, and a guaranteed minimum standard of living provided in what was once her own household, effectively bound widows to these contractual arrangements and ensured their "prudent" behaviour.

These provisions were meant, as well, to give the husband assurance that his widow would continue to enjoy the familial setting and the domestic arrangements to which she had become accustomed. No longer mistress of her own household, she would be surrounded nevertheless by familiar people and objects, an environment which would help to ease her reversion to single status. "It is my particular injunction," wrote one man who left his wife in better than average circumstances, "that my children and wife shall remain in love and friendship to each other. . . ."[32] Evidently it was a condition more easily willed than carried into effect. Susanna Moodie fretted that widowhood in a daughter-in-law's household meant "ironing the fine linen, or boiling over the cook-stove, while her daughter held her place in the drawing room."[33] Frances Stewart, in her reminiscences, described widowhood as a state of being "bewildered, weak and confused," a continuation of a lifetime of never being "allowed . . . to think or act but as . . . guided or directed. . . ."[34] Such were the perceptions and the experience of widowhood among gentlewomen.[35] Nevertheless, the contractual arrangements made by their deceased husbands undoubtedly guaranteed most women at least a tolerable existence as widows. In any event, as long as capital invested in land remained landed property, these were the only arrangements they could confidently anticipate.

The transmission of property from one generation to the next under this preferential system of inheritance, then, inevitably altered the circumstances and expectations of those affected by it in a variety of ways. Principal heirs inherited a legacy of debt and familial obligations, additional burdens to bear at a time when their own young families' needs already strained their resources. Over the long term their patrimony would compensate them, but in the short term they would begin their lives as independent farmers at some disadvantage to their own security. Sons who were residual heirs fared better than they would have under an impartible system, worse than they might have under a system of partible inheritance. Travelling money, capital to invest in a farm, trade, business, or profession, in short, a modest start in life in some other place, was the usual extent of their legacies. Wives and daughters were perhaps justified in equating death and inheritance with "domestic calamity." The sense of personal loss was accompanied, or was shortly followed, by a real loss of status within their households in return for a guaranteed minimum level of continued social security. But the land-poor farmer and his equally land-poor heir had little else save food, shelter, and pocket money to offer without jeopardizing their investment. By the 1860s, protecting it had become an art, skilfully and commonly practised by an entire generation, an entire community, of farmers. Their sons, as table 7 illustrates, followed their example. The impartible-partible system of inheritance persisted until the twentieth century.

The wholesale adoption of a new system of inheritance, in this case one which was neither impartible nor partible but attempted to achieve the objectives of both in response to a crisis, is of great importance. Any system of inheritance, as two scholars have recently argued, "sets limits, creates problems and opportunities, and evokes certain types of behaviour which conform to it or avoid its consequences."[36] It has been suggested, for example, that in rural societies single heir systems of inheritance and their variants tend to retard population growth by restricting the availability of land to a relatively fixed number of households. This in turn promotes delays in the age at which young couples anticipating a patrimony may marry and limits the number of new families to those who can expect such a patrimony. Children denied access to land will either remain celibate or emigrate in search of new economic opportunities. Fewer marriages, later marriages, celibacy, and emigration slow the rate of population growth, protect favourable family/land ratios, and promote particular types of family structures — extended families — in which parents and still-dependent married children, or married children and their celibate brothers and sisters, share the same roof. Conversely, it is supposed that perfect partibility, distributing land equally among surviving children, encourages higher rates of marriage, earlier family formation, rapid population growth, and the proliferation of relatively simple family structures consisting of parents and young children.[37]

These examples greatly oversimplify the impact of either system and ignore entirely the subtle effects which both patterns, or any of their variants, are capable of producing. The two extremes merely illustrate the widely held assumption that in societies where family formation presupposes an economic foundation of real property, any alteration in the circumstances under which land becomes available to new families necessarily provokes changes in the other direction: earlier or later ages at marriage; more or fewer children (larger or smaller families) depending on the age at marriage; higher or lower rates of emigration, particularly among the young; changes in the structures of households and families as children remain home-bound longer awaiting land, or leave home early to occupy land of their own. Clearly the implementation of the "Canadian" system of inheritance in Peel County after 1850 represented a permanent alteration in the conditions under which land became available to subsequent generations of children. Moreover, in spite of its egalitarian intent, it was a system of preferential inheritance[38] which restricted access to land in order to maintain customary man/land ratios in the face of mounting demographic pressure. Its consequences — inequality, insecurity, deprivation, and "domestic calamity" for some survivors, for others debt, prolonged dependence, and protracted familial obligations — were far-reaching. In theory, and in fact, the men and women of the next generation were bound to conform to these limitations. They could not avoid the problems which this new system of inheritance created for them, but they could attempt to protect their own children from repeating their experience.

One last example from the experience of a Peel County family will perhaps underscore these generalizations by placing events in a broader historical context. The history of the Leslie family, as reconstructed by Richard Houston in his brilliant genealogy of the Standish family of Esquesing Township,[39] illustrates the intergenerational effects of land availability in Peel County. John Leslie of County Tyrone, Ireland, arrived in Upper Canada in 1818 and acquired a grant of land on the western limits of Chinguacousy Township. In time, the prolific Leslie clan's holdings exceeded 1100 acres. John Leslie's three sons were all freeholders in Peel or Esquesing. The five sons of his eldest son George (all born between 1827 and 1846) all became freeholders in Peel. But of the five sons of George Leslie's eldest son John (b. 1827) only two became freeholders of family lands. The other three, and two of their four sisters who were married to farmers, took up farming, but in Manitoba and, subsequently, in British Columbia and Alberta. Among the Standish family and their close relatives in Peel, the Leslies, the Reeds, and several others, family farms were never subdivided into units of less than 100 acres, the proceeds of the sale of land to sons were the customary sources of daughters' legacies, and prolonged dependencies in their fathers' houses were the traditional lot of sons fortunate enough to be able to anticipate, as land became scarcer, a farm amid the other homesteads of the clan. The Leslies were exceptional in the duration of their commitment to Peel. But who would carry on the family's traditional loyalty to Chinguacousy Township in a narrowing sphere of economic opportunity became a matter of hard, practical decisions given the force of contractual obligations binding parents and children to the dictates of limited space.

Unquestionably, the loss of rural population experienced by this community in the 1860s had much to do with the attraction, elsewhere, of new or better economic opportunities associated directly with the availability of cheaper and more abundant land, or with non-farming opportunities created by the movement of population to those areas. Similarly, it would be unwise, in attempting to explain this loss of population, to ignore the climate of uncertainty, however fleeting, which the operation of external forces created in this local economy. But as the history of land occupancy in mid-nineteenth-century Peel County clearly demonstrates, the circumstances which propelled population out of rural Peel on the eve of Confederation had less to do with economic stagnation than with a considerable act of faith in the local economy on the part of established farmers. Anticipating a rising standard of living not only for themselves but for their sons, they either expanded their homesteads or placed legal restrictions on the availability of land in order to maintain man/land ratios which they had come to associate with prosperity. These actions were largely responsible for that movement of population — those who could not acquire land, those displaced off of it, and those to whom land was denied — away from Peel's rural townships between 1860 and 1870.

Thus, Peel's farm families emerged from the 1860s with a more favourable population/land ratio (84 per 1000 acres) than had existed two decades earlier (99 per 1000). Fewer people cultivating more acres meant that even though yields of wheat per acre declined by 16 percent between 1850 and 1870, and the total volume of wheat produced in 1870 was 90 000 bushels (14 percent) short of the 1851 harvest, surplus production remained virtually the same in spite of the ravages of nature. Per capita production of wheat in 1870 (24 bu.) was only marginally less than in 1851 (27 bu.). In the short run, of course, some ground was lost. The wheat crop of 1870 represented only 60 percent of the bumper harvest of 1860 — 934 000 bushels. It is clear that income losses resulting from declines in wheat production were offset by the continuing demand for the county's other field crops — hay, oats, barley, and peas — and by alternative areas of farm production, especially livestock and dairy produce which had already begun to play an important role in this farm economy (see table 10). Moreover, lower freight rates and the introduction of mechanized implements[40] represented just two of the factors of the costs of production which had become more favourable to the producer.

For all these reasons, the outlook for Peel's rural economy at the outset of the 1870s must have been an optimistic one, but one tempered by the memory of recent events. To the extent that this rural society was prepared for the new circumstances of agrarian prosperity or mere survival, as the case might be, in post-Confederation Ontario, its hopes lay in the strategies of social and demographic adjustment adopted during the two preceding decades. Farm expansion and its corollary, limiting accessibility to land among the rising generation of men, were not the only measures necessary to bring about this transition. But they were critical. First, they established the purpose of the exercise: to maintain family/land ratios historically associated with rural prosperity in Ontario. Then they created the conditions which made a secondary, though equally vital set of adjustments necessary. The land and demographic squeeze which beset one generation of these farm families became the inheritance of the next, literally as well as figuratively. One generation solved the urgent problem of too many people competing for too little land by applying financial and legal solutions suited to the immediacy of the problem. But neither debt nor domestic calamity were permanent solutions to the problem of economic opportunity and social security in a mature, established society. It remained for the next generation to sort out the permanent social implications of these events and to act accordingly.

TABLE 10

Selected Summary Statistics for Agriculture in Peel County, 1850–70

	1851	1861	1871
Total acreage improved (%)	51	65	73
Improved acreage in wheat (%)	29	32	18
Total acreage cropped (%)	30	49	60
Total cropped acreage in wheat (%)	49	42	27
Total acreage in wheat (%)	15	20	17
Wheat production (bushels)	659 575	934 139	569 126
Wheat concentration index*	0.404	0.462	0.282
Milch cow population	8107	9809	10 500
(% increase)	—	21	7
Butter production (lbs)	491 882	741 100	728 720
(% increase)	—	51	—

SOURCES: *Census of the Canadas, 1851–2,* vol. 2, table 6; *Census of the Canadas, 1860–1,* vol. 2, table 11; *Census of Canada, 1870–1,* vol. 3, table 11, 13.
*The wheat concentration index is the ratio of wheat acreage per 1000 cropped acres to the acreage of other field crops per 1000 cropped acres.

Notes

1. S.D. Clark, *The Developing Canadian Community,* 2nd ed. (Toronto, 1968), 3–4; R.A. Billington, *America's Frontier Heritage* (New York, 1966), 194.

2. Billington, *America's Frontier Heritage,* 25; M.H. Watkins, "A Staple Theory of Economic Growth," *Approaches to Canadian Economic History,* edited by W.T. Easterbrook and M.H. Watkins (Toronto, 1967), 61.

3. Rev. G.W. Warr, *Canada as It Is; or, The Emigrant's Friend and Guide to Upper Canada . . .* (London, 1847), 78.

4. R.L. Jones, *History of Agriculture in Ontario 1613–1880* (Toronto, 1948), 54; and see Kenneth Kelly, "The Evaluation of Land for Wheat Cultivation in Early Nineteenth-Century Ontario," *Ontario History* 62 (1970): 57–64.

5. John Lynch, "Agriculture and Its Advantages as a Pursuit," *Journal and Transactions of the Board of Agriculture of Upper Canada* 1 (1856): 199, as quoted in Kenneth Kelly, "The Transfer of British Ideas on Improved Farming to Ontario during the First Half of the Nineteenth Century," *Ontario History* 63 (1971): 103–11.

6. The coefficient of correlation, r, is 0.35, significant at 0.09.

7. Warr, *Canada as It Is,* 59.

8. I am indebted to a former McMaster graduate student in historical geography, Judy Hubert, for providing me with the results of her multiple regression analysis of the determinants of farm value. The land capability factor employed was derived from the *Canada Land Inventory Soil Capacity Classification for Agriculture* (Ottawa: Department of the Environment, 1965). Since the inventory is premised on modern determinants of soil capacity it is difficult to say what relationship it bears to the nineteenth-century farmer's perception of soil quality.

9. The 1861 published data are incomplete insofar as they refer only to farmer-occupiers. However, by 1861, 24 percent of Peel's farmers occupied more than 100 acres comprising 47 percent of farm lands held. The data cited here for 1851 and 1871 are similarly from published aggregates.

10. Samuel Philips Day, *English America; or, Pen Pictures of Canadian Places and People* (London, 1864), 1: 193.

11. Anna Jameson, *Winter Studies and Summer Rambles*, edited by J.J. Talman and E.M. Murray (Toronto, 1943), 53; William Cattermole, *Emigration; the Advantages of Emigration to Canada* . . . (London, 1831), 166; Thomas Conant, *Upper Canada Sketches* (Toronto, 1898), 177; Patrick Shirreff, *A Tour through North America Together with a Comprehensive View of Canada and the United States*. . . (Edinburgh, 1835), 170.

12. The "inheritance motive" as a determinant of economic and demographic behaviour and attitudes has particularly interested historical economists in recent years. See R.M. McInnis, "Childbearing and Land Availability: Some Evidence from Individual Household Data" (Behavioural Models in Historical Demography Conference, Philadelphia, 1974); Richard Easterlin, "Does Human Fertility Adjust to the Environment?" *American Economic Review: Papers and Proceedings* 61 (1971): 399–407; and, for an interesting comparison with colonial New England, Philip Greven, Jr., *Four Generations: Population, Land and Families in Colonial Andover, Massachusetts* (Ithaca, 1970), esp. 222–58.

13. See table 11.

TABLE 11

Means, Trend Values, and Three-Year Weighted Averages for Cost of Land Per Acre, Peel County, 1840–70

Date	Mean (y) ($)	Units (N)	x	x^2	xy	Trend Value ($)	Three-Year Moving Avg.
1840	8.30	0	15	225	−124.50	13.99	
1	8.00	1	14	196	−112.00	16.18	9.15
2	11.15	2	13	169	−144.95	18.37	28.45
3	66.19	3	12	144	−794.28	20.56	30.82
4	15.13	4	11	121	−166.43	22.75	31.03
5	11.79	5	10	100	−117.90	24.94	12.31
6	10.02	6	9	81	−90.18	27.13	12.40
7	15.40	7	8	64	−123.20	29.32	12.98
8	13.53	8	7	49	−94.71	31.51	12.80
9	9.49	9	6	36	−56.94	33.70	15.45
1850	23.34	10	5	25	−116.70	35.89	19.06
1	24.34	11	4	16	− 97.36	38.08	22.75
2	20.56	12	3	9	− 61.68	40.27	24.84
3	29.61	13	2	4	− 59.22	42.46	29.82
4	29.90	14	1	1	− 39.90	44.65	37.25
5	42.85	15	0	0	0	46.84	46.04
6	55.38	16	1	1	55.38	49.03	56.87
7	72.27	17	2	4	144.54	51.22	121.86
8	237.94	18	3	9	713.82	53.41	115.36
9	35.88	19	4	16	143.52	55.60	104.72
1860	40.35	20	5	25	201.75	57.79	57.29
1	95.64	21	6	36	573.84	59.98	106.33
2	183.02	22	7	49	1281.14	62.17	102.69
3	29.42	23	8	64	235.36	64.36	82.04
4	33.69	24	9	81	303.21	66.55	45.18
5	72.44	25	10	100	724.40	68.74	50.86
6	46.45	26	11	121	510.95	70.93	56.90
7	51.82	27	12	144	621.84	73.12	48.02
8	45.79	28	13	169	595.27	75.31	45.96
9	40.28	29	14	196	563.92	77.50	49.42
1870	62.19	30	15	225	932.85	79.69	
	1452.16	31		2468	+7601.79 −2199.35		

$Y_1 = 46.84 + 2.19X_1$ $N = 1916$ 5402.44

NOTE: that the *mean* is the average value of an acre of land purchased in a given year; the trend *values* locate the straight line which best describes the long-term trend of land prices; and the *three-year moving average* is the average of the values for a given year, the year preceding it, and the year following it, and is designed to smooth out anomalous irregularities in the curve.

14. Paul W. Gates, *The Farmers' Age: Agriculture 1815–1850: The Economic History of the United States* (New York, 1962), 3:405.

15. See David Gagan, "The Security of Land: Mortgaging in Toronto Gore Township, 1835–1885," *Aspects of Nineteenth-Century Ontario* edited by F.H. Armstrong, H. Stevenson, and D.J. Wilson (Toronto, 1974), 148.

16. Ibid., 137–8; and W.T. Easterbrook and Hugh G.J. Aitken, *Canadian Economic History* (Toronto, 1965), 507.

17. Cited in Jones, *History of Agriculture*, 203.

18. H.J. Habbakuk, "Family Structure and Economic Change in Nineteenth-Century Europe," *Journal of Economic History 15* (1955): 1, argues that this problem was faced by peasant families throughout nineteenth-century Europe. It is also clear that they frequently adopted the same inheritance systems in response. See the reference to Berkner and Mendels, note 36.

19. Susanna Moodie, *Life in the Clearings versus the Bush* (New York, 1855), 138.

20. See J.F. Cooper, "Patterns of Inheritance and Settlement by Great Landowners from the Fifteenth to the Eighteenth Centuries," *Family and Inheritance*, edited by J. Goody and J. Thirsk, (Cambridge, Eng., 1976), 197.

21. This system was first described and labelled by A.R.M. Lower in *Canadians in the Making* (Toronto, 1969), 336.

22. Peel County, Surrogate Court, Wills, vol. 1, 1867, will of J.V. Unless otherwise noted data for this analysis have been computed from Ontario Archives (hereafter OA), York County, Probate Court, Wills, 1800–67; Peel County, Surrogate Court, Wills, 1867–90; OA, Home District, Probate Court, Wills, 1800–1867.

23. J. Sheridan Hogan, *Canada: An Essay* (Montreal, 1855), 65–66.

24. Jones, *History of Agriculture*, 247, notes that the 1871 fall wheat crop in areas not affected by midge was the best in several years, and that the Franco-Prussian War had created a market for it.

25. Gagan, "The Security of Land," *Aspects of Nineteenth Century Ontario*, 143.

26. Ibid.

27. OA, York County, Probate Court, 1800–67, Wills No. 13590, 264; Peel County, Surrogate Court, Wills, 1867–90, Will No. 29.

28. Ibid., Will of J.M., No. 66.

29. Ibid., Will of J.H., No. 12716.

30. OA, Home District, Probate Court, Wills, 1800–67, Will of T.W., No. 09577, for example, orders that if the wife remarries the children are to be taken from her and housed elsewhere.

31. Peel County, Surrogate Court, Wills, 1867–1900, Will of N.A., No. 47.

32. OA, York County, Probate Court, Wills, 1800–67, Will of J.N., No. 338.

33. Moodie, *Life in the Clearings*, 291.

34. E.S. Dunlop, ed., *Our Forest Home: Being Extracts from the Correspondence of the Late Frances Stewart* (Toronto, 1889), 80–81.

35. These attitudes and other aspects of the experience of nineteenth-century Ontario farm women are discussed at length in Rosemary R. Ball, " 'A Perfect Farmer's Wife': Women in Nineteenth Century Rural Ontario," *Canada: An Historical Magazine* 3 (1975): 2–21.

36. Lutz Berkner and Franklin Mendels, "Inheritance Systems, Family Structure and Demographic Patterns in Western Europe, 1700–1900," *Historical Studies of Changing Fertility*, edited by Charles Tilly (Princeton, 1978), 216. As this essay makes abundantly clear, it is a misnomer to call the preferential system of inheritance found in Peel a "Canadian" system of inheritance. Its operation was well known in Europe long before it was implemented in rural Ontario.

37. Habbabuk, "Family Structure," 5–7.

38. Berkner and Mendels, "Inheritance Systems," 217.

39. J. Richard Houston, *Numbering the Survivors: A History of the Standish Family of Ireland, Ontario and Alberta* (Agincourt, 1979), 104–8, 118–21.

40. D.A. Lawr, "The Development of Farming in Ontario, 1870–1914: Patterns of Growth and Change," *Ontario History* 64 (1972): 240–51.

Engine No. 209, "Trevithick," built in the Grand Trunk Railway shops, 1859.

CANADIAN RAILWAYS AS MANUFACTURERS, 1850–1880†

PAUL CRAVEN AND TOM TRAVES

Most accounts of Canadian industrialization in the mid-nineteenth century attribute a dual role to the railways. First, by breaking down the old "tariff of bad roads" that protected small local markets for artisanal producers, they laid the groundwork for the concentration of industrial production in a handful of metropolitan centres. Second, it is often recognized that the railway companies were themselves important markets for a wide range of commodities, and so helped to create the opportunity structure for new investment in manufacturing. While the significance of the railways in the development of the market is indisputable, however, it is less frequently recognized that the railways were important industrial *producers* as well. Indeed the well-worn argument that railways represented commercial, as *opposed* to industrial, capital becomes quaintly irrelevant once it is realized that these companies owned and operated some of the largest and most sophisticated manufacturing plants in the Canadian economy from the early 1850s on.[1]

Railways were not just simple transportation companies. To understand their operations and management from their inception in the 1850s it is necessary first to appreciate the range of functions they performed in the daily course of business. In some respects they operated almost like states unto themselves; their company rules had the force of law, they employed their own police, and their executives, as the Grand Trunk's goods manager put it, were "as important as generals in an army or Ministers of State."[2] By 1860 the typical large railway, like the Grand Trunk or the Great Western, had the capacity to rebuild its line and repair its tracks, to manufacture its own cars and locomotives and even a good part of the machinery and equipment used in these manufacturing processes, to communicate telegraphically, to store and forward freight, to operate grain

†*Historical Papers/Communications historiques* (1983): 254–281. Research for this paper, and for the larger Canadian Railways Industrial Relations History Project of which it forms a part, has had the generous support of the Social Sciences and Humanities Research Council of Canada. The authors gratefully acknowledge the research assistance of David Sobel and Rose Hutchens.

elevators and steamships, and to maintain large depots and complex administrative offices, all in support of its basic service as a common carrier. In short, the railways were Canada's first large-scale integrated industrial corporations.

This essay focusses on one aspect of integrated railway operations, the manufacturing activities of the railways' locomotive and car departments. By describing the nature and scope of these activities, and some features of the plant, organization and technology that sustained them, it is intended to contribute towards a reassessment of the railways' place in the history of Canadian industrialization.

The Scope of Manufacturing

The Grand Trunk and the Great Western, in common with some smaller roads, built extensive car shops as part of their original construction program in the early 1850s, but at the outset they leased these structures to private contractors who equipped them to supply larger orders for cars. Although they had to cope with eager competition from British and American car builders, and had to import such crucial parts as wheels and axles, independent Canadian car manufacturers were able to realize their considerable transportation cost advantage to dominate the local market. Dissatisfaction with the quality of the product, and even more pressing difficulties with financing large purchases, soon brought the railway companies to the view that it would be both cheaper and more efficient to build some of their cars themselves. In March 1855, the cash-poor Great Western attempted to cover its debts by foisting GWR bonds on its principal suppliers; shortly thereafter the company cancelled outstanding contracts and began building its own cars. "It is believed that a considerable saving, both in first cost and repairs, may be effected," its president explained, "by the company building cars in their own workshops, besides insuring the use of none but the best materials, which is the greatest safeguard against accidents. . . ."[3]

The Grand Trunk entered the car business for exactly the same reasons. After its major supplier refused to do any more work on credit, the GTR board accepted its chief engineer's proposal to operate the company's Point St. Charles workshops on its own account. By July 1857 the GTR car works were supplying half the road's requirements, and the board was so impressed with this success that it decided to construct an iron foundry, rolling mills and machinery to produce its own rails as well.[4]

The more complicated task of building locomotives was not undertaken until a little later. Independent Canadian suppliers certainly were active in this market as in cars, but at first the bulk of the orders went to large producers in Britain and the United States. While there was a certain bias in favour of the British engines, not only because they were heavier and more substantially built, but also because of the preponderance of British capital invested in the Canadian railways, American locomotive builders were able to capture a substantial share of the market because of shipping costs and the readier availability of spare parts. Still, there were complaints about quality from both sources and some British engines proved to be unsuitable for the sharp curves and rough roadbeds characteristic of the Canadian lines. Gradually such Canadian suppliers as Kinmond Brothers (Montreal), Daniel C. Gunn's works (Hamilton), William Hamilton's St. Lawrence

Foundry (Toronto), Good's Foundry (Toronto), and the Canadian Locomotive Works (Kingston) began production. By 1857 the Grand Trunk was placing orders for eight engines from British manufacturers, seven from Americans, and thirty-two from Canadian builders.[5]

Both the Grand Trunk and the Great Western began to consider building locomotives in their own shops, not only for the familiar reason, that it would "doubtless effect a considerable saving in expense," but also because it could furnish slack-time employment for skilled shopworkers in whose recruitment and retention the railways had a large investment. Grand Trunk shops turned out the *Trevithick* in May 1859, and the Great Western's *George Stephenson* was put to work a few months later.[6]

Between January 1864 and December 1873, the Grand Trunk shops built forty-nine new locomotives, or five per year on average. In the same period, they produced 1224 new freight cars (122 per year) and rebuilt, thoroughly renovated or converted substantial proportions of their existing stock. Over the ten years, the Grand Trunk built 172 new passenger cars (seventeen per year). In 1880, when the pattern of shopwork characteristic of the early 1870s had been reestablished after the disruptions occasioned by the change of gauge, the Grand Trunk built eighteen locomotives, thirty-one new passenger cars and 550 new freight cars, as well as converting, rebuilding or thoroughly renovating fifty-two passenger and 1414 freight cars. The shops also manufactured or remanufactured substantial quantities of parts to be used in repair; in the early 1870s, for example, the GTR car shops were turning out approximately six hundred new and renewed trucks per year, as well as between a thousand and fifteen hundred additional new and renewed axles.[7]

Similarly, the Great Western's locomotive shop manufactured or rebuilt sixty-eight engines — four a year on average — between 1860 and 1876. Like the Grand Trunk's it also produced parts and components used in locomotive manufacture and repair. For example, in the year ending 31 January 1871 the GWR turned out five crank axles (four steel, one iron), eleven straight engine axles, eleven truck axles, twenty-two tender axles, sixty-four axle boxes, twenty-six pistons, eight eccentric pulleys, four eccentric straps, twenty-one crank pins, three cross heads, nine driving wheels (eight cast iron, one unspecified), 389 chilled wheels, forty-five engine springs, sixty tender springs, eleven engine bells, 118 steel tires, two tender trucks, one connecting rod, four valve spindles, two tender frames, and two flue-sheets (one copper, one steel), as well as completing three new boilers to be used in rebuilding locomotives and beginning work on three others. The Great Western's car shops were equally busy with new construction and rebuilding.[8]

Figures like these seriously underestimate the extent of manufacturing activity in the car and locomotive departments of the major railways, however. First, the published reports provide little or no systematic information about the production of all sorts of parts and components, although we know from various sources that a wide range of such things, such as iron bridge castings, locomotive boilers, springs, cast iron and wrought iron wheels, and lamps of various descriptions, were made in quantity by the shops, as well as such items of operating equipment as semaphore signals.[9]

Second, there is a dearth of systematic quantitative information about the manufacture of tools and machinery for use by the railway shops themselves. Again, we know that they produced a wide range of such equipment, from the machinery for turntables and grain elevators to such sophisticated machine tools as the "powerful drilling machine with six drills . . . for drilling the iron skeletons for our new trucks, and a similar machine with fine drills . . . for boring the wood-work of the same trucks," which the Grand Trunk built in 1869; "by the use of these and other labour-saving machinery we are enabled to build trucks at a much lower cost than in former years."[10]

Third, and perhaps most important, it is necessary to consider the extent to which shopwork characterized as "repair" really amounted to manufacturing activity. On the Great Western, it was said that "a first-class car . . . only lasts nine years, or, in other words, at the close of a nine years' servitude, the repairs will have been so numerous and extensive that not one atom of the original car remains in use." The Grand Trunk's mechanical superintendent said that much of the "general repairs" consisted in "actual rebuilding of cars," and warned not to take the construction figures as a "measure of the actual work done towards maintenance inasmuch as a very large number of cars receive from one half to four fifths of new material into their construction, none of which are reckoned as new cars."[11]

The work of the railways' car and locomotive shops might be classified under five headings: maintenance, repair, renewal, replacement, and capital construction. Replacement and capital construction involved essentially the same sorts of activity — building cars or locomotives "from scratch" — but for the most part they were reported differently in the railways' accounts.[12] Great Western (subsequently Grand Trunk) locomotive superintendent Richard Eaton defined renewals as "that class of work which adds new and additional life to the Engine, beyond its average term of fifteen years. Consequently new fire boxes, Tubes, Tyres or Wheels, supplied to Engines under the ordinary heavy repairs cannot be considered as renewals, as these, and other articles, are necessary to the life of fifteen years alone."[13] At the other extreme maintenance might be distinguished from light repairs by limiting it to routine cleaning, lubricating, and so forth.

Expenditure on Manufacturing

In attempting to draw the line between manufacturing and other types of activity in the locomotive and car departments, there is a risk of making the distinctions unnecessarily fine. In contemporary discourse, we are prepared to consider simple parts-assembly operations to be manufacturing plants, and workers who sweep the floors and keep the tools to be production workers. It is difficult to see why any greater terminological precision should be required of nineteenth-century industry. The most sensible demarcation between manufacturing and nonmanufacturing activity in the locomotive and car departments is that between light repairs and maintenance. In practice, the distinction may be drawn (where the data permit) between "running repairs" or "front-shop" work, and "back-shop" work; in other words, between repair work done in the main car and locomotive shops, and repairs done in the engine houses and car sheds, or at minor running shops along the line. This is more or less the distinction embodied in the modern Standard Industrial Classification, which views in-shop repair work as manufacturing activity, and maintenance and running repairs as a service incidental to transportation. It is a reasonable compromise between theoretical rigour and practical applicability.[14]

Unfortunately, it is not possible on the basis of the available data to separate maintenance from other mechanical department activities, or running repairs from work done in-shop, on any really satisfactory basis for the period of this paper. Mechanical superintendents on the larger railways reported in some detail the volume of repair and renewal activity of various sorts, but these reports almost always excluded running repairs; thus Eaton reported on "heavy," "medium," and "light" engine repairs on the Grand Trunk, but noted that his figures did not include "those repairs done in Steam sheds, or which only occupied a week or so in the repair shops." His successor Herbert Wallis used a similar three-fold distinction, "without taking into account the light or running repairs done at our *ten* outside Loco. Stations," but included engines which had been three days or more in the shops under "light repairs." In reporting on repairs in the car department, he listed "the more prominent items, leaving out of the record all Cars less than twenty-four hours under repair, and upon which a large staff are continually employed."[15]

Two data series are available. One, to be found for the most part in the mechanical superintendents' reports on the larger railways, provides information on the range of shopwork and some quantifiable material on the volume of certain activities. The other consists of mechanical department expenditures summarized in the railway company accounts. The first series does not report systematically on out-of-shop and maintenance activity, while the second does not systematically distinguish between manufacturing and maintenance expenditures. The first type of data has been drawn on extensively in the first part of this essay. Here we turn to the financial series in an attempt to estimate the value of manufacturing activity in the railway mechanical departments.

Manufacturing activity in locomotive and car departments appears in both the capital and revenue accounts. Railway accounting practices were inconsistent in this period (especially in the earlier years), and one suspects that the assignment of an item to one or the other frequently depended on a political assessment of the shareholders' collective frame of mind rather than on any theory of industrial finance. New equipment built in the railway shops was sometimes assigned to capital and sometimes to revenue. Renewals and replacements were frequently charged to revenue simply because they brought the department's stock up to numerical strength, without any regard to the substantial improvement of the stock that they often represented. Unfortunately, the schedules of additions to capital account reported by the major railways are very difficult to work with. The information they provide is incomplete, and items are sometimes accounted for years after the expenditure has been made. About all that can be said of the capital account data is that the railway shops evidently produced a substantial

FIGURE 1

Great Western Rwy: Trends 1859–76

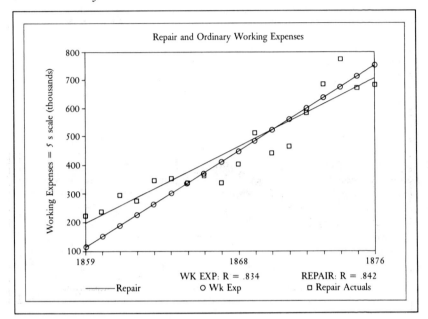

Repair and Ordinary Working Expenses

WK EXP: R = .834   REPAIR: R = .842

——— Repair   o Wk Exp   □ Repair Actuals

annual volume of rolling stock over and above the expenditure shown in the revenue accounts.

The locomotive and car repair schedules in the revenue accounts supply a more satisfactory basis for estimating the value of manufacturing activity in the railway mechanical departments. Tables 1 and 2 summarize the locomotive and car repair schedules in these accounts for the Great Western (1858–76) and Grand Trunk (1861–80) respectively, while figures 1 and 2 illustrate the growth trends. "Repair" in these schedules included new construction (on account of renewals or otherwise charged to revenue), rebuilding, conversion, and so forth — in short, the whole range of shopwork as discussed above. Our tabulations incorporate a number of adjustments for the inclusion of nonmanufacturing items and the exclusion of costs that may properly be attributed to manufacturing.

The total expenditure on locomotive and car repair shown in the tables should be taken as a minimum estimate of expenditures on manufacturing in the mechanical departments. It ignores entirely expenditure on capital account (which fluctuated widely from year to year and which, as discussed above, cannot be systematically quantified), and it does not take into account other costs of manufacturing which are charged elsewhere. Among the latter are manufacturing-related expenditure in the storekeepers' departments, and possibly some transportation expenditures as well. In sum, it is a conservative claim that the Great Western mechanical departments expended a quarter of a million dollars on manufacturing activity in 1859, and over three-quarters of a million in 1874; or that the

FIGURE 2

Grand Trunk Rwy: Trends 1862–80

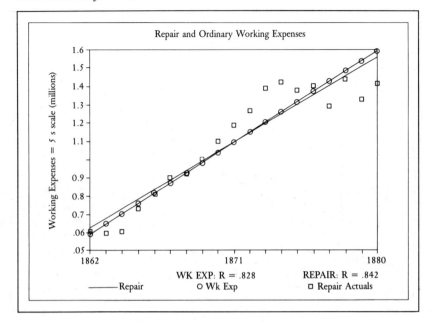

Grand Trunk spent over $600,000 a year on mechanical department manufacturing in the early 1860s and about $1.5 million annually in the later 1870s. Manufacturing expenditure on revenue account grew steadily over the period as a proportion (approximately 20 percent) of total ordinary working expenses.[16]

It should be noted that these expenditure figures are not equivalent to census value-added statistics, in that they include no profit component and, so far as we can ascertain, no market price adjustment for materials and components manufactured by the railway companies themselves. But even on a straight comparison of mechanical department expenditures to census value-added figures for other manufacturers, it appears plain that the railways were among the largest manufacturing firms in Canada in the period, and quite possibly the largest bar none. Table 3 draws together returns from car factories, engine builders and railway shops in the 1871 manuscript census. It is clear that the central car and locomotive shops on the two largest railways—the Grand Trunk's at Brantford and Montreal, and the Great Western's at Hamilton — were as big as the largest independent establishments in those industries, and that as *integrated*, multiplant manufacturers the larger railways were bigger by far — in terms just of *manufacturing* employment, consumption of materials, and output—than any of the independent firms. The exclusion of the railway company facilities from the aggregate tables published in the 1871 census reports resulted in a grossly distorted picture of the scale and organization of the Canadian railway supply and heavy engineering industries.[17]

TABLE 1

Great Western Railway Mechanical Expenditures on Revenue Account 1858–1876

For Year Ending 31 July —	1859	1860	1861	1862	1863	1864	1865	1866	1867
Revenue Account ($)									
Ordinary Working Expenses	1056514	1093184	1150179	1185289	1289903	1296856	1276358	1407214	1670578
Locomotive Repair:									
Materials, fuel & light	63324	59491	80305	69437	77361	77351	73418	77648	75410
Wages	100497	106150	99041	98407	102688	101051	96301	93765	91918
Car Repair:									
Materials	24955	25215	55563	57998	91080	105135	90019	103756	102771
Wages and salaries	42451	47780	61844	48426	77320	73255	83021	92831	71568
Total Loco. & Car Repair	231227	238636	296753	274268	348449	356793	342759	368000	341666
Loco. & Car Repair as % of Working Expenses	21.89	21.83	25.80	23.14	27.01	27.51	26.85	26.15	20.45

For Year Ending 31 July —	1868	1869	1870	1871	1872	1873	1874	1875	1876
Revenue Account ($)									
Ordinary Working Expenses	1928958	2132458	2389675	2591103	3116615	3864456	4161520	3626863	3440306
Locomotive Repair:									
Materials, fuel & light	81114	83235	71599	57584	113910	136078	178196	146525	139111
Wages	96348	107546	84963	98744	98410	·97593	100868	91526	99193
Car Repair:									
Materials	131396	158090	168116	193830	238691	250913	293055	260581	322161
Wages and salaries	100243	167980	120675	119753	140364	200451	202445	171054	123399
Total Loco. & Car Repair	409100	516851	445353	469910	591375	685034	774564	669686	683864
Loco. & Car Repair as % of Working Expenses	21.21	24.24	18.64	18.14	18.97	17.73	18.61	18.46	19.88

TABLE 2

Grand Trunk Railway Mechanical Expenditures on Revenue Account 1861–1880

For Year Ending 30 June —	1862	1863	1864	1865	1866	1867	1868	1869	1870	1871
Revenue Account ($) Ordinary Working Expenses	3216588	3048838	2950474	3830136	3995466	4217006	4368914	4527229	4887459	5311995
Locomotive Dept.:										
Materials for repair	143824	103893	102804	129216	152364	175409	164223	172570	228051	235428
Wages for repair	124174	135461	146680	143178	168034	196168	197975	210555	208419	210160
Repairs to tools &cc	23709	32640	37366	52821	63889	77639	74613	96416	81158	85086
Workshop fuel	18484	11608	9350	11350	13216	14999	19896	17909	17138	20041
Car Dept.:										
Materials for repair	148224	175113	160665	220460	238833	240378	258453	266191	315548	351471
Wages for repair	138689	136579	148101	178113	177629	191016	202248	233758	249138	284508
Repairs to tools &cc	8523									
Total Loco. & Car Repair	605625	595293	604966	735138	813964	895608	917406	997399	1099450	1186694
Loco. & Car Repair as % of Working Expenses	18.83	19.53	20.50	19.19	20.37	21.24	21.00	22.03	22.50	22.34

For Year Ending 30 June —	1872	1873	1874	1875	1876	1877	1878	1879	1880	1881*
Revenue Account ($) Ordinary Working Expenses	5769919	6429224	7399655	7959598	7761781	6905539	7182064	6715908	6940761	3919473
Locomotive Dept.:										
Materials for repair	209776	234646	223214	203710	219670	150559	213649	181678	237820	135126
Wages for repair	243216	263539	219490	213401	241849	259164	308569	303564	323949	172079
Repairs to tools &cc	91586	101329	111358	110429	115588	111135	118350	106435	95953	55375
Workshop fuel	24160	29739	32116	36630	37549	32454	29721	26346	25046	12445
Car Dept.:										
Materials for repair	386651	425073	469196	438340	432614	384809	389330	345169	357795	184970
Wages for repair	311923	332654	366460	378264	348530	354279	381120	365284	367876	200119
Repairs to tools &cc										
Total Loco. & Car Repair	1267313	1386979	1421834	1380774	1395799	1292399	1440739	1328475	1408439	760114
Loco. & Car Repair as % of Working Expenses	21.96	21.57	19.21	17.35	17.98	18.72	20.06	19.78	20.29	19.39

*First half of fiscal year.

TABLE 3

Census of 1871: Car Factories, Engine Builders and Railway Shops (see text)

Establishment	Total Employees	Annual Wages	Motive Power	Value of Material	Value of Product
1. Independent Car Factories from Aggregate Census					
John McDougall & Co., Car Wheel Factory, Montreal (West)	60	36000	15 HP	85000	144000
James Crossen, Railroad Car Manufactory, Cobourg, Northumberland Co.	40	12000	N/A	22000	150000
Toronto Car Wheel Company	20	6000	20 HP	40000	54000
A. Holmes, Montreal Car Works, Hochelaga	20	2500	Manual	20000	120000
Wm Hamilton & Sons, St. Lawrence Foundry, Machine and Car Shop, Toronto (East)[a]	200	100000	60 HP	35000	150000
2. Independent Engine Makers from Aggregate Census[b]					
Hyslop & Ronald, Steam Engine Factory, Chatham, Kent Co.	42	18000	Shared: 50 HP	6000	50000
C. H. Waterous & Co., Manufactory of Steam Engines, Boilers, &c, Brantford, Brant Co.	118	40573	40 HP	19700	120000
F. G. Beckett & Co., Manufacturers of Locomotives, Steam Engines, Boilers &c., Hamilton	120	40000	50 HP	40000	100000
Charles Levey & Co., Steam Engine Factory, Toronto (West)	46	10000	30 HP	20500	70000
Hamilton & Martin, Engine Builders and Machinists, Toronto (East)	9	7000	8 HP	2400	25000
Canadian Engine & Machinery Co., Locomotive and Car Factory, Kingston	173	75000	20 HP	201058	306000
Davidson & Doran Machine Shop, Kingston[c]	47	11000	15 HP	12000	40000
George Brush, Eagle Foundry and Machine Shop, Montreal (West)	80	25000	20 HP	25000	80000

TABLE 3 (continued)

Census of 1871: Car Factories, Engine Builders and Railway Shops (see text)

Establishment	Total Employees	Annual Wages	Motive Power	Value of Material	Value of Product
E. E. Gilbert, Engine and Machinists Works, Montreal (West)	145	50000	40 HP	46500	120000
W. P. Bartley & Co., Engine Works and Foundry, Montreal (West)	222	49200	Water: 160 HP	36250	128175
3. Railway Shops from Manuscript Census					
Grand Trunk: Point St. Charles shops[d]	790	250000	185 HP	500000	750000
Grand Trunk: car and loco shops, Brantford	315	182000	30 HP	82000	326000
Great Western Locomotive Shop, London	34	12786	35 HP	2330	20000
Great Western: Hamilton return[e]	984	500000	N/A	N/A	N/A
Northern: Toronto (West) return[e]	561	215808	139 HP	34533	N/A

a. Hamilton's was not included under car shops in the aggregate census. Its return suggests that car building was its principal business at this date, however.
b. One shop in Co. de Quebec and one in Montreal (C), each employing 5 men, are excluded.
c. Not included in aggregate census: principal product seems to be steam engines.
d. "Running shed, Repairs to Engines, Pattern Shops, Brass Foundry, Fitting Shops, Car Shops, Saw & Planning Shops, Blacksmith & Carpenters Shops." The product was reported as "Engines, cars & repairs."
e. These returns seem to include other railway facilities besides the shops. On the Northern's return the enumerator noted that the quantities and value of products could not be ascertained, "as the Company are manufacturers or producers merely on their own Account."

The Principal Shops

In June 1853, the Great Western's chief engineer informed the company's shareholders that their car factory, blacksmith's shops, setting-up shop, paint shops and machine shop at Hamilton were well advanced towards completion, and that similar plans had been approved for London. Later that summer the *American Railroad Journal* reported that GWR machine shops, depots and warehouses were being built, "of a size calculated to astonish even those who had made the largest calculations as to Western progress." The car factory was "not only the largest workshop of the kind, but perhaps, the most extensive manufacturing establishment of any description in Western Canada," exhibiting "the most efficient specimens of labor saving machines that we have ever witnessed."[18]

By 1857, when a local journalist visited the plant, the locomotive shop had between twenty and thirty locomotives under repair daily. Twelve tracks, each capable of holding two engines, passed through the ground floor of the erecting shed.

> The first room we entered seemed to be the general hospital, in which the sick giants were disposed in long rows and supported at a considerable height, on wooden blocks and beams. Passing in we came to two rows of ponderous machines. There were drilling machines, boring holes of various sizes through any thickness of metal. There were planing machines which dealt with iron and brass as if they were soft wood, and rapidly reduced the blocks of metal to the necessary form — machines which cut iron as if it were paper, and punched holes through quarter inch plates as easily as you would punch a gun-wad from a piece of pasteboard. Lathes of all imaginable shapes and sizes, for doing all imaginable things, and in short, the complete furniture of a first class establishment.

The upper floor of the building held the carpentry shop, 165 feet long by 83 wide, where lathes, shapers, planers and drilling machines were used to build buffers and cow catchers. The machinery was run by a sixty-horsepower engine, built at Chippawa, and shared between the locomotive and car departments, which also shared the services of a brass foundry, a coppersmith's shop and a smithy in which cranks, wheels and rails were manufactured and repaired in the glow of twenty-five or twenty-six forges.[19]

The car shops built and repaired rolling stock, manufactured furniture for the stations, and cut timber for fences and bridges. In the machine shop cast-iron car wheels were made and repaired with the use of "machinery the most powerful, and at the same time the most delicate. . . . One engine cuts through, with ease, bars of cold iron, an inch thick and three inches broad, while others turn the edges of the wheels so accurately that they do not differ the thousandth part of an inch from a true circle." The car department built baggage racks in the brass foundry, and kept cabinet, upholstery, finishing and paint shops at work, along with shops for making water coolers, signal lamps, stationary signals, hand cars, and gas fittings for stations. There was also a huge body-building shop, 300 feet by 50, to assemble the cars.[20]

When Richard Eaton became locomotive superintendent in 1858, he took charge of a planned expansion in the shops' capacity. By midyear he was able to report that the greater part of the improvements had been made: "the steam hammer, tyre furnaces, stores and coppersmith's shop are complete; and the tanks, plates, and crane for fixing and blocking the tyres are also erected and but little remains to complete the blocking machinery. . . . The travelling steam crane for large lathes &c and the few remaining improvements are in a very forward state. . . ." A fifty-hundredweight Nasmyth steam hammer had been ordered from England, and Eaton had a blooming furnace for working up wrought iron scrap installed and in production by the end of the year. The hammer was used to beat the heated scrap into plates an inch thick. A drawing published in 1863 shows it towering four times the height of the men crowded around it, forging a

14-foot, 1600-pound shaft for the stationary engine. Next door was the boiler shop with its riveting machines, drills, and "a large punching and shearing machine which will clip you off a piece of boiler plate half an inch thick and ten inches wide in a shorter time and with less manual labour than is required to cut as much cheese."[21]

A year later, the shops boasted an elaborate heating apparatus, which distributed the waste steam from the stationary engine and steam hammer furnace through a mile of piping; the whole system was extended the following year so that more than two miles of heating pipes snaked their way through the Hamilton works. Eaton undertook an extensive rearrangement of the shop machinery, added a hoist for moving materials between floors, rebuilt some wooden buildings in masonry, and supplied new lathes, new forges for making wrought-iron wheels, and a steam riveting machine for iron-bridge construction.[22] A report from late November 1860 gives an impression of the nature and rhythm of shopwork in this period:

> The Plates for Boilers for next pair of Engines have also been ordered from England and will arrive here about the middle of January next, and the Wrought Iron Framing, Driving Wheels and remaining Iron Work, will be put in hand on 3rd December (next Monday) at which time the Blooming Furnace will be put to work in order to use up the scrap iron. The Blooming Furnace will be kept to work until we have provided all the heavy forgings required for new Engines and for general use during the ensuing 12 months. A considerable portion of the Castings required for next year's new Engines are already made and the best use will be made of all the men and machines we can spare from the regular repairs in order to forward the new Engines and other improvements that are being made in the Locomotive Stock.[23]

The plant and equipment were expanded further over the succeeding years. The flooring was relaid and lorries and tramways installed to expedite the movement of heavy materials and parts. New furnaces for brass moulding and heavy iron work were added. By 1869 the stationary engine required new boilers and pistons, which were built in the shops; when they were completed the engine was fully refitted. New machinery was built or purchased — a radial drill, a screw-cutting lathe, a car wheel boring machine, nut- and bolt-making machinery, an improved hydraulic car wheel press, and a hydrostatic locomotive wheel press. By 1870, when additional carshop facilities were badly needed, there was no room for expansion at Hamilton so work began on a new car facility at London. The following year it became clear that the existing overcrowding at Hamilton posed a serious fire risk, and the Great Western management began to discuss moving the entire car department to London. Two hundred and fifty GWR carshop workers moved from Hamilton to London in November 1874, when this transfer was made; the decision may have been hastened when fire broke out at Hamilton in September 1873, although it caused little damage. In the interim, the Hamilton shops were hard-pressed.[24]

The Great Western established a locomotive repair shop in London as part of its original plant in the 1850s, and for a time the outside locomotive department (locomotive running) was headquartered there. A journalist visiting the works in 1857 described the round-house with its metal-working lathes, drilling and bolt-making machines, and eight blacksmith's forges, whose draft was supplied by a steam rotary fan, "for making of that work which cannot be done by machinery." The whole was powered by a sixty-five-horsepower horizontal engine. This was evidently a running shop, although some heavy repairs may have been done there, and there was talk at the time of expanding its capacity by introducing steam hammers. Under Eaton's program of shop improvement, though, the heavy repair work was to be done in the Hamilton shops, and the stationary engine and machinery were removed to the newly consolidated Hamilton works in 1858. "This will make thirty or forty dwellings in the city vacant," complained a local newspaper, "and materially decrease the population, which has already been more than sufficiently thinned."[25]

The tables were turned some fifteen years later when London became the new locale for the Great Western's principal carshops. "The removal of this large population from Hamilton, while depressing matters a little in the ambitious city, has considerably enlivened the town of London East, where the demand for house room is just at present unusually brisk." The total cost of the shops, sidings and machinery amounted to about £50,000, or a quarter of a million dollars. About $150,000 of this was paid to a London contracting firm, Messrs. Christie & Green, while the remainder was accounted for in work done by the Great Western itself and in purchases of new machinery. There were six buildings,

> all of them of extraordinary size, and with the exception of that used for the storage of dry lumber, are built of brick with slated roofs. They cover an immense area of ground, though clustered as closely together as convenience would allow. There is the blacksmith shop, the machine shop, the iron repair shop, the wood-working department, the storehouses for iron, coal, and other necessaries, and the offices, all in close proximity. A huge transfer table is used to convey the work from one department to another, and the numerous rail tracks that are seen in each building show that the shops are intended to accommodate almost any amount of work.[26]

After the car department's move to London, the buildings it had vacated at Hamilton proved to be too small for the locomotive department there to use. In October 1874 two large shops were dismantled, placed on twenty-car trains, and reerected at Suspension Bridge to replace running repair sheds that had been destroyed by fire there. The Great Western's principal locomotive shops remained at Hamilton for some years after the company's absorption into the Grand Trunk system in 1882. In 1889 their machinery and staff were transferred to the enlarged Grand Trunk motive power shops in Stratford, and the Hamilton shops were closed.[27]

The first substantial railway shops in the Montreal area were those of the Champlain & St. Lawrence, at St. Lambert (South Montreal) across the river from the city. In 1852 the terminus included a machine shop 100 feet by 50, a boiler house 25 feet square, and a blacksmith's shop 50 feet square. Together with the station buildings, engine house and workingmen's cottages they occupied an area of about twenty acres, and promised to be the making of a "handsome compact railway town." In the same year, the St. Lawrence & Atlantic, a Grand Trunk constituent, was soliciting tenders to build a car repair shop at nearby Longueuil. When the Grand Trunk commenced to build its own terminus and shop facilities, however, they were located on the island, at Point St. Charles.[28]

In 1854, when the line was taken over from the contractors, the Grand Trunk's chief engineer explained the works under way at Point St. Charles:

> It is intended to get in the foundations for the Station Buildings, at Montreal, throughout this season, these extend to an aggregate length of 3000 feet, in sundry buildings, varying from 40 to 90 feet in width, some of which are two stories in height, and consist principally of Passenger Stations, Goods Warehouses, Locomotive erecting shops, Engine Stables, Car erecting shops, Smiths, and Foundry shops. It is proposed to complete the Car and Smiths shops this season, so as to admit of commencing the construction of the car rolling stock, which is to be built upon the premises. The remaining buildings of this establishment being so far prepared this autumn, will be readily advanced to completion next year.[29]

By the beginning of 1855, the works were advertising for bolt-makers and coppersmiths, and car building (by contractors) had so far advanced by the spring of 1856 that a shopworkers' protest meeting was held to denounce the *Pilot* and other local newspapers for their disparaging remarks about the quality of the cars. The works had their own sawmill in 1856; by 1857, when the Grand Trunk was building cars on its own account, its locomotive superintendent could speak of the "ample and well appointed workshops" which "have no equal either in extent or in completeness of arrangement on this side of the Atlantic." Some idea of the scale of these works is suggested by a report that they were illuminated by seven hundred gas lights; by 1858 the company was considering spending $20,000 for the plant to make its own gas at a price 40 percent below that charged by the Montreal Gas Company.[30]

When W.S. Mackenzie succeeded Frederick Trevethick as locomotive superintendent in 1859, he predicted the need for substantial additions to and mechanization of the shops, including the introduction of steam hammers, which had come into use on the Great Western the previous year. There appears to be no record of whether he was successful in persuading his board to update the facilities, but when C.J. Brydges left the Great Western to become the Grand Trunk's general manager in 1862 it quickly became apparent that the company's shop arrangements were in terrible disarray. Brydges appointed Henry Yates and Richard Eaton to investigate the working of the mechanical and fuel departments, and they found room for considerable improvement. Repair facilities were scattered among numerous shops and running sheds along the line, several of them located very inefficiently; responsibility for the car stock was diffused; there was no effective renewals policy in force; the locomotive stock required to be standardized; and the stores department was in total disorder. Most importantly for this discussion, they recommended a thoroughgoing consolidation of repair shops, closing many of the smaller ones, converting others into running shops, and concentrating heavy repairs and car and locomotive building at Point St. Charles.[31]

Under Eaton's superintendency, the facilities and equipment at Point St. Charles were rapidly improved. In 1863 the shops built a 10-inch hydraulic power press and a very large mortising machine, and screwing and drilling machines were purchased. The machinery was rearranged and covered ways were built between the smiths, erecting and machine shops. More repairs were done to the shops the following year, and new lathes and machines were added. In 1865 work on the shops was "extraordinarily heavy," and Eaton reported that the company was deficient in shop room for more than fifty engines. Heavy expenditures on shop facilities and machinery continued throughout the 1860s, and by 1869 work was under way on a new paint shop, 270 feet by 40, and a saw and planing mill, 170 feet by 63, at Point St. Charles.[32]

New machinery was added in 1870, and in the same year a fireproof storage building for paints and varnishes was erected and a steam-heating system of the same sort introduced on the Great Western was put into operation. In 1872 new machinery was added, the existing machinery was rearranged, and the steam hammer was placed on new foundations. In 1873 the company bought an additional 40.6 *arpents* of land adjacent to the shops from the Grey Nunnery, in preparation for further expansion, and "extensive additions" were made during the year. In March 1875, the two principal car shops at Point St. Charles, with all their machinery, were destroyed by fire, but by the end of the year they had been replaced. Two years later the car shops were expanded, and additions were made to various of the locomotive shops as well. Over the course of the next several years, there were substantial additions to the stock of machinery. In 1880, "in consequence of the greatly increased work being done at Point St. Charles," the boiler shop was extended 95 feet, the smith's shop 44 feet, the passenger car shop 300 feet, and a new tube shop was erected.[33]

At Brantford, the old Buffalo, Brantford & Goderich company had agreed as one of the terms of its 1854 municipal bonus to erect a "large and commodious machine shop" in the town within fifteen months. A paint and finishing shop for cars, 150 feet by 40, collapsed while under construction in 1854. When the BB&G became the Buffalo & Lake Huron in 1856, Henry Yates was hired away from the Great Western to become its mechanical superintendent, and he brought some skilled shopworkers with him from Hamilton. By August of that year, the company's general manager was able to report that "the workshops are beginning to exhibit some signs of order and arrangement — we are obliged to create everything as we want it," and by November he expressed great satisfaction at the "interior economy" of the shops. The following year, the Brantford works began producing cars for the line, and in 1858 they began rebuilding some old BB&G engines.[34]

When the Grand Trunk absorbed the Buffalo & Lake Huron in 1868 it took over and operated the Brantford shops, leasing the old company's cars from the Brantford Car Company. The railway centralized its locomotive repair facilities at Toronto, transferring most of the engine shop mechanics from Brantford to the shops at Queen's Wharf and placing the former Brantford foreman, Thomas Patterson, in charge. The GTR's Toronto facilities had never been adequate, however; in 1862 Eaton and Yates had singled them out as being the most inconvenient in terms of location and arrangement of any on the line. In the general shops consolidation program of the early 1870s it became apparent that Toronto offered insufficient room for expansion, and Stratford, at the geographic centre of the district, was selected as the site for new locomotive repair shops. Construction began in June 1870 on a 300 foot by 90 workshop building, a storehouse 100 feet by 40, and a roundhouse; all were of brick on cut stone foundations. The shops were illuminated with ten thousand panes of glass (most of which were to be broken in a hailstorm three years later), and a local firm got the glazing contract. Another won the contract to supply castings. When the Stratford shops were completed in 1871, the Queen's Wharf machinery and workforce were transferred there, again under Patterson's general foremanship.[35]

The same consolidation program saw Brantford chosen as the site for a new freight car factory, constructed by Henry Yates at a cost of $31,000. When it began operations in 1871 the Brantford works was the largest in Canada. Capable of admitting fifty cars at a time, it was "provided with every possible labour-saving convenience, the machinery from the old shops having been transferred to it, and arranged to the best advantage, in order to facilitate the preparation of material and to reduce the cost of repairs." Besides carrying out a substantial proportion of the GTR's car repairs, Brantford was to be the company's chief freight car building facility. The "monster workshop" was 336 feet by 144, and 21 feet high. It had five sets of track running along its length and one across its width, with turntables at every intersection. The outside tracks were for repairing Pullman cars, and the three inside ones for freight car building and repair. It was built of brick on stone foundations, and with an iron-truss roof containing seventeen skylights of about 150 square feet each; additional illumination was provided by fifty-four windows. A 30 foot by 20 foot engine room, complete with "monster smoke stack, such as one has never before seen in Brant City," was connected at one side. On the same site stood the old engine house, now converted for car repairs, and a number of specialized workshops, stores buildings and machine rooms.[36]

Shop Practice

It remains to consider briefly some features of organization and practice that characterized the railway shops in the years before 1880. A substantial amount of technological innovation took place in the shops, not only in the form of "tinkering," but also in terms of systematic experimentation. Alongside this must be placed a dual concern with standardization, first with regard to the economy of interchangeable parts, and second to the standards which were imposed by necessity where several companies shared traffic and equipment. These industry standards sometimes restricted innovation. Finally, shop practice was informed throughout by an anxious interest in cost-saving. This found expression not only in the extensive recycling of old equipment and materials and the introduction of labour-saving machinery, but also in the evolution of relatively sophisticated cost-accounting methods and the development of renewals policies.

Most of the mechanical superintendents and at least some of the foremen developed and often patented technological innovations, many of which found their way into the everyday practice of the shops. To take only a few examples among many, Richard Eaton patented a steel locomotive boiler and heater, Henry Yates an improved firebox, and Samuel Sharpe a lateral motion truck and a ventilating apparatus for passenger cars. W.A. Robinson invented a rear-view mirror for engine cabs, Great Western engine shop foreman Joseph Marks had several patents to his credit, including a spark-arresting smokestack that was widely advertised in the industry press, and a Grand Trunk locomotive shop foreman (subsequently foreman of the Kingston Locomotive Works) named Nuttall invented a car lifting and truck transfer device which was indispensable to the company's operations during the transitional years of the gauge change.[37]

Innovation was accompanied by rigorous experimental testing of certain kinds of equipment. The best example is likely wheels, for the debate over the relative merits of cast iron and wrought iron wheels, and of steel tires, continued over the whole period. To some degree the technical questions were tangled up with the rival claims of British suppliers and North American practice, for wrought iron had become so firmly established as the British standard that the Canadian railways' British proprietors were susceptible to enthusiastic lobbying by English and Scottish manufacturers. In 1856 the Great Western's directors decided to replace cast iron driving wheels with English wrought iron wheels, "which, it is expected, will have a very beneficial result, both in respect to safety and ultimate cost for repairs." But three years later Robert Gill, chairman of the railway's English board, told the shareholders that "it was a very extraordinary fact that these wheels, which were cast in America, with charcoal, were found to be more durable and less liable to accident than wrought iron wheels. . . . It was a long time before the Board would give in, but at length they were obliged to let the fact of the small percentage of breakage of these [cast iron] tyres prevail over their own prejudices."[38]

This hardly ended the affair, however, for the wheels question was placed on the agenda of practically every shareholders' enquiry into the workings of the Canadian railways. The mechanical departments responded by manufacturing their own wheels in both cast and wrought iron, ordering test quantities from various manufacturers (including, in 1869, the Intercolonial Iron and Steel Company of Londonderry, Nova Scotia), and conducting exhaustive tests. The battle was still raging when, in 1873, the Grand Trunk's president invited the proprietor of an English railway car company to visit Canada and report on the GTR's rolling stock. He reported in favour of his own brand of wheels and tires, saying "it is almost impossible to estimate the evil effects of the use of Cast Iron Wheels upon your permanent Way. . . . I have no doubt that it would be found that the use of Cast Iron Wheels has been the cause of thousands of rails breaking. . . . I consider it would be an act of barbarism to destroy that road by perpetuating the use of your Cast Iron Wheels."[39]

The GTR management accordingly ordered another test of the English wheels, and two years later mechanical superintendent Wallis supplied an exhaustive accounting of every wrought iron wheel removed from service in January 1875, showing the nature of the defect and the number of miles run, and comparing the experience of wrought and cast iron wheels. This was only the opening salvo in an exchange of information and opinion that lasted for most of the year and resulted in general agreement among the company's officers in Canada that the existing types of English wheels were impracticable. In September the Grand Trunk managers awarded contracts to Canadian firms for the supply of cast iron engine, truck and car wheels, but agreed to try a further test of twelve English wheels with steel tires, made to the mechanical superintendent's new specifications. These were evidently a success, for at the end of 1877 the locomotive superintendent reported that "with regard to our Passenger Cars, we have, after two years' trial, adopted the standard English steel tyred car wheel of 43 inches diameter, in place of the cast iron chilled wheel of 33 inches, and so far as introduced these wheels have given satisfaction, having produced a marked general economy and improvement."[40]

The technological sophistication of the locomotive and car departments and their interest in mechanical invention and improvement seems to run contrary to T.C. Cochran's judgment that innovation was a talent not much looked for in American railway managers because of the difficulty of gaining competitive advantages in an industry that placed such a premium on co-operation. But in Canada, at any rate, the relationship between innovation and interindustry co-operation was fairly complex. Over the period, it was indeed increasingly true that the need to accommodate "foreign" traffic, and to have the company's rolling stock operate on "foreign" lines, precluded certain unilateral changes. On the other hand, technological superiority occasionally led to interindustry co-operation, as when the Grand Trunk agreed to let the Great Western run over its line to Portland for a year, in exchange for having the GWR mechanical department build it a terminal elevator at Toronto. And the need to conform to industry-wide standards could sometimes be a positive spur to innovation, as for example with the variety of appliances developed on both the Grand Trunk and the Great Western to cope first with breaks of gauge with connecting lines, and subsequently with breaks of gauge on their own main lines once the project of changing to the standard North American gauge was begun.[41]

Most significantly, though, technological developments were crucial to the railways' continuing efforts to reduce their costs. Certainly the attention of those in charge of the mechanical departments was constantly drawn to the need for reducing costs; indeed, it was the perception that in-house production could lead to substantial economies that accounted for the railways' role as large-scale manufacturers in the first place. But a sophisticated mechanical superintendent realized, and considered it part of his job to persuade his general manager and board of directors, that true economies could not be secured through simple cost-cutting. "No exertions or expense has been spared, in order to increase the efficiency and durability of the Engines," Eaton reported, "because such is the only way to effect real economy, and advantage to the Company. Our general reductions in expenses are due to the prevention of waste, and not to any false economy in repairs."[42]

Achieving "real economy" was an extremely complex task. Among its components were the establishment of standards permitting mechanization and interchangeability of parts, rational shop arrangement, the reduction of waste through heroic efforts at recycling used materials, experimentation with new materials and techniques, and effective accounting for expenditures and depreciation. Taking all these elements together, advanced railway shop practice in the three decades before 1880 bore a striking resemblance to several of the important "discoveries" of the new industrial management theorists of the early twentieth century.[43]

Standardization of equipment and parts was an important aspect of workshop economy. "Nothing tends so much to increase the working expenses of the Locomotive Department in this Country than by the adopting or ordering more than two or at most three classes of Engines," reported Eaton and Yates in 1862. "However great a number may be required they should be of one build and design, for apart from the comparatively smaller expenditure required for Patterns, Castings, Spare Gear, &c necessary to be kept always on hand, the advantages and saving arising from the use that could be made of parts of Engines under repairs during the Winter to meet emergencies could be of the greatest possible benefit to the Company."[44]

They estimated that standardization would reduce the proportion of engines under repair by at least 20 percent, and would mean extensive savings in labour and materials costs. They noted that the Grand Trunk locomotives were of a "great variety of Patterns and build which have been supplied from no less than fourteen different establishments, the varieties of Engines being still further increased from the fact of several of the same firms having furnished several lots of Engines of different kinds, from designs of their own, some of which have been found quite unsuitable for the road and Traffic, until important alterations and additions had been made by the Company," a fact which of course further varied the stock. Indeed, the more different kinds of engines a railway possessed, the more engines it needed to do the work because it could not achieve speed and efficiency in upkeep and repair.

Eaton and Yates recommended that a uniform standard for all leading dimensions be established and adhered to in altering the present stock and supplying new engines, so that in the course of time "a tolerable near approach to uniformity" might be achieved. Both the Grand Trunk and the Great Western adopted such standards for building new engines in their own shops, and they supplied specifications to the Kingston Locomotive Works as well. By 1868 the Great Western had five of these built at Kingston: "they are similar in all essential parts to the new standard freight engines built in our own works, with which their parts are interchangeable." The shops seem to have managed a judicious balance of standards and innovation. "I am using every means to secure a powerful Engine having only a moderate weight," wrote Eaton in 1867. "For obtaining this desirable object we are making the Boiler and other available parts of Steel, and substituting wrought- for cast-iron wherever it is possible to do so. I may also state that although differing in some details all the essential parts — such as wheels, axles and Machinery — will be strictly uniform with the Grand Trunk standard."[45]

Rational shop arrangement and recycling waste also produced efficiencies and economies. As we saw in the earlier discussion of the development of the railways' physical plant, the mechanical superintendents often rearranged their heavy machinery, sometimes in concert with the development of new equipment, and introduced hoists, tramways, overhead cranes and other appliances for the easy movement of heavy machines and materials. The kind of savings such integration involved is suggested by Eaton's account of the new furnace installed to heat scrap to be worked by the Great Western's steam hammer in 1858:

> The objects aimed at were, to get the fullest possible benefit from the enormous amount of waste heat evolved from the furnace, and we shall be able not only to raise steam for working the Steam Hammer, but there will be an overplus to assist the Stationary Engine, instead of taking from it as before, and from the same waste heat we shall be able to do all the Spring Makers Work and to re-heat for forging the same quantity of iron which is done by one of our largest Smiths Hearths, consequently saving the amount of Coal used by that hearth.[46]

Along with shop rearrangement went the shops consolidation programs undertaken by both the Great Western and the Grand Trunk. The effects of these have already been described; their purpose was stated succinctly by Eaton and Yates when they recommended that car renewals and repairs be concentrated at Point St. Charles, "where under a well regulated System with every appliance in the way of tools and machinery, the work can be done at a much less cost than by workmen employed at out of the way stations and under no regular supervision."[47]

Efficiencies and economies were also accomplished by recycling waste. The steam heating system installed at Point St. Charles was fuelled exclusively by sawdust and small cuttings from the woodworking shops. Eaton reported of the first engine constructed by the Great Western that "the Framing has been made by ourselves from our own scrap iron, the inside and outside connecting rods and the valve motion &c are made from worn out Lowmoor Tyres, the Piston Rods and Slide Bars we have made from old broken springs, and the greater part of the Cylinders consist of old Car Wheels, there being no better metal in the world for that purpose." Two years later he was proposing to use the machinery from one or two old locomotives to drive the company's proposed rolling mills. In 1874 the Grand Trunk's mechanical superintendent proposed to convert sufficient broad gauge car trucks to the standard gauge to be used for about one thousand new cars; some of the new car bodies would be built in the GTR shops and others would be contracted for. The same year, the Grand Trunk's storekeeper noted that "it will not be necessary to contract for Washers as they can be more economically made in the Company's shops out of the old sheet Iron on hand by the breaking up of the old broad guage [sic] tenders."[48]

Railway shop accounting is really a subset of the much larger topic of railway accounts and statistics generally, a subject too broad to be considered fully here. Concern about the keeping of adequate workshop accounts began with the inception of railway operations; in December 1854, some months before the Great Western's board decided on a policy of tendering for expenditures over £1000, it instructed the managing director and secretary to report "as early as possible upon the system of accounts to be kept in the Mechanical Department."

Shop bookkeeping seems to have involved establishing a separate account for every piece of rolling stock (adjusted from time to time by a census of cars), along with additional accounts for major pieces of machinery, for tools and for general shop maintenance. Wages and the cost of materials for repairing the stock would be charged to the appropriate account, so that it was possible, however tediously, to establish the costs of repair (and of running) for each item or class of equipment, compile comparative statistics such as those already discussed for wrought iron versus cast iron wheels, and to prepare, as a matter of course, half-yearly tabulations of costs of various kinds per mile run in the various types of service. By 1875 at the latest, shopworkers' daily work records were organized so as to show the allocation of working hours to each item of equipment. In principle, this might have enabled long-term efficiency checks on individual workers, or the tracing of faults in workmanship back to the individual responsible, although there is no evidence that such use was in fact made of these records. In any event, the detailed record-keeping systems in use in the railway shops and, with a complex system of cross-accounting, in other branches of the railway service, amounted to real cost-accounting, far removed from the simple double-entry bookkeeping systems that characterized most other industry in the period. This accounting system was the backbone of shop practice, for without it the superintendents' claims to be achieving real economies through judicious expenditure could hardly have been justified.[49]

Summary and Conclusions

While the railways have long been a favourite topic of Canadian economic historians, little attention has been paid to aspects of their activities other than finance and construction. For the most part, they have been viewed as transportation companies pure and simple. But this distorts the reality: the major railways were transportation companies, to be sure, but they were very large, vertically and horizontally integrated transportation companies, whose activities covered a much broader range of economic endeavour. In the period before the National Policy (and perhaps for many years later as well) the major railways were, *inter alia*, among the biggest manufacturing firms in the economy.

From the beginning, the railway companies erected the plant to build their own cars, leasing it to independent contractors. They took over these car works and operated them themselves for three principal reasons. First, they considered (with good reason given that they already owned the physical plant and had a substantial workforce engaged in repairs) that they could build cars more cheaply than the contractors. Second, they were unhappy with the quality of the contractors' product. Finally, manufacturing activity of this sort offered alternative employment for shopworkers in periods of slack traffic, thereby protecting the railways' substantial investment in labour recruitment. From manufacturing cars it was a short step to manufacturing locomotives and other railway equipment as well, wherever it was cost-effective, in the broadest sense, to do so.

With the growth of the system, the scope of shopwork expanded. Parts and components that had formerly been purchased from outside suppliers as a matter of course, and had often to be imported at great expense and with some uncertainty, were now frequently made in the railways' own works. Heavy investments in new shop capacity were made, and existing facilities were consolidated and modernized. Operating under an imperative to keep costs low, both in shopwork and in the train running that it supported, the works invested heavily in machinery, some of it made in the shops, attempted to improve the efficiency of equipment through innovation, experiment and exhaustive testing, and instituted sophisticated systems of cost control. As a result, the railway shops were not only among the largest manufacturing establishments in the Canadian economy, but were among the most advanced technologically and managerially as well.

If this is accepted, then it appears evident that traditional views of the railways' place in Canadian industrialization require some revision. The distinction between "commercial" railways and "industrial" factories is plainly absurd, and should be abolished. The view that the railways' contribution to industrialization consisted of expanding the effective market for domestic industry is no longer adequate. It must be supplemented by enquiries about the interaction between the railways' manufacturing activities and the rest of the industrial economy. In particular, the broader industrializing effects of the railways' shop location decisions, in terms of the local labour force, sources of supply (including the surplus materials and equipment that the railways placed on the market), and the independent railway supply industry deserve examination. It may be that in the final analysis one of the critical questions to be asked about the development of Canadian manufacturing is why other producers in the economy took so long to follow the railways' lead.

Notes

1. In December 1862, the Great Western's Inside Locomotive Department (i.e., shops as distinct from running trades) employed 255 men at Hamilton, and the Car Department 265; see Hamilton Public Library, GWR Mechanical Dept. Paysheets. In early 1860 the company held a dinner for six hundred men to celebrate the completion of the first locomotive built entirely in its shops; see Hamilton *Spectator*, 10 Feb. 1860. The Grand Trunk published a breakdown of employment and wages in its locomotive department in its *Report* for the half-year ending 31 June 1859, showing 684 men employed in its locomotive shops alone.

2. Myles Pennington, *Railways and Other Ways* (Toronto, 1894), 119.

3. Public Archives of Canada (hereafter PAC), RG 30, Canadian National Railways Papers (henceforth *CNR*), vol. 1, 24 Aug. 1855, Report of G.L. Reid, Chief Engineer to the Shareholders; ibid., 4 June 1853; *CNR* 1000, 11 Dec. 1856; PAC, John Young Papers, 20 Apr. 1852; *CNR* 2, 2 Sept. 1853; 2 Feb. 1855; 2 Mar. 1855; 30 Mar. 1855; Hamilton *Spectator*, 15 Sept. 1855.

4. *CNR* 1000, 11 Dec. 1856; Montreal *Pilot*, 1 Aug. 1857.

5. Toronto *Globe*, 28 Apr. 1853; W.M. Spriggs, "Great Western Railway of Canada," *Bulletin of the Railway and Locomotive Historical Society*: 51; John Loye, "Locomotives of the Grand Trunk Railway," ibid.: 25. The rivalry of British and American locomotive builders was regularly vented in industry periodicals on both sides of the Atlantic. For a contemporary comparison of costs and labour content see *American Railway Review* 5 (1862): 230, copying *The Engineer* (London), 22 Nov. 1861. Independent Canadian producers were extremely vulnerable to recession, and only the Kingston works survived as a locomotive builder to the end of the century. See W.G. Richardson, "The Canadian Locomotive Company in the Nineteenth Century" (paper presented to Canadian Historical Association, Annual Meeting, Kingston, 1973). Hamilton *Spectator*, 9 Aug. 1856, 28 Feb. 1857, 3 Sept. 1857 and 4 Jan. 1858; Toronto *Globe*, 28 Apr. 1853; Toronto *Leader*, 6

Feb. and 24 Mar. 1854; *CNR* 2, no. 1148, 16 Jan. 1857; *Railways and Other Ways*, 86; *Dictionary of Canadian Biography*, X (Toronto, 1972), 330f. [William Hamilton]; Bryan D. Palmer, *A Culture in Conflict* (Montreal, 1979), 14; Montreal *Pilot*, 1 Aug. 1857; Montreal *Gazette*, 30 Apr. 1852; *CNR* 2, no. 709, 8 June 1855. Hamilton's abandoned the locomotive and general machine business to specialize in producing railway cars and railway iron; see Toronto *Mail*, 18 Apr. 1872.

6. Hamilton *Spectator*, 25 Jan. 1861. See Paul Craven and Tom Traves, "Dimensions of Paternalism: Discipline and Culture in Canadian Railway Operations in the 1850s," in C. Heron and R. Storey, eds., *On the Job* (Kingston, 1986), 47–74. Hamilton *Spectator*, 10 Feb. 1860; Hamilton *Times*, 12 May 1859; Toronto *Globe*, 17 May 1859.

7. The data in this paragraph are calculated from mechanical (or locomotive) superintendents' reports and associated tables published in the Grand Trunk's half-yearly *Reports* (varying titles) for the appropriate dates. We have so far been unable to compile a wholly unbroken run of these reports from mid-1854 (when the first one appeared) to mid-1863. The December 1873 cut-off date is used here because the Grand Trunk's change of gauge substantially altered the pattern of shopwork in the years immediately following.

8. For details on locomotive components and construction see, for example, Matthias N. Forney, *Catechism of the Locomotive* (New York, 1883). The figures in this paragraph are calculated from the Great Western's *Reports* for the appropriate dates.

9. *CNR* 7, no. 1597, 27 Aug. 1861; no. 1643, 15 Jan. 1862; GTR *Report*, half-year ending 30 June 1869, p. 11; GWR *Report*, half-year ending 31 Jan. 1861, p. 27; Hamilton *Spectator*, 9 Aug. 1860; *CNR* 1042, 28 Nov. 1879; *CNR* 6, no. 1649, 26 Feb. 1864.

10. *CNR* 7, no. 1380, 20 May 1859; ibid., nos. 1651–2, 11 Mar. 1862; GTR *Report*, half-year ending 30 June 1869, 11.

11. Hamilton *Spectator*, 4 Mar. 1857; GTR *Report* for half-year to 30 June 1864; ibid., half-year to 30 June 1865. "Maintenance" here meant keeping the car stock up to numerical strength.

12. It was not until well into the 1860s that the larger railway companies worked out even a moderately consistent accounting response to the problem of depreciation; previously, new equipment had frequently been charged to revenue account, and renewals to capital.

13. *CNR*, no. 1643, 15 Jan. 1862.

14. Dominion Bureau of Statistics/Statistics Canada, *Standard Industrial Classification Manual* (Ottawa, 1948); ibid (Ottawa, 1960); ibid (Ottawa, 1970); ibid (Ottawa, 1980). The latest revision is somewhat opaque in its criteria as compared to earlier versions.

15. Canadian National Railways Library, Richard Eaton, ms. half-yearly report of mechanical superintendent, GTR, for 31 Dec. 1864; GTR *Report* for half-year ending 30 June 1878, 12; ibid., half-year ending 31 Dec. 1879, 14; ibid, half-year ending 30 June 1878, 13.

16. Car and locomotive renewal funds have been included in the tables whether or not they were reported separately in the original accounts. On both railways, mechanical department expenditures increased rapidly during the change of gauge due to new construction and (especially) the herculean task of conversions. In the years immediately following the change, repair and renewal expenditures dropped sharply since so much of the stock was new or had recently undergone extensive rebuilding. These factors account for the larger departures from trend in the Figures.

17. "Engine builders" included manufacturers of all manner of steam engines, not merely locomotives. A detailed systematic examination of the industrial schedules for locations other than those surveyed here might well turn up other misclassified and/or omitted establishments. The published report should be used with the greatest caution: Canada, *Census (1870–1)* (Ottawa, 1875), vol. 3.

18. *CNR* 1, p. 17: Report of John T. Clark, 4 June 1853; *American Railroad Journal*, 27 Aug. 1853.

19. Hamilton *Spectator*, 28 Feb. 1857.

20. Ibid., 4 Mar. 1857.

21. Ibid., 7 Oct. 1857; *CNR* 6, 31 July 1858; *CNR* 7, no. 1308, 17 Dec. 1858, ibid., no. 1319, 31 Dec. 1858; *Canadian Illustrated News*, 14 Feb. 1863.

22. *CNR* 7, no. 1441, 18 Nov. 1859; GWR *Report* for half-year to 31 Jan. 1860; GWR *Reports*, half-years to 31 Jan. 1860 and 31 July 1860; *CNR* 7, no. 1474, 10 Feb. 1860; *CNR* 6, no. 1142, 28 Nov. 1860.

23. *CNR* 6, no. 1142, 28 Nov. 1860.

24. GWR *Reports*, half-years to 31 July 1862, 31 July 1865, 31 July 1869, 31 Jan. 1870, 31 July 1870, 31 Jan. 1871, 31 Jan. 1872 and 31 Jan. 1873; *CNR* 4, no 3335, 23 June 1871; ibid., no. 3341, 29 June 1871; GWR *Report* for half-year to 31 Jan. 1875; London *Advertiser*, 10 and 25 Nov. 1874; London *Free Press*, 11 Nov. 1874; *CNR* 4, no. 4096, 18 Sept. 1873; GWR *Reports*, half-years to 31 July 1873 and 31 Jan. 1874; *CNR* 8, 5 Nov. 1873.

25. Hamilton *Spectator*, 12 Mar. 1857, copying London *Prototype*; Toronto *Leader*, 7 Apr. 1858, copying London *Journal*.

26. London *Advertiser*, 10 and 21 Nov. 1874; GWR *Reports*, half-years to 31 July 1870, 31 July 1873, 31 Jan. 1874, 31 July 1874, 31 Jan. 1875 and 31 July 1875; *CNR* 4, no. 4112, 9 Oct. 1873.

27. *CNR* 4, no. 3965, 10 Apr. 1873; London *Advertiser*, 16 Oct. 1874; Canadian National Railways Library, Montreal, H. Spencer, "An Historical Review of the Canadian National Railways Motive Power Shops, at Stratford, Ont., from its Inception in 1870 to August 1951," unpublished typescript.

28. Montreal *Gazette*, 2 and 18 Feb. 1852, 10 Aug. and 30 Nov. 1853; Montreal *Gazette*, 17 Sept. 1852. In the United States, the Grand Trunk had substantial engine shops at Gorham, New Hampshire and at Island Pond, Vermont, and a major car shop at Portland, Maine. These American facilities are not discussed further in this paper. Montreal *Gazette*, 15 and 16 Feb. 1855; Montreal *Transcript*, 25 Sept. 1857; GTR *Report*, 1855.

29. GTR *Report*, 1854.

30. Montreal *Gazette*, 15 Jan. and 2 Oct. 1855, 10 May and 22 July 1856; GTR *Report* for half-year to 30 June 1857; *Journal of the Franklin Institute of the State of Pennsylvania*, 3rd ser., 36 (July 1858).

31. GTR *Report* for half-year to 30 June 1859. For an engraving of the Grand Trunk workshops in 1860, see C.P. DeVolpi and P.S. Winkworth, eds., *Montréal: Recueil Iconographique* (Montreal, 1963), vol. 1, 137. The Eaton-Yates report was predicated on the contemplated merger of the Grand Trunk and Great Western, so they proposed to make Montreal the focal point for repairs and renewals on the Portland to Toronto section, and Hamilton for the western section. When the merger plans fell through, their major recommendations were adapted for the Grand Trunk alone. *CNR* 1001, 9 June 1862; *CNR* 10190, fo. 77.

32. Canadian National Railways Library, GTR, ms. Locomotive Superintendent's Reports, half-years to 31 Dec. 1863, 30 June 1864, 30 June 1865 and 30 June 1868; GTR *Reports*, half-years to 31 Dec. 1868 and 30 June and 31 Dec. 1869.

33. GTR *Reports*, half-years to 30 June 1870, 31 Dec. 1870, 30 June 1872 and 31 Dec. 1872; 92 *CNR* 1039, 6 Dec. 1873; GTR *Reports*, half-years to 31 Dec. 1873, 30 June 1875, 31 Dec. 1875 and 31 Dec 1877; *CNR* 1042, 20 May 1880; GTR *Reports*, half-years to 30 June 1880 and 31 Dec. 1880.

34. Brantford *Expositor*, 14 Mar. 1854 and 15 July 1870; University of Western Ontario, Regional History Collection, published evidence in *Whitehead v. Buffalo*, II: 36 (Barlow to Heseltine and Powell, 5 July 1856); II, p. 44 (Barlow to Heseltine and Powell, 16 Aug. 1856); II, p. 55 (Barlow to Powell, 15 Nov. 1856); I, p. 111 (Barlow to proprietors, 16 Feb. 1857); III (*Report* for half-year to 31 July 1857); I, p. 122 (Powell to proprietors, 21 Sept. 1857); III (*Report* for half-year to 31 July 1858).

35. *CNR* 10190, fo. 77. See generally, H. Spencer, "Canadian National Railways Motive Power Shops," 113; Stratford *Beacon*, 12 Aug. 1870, 4 Nov. 1870, 11 Nov. 1870, 11 Apr. 1873, 16 May 1873, 13 June 1873 and 18 July 1873, Stratford *Herald*, 15 June 1870 and 10 and 24 May 1871.

36. *CNR* 1038, 6 May 1871; Brantford *Expositor*, 7 Oct. 1870, 2 June 1871, 14 July 1871 and 28 July 1871; GTR *Report* for half-year to 31 Dec. 1871.

37. *The Engineer* (London), 9 Mar. 1860, 155; *Whitehead v. Buffalo*, III, *Report* for half-year to 31 Jan. 1858; Montreal *Transcript*, 6 Nov. 1857; Hamilton *Spectator*, 28 Aug. 1860 and 27 Apr. 1863; *Canadian Illustrated News*, 6 Dec. 1862; *Canadian National Railways Magazine*, Aug. 1934; *American Railway Review* 5 (1862): 210; Stratford *Beacon*, 1 Aug. 1873, and see Montreal *Transcript*, 8 Oct. 1857; *CNR* 1039, 3 June 1873.

38. *CNR* 1, Report of R.W. Harris, 12 Mar. 1856; ibid., Car Superintendent's Report, 18 Feb. 1859; Hamilton *Times*, 26 Apr. 1859. Discussions of the inadequacies of wrought iron wheels and the superiority of cast iron occur regularly in the mechanical superintendents' half-yearly reports; the most common problem with the English wheels was their high rate of winter breakage.

39. University of Western Ontario, Regional History Collection, Thomas Swinyard Papers, v. 1430, Swinyard to Livesey, 28 Dec. 1869; *CNR* 1039, 22 Oct. 1873; London *Advertiser*, 19 Mar. 1874.

40. Canadian National Railways Library, Wallis to Hickson, ms. report on steel wheels, 2 and 3 Mar. 1875; ibid., ms. bundle, "Correspondence and Reports on English Steel Tyred Wheels," Hannaford to Hickson, 26 Aug. 1875; *CNR* 1040, 21 Sept. 1875; GTR *Report* for half-year ending 31 Dec. 1877.

41. Thomas C. Cochran, *Railroad Leaders, 1843–1899* (Cambridge, Mass., 1953), 147ff.; GTR *Report* for half-year to 31 Dec. 1877. The argument that interdependence of firms prohibited unilateral innovation was advanced by several railway managers to excuse their failure to introduce certain safety appliances that might reduce the frequency of accidents to brakemen; see Ontario, Select Committee on Railway Accidents, *Report*, 1880, passim; *CNR* 7, #1617, 18 Oct. 1861.

42. GWR *Report* for half-year to 31 Jan. 1862; Canadian National Railways Library, GTR, ms. Locomotive Superintendent's Report for half-year to 30 June 1864.

43. A very important difference, however, arose from the fact that "scientific management" assumed a fully formed labour market, while the railway managers had to incorporate the retention of skilled workers into their economy project. But by the late 1870s this was beginning to change, and the railway shops found it possible for the first time (with some minor exceptions in the crisis of the late 1850s) to reduce the size of their workforces, where earlier they had only reluctantly reduced the length of the working day. In terms of *labour* management, then, it would strain the argument to say that the railways of the 1860s and 1870s anticipated scientific management, but in terms of industrial organization and cost-control methods of other kinds, they were in the vanguard of managerial innovation.

44. *CNR* 10190, fo. 77, 31 May 1862.

45. Canadian National Railways Library, GTR, ms. Locomotive Superintendent's Reports, half-years to 31 Dec. 1864 and 30 June 1867; GWR *Report* for half-year to 31 July 1868.

46. *CNR* 7, no. 1319, Locomotive Superintendent's Report for half-year to 31 Dec. 1858. One of the fullest discussions available of railway workshop layout was published by the Grand Trunk's Master Mechanic at Stratford in 1889; see J. Davis Barnett, "Work Shops, Their Design and Construction," Engineering Institute of Canada, *Transactions* 3 (1889): 1.

47. *CNR* 10190, fo. 77, 31 May 1862.

48. GTR *Report* for half-year to 31 Dec. 1870; *CNR* 7, no. 1467, 27 Jan. 1860; no. 1643, 15 Jan. 1862; ibid., no. 1039, 2 Oct. 1874 and 23 Sept. 1874.

49. *CNR* 2, no. 501, 5 Dec. 1854; the tendering policy was adopted in May 1855 (ibid, no. 662); GTR *Report* for half-year to 30 June 1859; Hamilton Public Library, GWR, ms. locomotive shop work records, 1875; on accounting practices in contemporary industry, see A.D. Chandler, *The Visible Hand* (Cambridge, Mass., 1977), 69ff.

Munificent Parsons and Municipal Parsimony: Voluntary v. Public Poor Relief in Nineteenth Century Toronto†

Stephen A. Speisman

During the course of an optimistic inaugural address delivered to the Toronto City Council in 1881, Mayor William Howland expressed the opinion that "the real prosperity of the town is due to our character as a religious people."[1] To the observer of the 1970s this statement might seem absurd, but to Howland's audience it was eminently logical and correct. Torontonians in the early decades of the nineteenth century desired to fulfil their responsibilities toward their unfortunate fellow citizens and to do so as a religious community. In fact, prior to 1900, the very religious character of Toronto militated against the assumption of social welfare responsibilities by the city government. For one thing, the dispensing of "charity" was considered a purely religious function, and so the absence of a strong church-state connection in Upper Canada freed government at all levels from this task.[2] Moreover, the diversity of religious denominations within the city had several interesting consequences in the field of private charity. It gave rise to a multiplicity of voluntary relief organizations, thereby diminishing whatever popular pressure there might have been for the assumption of relief functions by the City. But as a result of jealousies between denominations, and their desire for independence, this diversity long prevented the development of a unified private approach to charity. Occasionally, it came to be realized that some problems were too large to be attacked by small groups, and in some instances, most specifically in the cases of the Hospital and the House of Industry, Protestant groups banded together in non-denominational enterprises. This phenomenon, however, was neither common nor widespread, and seldom before the 1880s and 1890s did it encompass non-Protestant groups.

If any philosophy can be said to have guided the Toronto approach to the problems of the poor, it was a combination of the tenets of Evangelical Protestantism and Manchester Liberalism. In this regard, Toronto was by no means

†*Ontario History* 65 (1973): 33–49. The author is grateful to Prof. J.M.S. Careless for suggesting this as a subject for research; to Mrs. S.I. Gerridzen, Librarian of the School of Social Work, University of Toronto; and especially to Mr. Scott James and Mrs. Glenna Tisshaw of the City of Toronto Archives, whose valuable assistance made enjoyable what would have been many tedious hours.

unique; it merely reflected those attitudes which prevailed throughout the English-speaking world in the nineteenth century and which have come to be called "Victorian." In essence, this body of belief encompassed the following principles. First, it was the Divine Will that some people in every society must be poor. But these "deserving" poor were immediately recognizable since the cause of their poverty, be it age, infirmity, or youthful innocence, was undeniably obvious. These poor, the Christian was morally bound to assist, without the imposition of any restrictions upon the recipient of the charity. Those, however, whose poverty was not immediately traceable to one of such causes, were to be designated "undeserving." Any able-bodied person, it was believed, could not fail to find work and to prosper if he desired to do so. Poverty for him, therefore, could be the result only of moral failure.[3] It was the duty of the Christian to find work for the able-bodied poor, preferably under unpleasant conditions such as those of a workhouse, where according to good Benthamite logic laziness would be cured and morals regenerated.

Secondly, assistance to the poor was to be given by Christians as religious individuals or in private voluntary associations. Only these could distinguish between deserving and undeserving poor. Moreover, voluntary performance of charitable acts promoted the salvation of the benefactor. Automatic state aid, on the contrary, especially that financed by poor rates, was considered indiscriminate by definition, tending, as Lord Shaftesbury remarked, "to debase a large mass of people to the condition of the nursery. . . ."[4] There was even the danger that well-meaning individual Christians might fail to examine the merits of the applicant for charity and recognizing the hazard, *The Toronto Globe* warned its readers that "Promiscuous alms giving is fatal . . . it is the patent process of the manufacture of paupers out of the worthless and improvident." As for a poor law, this was "a legislative machine for the manufacture of pauperism. It is true mercy to say that it would be better that a few individuals should die of starvation than that a pauper class should be raised up with thousands devoted to crime and the victims of misery."[5]

A third principle of this Victorian attitude toward the poor, originated in the theories of Malthus and revolved around the belief that one should not be too generous with one's charity lest poverty, a natural means of population limitation, be totally eliminated. There is little doubt that this belief, coupled with the fear of creating a pauper class, was responsible to a considerable degree for the failure to institute a poor law in Upper Canada, even after municipal government became available to enforce one. Fortunately, however scientific Victorian Torontonians attempted to be, their religious nature simply would not permit them to tolerate outright starvation.[6]

Finally, Victorians had immense confidence in their society, a feeling which increased with each year especially following the great Exhibition of 1851.[7] They were proud of the prosperity they had wrought and of the Empire they were creating. Yet simultaneously, they felt guilty and vulnerable. As pious Christians they could not but feel uncomfortable in their luxury while others did not share it. Furthermore, with Edmund Burke they saw poverty as breeding social revolution,[8] and if Victorians feared anything, it was drastic social change. Consequently, philanthropy became for many a means of assuaging that guilt and of preventing an alienated multitude from destroying the society responsible for it. Just as public health projects were first undertaken in England as a means of protecting the rich from infection, so welfare ventures served a similar protective function. This was the case in Toronto no less than in Europe.

The exact origins of relief work in Toronto are obscure. No doubt, as in every pioneer community, individual householders at York must have extended aid to those who requested it. In addition, there had existed very early in the nineteeenth century a society for the "relief of strangers in distress,"[9] but one cannot be certain who comprised it or what precisely were its functions. A discussion of organized service to the poor in the city and the tension between the private and public sectors begins, however, with the York Hospital. Although the establishment of military hospitals was considered the legitimate preserve of government, civilian institutions, caring as they did in the early nineteenth century only for those who could not afford to have medical care at home, were classified as charities. It is not surprising, then, that the hospital at York began as a private enterprise, indeed, almost as an afterthought.

In response to the war with the United States, the Loyal and Patriotic Society of Upper Canada had begun in 1813 to collect money for a military hospital and had persuaded the provincial authorities to grant a parcel of land on the Garrison Common east of Fort York. However, by the time the land had passed officially to the society in 1818, the war had ended and the project appeared lost, since private donations to the fund had fallen off as soon as the crisis passed, and it would have been unthinkable to expect the government to support a campaign for what must now be exclusively a civilian institution. Fortunately, the society found itself in that year with an unexpected supply of funds. The organization had planned to reward outstanding members of the militia with gold medals at the completion of the conflict, but the eligible candidates were so numerous that another form of appreciation had to be found.[10] The medals, which had already been ordered, were then defaced and put up for sale, with the money realized being used to endow the new hospital at York.

By 1820 the hospital was rising at King and John Streets, and already it reflected that upper class leadership which was to remain characteristic of Toronto philanthropy throughout the century. The first board and trustees included such illustrious men as the Rev. Dr. John Strachan, James Bâby, John Beverley Robinson and William Allan. Despite the impressive patronage, however, private funds were insufficient to allow the unfinished premises to be fitted up. The provincial government agreed to complete the structure only in 1824, after the Parliament buildings had been destroyed by fire and it was needed to house the legislature.

Almost from its inception, the hospital was beset with difficulties. It was constantly under public attack, the doctors being suspected of performing medical experiments on patients. Moreover, rivalry between the students of Trinity College Medical School and those of Dr. Rolph's Toronto School of Medicine erupted in 1855 in an ugly investigation of the hospital's management, with charges of malpractice and drunkenness being exchanged. In 1854, when the institution was moved to what is now Gerrard Street near Parliament Street, there were complaints that its location was inconvenient and that the area was conducive to ague. As the historian of the hospital remarks, "the whole discussion revealed a state of affairs hardly in line with the modern requirements of a hosptial."[11]

Since the terms of its endowment provided that the hospital was to serve the entire province, the local officials of York, and their successors after incorporation, tended to leave maintenance of the institution to the provincial government; the latter, however, considered it a charity and so preferred to leave it in private hands. As a result, it was not until 1841 that the provincial government offered a minute annual grant,[12] whereas the city officials refused until the end of the century to accept any definite financial commitment. The situation grew so serious that in 1868 the hospital had to close for lack of funds. Only after the Roman Catholics under Archbishop Lynch offered to take over the institution and heated opposition arose from Protestant citizens did the city offer "a small grant" to allow the hospital to reopen.[13] Even so, when the directors asked the council for an annual grant to prevent a recurrence of the incident, the latter refused, insisting that charity should sustain hospitals.[14] If the provincial government had not provided an emergency appropriation the hospital doubtless would not have survived, but even this sector of government was not generous. When remodelling became necessary in 1875, it had to be financed entirely by private funds, with later additions being sponsored by wealthy citizens such as William Gooderham Sr., James Worts, William Cawthra. Andrew Mercer and Joseph Flavelle. Not until 1914, when the College Street hospital was opened, did the city contribute any substantial sum.[15]

Although the sick poor could be cared for with reasonable efficiency after the 1820s, there was no organized provision for children, for the aged, the unemployed or for the able-bodied poor in general, nor did the local officials at Toronto display any inclination to alter the situation. In 1836 an irate citizen complained to the mayor of his disappointment in a meeting held at City Hall, at which, apparently, a proposal to establish a workhouse had been defeated. Voicing the typical nineteenth-century fear of a potentially dangerous pauper class, he pleaded for "a more permanent and extended mode of relieving the *industrious* poor." "It is [a] matter of astonishment to me," he continued, "that the Citizens of Toronto should be so blind to their own interest. . . . " Private givers of charity, he charged, rendered themselves "accessory to the degradation and vice which the proposed plan is calculated to remove. . . ." A workhouse, on the other hand, would not only relieve the public from the annoyance of beggars but also would inculcate in these mendicants the "principles and habits of industry and moral virtue."[16]

Such exhortations fell upon deaf ears, but the depression of 1837 could not be ignored. Probably in response to it, the city provided an old house on Richmond Street for use as a House of Industry.[17] Although a small sum of money accompanied the building, most of the necessary funds were raised by private subscription. In fact, initiative for the founding of the workhouse came not from the municipal authorities but rather from concerned private citizens. Their purpose was to set up an institution on the English model, "whose tendency is to discriminate between actual and pretended poor and to distribute charity accordingly."[18] The result would be the elimination of street begging, the forcing of the city's indolent to work — preferably in the countryside — the prevention of immorality, and the better care of the deserving poor by the reduction of monetary waste.[19] In line with the Benthamite principle of "less eligibility," most assistance provided was to be institutional. Male inmates were to break stone for the city roads, whereas women were to knit and to sell their products for the support of the workhouse.

Neglected children were also to be cared for at the House of Industry. Well into the century, baskets were placed on the porch so that mothers who found it necessary to abandon their infants could leave them there, ring the bell, and then disappear.[20] For the most part, the children lived at the House of Industry until they were old enough to be apprenticed, in the interim having been provided with rudimentary education. However, the officials of the institution sought whenever possible to place the children in foster homes, not only in Toronto but also in the surrounding rural areas. Actually, the latter was preferred.[21] In a fashion typical of the nineteenth century, these embryonic children's aid projects were based as much on the protection of society as they were philanthropic. As a contemporary writer phrased it:

> Nothing could be more . . . dangerous to the citizens at large, than to have a number of idle and vagrant children thrown upon our streets to beg for a living, while they are constantly shut out from those moral and religious influences which form the principal elements of civilized life.[22]

In July 1852, the House of Industry expanded its services to provide temporary accommodation for transients on the model of the night asylums for the homeless poor in England and Scotland. Following the English practice, applicants were limited to one night's free lodging with supper and breakfast. Here, especially, Benthamite practices were applied. Lodgers were obliged to chop wood each morning or be denied admission the next day. The importance attached to this device is illustrated by the fact that it was retained well after 1900, even though the institution had difficulty disposing of the wood. Moreover, conditions in the transient quarters were kept as unpleasant as possible. As late as 1891, a member of the Board of Management remarked that the city jail was "ten times more comfortable than our quarters. . . ."[23] Despite the deterrent, there appears to have been enthusiastic response to this "casual ward," as it was called; from its inception until December 1854 it accommodated 2620 people.[24] This is by no means surprising, for the casual ward was virtually the only service of its kind until about 1915 when a section of the Toronto General Hospital was set aside, under city grant, as the Municipal Lodging House.

The House of Industry had also provided some outdoor relief from the beginning.[25] Attempts likely were made to keep this to a minimum, but no systematic method was adopted until 1858 when a member of the board was appointed to inquire personally into the needs of those requesting "outdoor assistance." The number of inspectors was increased as the century progressed, but never in the period of this study did they exceed ten.[26] While the practice of investigation was in accord with the philosophy of helping only the deserving poor, it was put into effect directly in response to a particular event, namely the depression of

1857. Administrative progress as a result of a specific stimulus rather than of general principles was characteristic of relief work in Toronto throughout the nineteenth century.

Outdoor assistance took the form of the provision of food and fuel. Food was distributed in "large," "medium," or "small" parcels, with no provision for illness in the home or for special diets. Only bread and milk were prepared in special quantities outside the general categories, the recipients being provided with tickets by the inspector to indicate the precise amount to which they were entitled. These were to be presented at the House of Industry, for the poor had to make their own arrangements for transporting whatever they received.

The increase in unemployment which accompanied the depression of the mid-1850s forced the House of Industry to further diversify its efforts by opening a soup kitchen. The service was an unqualified success, and so by 1859 the institution was able to boast that Toronto "refuses aid to none who need and deserve it."[27] Such a statement was certainly unwise, for by 1861 other municipalities were sending their poor to the Toronto workhouse, with the result that the board had to send many back and to charge the neighbouring towns to provide for their own.

The towns of the hinterland continued, however, to urge their poor to seek aid in Toronto, thus swelling the ranks of the local unemployed. The destitute also poured in from the surrounding rural areas and from Europe. In fact, there was even an influx from the United States.[28] The House of Industry with some reluctance undertook to care for new arrivals during their first year's residence.[29] Furthermore, after 1864 the institution accepted incurables who had been refused admission to the hospital.[30] The functions of the institution increased with each passing year and, despite protests that it was intended only for temporary relief,[31] the House of Industry was compelled to assume long-term responsibility for the poor.

The House of Industry quickly found itself in a financial position comparable to that of the hospital. Although the province supplied a regular grant after 1841, this bore little relation to the extent of the services provided.[32] And in the decade following Union the city would condescend to help only when the institution threatened to close.[33] The circumstances of the depression forced the Toronto Council in 1858 to appropriate $1000 annually to the House of Industry, but this was not nearly adequate and the Board of Management was constantly asking for advances on the following year's grant.[34] This they received without much difficulty, and the size of the municipal grant increased as the century progressed, but funds were never sufficient. In 1886 lack of money continued to prevent the establishment of a dispensary in connection with the institution.

Although the civic authorities accepted a measure of responsibility for the poor through grants to the workhouse, they were reluctant to trouble themselves with administration. The Board of Management, therefore, remained entirely a private body. The city council occasionally took some independent positive steps. For instance, in exceptional cases they paid for the boarding of orphaned infants in private homes.[35] In 1860 there were plans afoot to establish a House of Refuge in connection with the recently erected city jail. The proposed institution, according to a contemporary report, was to duplicate many of the services already provided by the House of Industry. In addition to relieving the deserving poor, the refuge would house "all persons leading a lewd or vagrant life . . . , all who spend their time in public-houses to the neglect of any useful calling, [and] . . . all idiots or such as from birth or from bodily infirmity or severe visitation are bereft of reason without hope of restoration."[36] As with the House of Industry, the purpose of the refuge was to make inmates "useful, industrious and profitable," and so they were to engage in shoemaking, tailoring and gardening. To this end, the new building was to contain the most modern workshop facilities.[37] However, the venture appears to have been undertaken half-heartedly, its purpose being more to rid the public of nuisance than actually to care for the poor. The refuge, announced the mayor, would "enable the Council . . . to suppress the vagrancy and mendicancy which are not creditable to our Municipal government [and which] are also so severe and annoying a tax upon the charitable public."[38] Consequently, even after the jail was opened in 1865, public relief services were minimal, the burden of the House of Industry remained overwhelming, and the bulk of the responsibility for aid to the unfortunate rested in private hands, especially with the city's religious organizations.

In 1898, one observer remarked that "In its charities Toronto stands in the first rank of Canadian and American cities. The various religious denominations spend annually thousands of dollars and private contributions towards charitable institutions amount in the aggregate to sum (*sic*) that are almost princely."[39] If the last point was perhaps exaggerated — as requests for civic aid on the part of local charities indicate[40] — Toronto already had, by the 1860s, no shortage of private philanthropic associations. In contrast to the House of Industry with its almost all-encompassing scope, these smaller institutions often served a more specialized function and almost without exception, they had religious antecedents. The majority were Protestant, and those not affiliated with a particular congregation were non-denominational in character. Although the administrators and volunteers of the hospital and the House of Industry were all men, volunteer work in the smaller institutions after 1850 was almost the exclusive preserve of women. But, even here, men retained control of administration.

The largest of these private Protestant charities, and one of the few exceptions to the rule of male administration, was the Protestant Orphans' Home which was established in 1851. Originally called the Orphans' Home and Female Aid Society, it was founded by a group of Anglican women, primarily wives and daughters of the Family Compact, and proposed to offer "relief and support to friendless orphans and destitute females," and to give them "religious and moral instruction."[41] The society soon confined its activities only to orphans, for financial support could be had most readily for this purpose. Funds came primarily from Toronto Anglican businessmen such as Robert Baldwin and Mayor Gurnett, but also from Orange and Oddfellow lodges, as well as from Anglican congregations throughout the province.

In the middle of the nineteenth century there was considerable opposition on the part of much of the male population to women's participation even in the volunteer aspects of charity work, lest they be exposed to the shocking and seedy side of life. That some, especially married women, should actually propose to run a corporation was considered scandalous. This apparently vehement opposition resulted in the stipulation being included in the act establishing the Protestant Orphans' Home that the lady directors were not to be bound in their actions by the wishes of their husbands, "usage of custom to the contrary notwithstanding."[42] Officially a Church of England institution, the home also accepted Roman Catholic children, but at the age of twelve, when the children were normally apprenticed out, they were sent only to Protestant families.

In 1853 the Magdalen Asylum and Industrial Refuge was established by a group associated with Holy Trinity (Anglican) Church. Also non-denominational, this organization sought to care for mentally deficient women and to rehabilitate those who suffered addiction or who had become immoral. Typically, the effort began as protection for society, "lest a greater evil come upon us."[43] The inmates were taught to do laundry, to sew clothing for important enterprises such as Sir Wilfred Grenfell's mission to Labrador, and to cultivate vegetables. Volunteers from the asylum constantly visited the local jail, held services there and invited female inmates to utilize their facilities upon release.

The years 1856 and 1859 respectively saw the founding of the Girls' Home and the Boys' Home by Protestant individuals who were unaffiliated with any particular denomination, but who considered their work a religious duty. These institutions were established because of "the alarming increase of Juvenile crime in the city, attributable to the dissolute character of parents. . . ."[44] Their purpose was to remove children from evil influence before they were drawn into criminal acts and to educate them in some trade. In the case of the Boys' Home, young people between the ages of five and fourteen were admitted, with the older boys being apprenticed to local merchants and craftsmen. Of these earnings, one-half went toward support of the home and the rest into bank accounts for the individual boys. With a characteristic eye upon the British models, the operation of the homes was to be "similar to those in such successful operation in London and [other] large cities."[45] It is interesting to note, however, that neither of these organizations originally intended to provide more than temporary care. The primary purpose of the Girls' Home was to be a public day nursery, while the Boys' Home proposed to care for children only until foster homes could be found for them. But by the 1860s, neither plan was adequate for the city's needs, and some arrangement for long-term care had to be made.

Assistance to the destitute was also attempted by the YMCA. The first association in Toronto had been founded in 1853, and although it had lasted only a few years it did succeed in setting up a "vigilance committee" to find jobs for "deserving young men."[46] However, when it was revived in 1864 under the guidance of Daniel Wilson, the "Y" extended its services to include relief of the poor in winter, reading to patients in hospitals, assistance to immigrants in finding accommodations and employment, and visiting of local jails. Closely tied to the university in its early years, the "Y" apparently seldom had a shortage of volunteers.

The twenty years following Confederation saw an even greater proliferation of private non-denominational charities. Daniel Wilson established a Working Boys' Home in 1867. The following year, a Newsboys' Home was opened "to inculcate . . . the habits of industry" in and to find better employment for these unfortunate waifs.[47] In 1877 an Infants' Home, operated by the Church of

England, was providing lodging and medical care for unwed mothers, deserted wives, and children of widowers, and infants under two years of age left destitute from a variety of causes.[48] By the end of the decade, the Women's Christian Association was operating a Prison Gate Mission for women recently released, and a Haven for women inebriates, unwed mothers and respectable, homeless women. Another group of women established a Nursing-at-Home Mission and Dispensary in 1885, providing medicine and nursing care with payment according to the means of the recipient, while a Methodist group connected with the Metropolitan Church organized a lodging house for neglected boys and homeless men. This service, which became the Fred Victor Mission after Hart Massey donated a building in 1894, also provided night classes, a gymnasium and an unemployment bureau.

The list of such charities is virtually endless, especially, after the depression of the 1890s added dozens more to it. Consequently, it defies description in detail. It is essential, however, to realize that although the variety of services provided by these organizations was enormous, they were not always provided well. Whereas institutions such as the Newsboys' Home measure up well in terms of facilities, others, such as the Men's Metropole and Shelter, apparently occupied dirty buildings which had no fire escapes. Undoubtedly these conditions were directly related to the degree of support received from both private and public sources. The latter especially was usually sorely deficient.

Individual Protestant churches apparently did well by their own congregants, but aside from the work done by exceptional individuals, seldom before the end of the century did they look beyond. As S. D. Clark remarks, church membership was dominated by the successful upper and middle classes.

> Respectability was a condition of membership in the church, and respectability was maintained by ignoring undesirable members of the population. Charitable contributors to the poor and sermons denouncing vice were means of preserving the isolation of these contaminating elements within the urban community. The psychological and philosophical assumptions of most of the leaders of the church, and the orthodox techniques of evangelization, made almost impossible the adoption of effective methods of dealing with problems such as the slum, crime, and prostitution.[49]

Some of the evangelicals such as the Salvation Army, and a few within the Anglican and Presbyterian churches, were engaged in rehabilitation work among convicts,[50] but this appears to have been unusual.

Benevolent societies in the city engaged in some relief work. The St. George's and St. Andrew's Societies, dating from the 1830s, provided for the poor of English and Scottish descent, while the Irish Protestant Benevolent Society began operating in 1870. They offered advice for immigrants and supplied those poor they deemed deserving with food certificates redeemable with local merchants. The Odd Fellows, Orange Order and the Sons of England did much the same, but tended to confine themselves to their own members. Labour unions, especially before the federal government removed the threat of prosecution in 1872, engaged in similar practices.

Although, for the most part, the non-denominational Protestant charities did not discriminate against Catholics, the latter preferred to establish independent relief machinery. Despite the relative poverty of most Toronto Catholics in the nineteenth century, and because of the Church's hierarchial structure and the system, Catholic charities in the city apparently operated more efficiently than did Protestant ones.

St. Paul's Congregation, the oldest Catholic parish in the city, had undoubtedly been providing some measure of assistance to the poor since its inception. The Ladies' Sewing and Relief Society had been operating since the 1820s, supplying needy children with shoes and clothes during the winter. But systematic relief did not begin until Bishop de Charbonnel invited the Sisters of St. Joseph to Toronto in 1851. In that year, the Sacred Heart Orphanage was opened, to be followed in 1857 by the House of Providence, which provided many of the same services as the House of Industry, except for the fact that no labour test was imposed. Like the Protestant institutions, these did not discriminate according to creed.[51]

The Catholic community also had its benevolent societies, these being divided according to sex. In 1853, men of St. Paul's organized the St. Vincent de Paul Society, which proposed to provide for the physical welfare of the poor. To this end, the society co-operated with the House of Industry, the latter supplying the organization with information on needy families. However, the members were concerned also with the education and religious well-being of their clients: consequently, they visited Catholic patients at the hospitals, bringing magazines and prayerbooks.

While the men were principally occupied with material relief for the Catholic community at large, the women of the parish established the Sodality of the Children of Mary in 1860, to develop their own spiritual welfare. Aside from their study and prayer meetings the Sodality soon provided important aid to the poor by assisting financially both the St. Vincent de Paul and the Sewing Societies. Funds were acquired by holding bazaars and garden parties.

Duplication of Protestant social services by the Catholics was practically achieved with the establishment in 1886 of St. Michael's Hospital. Actually, the venture began as a combination Sunday school, young men's reading room and young ladies' boarding school. Apparently it was felt that the General Hospital was providing inadequate service — or perhaps an improper atmosphere — and so the school facilities, which consisted of a former Baptist church on Bond Street, were converted into a hospital.

Jewish and Negro welfare services, like the Catholic, tended in the nineteenth century to develop parallel to but separate from those of the white Protestant majority. Negro organizations saw their greatest activity in the 1840s and 50s when it became necessary to assist fugitive slaves. In this period, several nameless societies were established in connection with the individual coloured churches, while women of all such congregations banded together in the Queen Victoria Benevolent Society. White abolitionists in Toronto also helped. The Toronto Anti-Slavery Society was "composed of some of the best and most influential ladies and gentlemen in the city . . . ,"[52] and these assisted the refugees by holding benefit concerts at St. Lawrence Hall. After the American Civil War, however, the number of Negroes in Toronto declined sharply, and while church aid undoubtedly continued, coloured charities did not become highly organized and diversified until the middle of the twentieth century.

Jewish philanthropy between 1850 and 1880 centred primarily around the single synagogue, the Toronto Hebrew Congregation. Although it served only Jews, the congregation did not limit itself to members. All needy Jews were supplied with clothing, unleavened bread for Passover, and hospital care.[53] After 1868 when the women of the congregation formed the Toronto Hebrew Ladies' Sick and Benevolent Society, Jewish charity took a more organized and expanded form. Sick members were paid $2.00 weekly to cover medical care and were provided with housekeeping assistance by volunteers from the synagogue. Members of the society collected money for the poor and imposed severe fines on themselves for neglect of duty.[54] By the late 1870s the organization had spawned the Ladies' Montefiore Benevolent Society, which devoted itself exclusively to the poor, and in the same period a (Ladies') Dorcas Society, the origin of which is unknown, was providing clothes and instruction in sewing for the needy. Jewish men's organizations which served much the same function as the St. George's Society began in 1875 with the establishment of the Toronto Lodge of B'nai B'rith. Those which followed in the 1880s and 90s, as the influx from Eastern Europe reached Toronto, were numerous. It is notable, however, that before 1900 they followed the pattern of the synagogue and tended to divide on lines of national origin. Moreover, they assiduously avoided assistance from public sources in the few areas where it was available.

The municipal officials of Toronto reacted with ambivalence to this multiplicity of charities throughout the second half of the nineteenth century. Although a revision of the Municipal Corporations Act in 1858 had empowered them to aid charitable institutions beyond hospitals and poorhouses, and to extend outdoor relief to the resident poor, the city council preferred to remain relatively aloof.[55] The degree of municipal assistance that private charity received appears to have depended upon how persuasive the directors of a given organization were in convincing the council of their need. The Magdalen Asylum, for instance, was able to obtain a grant of land from the city as early as 1856, but very little financial relief. Institutions such as the Newsboys' Home had to be supported entirely from private funds.[56] Organizations such as the St. George's Society received only the occasional grant for relief work,[57] whereas the Protestant Orphans' Home enjoyed a substantial annual grant. The success of the latter probably stemmed from its constant invitations to the council to visit the home and to see the need. The House of Providence used the same method of persuasion.[58] In fairness to the municipal officials it should be mentioned that charitable institutions often received tax refunds and the free use of civic facilities for charity balls and meetings. However, this was never automatic; the organizations involved had to petition the council each time they desired exemption.[59] Moreover, the council constantly pleaded poverty, insisting that since it contributed so generously to the House of Industry, it could afford very little for other institutions.[60]

At least by the 1870s many of the larger private philanthropic organizations had succeeded in wrestling a small annual grant from the city fathers' tight fists. But seldom, once the money was relinquished, did the municipality concern itself with the workings of these organizations or with the extent of the services provided. Admittedly, in the case of the Magdalen Asylum, the city demanded representation on its administrative board in return for the land grant, but until late in the century this practice was most unusual.[61] By the 1880s, many of those institutions dealing with children were supplied with teachers by the council; this was the case for instance with the Boys' Home and with the Protestant Orphans' Home. But the city was inconsistent in this regard; such institutions as the Newsboys' Home had to depend upon volunteers.[62] It appears that only in the case of the Infants' Home, where the city paid five dollars a month for each foundling cared for, did municipal aid correspond closely to the actual workings of a particular agency. Indeed, the directors of the home boasted in 1880 that the institution was "more closely connected with our civic machinery than any other of our city charities. . . ."[63]

This relative indifference on the part of the city resulted from the belief that charity was a private matter. Consequently, before the 1890s Toronto had no specialized department within the city government for poor relief administration. Responsibility for the distribution of money rested in theory with the council but in fact with the mayor. The chief magistrate often delegated one of the councillors to deal with charity requests on a part-time basis, but usually he performed the function himself.[64] In this capacity, the mayor, in addition to subsidizing philanthropic organizations, was empowered to relieve indigent individuals by paying, for example, for hospitalization and by operating soup kitchens. Such action, however, appears to have been rare.

As a result of this municipal attitude, the lack of government machinery, and the enormous number of unco-ordinated private charities, the poor of Toronto until late in the nineteenth century were being served very badly indeed. Philanthropic organizations were constantly short of funds. Although most received an annual provincial grant, this, like the contributions of the city, was not commensurate with the services provided. Charity balls, garden parties, concerts and door-to-door collections brought in private funds, but if these usually sufficed to keep the various institutions in operation, they were rarely enough to permit much necessary expansion. Indeed, some institutions had to set their inmates to work doing laundry in order to maintain themselves.[65]

The difficulty in staffing Toronto's charitable institutions and in finding capable volunteer visitors aggravated the problem of the poor. Considering the importance which Victorians attached to voluntary philanthropy, it is not surprising that little provision was made before 1900 for the training of professional charity workers. In fact, the few who did consider themselves professionals were looked upon with disdain. This was true even in British and American centres which were often far ahead of Toronto in attitudes toward efficient philanthropy. As a result, the usual practice in Toronto institutions was to employ an untrained man as superintendent, while his equally unsuitable wife served as matron. Sometimes as in the case of the House of Industry, the two were conscientious and performed with relative efficiency; in other instances, however, the use of such personnel must have been disastrous. As early as 1860, some residents of the city had become aware of the inadequacies of the system. In that year, for example, when the municipality was planning to open a House of Refuge in connection with the jail, the council was warned that the improper selection of a keeper would ruin the project and that there were very few available who could fill the office satisfactorily.[66] A half century would pass, however, before any systematic attempt would be made in Toronto to provide qualified welfare workers.

Prominent critics of the whole voluntary approach to philanthropy could be heard in the city at every period of economic difficulty, and they spoke with increasing frequency as the effects of Toronto's growing metropolitan position within the province became evident. For example, in 1857 Strachan drew the attention of the mayor to "the distressing state of our poor." Their numbers, he wrote,

> are now felt to be getting far beyond voluntary charity, whether individual or associated, — a fact generally acknowledged by all who have given the subject serious consideration. —
> Toronto, from its central position has become a sort of reservoir, and a place of refuge to the indigent from all parts of the Province. It is true the different Christian denominations are doing their best, as they have always done, to mitigate the suffering . . ., and for many years, their labours were successful. But latterly, the poor have so greatly multiplied, that their utmost exertions have been found unequal to satisfy many sad cases of destitution.
> On the whole it appears to me that the period has arrived, when some public aid should be given, not to supersede, but to strengthen and encourage voluntary charity. This may be done in the shape of a slight assessment. . . .[67]

The city's sporadic financial assistance to charities had been gratefully received, the Bishop continued, but it had gone only "a very little way to remedy the evil." Aware of the opposition to anything resembling a poor law, Strachan insisted that the objections were based upon "favourite theories and false philosophy"[68] and that some Torontonians had forgotten "that to make provisions for the really poor is a Scriptural doctrine, highly becoming a Christian nation, and as wise as it is beneficial." Had not England's Poor Law been "the glory of the nation" and had it not saved her from the anarchy and revolution that had engulfed other nations?[69]

Such exhortations to civic involvement in relief services for the most part went unheeded. The municipal officials would continue their haphazard approach for decades; indeed, a poor rate would never be levied in Toronto. Well into the twentieth century, municipal authorities refused, as a rule, to undertake direct involvement in welfare and relief work, nor would they countenance the suggestion that they at least enter into equal partnership with private philanthropic associations. They were content to absolve themselves through grudgingly dispensed grants, leaving the bulk of the responsibility to the religious conscience of the private citizen.

If any significant progress in the field of philanthropy was achieved in Toronto as the new century approached, this was due to a revision throughout the English-speaking world of the whole philosophy of relief work, to the rejection of moral judgment of the poor and to its replacement by a genuinely scientific environmentalist approach. This change of attitude emerged in Toronto almost entirely in the private sector and often came to fruition within those religious institutions which were already engaged in welfare work, and which possessed facilities easily adjusted to suit the scientific approach. In this atmosphere charity organization societies, settlements and especially professional social work could develop. Only after these had provided the rationale, the machinery and the personnel for equitable and efficient distribution of relief did city authorities begin to participate actively.

Notes

1. *Minutes of Proceedings of the Council of the Corporation of the City of Toronto* (hereafter *Toronto Council Minutes*), 1881, Appendix 1.
2. The term "welfare" did not come into common use until the decade following 1900. See B.A. McKenzie, "The Impact of Social Change on the Organization of Welfare Services in Ontario 1891–1921: Care of the Poor in Toronto" (M.A. thesis, University of Toronto, 1966), 1.
3. This particular aspect of Victorian thought was more prominent in Canada and in the United States than in Britain, since North America was the habitat of the self-made man of the frontier. Success was commonplace here, at least in popular mythology.
4. Quoted in K. Woodroofe, *From Charity to Social Work* (Toronto: University of Toronto Press, 1962), 16. Although Shaftsbury did not utter this statement until 1883, it is expressive of sentiments which were already common much earlier in the century.
5. *Globe*, 27 Feb. 1874, quoted in R.B. Splane, *Social Welfare in Ontario 1791–1893* (Toronto: University of Toronto Press, 1965), 16.
6. Splane attributes this tendency to a collective memory of pioneer days in the province, when all were in need and all helped. *Social Welfare in Ontario*, 17.
7. For examples of this attitude, see A. Briggs, *The Age of Improvement* (London: Longmans, 1964), chaps. 8 and 9.
8. Edmund Burke, *Reflections on the French Revolution*, cited in Woodroofe, *From Charity to Social Work*, 12.
9. C.K. Clarke, *A History of the Toronto General Hospital* (Toronto: William Briggs, 1913), 26.
10. There are many versions of this incident and varying reasons put forth as to why the medals could not be used. The one cited here is related by Jesse Middleton, *The Municipality of Toronto: A History* (Toronto: Dominion Publishing Co., 1923), 2:631.
11. Clarke, *Toronto General Hospital*, 62.
12. Splane, *Social Welfare in Ontario*, 40.
13. Clarke, *Toronto General Hospital*, 72.
14. The provincial land grant of 1818 included not only the original lot on the Garrison Reserve, but also several other properties in and around York. Therefore, in 1868, the city council argued that the institution should sell some of its land to support itself. This was not the first instance of municipal refusal. In 1847, the secretary of the Toronto Hospital had written of the great discourtesy shown by the city council toward the advocates of a hospital for sick immigrants. George Ryerson to Charles Daly, 5 June 1847, City of Toronto Papers, Ontario Archives (hereafter OA).
15. Middleton, *The Municipality of Toronto*, 2: 636.
16. B. Turquand to Mayor T.D. Morrison, 28 Dec. 1836, City of Toronto Papers, OA. The proposed institution would, in addition to its other functions, supply employment, clothing and education to indigent children. Turquand maintained that the collections of the Church of England alone, would pay for its erection, whereas the work performed by inmates would finance the staffing.
17. The institution found larger quarters in 1842 on Shuter Street and finally, in 1848, it could be housed in a building erected especially for the purpose. This structure still remained in use in the late 1960s.

18. Early report of the House of Industry, quoted in D.C. Card, "History of Direct Relief in Toronto" (unpublished paper, Dept. of Social Science, University of Toronto, 1938), 2.

19. House of Industry report, quoted in Card, "History of Direct Relief in Toronto."

20. Card, "History of Direct Relief in Toronto," 3.

21. *100th Annual Report of the House of Industry City of Toronto for the Year 1936–37* (Toronto, 1937), 9.

22. Ibid.

23. Rev. A.H. Baldwin to the Royal Commission on Prisons, "Report of the Commissioners Appointed to Enquire into the Prison and Reformatory System of Ontario," *Ontario Legislative Assembly Sessional Papers*, 1891, no. 18 (hereafter "Report into the Prison and Reformatory System"), 112.

24. "The House of Industry," historical sketch of the House of Industry, c. 1900, typescript, University of Toronto Archives, unpaginated.

25. Splane, *Social Welfare in Ontario*, 72.

26. Card, "History of Direct Relief in Toronto," 5. The inspectors or "visitors," were all volunteers, being primarily upper-class men, usually clergymen and doctors. Even the mayor and aldermen participated in their private capacities ("House of Industry Report, 1890", cited in "The House of Industry"). Once a visitor recommended a family for relief, aid was not given automatically. On the contrary, the merits of each case were discussed by a committee of the board which met twice weekly ("House of Industry Report, 1881" in *Toronto Council Minutes*, 1881, Appendix 36). By the twentieth century, methods of inspection had become reasonably well organized, with each visitor being assigned a specific district upon which to report. In the latter period, volunteers assisted members of the board in this capacity. These continued to come from the upper strata of society (Rev. H. Francis Perry, President of the Associated Charities, "Methods, Motives and Aims of Organized Charity," address to the General Ministerial Association, c. 1908, typescript, University of Toronto Archives.)

27. "Report of the House of Industry, 1859," quoted in "The House of Industry."

28. "Annual Report of the Toronto House of Industry, 1876," cited in "The House of Industry."

29. "Annual Report of the Toronto House of Industry, 1874," quoted in "The House of Industry."

30. "Annual Report of the Toronto House of Industry, 1864–65," quoted in "The House of Industry."

31. "Annual Report of the Toronto House of Industry, 1878," quoted in "The House of Industry."

32. Splane, *Social Welfare in Ontario*, 40, 41.

33. For instance, see W.M. Westmacott (Secretary of the House of Industry) to Mayor W.H. Boulton, 17 May 1874, City of Toronto Papers, OA.

34. See, for example, *Toronto Council Minutes*, 1860, Appendix 12.

35. *Toronto Council Minutes*, 1861, Appendix 116.

36. "Board of Jail Inspectors Report # 3," in *Toronto Council Minutes*, 1860, Appendix 189.

37. Ibid.

38. "Final Report of the Mayor," *Toronto Council Minutes*, 1860, Appendix 189.

39. C.S. Clark, *Of Toronto the Good: A Social Study* (Montreal: Toronto Publishing Co., 1898), 3.

40. For instance, see *Toronto Council Minutes*, 1860, entries no. 484 (Toronto Lying-in Hospital), no. 225 (Boy's Home), and no. 616 (Public Nursery), which are typical of requests made throughout the nineteenth century.

41. Act to Establish an Orphans' Home, quoted in Splane, *Social Welfare in Ontario*, 224.

42. Quoted in Splane, *Social Welfare in Ontario*, 224.

43. "A Trio of Benevolent Institutions" (Toronto: The Industrial Refuge, c. 1910), 5.

44. "Annual Report of the Boys' Home, 1860," included in a collection of documents related to children's homes in Toronto, Social Work Manuscripts, University of Toronto Archives.

45. Ibid. The homes followed closely the suggestions made in 1851 by a select committee of the British House of Commons on the education of destitute children (Splane, *Social Welfare in Ontario*, 229). However, whereas local rates financed such activities in Britain, in Toronto the effort was purely voluntary.

46. *An Historical Sketch of the YMCA* (Toronto: YMCA, 1913), 14.

47. "Report into the Prison and Reformatory System," 729. As a result of the detailed report of its superintendent before the Prisons Commission of 1891, an unusual amount of information survives concerning the operation of the Newsboys' Home. Boys between the ages of nine and sixteen were

admitted. Entry was voluntary, but the boys' backgrounds were investigated upon application. There were few restrictions upon them; however, the boys were expected to be clean and to be in by a certain hour at night. In the evenings, classes were given by volunteer university students.

In 1891, applicants were expected to pay 10¢ a day or $1.30 a week for breakfast, supper and a bed. No one of good character, however, was turned away for lack of funds (729). J.J. Kelso told the Commission that in the home "There are nice clean beds . . . with texts on the wall or over the bed, and appropriate mottoes" (423), an indication that the institution still maintained its original purpose.

48. It appears that the Infants' Home, like the Girls' and Boys' Homes, was forced by circumstances to alter its activities. Its charter indicates that it was intended to provide day care for the children of working mothers and institutional care only for homeless infants. From the beginning, however, it was prepared to accept children from other municipalities in Ontario ("Charter of the Infants Home and Infirmary of Toronto 1877," Social Work Manuscripts, University of Toronto Archives).

The institution had great difficulty getting into operation. The ladies' group responsible for it had been attempting to provide services as early as 1850, but they made little progress until the 1870s, when they were able to obtain a house at Yonge and Bloor Streets. Nobody wanted the building, it seems, since it was reputed to be haunted ("History of the Infants Home," typescript, University of Toronto Archives). Once under way, however, the administrators of the home wrote to similar institutions throughout the United States and Canada to determine the best method of operating it.

49. S.D. Clark, *The Social Development of Canada* (Toronto: University of Toronto Press, 1942), 392. Clark was referring to the province as a whole, but the generalization certainly fits Toronto.

50. G.T. Denison, *Recollections of a Police Magistrate* (Toronto, Musson, 1920), 257.

51. E. Kelly, *The Story of St. Paul's Parish, Toronto* (Toronto: St. Paul's, 1922), 197.

52. "Voice of the Fugitive" (Negro paper published at Sandwich, Ont., 8 Oct. 1851), quoted in D.G. Hill, "Negroes in Toronto, 1793–1865," *Ontario History* 55 (1963): 81.

53. Minutes of the Toronto Hebrew Congregation, 20 Nov. 1864.

54. By-Laws and Regulations of the Chebre Gemilas Chesed or Toronto Hebrew Ladies' Sick and Benevolent Society, 1868.

55. Actually, Toronto had been able to extend such assistance as early as 1846; in fact, the city council had, contrary to the English practice, been empowered to levy taxes to finance outdoor as well as institutional relief. The 1858 amendment merely eliminated some of the ambiguities concerning this authority. Splane, *Social Welfare in Ontario*, 73–75.

56. "Report into the Prison and Reformatory System," 729.

57. *Toronto Council Minutes*, 1875, entry no. 1302.

58. E.g., ibid.

59. The council minutes of almost any year during the nineteenth century will support this fact.

60. E.g., *Toronto Council Minutes*, 1862.

61. The House of Industry, however, which was considered a semi-public institution, had city representation at least from 1850. The same was true of the General Hospital.

62. City of Toronto Charities Commission 1911–12, "Institutions Report." See also *Toronto Council Minutes*, 1881, Appendix 36.

63. *Infants Home Year Book 1880*, quoted in Infants Home, *50th Annual Report* (Toronto, 1925).

64. *Toronto Council Minutes*, 1881, Appendix 36.

65. For instance see "History of the Haven," typescript, Social Work Manuscripts, University of Toronto Archives, 2.

66. "Board of Jail Inspection, Report #3," *Toronto Council Minutes*, 1860, Appendix 74.

67. Strachan to Mayor Hutchison, 30 Nov. 1857, City of Toronto Papers, OA.

68. He was doubtless referring here to the commonplace belief that public relief breeds pauperism.

69. Ibid. Note Strachan's appeal to the middle-class fears of the period, which he certainly shared himself. The Bishop's letter suggests that perhaps Torontonians were not as generous at mid-century as C.S. Clark would have us believe was true in 1890s (*Of Toronto the Good*, 13). "At present," Strachan wrote, "comparatively few of the inhabitants give anything considerable to the poor, and many of the wealthy give nothing, or such a miserable pittance as would shame them if known."

THE ORANGE ORDER IN TORONTO:
RELIGIOUS RIOT AND THE WORKING CLASS†

GREGORY S. KEALEY

Toronto, like other North American cities, received part of the massive emigration from the British Isles in the nineteenth century. On arrival these immigrants immediately created institutions to alleviate the dislocating effects of the transatlantic voyage, and in Toronto the predominance of Protestant immigrants made the Orange Order one of the largest ethnic voluntary associations there. The city even became known as "The Belfast of Canada."[1]

The order's importance in the political sphere and the Orangemen's propensity to engage in riot and other forms of collective violence have gained them some historical attention. Unfortunately most Canadian historians, in their haste to deplore such illiberal behaviour, have failed to explore seriously the culture that generated these collective actions; instead, they focused concern on the vagaries of Orange leadership in national politics, ignoring the order's social composition, its constellation of ideas, its roots in traditional Irish society, and its important local functions. More specifically, historians of the Canadian working-class experience have been satisfied with an easy dismissal of ethnic and religious associations as being detrimental to the emergence of some ill-defined notion of class-consciousness.[2] Yet, closer study demonstrates that Orangeism offered Toronto workers a profoundly ambiguous heritage — a set of traditions which, on the one hand, aided Protestant workers in their struggle to exist in the industrializing city but which, on the other hand, led them, on occasion, to riot against their Catholic fellow workers.

The Orange Order's most perceptive student, H.C. Pentland, has argued that until 1870, "Orangeism and the moderate political conservatism which it built represented the artisan well at a time when capitalism had not advanced enough to subordinate all other divisions to the one between capitalist and proletarian."[3]

†Gregory S. Kealey, *Toronto Workers Respond to Industrial Capitalism, 1867–1892* (Toronto: University of Toronto Press, 1980), 98–123.

This article will explore the implications of that assertion by analysing the cultural roots and developing beliefs of the Orange Order generally, and then turn to a specific analysis of the order in industrial Toronto — its class composition and collective behaviour. An examination of its political impact on the Toronto working class will be left for later analysis.

TABLE 1

Toronto Population, 1848–91

| Year | Population | Increase by decade | |
		Number	Percentage
1848	23 503		
1851	30 775	7 272	31
1861	44 821	14 046	46
1871	56 092	11 271	25
1881	85 415	30 323	54
1891	144 023	57 608	67

SOURCE: Canada, Census, 1848–91

A few demographic characteristics of the Toronto population will aid our consideration of Orangeism. The rapid economic development that we have described earlier led to significant population growth. The city grew steadily each decade but leaped ahead in the 1850s (see table 1). The population was notably homogeneous throughout these years, Irish Catholics being the only significantly "foreign" group in the city. Inadequacies in published census data do not permit a total reconstruction of the population by birthplace; however the trends, as shown in table 2, indicate that the number of Canadian-born persons increased significantly over the four decades. The slight decline in Canadian-born persons between 1848 and 1851 was probably caused by the influx of Irish famine migrants. By 1891 65 percent of the population were native-born and 24 percent were of American, English, or Scottish origin.

The city's religious pattern demonstrated a similar homogeneity, being overwhelmingly Protestant and throughout these years becoming increasingly so (see table 3). The Catholic population declined from a high of 27 percent in 1861 to only 15 percent in 1891. Of the Protestant churches, the Methodist grew the most, although the Baptist and Presbyterian also increased their membership. The percentage of Anglicans declined slightly but they remained by far the largest group, claiming almost a third of the city's souls in 1891.

This ethnic and religious homogeneity made Toronto quite different from other major North American cities such as Montreal, with its large French-Canadian population, or New York, with its much higher proportions of foreign-born. Despite the relative homogeneity, however, significant ethnic and religious conflict between the various elements of the working class did occur in this period.

The Orange Order in Toronto provides us with a particularly successful example of the adaptation of an old-world culture to the contingencies of a new society. This chapter suggests some reasons for the order's success and demonstrates

TABLE 2

Ethnic Structure of Toronto, 1848–91

Birthplace	1848 No.	%	1851* No.	%	1861* No.	%	1871 No.	%	1881 No.	%	1891 No.	%
England	3 789	16	4 958	16	7 112	16	11 089	20	14 674	17	22 801	16
Ireland	1 695	7	11 305	37	12 441	28	10 336	18	10 781	13	13 252	9
Scotland	9 044	39	2 169	7	2 961	7	3 263	6	4 431	5	6 347	4
France			113	0.4	66	0.1	61	0.1	67	0.1		
Germany	59	0.3			336	0.7	336	0.5	492	0.6	799	0.6
Canada	8 119	35	10 433	34	19 490	44	28 578	51	51 489	60	93 162	65
United States	753	3	1 407	5	2 031	5	1 997	4	3 357	4	5 086	4
Other	44	0.2	402	1	854	2	209	0.4	1 124	0.1	2 576	2
Total	23 503		30 775		44 821		56 092		86 415		144 023	

* Data available only on ethnicity by origin, not by birth.
SOURCE: Canada, Census 1848–91.

TABLE 3

Religious Affiliation in Toronto, 1848–91

Denomination	1848		1851		1861		1871		1881		1891	
	No.	%	No.	%	No.	%	No.	%	No.	%	No.	%
Anglican	8 315	35	11 557	38	14 125	32	20 668	37	30 913	36	46 804	33
Presbyterian	3 655	16	4 544	15	6 604	15	8 982	16	14 612	17	27 449	19
Methodist	2 965	13	4 123	13	6 976	16	9 596	17	16 357	19	32 505	23
Baptist	528	2	948	3	1 288	3	1 953	4	3 667	4	6 909	5
Congregationalist	575	3	646	2	826	2	1 186	2	2 018	2	3 102	2
Lutheran	22	0.1	7 940				343	0.6	494	0.6		
Roman Catholic	5 903	25	7 940	26	12 135	27	11 881	21	15 716	18	21 830	15
Jewish	27	0.1	57	0.2	153	0.3	157	0.3	534	0.6	1 425	1
Other and not given	1 513	6	178	0.6	1 834	4	594	1	255	0.3	4 739	3
Total	23 503		30 775		44 821		56 092		86 415		144 023	

SOURCE: Canada, Census, 1848–91.

not only its adaptation to the new world, but also its transition from rural, pre-industrial roots to a society based in an urban industrial world. The internal tensions engendered by the changes were great. The ever-shifting, but successful, resolution of these tensions allowed Orangeism to remain an important factor in Toronto working-class life throughout the nineteenth century despite the changing nature of the city and its working class.

An analysis of Orangeism in Toronto must begin with the origins of the order in Ireland. The Irish countryside was permeated with agrarian secret societies as early as the mid-eighteenth century. The original groups — the Steelboys, Whiteboys, Rightboys, and Oakboys — were primarily economically motivated in that they sought to protect the interests of agricultural labourers and small cottiers against farmers and landlords, regardless of religious affiliation. These movements existed in both the north and the south and were successful in achieving limited aims:

> Although the agrarian secret societies failed to achieve tithe reform in the years before the Union, they may have prevented the type of wholesale eviction which took place in Scotland in the last half of the eighteenth century . . . secret societies succeeded to some extent in enforcing tenant rights and other regulations which they believed necessary for their protection.[4]

Nevertheless, the existence of deep hatred between Protestants and Catholics made it relatively easy for the landlords to transform these economic struggles into sectarian strife. In addition, the success of the American and French revolutions transformed the nature of rebellion in Ireland, as well as in the rest of the world. The ability of Jacobin agitators, such as Wolfe Tone, to unite the Defenders, a Catholic agrarian secret society, with his United Irishmen, an urban revolutionary grouping, led to a similar union among Protestant peasant groupings. The Peep o'Day Boys evolved into the Orange Order and took on an avowedly sectarian, anti-Catholic, and anti-revolutionary cast. The revolt of 1798 further reinforced these tendencies. Although agrarian secret societies re-emerged in pre-famine Ireland, their potential for linking the Protestant and Catholic lower classes was gone. Sectarian warfare had gained primacy, and ruling-class interests now possessed the co-operation of societies such as the Orange Order which provided "an invaluable link between ascendancy power in terms of land on the one hand and the Protestant farming and working classes in Ulster on the other."[5] Although the order served this function in periods when Ireland's British connection was in question, it continued to be troublesome to the established authorities at all other times.

A movement of lower-class forces which never could be quite trusted, Orangemen found their society outlawed on numerous occasions throughout the nineteenth century. Thus, even in Ireland the Orange Order arose from a curious conjunction of peasant revolt and patriotic reaction. This legacy could only grow more ambiguous when transferred to a country where the economic underpinnings of sectarian strife were far less prominent.[6] For, in Ireland "religion had determined the side on which a man stood, but the struggle had been one for land and power, and religion had been the badge of difference rather than the main bone in the dispute."[7] In Canada, land would not be an issue, but power was quite a different question.

Orangeism came to Canada with British troops and with Irish Protestant immigrants in the first years of the nineteenth century. Initially the lodges among soldiers were founded on the authority of the Irish Grand Lodge and the rituals, songs, degrees, and forms of organization were totally imitative of Irish practices. The formal history of a separate Canadian Orangeism begins in 1830 when Brockville's Ogle Gowan, an Irish immigrant with Orange leadership experience, called together representatives from central Canada's scattered pioneer lodges and knit them into a new Grand Lodge of British North America.[8]

In these early years, Gowan did much to separate Canadian Orangeism from pure Irish models. After the proscription of the Orange Order in Ireland, Gowan had been a major force in creating the new Orange Patriotic and Benevolent Society, wherein the militaristic and sectarian sides of Orangeism were de-emphasized, and instead, fraternal and benevolent functions were developed. Although unsuccessful in Ireland, this emphasis was well-suited to Canadian conditions. Partially because of his personal political aspirations, Gowan moved toward a broader definition of Orangeism as a type of immigrant-aid society which might at times even ignore religious differences. This interest was evident in his alliance with Catholic Bishop Macdonnell before the Rebellion of 1837, at which time the threat of republicanism united both Orange and Green. The early growth of the order was largely due to Gowan's ability to implement these benevolent aims and thus adapt successfully the old institution to its new home.[9]

This is not to deny the order's militant Protestant British identification or its sizeable representation in the Canadian militia. A Canadian tradition of patriotic armed struggle was being created alongside the glorious Irish past. Thus, for Canadian Orangemen the 1837 Rebellion came to be almost as celebrated in song and verse as the Battle of the Boyne. Violent encounters with Irish Catholics in Canada, such as the 1849 Slabtown affair, were juxtaposed with famous Irish encounters such as the Diamond.[10] Thus a Canadian heroic mythology emerged to replace the Irish past — no doubt a prerequisite for the order's successful adaptation to Canadian soil.

Although updated and revised throughout the century, the basic aims of Canadian Orangeism were formulated quite early. Certainly by the mid-forties the standard *Laws, Rules and Regulations* had been devised. Members were committed to four duties: (1) to uphold the principles of the Christian religion; (2) to maintain the laws and constitution of the country; (3) to assist distressed members of the order; and (4) to promote other "laudable and benevolent purposes" consistent with Christianity and constitutional freedom. The latter two duties demonstrate how integral the social welfare function was to the Canadian order, unlike its Irish parent. Nevertheless, that Orangemen were quite capable of ignoring these principles will be seen later in their willingness to engage in various illegal collective actions.[11]

Ritual played a crucial role. All Orange candidates swore a sacred oath before entrance into the order. Allegiance to the monarch was part of the oath, but on the condition that the crown uphold the Protestant religion and constitutional rights. This surprising qualification from a proudly loyal organization demonstrates again the ambiguities in the Orange tradition, and shows the depth of Orange suspicion for constituted authority. The oath also committed the initiate to uphold the Empire, to fight for justice for all brother Orangemen, to hold sacred the name of William, to celebrate William's victory every 12 July, to refrain from becoming a papist, never to disclose or reveal the secret work of the order, and lastly, to support and maintain the Loyal Orange Institution.[12]

The solemn oath formed part of the ritual of most nineteenth-century secret societies. In societies involved in transgressions of the law, these oaths represented a potent method of allying and binding the initiate to his new brothers. Even in Canada, where much of the necessity for absolute secrecy was lacking, these oaths continued to be important. In the Orange Order the oath was only the initiation part of an elaborate ritual inspired by Masonic forms. For example, the order had five degrees to which one graduated in a hierarchical order through faithful service: the Orange, the Purple, the Royal Blue, the Royal Arch Purple, and the Royal Scarlet. Initiation into each of these involved a unique ceremony with a ritual introduction, a prayer by the chaplain, an obligation or oath on the part of the candidate, a ritual investiture, and finally a charge to the recipient by the Grand Master of the lodge, or by a more important official in the case of the highest degrees. The oaths and charges depict an interesting symbolic ascent with degree representing greater responsibilities and duties: the Orange simply emphasized faithful personal performance; the Purple called upon the member to scrutinize his brothers and proffer criticism and advice where necessary; the Blue reiterated that charge and called for yet greater diligence; the ritual for the Royal Arch Purple cautioned that "The mysteries and solemnity of this degree require that the utmost respect, order and decorum be observed by all the brothers. No one shall be admitted into the lodge room in a slovenly or unbecoming dress, nor without a sash appertaining to the order. . . . No brother shall engage in any levity." The charge of the degree demanded that the new holder take an increased interest in the well-being of his brothers. The final and most solemn degree was the Royal Scarlet. Its ceremony was full of blood imagery drawing on biblical accounts of the Passover. After being invested with a sword, spurs, a scarlet mantle, and a cord and tassel, the candidate was charged to use his sword "in defense of our glorious institution" and "to war against the enemies of destitute widows, helpless orphans, and the Protestant faith."

The function of this hierarchy of degrees was undoubtedly to provide additional interest and incentive to persevere and to obey Orange strictures in order to attain the reward of a higher degree. An Orangeman's achievements were visible to the entire community in each 12 July parade. For each degree and office carried with it a distinctive regalia.[13]

Special rituals accompanied other important events, such as the dedication of a new Orange Hall and funerals. Funerals had played a crucial role in traditional Irish society. A Harvard anthropologist, reporting on the Irish countryside in the 1930s, was so impressed with the vibrancy of funeral custom that he argued: "The most important secular ceremony of rural life is the wake and funeral. . . . Every man in death can command a multitude. To stay away, to make no recognition of the day, is to give deadly affront."[14] The Orange ceremony involved a eulogistic review of the decreased brother's achievements, a renewal of the solemn oaths of the remaining Orangemen over the grave of their late brother, "sealed" by dropping the rosette of each member's degree into the open grave. These Orange rituals must have been very powerful for members of the lodges.[15]

TABLE 4

Orange Lodges in Toronto, 1860–90

Year	Number	Year	Number
1860	20(21*)	1884	32
1865	20	1885	36*
1870	17*	1886	36
1875	26*	1888	39
1879	31	1890	45(50*)
1880	31*	1895	56*

*Figures from Houston and Smyth, "Toronto, the Belfast of Canada," Fig. 1.
SOURCE: Saunders, *The Story of Orangeism*; Grand Lodge, *Annual Reports*; Toronto *Globe*; Toronto City Directories

Toronto, the Belfast of Canada, was the acknowledged centre of nineteenth-century Canadian Orangeism. The tenacity of Orange traditions in rural areas of Ontario has misled some modern observers into assuming that the order was weaker in the cities. A closer look at the Orange Order in Toronto should correct this error.[16]

Data on the early organization in Toronto are limited,[17] but it is known that lodges were already in existence before Gowan's 1830 reorganization (they are not important for our purposes). Subsequently approximately twelve lodges were founded in Toronto in the 1830s, seventeen in the 1840s, and fifteen in the 1850s; however, by 1860 only twenty of these still functioned.[18] The 1860s was a period of organizational quiescence and by 1871 attrition had reduced the number of lodges to seventeen, totalling 1494 members. The next five years saw the order grow quite rapidly and in 1876 there were twenty-six lodges with 2215 Orangemen. By 1880 the number of lodges had grown to thirty but membership had fallen off to 1724 and by 1883 there was a further decline to 1632. Membership continued to decline slightly until the late 1880s. Those years saw the order grow in Toronto at an unprecedented rate. From thirty-two lodges in 1884, the order grew to thirty-six by 1886, thirty-nine by 1888, added seven lodges in 1889 and by the end of 1891 had grown to over fifty lodges (see tables 4 and 5). Although statistics of individual membership are not available for the late eighties, a conservative projection based on the lowest average number of members per lodge from the previous years would suggest that by 1892 Toronto Orangemen numbered well over 2500. Houston and Smyth's detailed study of Orange membership in Toronto in 1894 argues that by that year there were approximately 4000 followers of King William in the city, and that because of the volatility of lodge membership, there were probably many ex-Orangemen as current members at any one time.[19] Thus the political and social importance of the order always transcended its official membership.

TABLE 5

Orange Lodges Founded or Reorganized in Toronto, 1860–90

Year	Number	Year	Number
1860–64	0	1880–84	2
1865–69*	0	1885–89*	14
1870–74	9	1890–91	7
1875–79	8		

*Houston and Smyth, in "The Orange Order in Nineteenth-Century Ontario," 43, claim one new lodge in the 1860s, fifteen as opposed to my seventeen in the 1870s, and thirteen as opposed to my sixteen in the 1880s. Their sources are varied but seem to come from GOLBNA, *Register of Warrants*, 4 vols., where the status of "reorganized" lodges might account for the variations.
SOURCE: Saunders, *The Story of Orangeism*.

The Orange Order in Toronto was overwhelmingly working-class in composition (see table 6). Contrary to earlier impressions, however, membership was not limited to successful artisans, since the lodges were filled with labourers, street-railway workers, grooms, teamsters, and others from the lower levels of Toronto's working class. No imaginative flights can transform Toronto Orangemen into a labour aristocracy.[20]

An analysis of lodge records reveals much about membership patterns. Four lodges were studied: Armstrong Lodge 137 and Virgin Lodge 328, both of Toronto Centre and founded in the 1840s; Boyne Lodge 173, also of Toronto Centre, founded in 1878; and Enniskillen Purple Star Lodge 711 of Toronto East, founded in 1872.[21] Each had a distinctive social character and all show a majority of working-class members, except Virgin Lodge whose unique emphasis on social control and intent to cater to middle-class sojourners in the city made this lodge unattractive to workers: "This lodge was originally opened, for the purpose of giving unmarried young men, students, or mercantile men, etc., a lodge where they could assemble together . . . and also of improving on the working and discipline of the Order, as carried out at that time, which was very lax in many lodges."[22] Its transformation, in 1869, into a benevolent and temperance lodge did not augment its attractiveness for working-class Orangemen. Armstrong Lodge had a less-pronounced majority of working-class members, with a number of socially prominent honorary members who played no role in the lodge life. They attended no meetings and paid no dues.[23]

Boyne Lodge 173 had a large number of street-railway employees from its inception. It grew from nine drivers and a conductor in 1878 to six conductors, six drivers, and twelve grooms in 1885. The lodge also contained seven teamsters and three coachmen in the latter year to round out the picture of a concentration of workers in horse transport. Enniskillen Purple Star, founded by Toronto brewer Thomas Allen, in contrast, had from its beginning a large number of brewery labourers and teamsters. Fifteen years later the lodge contained five machinists from one shop, a number of teamsters and building trades workers employed by the same contractor, and several labourers from the Toronto Gas Works. Most of the members of this lodge lived in a neighbourhood bounded by Parliament St., Queen East, River St., and Spruce St.

TABLE 6

Membership of Selected Lodges by Trade, 1872–92

	Virgin Lodge 328 1872	Enniskillen Lodge 711 1872–74	Boyne Lodge 173 1878	Boyne Lodge 173 1885	Armstrong Lodge 137 1885–91	Enniskillen Lodge 711 1887	Enniskillen Lodge 711 1890–92*
Professionals	2	0	0	1	2	1	1
Government employees	2	0	0	0	0	1	0
Manufacturers	0	1	1	0	1	1	0
Merchants	4	3	1	9	5	3	4
Master craftsmen	2	1	4	0	2	4	1
Clerks	5	1	4	5	8	4	2
Non-working-class total	15	6	10	15	18	14	8
Artisans	8	7	17	21	9	35	16
Unskilled	6	15	32	56	19	33	12
Working-class total	14	22	49	77	28	68	28
Percentage	48.3	78.6	83.1	83.7	60.9	82.9	77.8
Total number with occupations	29	28	59	92	46	82	36
Total number listed	48	72	94	121	90	152	80
% with occupations of total listed	60	39	63	76	51	54	45

*New members only.
SOURCE: Manuscript Lodge Records, Metropolitan Toronto Central Library

Each Orange lodge, then, possessed its own history, and some articulated specific idiosyncratic aims. The splitting of the city into three Orange districts in 1876 provided a further rationale for choosing which lodge to belong to. The split was intended "to foster a friendly rivalry that will induce to the benefit of our order." (No doubt the new districts, which conformed to Toronto's federal electoral divisions, were also intended to be politically efficient.) A prospective member chose a lodge (and was chosen) on the basis of job-associated friendships and neighbourhood ties. The concentration of workers from single workplaces implies that the lodges were perhaps used as forums for job-related controversies. Lodges in the new working-class suburbs showed higher concentrations of working-class members and probably provided ample time for issues of community concern. This framework, where job, neighbourhood, and leisure came together, contrasts sharply with more modern patterns in which the three are separated.

Recent work by Houston and Smyth confirms these findings. In their sample of 325 Toronto Orangemen in 1894, they found almost 67 percent to be working-class. In three Toronto lodges examined, they found each to range from 43 percent to 50 percent in working-class membership. They also found similar patterns of workplace-related membership. Finally, and perhaps most important, they point out that "financiers and large industrial capitalists" were not represented in the order.[24] Admittedly, their emphasis throughout is on the social mix of the order, being more impressed by its cross-class profile than by its working-class majority. The middle-class elements they point to, however, tend to be professionals and small-shop owners. The former, who often depended on the order for their business, and the latter, who shared that dependence, were often upwardly mobile, graduating from the working class on only the most tenuous basis. In my opinion, rather than middle-class members dictating Orange standards, it is more likely that it was the working class that exercised control, especially at the lodge level.[25]

If the membership of the lodges was predominantly working-class, then what was the class background of the leaders? Did middle- and upper-class Orangemen exercise a pervasive control over lodge office? An analysis of the occupations of Orange leaders in Toronto suggests not. A survey of lodge masters from 1871 to 1888 indicates that although middle-class members held the majority of masterships in the 1870s, this reversed in the 1880s (see table 7). Further, when one extends the analysis to include all lodge offices, the role of working-class members increases strikingly (see table 8). Although the middle class supplied a disproportionate number of Orange leaders, their control was far less pervasive than has been previously claimed. Tables 7 and 8 probably exaggerate the non-working-class role, for three of the categories are open to further investigation. Both the government-employee and clerk categories include a number of patronage appointees who, though working-class in origin, earned jobs as Orange leaders, not the reverse. Similarly, the merchant category includes many small publicans and grocers, traditional avenues of limited social mobility for a select few workers. Again Houston and Smyth's analysis confirms my own. The proportion of leaders who were working-class in the three lodges they examined was as follows: 50 percent, 10 percent, and 88 percent.[26]

TABLE 7

Lodge Masters by Trade, 1871–88

	1871	1876	1878	1880	1886	1888
Professionals	1	0	2	3	4	1
Government employees	1	1	0	3	1	2
Manufacturers	1	1	0	0	0	2
Merchants	1	4	7	4	5	5
Master craftsmen	2	2	2	1	3	0
Clerks	1	1	2	2	1	2
Non-working-class total	7	9	13	13	14	12
Artisans	3	5	3	3	15	9
Labourers and unskilled	0	4	1	4	5	7
Working-class total	3	9	4	7	20	16
Working-class percentage	30	50	24	35	59	57
Number identified	10	18	17	20	34	28
Total number	17	27	29	30	35	39
Percentage identified	59	66	58	66	97	71

SOURCE: See note 27.

TABLE 8

All Orange Lodge Officers, 1871–86

	1871	1878	1886
Professionals	3	9	8
Government employees	4	8	9
Manufacturers	2	0	4
Merchants	9	21	14
Master craftsmen	4	3	11
Clerks	8	11	23
Non-working-class total	30	52	69
Artisans	51	42	91
Labourers and other unskilled	19	10	47
Working-class total	70	52	138
Working-class percentage	70	50	67
Number identified	100	104	207
Total number	190	197	315
Percentage identified	53	52	66

SOURCE: See note 28.

Final conclusions concerning the class affiliation of Orange leaders must await further study of individual leaders. In Toronto working-class individuals not only became lodge officers but also filled more eminent positions. For example, the editors of *The Orange Sentinel*, the order's most influential organ, were prominent trade unionists; E.F. Clarke had been a leader in the printer's strike of 1872 and his co-editor, John Hewitt, perhaps the most important theorist of the nine-hour movement, had been international vice-president of the coopers union. Two other prominent Toronto Orange leaders who played important trade-union roles were J.S. Williams, a printer and editor of the *Ontario Workman*, and Robert Glockling, a bookbinder and District Master Workman of the Knights of Labor. Orange bands were always prominent features at labour demonstrations throughout this period. Clearly, the ties between organized labour and Orangemen suggest that easy assertions about the order's preference for "leaders with social prestige" should be regarded with considerable scepticism.[29]

The rapid growth of Orangeism in Toronto may have been precipitated by a combination of national and local issues of sectarian strife, but what kept men in the order when the tides of religious struggle retreated? What was the basis for the continued success of an institution, which, as writers and pundits constantly asserted, had no reason for existence in a country with freedom of religion and no great land question? What motivated Toronto workers to maintain their Orange identities?

The answers to these questions lead one to an appreciation of the breadth and the strength of Orangeism. The order offered much to many quite different people. For some, there was the obvious patriotic and Protestant-defender appeal. For others, there was the confidence that came from belonging to a society which would help carry them through the difficulties of working-class life: if you were unemployed, you could depend on your lodge brothers for aid; if you were sick, the lodge would provide a doctor free and pay any additional medical expenses; or, if you died, the lodge would pay your funeral costs and pave your path into the next world with an impressive ritual, as well as providing financial aid to your widow and orphans. These benevolent functions tended to be informal until the 1880s when, faced with the competition of a whole series of fraternal societies specializing in insurance and other types of aid, the Orange Order formalized their systems into the Orange Mutual Benefit Society.[30]

There was, in addition to these practical advantages, the camaraderie and fraternity of the lodge. Here one found a male society away from women and the pervasive influence of the middle-class-inspired cult of domesticity. Faced with the increased size of their workplaces and their city, these men turned to institutions such as the Orange lodge to recreate the old familiar intimacies of smaller communities. Others probably joined in the expectation of personal gain or, at least, increased security. It was clear that in Toronto there was a whole series of corporation jobs which served as retainers for an Orangeman's faithful service. Although never as formalized as Tammany, the Orange Order served similar uses in machine politics. Orange-controlled jobs included the post office and the customs house at the federal level, and the gasworks, waterworks, police and fire departments at the corporation level. Houston and Smyth point out, for example, that in 1894 LOL No. 207 had four members who gave their address as the Parkdale fire station and LOL No. 781 had eleven firemen as members.[31] *The Irish Canadian*, no friend of Toronto Orangemen, complained in 1876 that the city had employed only two Catholics, who were subsequently fired. In the 1880s, *The Irish Canadian* ran a series of editorials exposing Orange jobbery in the civic corporation.[32] In 1885, for example, the paper systematically analysed the civic list and found only twenty-one (6 percent) Catholics in a total of 327 city positions. This included four Catholics in the 73-member fire department and fourteen in the 159-member police force.[33]

For those who were more ambitious the possibility existed of making a larger mark and receiving the sinecures that came from higher political intrigue. And for the most ambitious there was the political route itself. For a generation of Conservative politicians, the order represented a method of breaking the stranglehold of Compact Tories on nominations. It should be noted, however, that this route was open to few Orangemen and probably played a minor motivational role. At the local level the merchant, undertaker, or tavern keeper living in a working-class neighbourhood found lodge membership a prerequisite for attracting clients. Each candidate for Orange membership probably mixed these motives in distinctive ways.[34]

The Orange Order's role in political life was especially important in Toronto, where politicians built or demolished their careers in proportion to lodge support. The order did not provide an easy path to prominence in public life, for the politician was caught between the Orangeman's continuing need and love for the traditional marches, songs, rituals, and informal riots and the emerging industrial society's demand for order and control. Ogle Gowan's own political career demonstrates the snares upon the path to political success and respectability. His first electoral success was entirely contingent on Orange poll violence — behaviour that he was later instrumental in attempting to suppress.

The conflict between Orange tradition and new societal demands continued throughout the 1850s, 1860s, and 1870s. Whereas Orange workers identified with the old ways and happier days before the alienating onslaught of industrialism, Orange leaders found themselves under ever-increasing social pressure to control their compatriots' excesses. Thus Gowan encouraged the inception of Temperance lodges in the 1850s, which constituted a major break with Orange tradition with its heavy emphasis on the social role of drink. Recognizing the implications of such a step, he argued: "Our institution is not confined, wholly, or even chiefly, to the uneducated classes of the community, but includes large masses of intelligent and educated men. Remove from them the mirth and hilarity of the festive bowl, and some other source of enjoyment must be provided."[35] As a solution, he suggested that "every lodge have its own library and reading room." After 1859, Orange lodges were forbidden to meet in hotels, taverns, or saloons. Throughout the 1850s Gowan also proposed that lodges set up saving banks, and that Orange bands be required to study music — until then an unheard of proposition.[36]

Virgin Lodge was avowedly orangized to stiffen Orange discipline and to socialize younger Orangemen to new models of Orange behaviour. Originally, the name Virgin, which they later adopted officially, was hurled at them as an insult by their more senior and less "controlled" brothers in the order. The various attempts to assert a new discipline over the membership were not totally successful in the 1850s. The conflict continued into the 1870s and 1880s and heated discussions of whether to drink or not to drink became as much a part of 12 July as King Billy and his white horse.[37]

Another example of the order's increasing concern for respectability was the creation, in 1875, of a Grand Lodge committee on regalia. This committee reported in favour of formalizing and regularizing the old traditional modes of dress: "The Time has come when this Grand Lodge should adopt a uniform regalia; wanting this, our processions fail to favourably impress the public, and the grotesque and ridiculous things often worn as regalia making a laughing stock not only of those who wear them, but of the Association." The committee went on to specify the different robes for every degree and office in the order, the elaborateness of which was so great that it encouraged the emergence of firms that specialized in manufacturing Orange regalia at exorbitant rates.[38]

The events of 12 July always created great problems for Orange leaders in Canada. The day was so deeply entrenched in the Orange calendar that each member had to swear to celebrate annually the Battle of the Boyne. In periods of great tension, civic authorities often exerted considerable pressure to prevent Orangemen from marching. Orange leaders co-operated with such injunctions only in the most extreme cases, and even then were often unable to prevent their members from marching. It was bad enough that Orangemen demanded to march, but, what was worse, they usually insisted on fighting also. July 12, March 17, and November 5 were days when riot became ritual.

These riots, at least in mid- to late nineteenth-century Toronto, were controlled and not particularly violent. Only extraordinary happenings transformed them into serious outbreaks of collective violence in which severe damage or injury occurred. One historian of Orangeism has noted: "Even in Ireland the disorders caused by the 12 July processions were relatively minor irritations, the real evil being the nightly raids on Catholic dwellings and the reprisals which grew out of a land question that had no counterpart in Canada."[39] In Toronto the riots maintained a "territorial" basis but they also took on an increasingly ritualistic aspect.[40]

Orangemen and Irish Catholics clashed twenty-two times in the twenty-five years between 1867 and 1892. On only two of these occasions did serious violence occur to fracture the pattern of restrained ritual riot. Before discussing these two events and what transformed them into bloody occasions, let us describe the calendar of sectarian conflict in Toronto.[41]

Twelve of the riots quite predictably took place on 12 July and 17 March (eight and four respectively). One coincided with the Orange celebration of the discovery of the Gunpowder Plot in November and four others occurred at Orange and Green picnics in August. Thus seventeen of the twenty-two riots accompanied celebrations of import in the annual Orange and Green calendars. The pattern should not surprise us, for collective violence of this kind is neither random nor spontaneous but is most often "given some structure by the situation of worship or the procession that was the occasion for the disturbance."

Parades, then, were at the centre of violence in Toronto. This parallels the Irish experience, for "where you could 'walk' you were dominant and the other things followed." In Toronto, however, this testing of territory took on a ritualistic aspect, seldom progressing to the Belfast model of house-wrecking. A more careful study of the events of 12 July and 17 March will clarify the ritualistic nature of this violence.[42]

The July riots were of three types: those prompted by Green aggression toward the Orange celebration, those prompted by Orange challenges to Green neighbourhoods, and finally Green retaliation post-12 July. The first type was quite rare in Toronto because of the predominance of Orangemen, but in cities which were demographically more balanced or more Catholic, as in Montreal, it became more prominent. This type did occur in 1870 when a foolhardy Green drove his cart, bedecked with green ribbons, through the 12 July procession. It should be noted that, although a risky business at best, he did attempt this disruption in the heart of a Catholic neighbourhood. An earlier example of Green interference occurred in 1833, when Irish Catholics imitated the Orangemen by marching with green flags, with one of their members astride a white horse obscenely mimicking King Billy. Not surprisingly, a riot ensued.[43]

Riots of the second type were the most frequent in Toronto. In 1870, 1876, 1877, and again in 1888, riots were caused by Irish Catholics who attacked Orange fife and drum bands as they marched through the heart of a Green residential area playing tunes such as "Croppies Lie Down," "Protestant Boys," and "The Boyne Water." In 1877 an Orange fife and drum band chose Cosgrove's Hotel, a centre of Irish Catholic activity, as a likely spot to serenade. When their lusty performance of "Protestant Boys" was greeted with stones and jeers, they fought back. A crowd then gathered and proceeded to stone Cosgrove's Hotel, successfully smashing all the windows. This same hotel was attacked and wrecked successively in 1870, 1875, and 1878 — the one example of the Irish model of wrecking in sectarian strife. Cosgrove was a prominent Green leader and, on occasion, served as marshal in the St. Patrick's Day procession. His tavern was reputed to be a meeting place for Toronto Fenians.[44]

The third type of riot, Green aggression after the 12th, was infrequent and occurred only in 1873 and 1874.[45]

Riots that took place on 17 March, St. Patrick's Day, were usually instigated by Orangemen challenging Green marchers, as in 1871 when an Orange carter drove his horse through a Catholic procession, or when Orange bands marched in Catholic neighbourhoods playing their favourite party tunes, as they did in 1872 and 1889. (The fourth incident of a 17 March riot will be discussed later.)[46]

Most of these riots, then, were highly ritualized and specific. They focused around the major fetes of the Orange and Green calendar but, unlike that in Belfast, the violence was usually quite localized and slight. The milder form of celebration had been true of an earlier period in Ireland, where "The marching around the countryside of large bands had about it something of the holiday spirit. Parties usually met by mutual agreement and exchanged shots and insults outside of effective range until the magistrates arrived."[47] In Toronto, the riots seldom involved shooting; sometimes the parties came close enough to exchange blows, but they showed more bravado than blood.

Some riots did occur outside of the fetes. A number of them involved the Orange Young Britons and the Young Irishmen, their Catholic counterparts, in altercations at dances and over female attention. These adolescent wings of the Orange and Green closely resembled modern street gangs. They were certainly among the most militant on either side and, when arrests occurred, it usually involved these youthful sectarians. The events of September 1870 suggest the street-gang analogy. A fight broke out between a number of Orange Young Britons, who had come to a "low" (no doubt, Irish Catholic) dancehall to avenge some slight that one of their more daring members had received there. The fight that followed set off a wave of riots that led one leading Orangeman, John Ross Robertson, to editorialize in his *Daily Telegraph* against these "Young Rowdies," who were motivated by nothing more than "a spirit of braggadocio and rowdyism." Orange leaders sprang to the defence of the Young Britons. At a protest meeting held after the conviction of some of their colleagues for riotous and disorderly conduct, one Orange leader proposed a motion condemning Robertson after denying that any of those arrested were Young Britons.

> The Orange and the Green have at all times lived in this city in peace and harmony, each pursuing tenets, religious and political, playing their own favoured music, religious and national, and celebrating their own peculiar anniversaries and fete days without offense, molestation, or interruption and that this joyous and happy state of society it has now for the first time been attempted to be interrupted by the foul and atrocious articles which have recently been printed in certain newspapers in this city.

The same speaker went on to condemn the actions of the police in intervening in the altercation. This is the clue to Orange fury in this case, for the convictions following these events were among the first brought down against these ritual riots. Young Britons previously arrested had escaped with nothing more than a reprimand from the police magistrate. Orange leadership rallied behind their members on this occasion for the last time.

The willingness of civic authorities to suppress Orange riots, and the support that Robertson lent them, symbolize the fact that Orange riots were on their way to becoming as much a memory as the Battle of the Boyne itself. This change, like others in the Orange Order, was bitterly resisted and was not accomplished overnight. Robertson's experience in attacking the Young Britons in 1870 was instructive: "The *Daily Telegraph* office was threatened with destruction: letters similar to those laid on the tables of obnoxious Irish landlords were received by the editor and reporters; and those taverns and shebeens in which the Young Britons concoct their fearful fights echoed with howls of vengeance against the *Daily Telegraph*." If that was the case, Robertson must have taken great satisfaction when Gowan, in 1873, made a motion that:

> Whereas a number of societies or orders such as the Orange Young Britons . . . have been introduced in Canada, or have been organized in the last few years. And whereas such societies have been allowed in some places to walk in public processions and otherwise identify themselves with the Orange Institution, without being under the control, or owing any direct responsibility to the Grand Lodge of the Order for their acts, words or proceedings; and it has become highly desirable and necessary that if such bodies are to be continued, they should be placed under the direct control of proper officers, responsible to the Grand Lodge.

This motion was carried in 1874, but the Young Britons chafed under the authority of the Grand Lodge and a number of them split from the order in the early 1880s. But conflict over the old Orange models and the new Orange design was present. One young leader argued for the new control:

> I would recommend the cultivation of the young mind . . . how much time do young men generally spend in frivolity or idleness; how much in what is worse—vicious indulgence: smoking, gaming, riotous and ribald conversation, or indolent lounging which ought to be devoted to the pursuit of knowledge and the attainment of business habits. . . . This is not as it ought to be. Every hour should be appropriated to some useful purpose. We should be as niggardly of time as is the miser of his hoarded treasure.

Following on that appropriate simile, he went on to propose that they should become "valuable members of society, efficient businessmen, and active moral agents." Things had moved a long way from the earlier "festive bowl."[48]

The conscious efforts of some Orange leaders to instil tougher discipline and to enforce a rigid control over their membership came to fruition in the 1870s. The slow disappearance of the social base for preindustrial Orange behaviour played as large a part as the conscious efforts of Orange leaders. But whatever the cause, of the twenty-two riots between 1867 and 1892 only four took place after 1878, and these were all clustered in the three-year period 1887–90. Perhaps even more persuasive was the changed nature of the descriptions of 12 July events in the Toronto press in the 1880s: reminiscence prevailed as writers reflected on how 12 July *used to be*. It was even noted that some of the traditional ritual dress had been dropped. "The striking white trousers have practically become a thing of history," wrote one journalist with a tinge of regret. *The Irish Canadian*, a Green paper, noted gleefully throughout the mid-1880s that the numbers were falling off at Twelfth celebrations and that the celebrations were now "quiet," "tame and flat." It also described the decline of the "broils that in years gone by disgraced the Orange anniversary," and emphasized the decline of the old traditions:

> And then the traditional grey horse is not as prominent and ubiquitous as was his wont—a circumstance not without significance as indicative of that fatal indifference which preceded the final collapse. . . . We refer to these trifles merely to show that the discipline of the Twelfth is not as rigid as it used to be, and it looks as if a horse of any colour will now serve where formerly it was treason to hint at anything but the sleekest grey.

The two exceptional riots of the 1870s and the O'Brien riot of 1887[49] provide further indications of changes in Orangeism in that period. The Jubilee Riots of 1875 were undoubtedly the bloodiest sectarian struggles in Toronto's history. The second most violent was the riot which greeted the Fenian leader, O'Donavon Rossa, when he lectured at a 17 March Hibernian celebration in 1878. In both cases the Orange crowds were aroused by the transgression of the informal limits set upon sectarian display by years of ritual riot. In both cases, Toronto Catholics seemed to be extending their territory beyond previous definition. Seventeenth of March marches were acceptable, but the importation of an Irish revolutionary to speak in Toronto was an affront that could not go unchallenged. Equally, processions with green ribbons and Hibernian slogans were acceptable, but a pilgrimage through quiet Toronto streets on the Sabbath, with symbols of Popery and apparently on the bidding of the Vatican, could not be allowed to pass unchallenged.[50]

The response of Toronto community leaders is instructive. They decided that they must defend the Catholics' right to religious procession. The entire police force and three companies of militia were utilized to assure Roman Catholics their right to march in 1875. In 1878, however, they did little to protect Rossa. The police took a severe beating on both occasions, but the copious arrests of 1875 contrast noticeably with the record of no arrests in 1878.

The use of Orange militia companies by an Orange mayor against an Orange crowd must have made it very clear to rioting Orangemen that their conduct no longer received tacit approval. It was, of course, partially this armed intervention that transformed the Jubilee Riots into a serious affray. A look at the twenty-nine men arrested reveals eleven identifiable Orangemen. The occupations of the arrested men represent a cross-section of Toronto's working class.[51]

The extraordinary nature of these Roman Catholic marches aroused Orange ire and, when combined with the aggressive attempt by the authorities to suppress the riot, changed the general form of Toronto ritual riot into a full-scale sectarian struggle. There was an important national context as well. The Guibord Affair was still working its way to a macabre close, and only weeks before the Toronto riots, a crowd of Roman Catholics had prevented the burial of Guibord's body in a Montreal Catholic cemetery, despite a court order to the contrary. Meanwhile, only a month before, the Catholic community had hosted an unprecedented August O'Connell Centenary for Hibernians from all over the province.[52] This was probably the largest Catholic demonstration ever held in Toronto. Local Orangemen thus had much on their mind when later they heard of plans for a procession to be held for Catholic bishops visiting the city. In addition, the Catholics planned to march on church visitations to gain indulgences which were connected with the Pope's declaration of 1875 as a jubilee year. All of this parading seemed as if Catholics were trailing coats, and the Orangemen requested that Archbishop Lynch cancel these affairs. He refused, and the processionists were met with a small riot on Sunday, 26 September. After these events, Orange leaders called a special public meeting. There, after speeches attacking Ultramontanism, they moved that both sides refrain from marching on the coming Sunday. Lynch again refused and instead demanded from the mayor that, if he forbade his laity to resist, they would be assured of police protection. To this the mayor reluctantly agreed.

The riot that ensued involved as many as 6000 to 8000 people, and the entire city core was out of control for a number of hours. Given the crowd's immense size, one is struck by its self-control. The pilgrims were attacked but there were few reported injuries, and the only property damage was incurred by every Orangeman's favourite Toronto target, Owen Cosgrove's Hotel. One scene, reported in the press, vividly portrays the irony of the situation. A fervid anti-processionist appealed to the crowd to attack a Catholic church by reminding them of the old days "when they walked eight deep" on 12 July. The crowd did not sack any churches that day. Although they might continue to walk eight deep on the Twelfth, the years of ritualized riot were all but over.

The events of 1878 were limited to one night of riot. Insulted by the Catholics' very attempt to bring Rossa to Toronto, Orangemen gathered to prevent the lecture from taking place. In this they failed and, when Rossa managed to elude them after the speech, they proceeded to stone the hall and later to attack Cosgrove's. After 1878 Toronto was to enjoy relative quiet until the late 1880s. Those years saw a few half-hearted attempts at religious riot but the times had changed. The re-emergence of anti-Catholic sentiments in various third-party movements, and the creation in the 1890s of the Protestant Protective Association, modelled on the nativist American Protective Association, suggest the breakdown of the old Orangeism and hint at one of its uses.[53]

The ritualized violence of Toronto Orangemen, which seldom exceeded a set of informal limits, was far less menacing than the nativist movements which replaced it in the 1890s. This restricted violence also prevailed in the 1850s, when the Brown wing of the Grit party exceeded the order in pushing anti-Catholic positions. Orangeism was never racist; its replacements were. The relative mildness of Canadian sectarian strife, when compared with events in the United States, suggests that the Orange institution, which was never strong in the United States, may have played a major role in tempering sectarian strife by institutionalizing elements of it. Shows of strife more often resembled rugged games than vicious riot.

The Orange Order played an ambiguous role in the life of the Toronto working class. Although clearly dividing the working-class community in two, it nevertheless provided some of its Protestant members with a number of strengths that were usefully carried into the realm of unionism. The Orange lodges trained their members in parliamentary procedure and taught them how to conduct and lead meetings. The order also provided leadership for the labour movement. Perhaps of more import, however, was the reinforcement that the order gave to old themes of working-class life. The virtues of mutuality, fraternity, and benevolence had roots deep in the preindustrial community, and institutions such as the Orange lodges succeeded in transferring them to the increasingly fragmented world of the industrial city. Rowland Berthoff has argued that similar, but less traditional, societies in the United States "stood in reaction against the social, cultural, and spiritual inadequacies of the nineteenth century. Ineffectual or insubstantial though they might be, they had at least begun the evolution of new institutions and a new community capable of satisfying eternal human needs in forms suited to modern society."[54]

The other aspect of the Orange tradition with a positive heritage for working-class achievement was its activism. The Orangemen carried with them an Irish dislike of constitutional authority and a willingness to impose their own justice. As one scholar has argued of their Green brothers, but which applies equally well to Orangemen:

> Rioting to secure . . . political recognition, or religious liberty as popularly construed can be explained by reference to Irish tradition and social organization. It was simply a continuation in Canada of all the devices, including oath-bound secret societies, developed extra-legally in response to legal, civil and religious deprivation. . . . The violence indicates not massive social disorganization but the persistence of a social order.

These traditions were carried on, he continues, in "early trade unionism and the political machine." Even in the extreme case of religious riot, "the violence is explained not in terms of how crazy, hungry, or sexually frustrated the violent people are, but in terms of the goals of their actions and in terms of the roles and patterns of behaviour allowed by their culture."[55]

The Irish background and the Toronto working-class experience then explain much about Orange actions, but explanations are not, of course, apologies.[56] The divisive influence of the Orange Order in Toronto's working-class community did exist, albeit mainly in the realm of politics. D.J. O'Donoghue and Alf Jury, two working-class leaders with Liberal party ties, often inveighed against the reactionary Orangemen, but one should treat the evidence of these political losers with extreme caution. For they were just as committed political partisans — all that differed was the party. E.F. Clarke's and John Hewitt's toryism must be weighed on the same ideological scale, not on one that registers only Orangemen. Irish Catholic liberalism was as disruptive to the emergence of a working-class party as Orange toryism.

A distinction must also be made here between the sectarian strife of religious riot and economic discrimination and that of partisan politics. Religious riot had all but disappeared by the 1880s, and riots to keep Catholics out of jobs did not occur in Toronto in this period. No examples of ethnic or religious riot at the workplace have been found. Partisan political strife, on the other hand, continued. Nevertheless, by the 1880s, common class issues emerged to unite Irish Catholic Liberal trade-unionists like O'Donoghue, Orangemen like Hewitt and Glockling, and even secularist Alf Jury and theosophist Phillips Thompson. In arriving at this point, many rival and mutually exclusive cultural traditions played a role, and Orangeism was by no means the least important.

Thus, by the 1880s, although the Orange Order was still a vibrant part of working-class life, in the economic sphere at least class had triumphed over ethnicity. In the political sphere . . . class emerged as only a momentary victor in 1886 but was submerged again thereafter in a tide of ethnic, religious, and partisan political strife.

Notes

1. Hector Charlesworth, *Candid Chronicles* (Toronto, 1925), especially his Foreword.

2. Martin Robin, *Radical Politics and Canadian Labour, 1880–1930* (Kingston, 1968), Introduction, esp. 5–6.

3. H.C. Pentland, "Labour and the Development of Industrial Capitalism in Canada" (Ph.D. thesis, University of Toronto, 1960), 259. Recent work by University of Toronto geographers Cecil Houston and William J. Smyth has added greatly to our knowledge of the Orange Order in Ontario. Although differing in emphasis, and despite their disclaimers, in most aspects I find their work compatible with my own interpretation. However, I disagree with their interpretation of the Orangemen's "garrison mentality," their dismissal of territoriality as a useful analytic device, and their insistence on the Order's cross-class membership. See especially their "The Orange Order in Nineteenth-Century Ontario: A Study in Institutional Cultural Transfer" (Department of Geography, University of Toronto, Discussion Paper No. 22, 1977), and "Toronto, the Belfast of Canada" (unpublished paper).

4. Maureen Wall, "The Whiteboys," in T. Desmond Williams, *Secret Societies in Ireland* (Dublin, 1973).

5. E.P. Thompson, *The Making of the English Working Class* (London, 1968), 470–71.

6. Kevin B. Nowlan, "Conclusion," in Williams, *Secret Societies*, 183.

7. J.C. Beckett, *The Anglo-Irish Tradition* (London, 1976), 45.

8. Hereward Senior, "The Genesis of Canadian Orangeism," *Ontario History* 60 (1968): 13–14; *Orangeism: The Canadian Phase* (Toronto, 1973), ch. 1–2; "Ogle Gowan," in *Dictionary of Canadian Biography* (Toronto, 1972), 10: 309–14.

9. W.B. Kerr, "When Orange and Green United, 1832–1839: The Alliance of Macdonnell and Gowan," *Ontario History* 34 (1942): 34–42.

10. For examples see William Shannon, *The United Empire Minstrel* (Toronto, 1852), 42–43; Shannon, *The Dominion Orange Harmonist* (Toronto, 1876), 27 and chronology. See also R. McBride, *The Canadian Orange Minstrel for 1860* (London, 1860), and *The Canadian Orange Minstrel for 1870: Written for the Purposes of Keeping in Remembrance the Dark Doings and Designs of Popery in This Country* (Toronto, 1870). The best description of the Slabtown Affair is provided by J. Lawrence Runnals, *The Irish on the Welland Canal* (St. Catharines, 1973). On 12 July 1849 Irish Catholics gathered to prevent the Orangemen from "walking," but when the Orangemen failed even to try, the Catholics settled for three cheers — one for the queen, one for the governor, and one for the pope. The Orangemen responded with a volley of shots which left two Catholics dead and four others wounded. For a similar event in Irish history, see H. Senior, *Orangeism in Ireland and Britain, 1795–1836* (Toronto, 1966), 16.

11. For examples, see Loyal Orange Institution of British North America, *Laws, Rules, and Regulations*, (Cobourg, 1846, and Belleville, 1850); *Constitution and Laws of the Loyal Orange Institution*, (Toronto, 1855).

12. Loyal Orange Institution of British North America (LOIBNA), *Forms to Be Observed in Private Lodges*, (Toronto, 1855).

13. For ritual see E.J. Hobsbawm, *Primitive Rebels* (London, 1959), 150–74; for Masonic roots see Senior, *Orangeism in Ireland*, 12, and Nowlan, "Conclusion," in Williams, *Secret Societies*, 183; for actual ritual forms see LOIBNA, *Charges to Be Delivered at the Initiation of Members* (Toronto, 1856); *Forms to Be Observed in Private Lodges* (Toronto, 1855); *Orange Ritual* (Belleville, 1874); *Forms of the Royal Blue Order* (Toronto, 1855); *Ritual of the Blue Order* (Belleville, 1864); *Forms of the Royal Blue Order* (Toronto, 1869); *Forms of the Purple Order* (Toronto, 1855); *Forms of the Royal Arch Purple Mark* (Toronto, 1855, 1869); *Forms and Ritual of the Royal Scarlet Order* (Cobourg, 1846, 1864); *Ritual of the Royal Scarlet Order* (Toronto, 1886).

14. Conrad Arensberg, *The Irish Countryman* (New York, 1937), 215–16.

15. LOIBNA, *Charges to be Delivered . . . and Services for the Burial of Orangemen, The Dedication of an Orange Lodge, and for the Installation of Officers*, (Toronto, 1856).

16. As late as 1969 partisan historians were still claiming that "in fact the Twelfth in Toronto is second only to that on the field at Finaghy" (M.W. Dewar, John Brown, S.E. Long, *Orangeism: A New Historical Appreciation* (Belfast, 1969), 17).

17. Much of it is drawn from Leslie H. Saunders, *The Story of Orangeism* (Toronto, 1941). However, Provincial Grand Lodge Proceedings, Toronto Orange Directories, Toronto City Directories, and the Toronto press have also been utilized. The extremely useful work of Cecil Houston and William Smyth, drawn from archival materials still held by the order, differs generally on the level of a few lodges only, and I have tried to cite their evidence when it is opposed to my own.

18. These figures and those following are from LOIBNA, Provincial Grand Lodge of Canada West, *Proceedings*, (Toronto, 1872, 1876, 1880, 1883).

19. Houston and Smyth, "The Orange Order," 5, 44–51 but esp. 50–51. This useful discussion clarifies some of the bewildering array of numbers used when discussing Orange membership.

20. Pentland, "Labour and the Development of Industrial Capitalism," 247ff. Pentland's work on the order is the most insightful we have, but he makes the error of assuming that "the typical urban Orangeman was a skilled worker, a craftsman" (257). However, he was quite aware of the Orange Order's predominant working-class membership and its importance. Both these insights have not been picked up by scholars writing after him.

21. The data are from the following sources: *By-laws of Loyal Orange Lodge, No. 328* (Toronto, 1846, 1852, 1856, and 1872); Lodge 137, Treasurers Book, 1889–1907 and Roll Book, 1885– ; Lodge 173, Minutes, 1883–1903 and Roll Book, 1883–1896; Lodge 711, Minutes, 1873–1906; Membership and Degree Book, 1890– ; Proposition Book, 1890– ; Roll Book, 1875–1895. The Manuscript Records of Lodges 137, 173 and 711 are all in The Baldwin Room of Metropolitan Toronto Central Library.

22. *By-laws of Loyal Orange Lodge, No. 328*, (Toronto, 1872).

23. Minutes, LOL No. 137.

24. Houston and Smyth, "Toronto, the Belfast of Canada," 11, 12–13, 14.

25. Ibid., and "The Orange Order in Nineteenth-Century Ontario," 6–7.

26. Houston and Smyth, "Toronto, the Belfast of Canada," 13.

27. For the opposite argument see Senior, "Orangeism in Ontario in Politics, 1872–1896," 136–37 in Donald Swainson, *Oliver Mowat's Ontario* (Toronto, 1972). Data on lodge masters were taken from the following sources: Thomas Keyes, *Orange Directory of Western Ontario* (St. Catharines, 1871); *Second Annual Orange Directory of Lodges, Meetings, Officers, etc. for Toronto* (Toronto, 1876); *Toronto Orange Directory, 1878* (Toronto, 1878); LOIBNA, Provincial Grand Lodge of Canada West, *Proceedings* (Toronto, 1888). These lists of masters were then traced in directories for occupational data.

28. The 1878 and 1886 data are from the above sources; the 1871 lists of all officers was complied from the lists appearing in the *Globe* after each lodge election was held.

29. Senior, "Orangeism in Canadian Politics," 136–37.

30. For all these functions see Minutes of Lodges 173 and 711. See also Lodge By-laws of the following Toronto lodges: Virgin No. 328, 1846, 1852, 1856, and 1872; Schomberg No. 212, 1882; McKinlay No. 275, 1874; York No. 375, 1866 and 1894; Enniskillen No. 711, 1898; and *Constitution and Laws of the Orange Mutual Benefit Society of Ontario West* (Toronto, 188?).

31. Houston and Smyth, "Toronto, the Belfast of Canada," 21.

32. Membership lists for the lodges studied and lists of lodge officers confirm this. See also patronage correspondence in Macdonald Papers, PAC, and *Irish Canadian*, 8 March 1876, 9 Oct. 1884, and 7 May 1885.

33. See especially *Irish Canadian*, 12 Nov. 1885 and 21, 28 Aug. and 11 Dec. 1884.

34. Senior, *Orangeism: The Canadian Phase*, esp. ch. 2.

35. LOIBNA, *Proceedings of the Grand Lodge* (Toronto, 1856).

36. William Perkins Bull, *From the Boyne to Brampton* (Toronto, 1936), 138.

37. *By-laws* (Toronto, 1872).

38. *Constitution and Laws* (Belleville, 1875).

39. Senior, "The Genesis of Canadian Orangeism," 27.

40. Sybil E. Baker, "The Orange and Green," in Dyos and Wolff, *The Victorian City: Images and Reality* (London, 1973), 789–814.

41. The data are taken from a daily reading of the Toronto press for the twenty-five-year period. The best Canadian analysis of Orange-Green conflict is Michael Cross, "Stony Monday, 1849: The Rebellion Losses Riot in Bytown," *Ontario History* (1971): 177–90. See also his "The Shiners War: Social Violence in the Ottawa Valley in the 1830s," *Canadian Historical Review* (1973): 1–26, for a fine description of pre-industrial Green organization.

42. Natalie Zemon Davis, "The Rites of Violence: Religious Riot in Sixteenth Century France," *Past and Present* 59 (1973): 51–91, and Baker, "The Orange and the Green," 790–97.

43. *Globe*, 23 July 1870, and W.B. Kerr, "The Orange Order in the 1820s" from *The Orange Sentinel* now on microfilm in the Toronto Public Library.

44. *Globe*, 13 July 1870, 11 July 1876, 13 July 1877, 13 July 1888; *Mail*, 19 June 1877, 13 July 1877.

45. *Globe*, 30 July 1873, 27 July 1874; *Leader*, 30 July 1873; *Irish Canadian*, 30 July 1873.

46. *Irish Canadian*, 22, 29 March, 5 April 1871; *Globe*, 6, 13 April 1871; 19, 20 March 1872; 19, 22 March 1889; *Telegraph*, 19 March 1872.

47. Senior, *Orangeism in Ireland*, 12.

48. For a discussion of the role of adolescent males in collective violence of a traditional sort, see Davis, "Rites of Violence"; for specific Orange data on boys, see Baker, "Orange and Green"; *Globe*, 2, 3, 5, 6, 12, 14, 20, 21 Sept. 1870. See also LOIBNA, Grand Lodge of Canada West, *Proceedings* (Toronto, 1873); Orange Young Britons, Grand Lodge, *Proceedings* (Toronto, 1878).

49. For a detailed discussion of the O'Brien riot see: Desmond Morton, *Mayor Howland* (Toronto, 1973), 77–82; Colonel George T. Denison, *The Struggle for Imperial Unity: Recollections and Experiences* (Toronto, 1909), 70–76; and *Globe*, 16, 18, 29, 21 May 1887.

50. *Globe*, 12 July 1888, 13 July 1889; *Irish Canadian*, 16 July 1885, 15 July 1886. For the events of 1875

see Martin Galvin, "Catholic-Protestant Relations in Ontario 1864–1875" (M.A. thesis, University of Toronto, 1962), and Galvin, "The Jubilee Riots in Toronto," *Canadian Catholic Historical Association Annual Report* (1959): 93–107. See also E.C. Guillet, *Toronto: Trading Post to Great City* (Toronto, 1934), 216–18.

51. For arrests and trials see *Globe*, 27, 28 Sept.; 4, 5, 9, 12 Oct.; 17–21, 28 Jan. 1876.

52. Ibid., 7 Aug. 1875.

53. *Globe*, 19, 20, 22, 27 March 1878; *Mail*, 19, 20 March 1878.

54. Rowland Berthoff, *An Unsettled People* (New York, 1971), 274.

55. Kenneth Duncan, "Irish Famine Immigration and the Social Structure of Canada West," *Canadian Review of Sociology and Anthropology* (1965): 39 and Davis, "The Rites of Violence," 91. For an excellent analysis of the utility of Irish cultural traditions for the emerging labour movement, see Michael A. Gordon, "Irish Immigrant Culture and the Labor Boycott in New York City, 1880–1886," *Labor History* 16 (1975): 184–229.

56. This rather obvious point is added to prevent further misreadings of the kind made by John Smart, "Archivists, Nationalists and New Leftists — Themes, Sources and Problems in English Canadian Labour History since 1965" (unpublished paper), esp. 14–17.

PRIVATE ELECTRICAL UTILITIES AND MUNICIPAL OWNERSHIP IN ONTARIO, 1891–1900†

KENNETH C. DEWAR

In June, 1897, the electrial utility companies of Ontario launched their first organized offensive against municipal ownership. Their objective was to secure an amendment to the Ontario Municipal Act that would protect the vested interests of local utilities and perhaps slow the reform movement then gathering momentum throughout the province. Two years later, they achieved success in the form of the so-called "Conmee Clauses," requiring municipalities to buy out privately owned local electrical and gas utilities before inaugurating their own systems.

Passage of the amendment may be seen as a minor, though not insignificant, incident in the history of the conflict over state ownership that culminated in the creation of the Hydro-Electric Power Commission of Ontario in 1906. It helped to shift the focus of conflict from the municipal to the provincial level of government at the turn of the century. At the same time, the campaign for the amendment is interesting in its own right. The movement for municipal ownership of civic services, a compound of reforming zeal, economic self-interest and pragmatic response to the administrative and political problems of urban growth, was then in its early stages. Yet the central importance of electric light and power, for street lighting, transportation and water pumping, if not yet for manufacturing, was already recognized.[1] The utility owners thus had some reason to feel a sense of both optimism and insecurity. Their campaign affords an opportunity to observe one industry's attempt to organize its members for political action, and to note the means it employed to present its wishes to the government. In the process, the owners and operators express a view of the role of the state at once flexible in its conception of the limits of government regulations, and fixed in its perception of government's responsibility to protect fundamental business interests.

†*Urban History Review/Revue d'histoire urbaine* 12, no. 1 (June 1983): 29–38.

The organizational vehicle of the campaign was the Canadian Electrical Association, formed in 1891 in an attempt to stabilize the fortunes of the lighting business.[2] Competition and rapid technological change had introduced an element of uncertainty into what had been at first a highly profitable line of enterprise. In order to encourage more co-operation and to help upgrade the technical expertise of "electrical men," a number of companies, assisted by the trade paper, the *Canadian Electrical News*, invited those associated with electrical lighting to join a new national body. Among the respondents, utilities predominated. They were joined by a few manufacturers — the "supply men" — and a few individual technicians, forerunners of the electrical engineering profession.[3] Like many other national associations of the time, the CEA was overwhelmingly Ontarian in its membership and concerns. In the late nineties, its Legislative Committee devoted itself wholly to meeting the threat of municipal ownership in Ontario.

John Yule, general manager of the Guelph Light and Power Company, a firm engaged in both gas and electricity production, initiated and led the efforts to secure protective legislation.[4] As President of the CEA in 1897, he called upon all members to set aside their differences and unite against a common enemy. "No business jealousies should find a place amongst us," he said in opening the annual convention; "rather ought we to help each other by exchanging opinions and experiences, and particularly should this be the case just now, when so many are face to face with that movement now prevalent in Canada for what is called municipal control."[5] He contrasted, with some bitterness, the acclaim which earlier had greeted the introduction of electric light with the persistent and growing movement which now threatened the very people who had risked their capital in the pioneer lighting business — "in most cases done for the purpose of improving their town and helping their community to keep up with the march of progress." Yule himself was not moved by any abstract concern for the rights of property: the local movement which some six years later was to result in the town's purchase of Guelph Light and Power was already gaining strength.

Yule's call to arms was representative, in tone and argument, of the utility companies' response to their critics. He dismissed the reformers as "local agitators." Yet at the same time, the moderation of his specific proposals revealed a flexible and fluid approach to the limits of state action, accompanied by, doubtless in part prompted by, a calculated respect for the strength of the movement. His essential concern was to protect the capital already invested in the electrical business: "The agitation is in the air and how best to save our property from complete confiscation is the question of primary importance. We do not dispute the right of municipalities to control and operate all their franchises, *if honestly and fairly entered into*." [My emphasis.] The greatest danger, that is, lay in something which he and his associates in the CEA had always feared: competition.

In this case the competitor, for all his disadvantages of inexperience and political meddling, would have the backing of the community's tax resources, resources to which the private company itself, as a member of that community, was required to contribute. Yule regarded as a "hopeful sign" that "a few of our leading newspapers are now recognizing that the practice in some European countries of government control of monopolies is the true remedy for any evils that may exist." He described the regulatory Board of Gas and Electric Light Commissioners which existed in Massachusetts, and also noted that in Great Britain local authorities were prohibited from entering competition with private companies. A British municipality was required to purchase the local company, according to rules and procedures set out in the Electric Lighting Act, before it entered the lighting business. If a purchase price could not be agreed upon, the matter went to arbitration. Yule thought that a combination of the British and Massachusetts legislation would offer an ideal environment for private companies. His sights were mainly focused, however, on achieving protection on the British model.

The *Canadian Electrical News*, which had become the official CEA journal, had arrived at much the same position. Three years earlier, in response to a series of municipal initiatives in London, Hamilton, Woodstock and Ottawa, the *News* had begun to devote more space and more serious consideration to the municipal ownership question than it had done previously.[6] Its editorials and articles reflected a mixture of anger and fear, of rigidity and flexibility, similar to that found in Yule's address. Occasionally, articles were printed that were sympathetic to municipal ownership, though these were always signed or, in one case, marked "Contributed."[7] More commonly, a stance that was basically critical was tempered by a cautious reluctance to prejudge the issue. In the summer of 1894, the journal carried an article on the Port Arthur Electric Railway, "the only street railway in America that is owned and operated by the town," and while it seized the opportunity to criticize construction expenditures, it also referred to the railway as "an interesting experiment in municipal undertakings [sic]," one which might in the future help to resolve the question of "the feasibility of towns operating their own railways."[8] Similarly, the journal firmly opposed a Toronto bylaw authorizing money for an electric light plant, but suggested it was too early, in light of the changing state of electrical technology, to make a decision involving so heavy a capital commitment.

> It is altogether certain, we believe, that the saving, if any (which might be made by a municipal plant) would be so very trifling as not to warrant the city in entering upon such an extensive undertaking, involving so large an outlay. . . . Whether or not it will ultimately be to the city's advantage to own and operate its own lighting plant, will be much better understood say five years hence than it can possibly be to-day, when the business is to some extent in a transition state.[9]

When the bylaw was defeated, an editorial congratulated the city's property owners on their wisdom, but again revealed the pragmatism of the journal's attitude: "We believe the decision to be a wise one so far as it related to Toronto and cities of large population."[10] The question might be resolved differently, in other words, in smaller centres, where the profitability of lighting was more doubtful but where demand was nonetheless present.

The *Electrical News* also acknowledged the justice of some criticism of the industry by its own appeals for improvements in company practice. In October, 1898, it reprimanded a number of unspecified companies for their cavalier treatment of customers. The editorial, entitled "Short-Sighted Methods," began, "From information to hand, we are of the opinion that the movement in favor of municipal control of electric lighting is being advanced by the unpopular methods of some of the private lighting companies." To operate successfully, utilities had to cater to public requirements. "Their object should be to please by every means the persons from whom their business derives its revenue." The companies in question were not doing so and, moreover, were not maintaining and renewing their equipment. "As might easily have been foreseen, the result of this line of policy has been forfeit of the sympathy and goodwill of the consumers on whom the success of the business must depend, and the dissatisfaction thus engendered has, in many instance, taken the form of active opposition and advocacy of municipal control."[11] This was a result which affected not only the parties directly concerned, but the entire industry.

This self-criticism, was, of course, exceptional. The image usually presented by the *Electrical News* and by vocal members of the CEA was of an industry engaged in an undertaking hazardous by its very nature, and made even more so by the threat of municipal ownership.[12] An especially destructive snowstorm in the winter of 1894 inspired the hope that the public would recognize the need for a "fair margin of profit" in a business vulnerable to sudden and serious damage.[13] The picture of uncertain profits first drawn at the time of the Association's creation recurred in subsequent years. When in 1894 a delegation of gas and electric company representatives opposed the assessment of "street plant" for taxation purposes, the risks of electric lighting enterprise were stressed: changing technology, low profit margins, "keen competition," including that of other illuminants, and the immobility of plant, once it was established.[14] At the same time, the *News* suggested it was "the public" itself which owned these enterprises. The original promoters typically sold their stock at a premium, thereby reaping "some of the reward due to their daring and ability," and the purchaser was generally a "steady," "sensible" man who was investing his small yearly surplus earned in business or a profession. His shares constituted part of the legacy which he left to his family. "These men," according to the *News* "their widows and unmarried daughters, are ultimately the principal owners of gas and electric companies in the larger towns. . . ."[15] This transfer of ownership had taken approximately a decade.

The companies, in this view, occupied a position of weakness in relation to the municipalities. The *News* argued that central station men were ignorant of each other's methods and operating conditions. It offered as evidence a letter from the manager of a plant in an eastern Ontario town to his counterpart in a western Ontario town requesting information about the other's lighting system and the nature of his municipal contract. "The municipalities have taken advantage of this state of things to force down the price of electric lighting, and in fact to almost dictate their own terms to the companies." The need for some sort of united defensive action was manifest, and the journal urged managers and owners to join and support the CEA.[16]

The Association devoted a session of its 1898 convention to a consideration of how the beleaguered company owner might best cope with his problems. The paper, delivered by A.A. Wright of Renfrew — "How to Overcome Some of the

Difficulties Encountered by Central Station Men" — and the discussion that followed, gave as much attention to municipal relations as to commercial and residential lighting. Wright, later a Liberal M.P., was a prominent charter member of the CEA.[17] His advice consisted mainly of two points. The first was to confine one's own political activity to the provincial and federal areas. Direct involvement in municipal politics would only make enemies who would then attack the municipal lighting agreement. Entire passivity, on the other hand, was likewise to be avoided: "I do not wish you to infer from this that you should not exercise your franchise when the day for voting comes around, but on the contrary let it be known that you and your employees always vote for the progressive and enterprising men of the town and as every aspiring alderman will want your assistance, you if you do not make too much noise, will generally manage when he is elected to get his."[18]

Secondly, Wright advised that every attempt should be made to terminate the lighting contract, usually annual in smaller centres, on the first of March. This could be done by informing the municipal authorities that the company's fiscal year began on that date. A "harmless looking saving clause" should then be inserted near the end of the contract, providing for thirty days' written notice of intent to terminate by either party, failing which the contract would be renewed for another year. Quarterly billing dates, finally, should be arranged to fall on the first of March, June, September and December. This strategy was predicated on the timing of Ontario municipal elections, held at the beginning of each year. The outgoing council, hopeful of the company's assistance in re-election, would "forget" to give notice. The new council normally met for the first time only at the end of January, when in any case little business was conducted. Electric lighting thus would escape attention until presentation of the March quarterly account, by which time it would be impossible to meet the requirements for notice of termination. Wright thought this might go on for some time!

During the discussion, he supplemented this advice by recommending the joint stock company as a form of organization. If "the most influential men in the town" could be enlisted as members of the board the company would secure an added "leverage on the council" and a hedge against the formation of a rival concern. More pessimistically, he advised his listeners to avoid street lighting altogether and to concentrate on the commercial and residential side of the business. J.J. Wright, manager of the Toronto Electric Light Company, added a cautionary note to the saving clause recommendation. It was impossible, he thought, to come right out and ask for it, "especially as one has to deal with a number of men who are not any too well up." One had to choose carefully an alderman who would sponsor it. In a similar vein, Yule warned of the fickleness of municipal councillors. The problem with gathering the support of influential men was that often their influence was transitory. He himself was thankful that in Ontario only property holders could vote on a bylaw, and they were not inclined to trust the councils "with any more money or property than they can get at present."[19]

Underlying the electric light industry's sense of municipal persecution was thus a solid distrust, bordering on contempt, for local authorities. Many of them, in A.A. Wright's words, "know nothing of arc lighting, except that it is not only necessary, but their special duty, to appear wise in order that they may look well after the interests of the town." More sympathetically, in his 1897 Presidential Address, Yule contrasted the situation in cities admired by municipal reformers, like Glasgow, Manchester and Birmingham, "where the civic ambition largely prevails amongst men of capital, leisure and ability, who give their time and talents to promote the common good," with that in Canada, where municipal affairs were managed "in odd hours snatched from business, by men who cannot afford to give the time and attention necessary to the successful management of an intricate and hazardous mercantile concern like the supply of electricity."[20] The problem of incompetence was compounded by the problem of corruption, as the *Electrical News* was quick to point out late in 1894 when the famous Toronto boodle case was exposed. Municipal institutions, it argued, were unfit to take over any industry.[21] For the utility companies, the Damoclean sword was suspended by the thin hair of a municipal politician.

The criticism directed by industry spokesmen at local authorities was not markedly different from that voiced by municipal reformers. The tone of reform criticism tended toward earnest concern, but Yule's words, for example, might have been lifted from the pages of the *Municipal World*. The same might be said of an *Electrical News* editorial of 1894:

> Without the slightest reflection upon the ability and integrity of the permanent civic officials, and apart from all questions of political influence or corruption, the lack of continuity of control inherent in our system of municipal government, and the control by men elected for other considerations than their especial fitness for the business in hand, place the civic corporation at such a disadvantage that in competition with it a private concern will earn a profit which is the wages of ability and fitness.

"Politics" would obstruct the best-intentioned efforts of permanent officials.[22]

Like the reformers, the companies were preoccupied by the lack of expertise found among local politicians. E. Carl Breithaupt presented the case against state ownership in a paper delivered at the CEA convention in the autumn of 1894. He offered evidence to demonstrate that private plants were superior in economy and efficiency to municipal ones. A large part of the explanation for this lay in the years of special training and experience required to operate an electric light plant successfully. What could one expect of a plant supervised or even in some cases managed by a committee of council, "a body of men who hold office for only one year, and who, while they are probably well versed in their own private business, usually have no knowledge of gas or electric light matters."[23] Continuity and expertise were required for efficient operation. Breithaupt also criticized municipal accounting practice, for its inaccuracy and for its tendency to charge items from one department, such as lighting, to the expenses of another, such as waterworks.[24] One *Electrical News* editorial in 1901 went so far as to commend the commission system of municipal utility operation because it removed management from politics and placed it under expert guidance.[25]

Each side, of course, approached the problem of inefficiency in municipal government from a different perspective. The reformers saw it as a flaw to be remedied. The companies usually saw it as an irremediable fact of municipal life.

In 1898, the city of Hamilton commissioned a report on the cost of installing and operating a lighting plant. When the report was presented, the *Electrical News* commented on it at some length, in terms which accepted a significant portion of the municipal ownership argument.

> We do not wish to be understood as condemning every case of municipal control off-hand, but we do say that in the majority of cases it has been found to be a mistake. Given the same system under municipal and under private control, and assuming that the management in both cases has the same dividend making efficiency, the former will have an advantage, for whereas the municipal plant is capitalized on money borrowed at 3.5 per cent, the private plant is expected to pay, say, 8 per cent, and the difference of 4.5 per cent is in favor of the first. Again, a new municipal plant properly engineered and managed, has, by reason of its greater efficiency of operation, a decided advantage over an old and inefficient plant which it is to replace. . . .

The fault in the argument lay in the assumption of comparable management. "In any case, the difference in cost of operation will not be so great but that by improper management the positions may be reversed, and municipal management, hampered as it usually is by local politics, is not in the best position to make the most of the above advantages."[26] It obviously was not in the interest of the companies that this problem be solved. Nevertheless, it was over the *possibility* of solving it that their argument mainly differed from that of the reformers.

By 1897 and 1898, however, the utility companies recognized that whatever their views of the practicability of municipal ownership, the movement, even if only a passing fancy, would not pass in the immediate future. A number of demonstrated failures to live up to its claims of greater economy and efficiency would be required before the municipalities recognized their mistake. The immediate necessity, therefore, was to secure protective legislation. "The function of a government," Breithaupt had argued, "is to regulate and control and to encourage enterprise on the part of its citizens by extending a protecting hand over the industries they establish." "Simple justice" required that if a municipal corporation decided to enter a business in which some of its citizens were already engaged, it offered to buy them out at a "fair and equitable price."[27] The *News* urged its readers to attend the CEA convention in June, 1897 and to use the Association as an instrument to prevent the "annihilation" of private lighting companies.[28]

During the convention, held that year in Niagara Falls, the Association adopted John Yule's recommendation that its Committee on Legislation be authorized to seek protective aid from Queen's Park. The committee, under Yule's chairmanship, got down to work immediately. It retained the legal services of Donald Guthrie, Q.C., a prominent Guelph Liberal and president of the Guelph Light and Power Company since its inception in 1870.[29] On his advice, the committee prepared a bill to be introduced to the Ontario Legislature, to amend the Municipal Act. It canvassed the lighting companies of the province for financial assistance and urged them to seek the support of their local Members. It contacted "leading" newspapers and, assisted by Guthrie and Z.A. Lash, who was paid by the Toronto Electric Light Company, it appeared before the Municipal Committee of the Legislature in January, 1898.[30]

The campaign for protection strained the unity of the Canadian Electrical Association. Yule apparently was afraid of certain problems right from the beginning. This, at any rate, would explain some of the remarks in his 1897 Presidential Address, the intent of which seemed to be to anticipate and head off possible ruptures. His explicit appeal to set aside "business jealousies" perhaps reflected a concern for the effects of competition on inter-company relations. A brief justification of the convention as time well spent reflected some unhappiness with the limited support the Association was receiving from the industry, and his denial that the organization existed "for the display of intellectual gymnastics" perhaps hinted at an old conflict over purpose between promotion of commercial interest and the advancement of engineering knowledge.[31] He concluded by assuring the electrical manufacturers that the utilities were most appreciative that, unlike their counterparts in the United States, they were not going after the municipalities as a way of maintaining their declining rate of growth in sales. It was not expected that the suppliers actually *refuse* to sell to municipalities. "But that they take a stand for the best interest of the business and do not lend themselves to helping in confiscating the property of those who had the courage to invest in electric lighting enterprises, is very much to be commended."[32]

If his purpose was indeed to paper over differences, Yule achieved only partial success. The commercial-professional conflict did not become evident until 1900, the year after the Conmee clauses had been passed. At that time a proposal was made that the Association amend its constitution to provide for a company membership as well as an individual one. More fees would result and legislative pressure might be facilitated. The objection was raised, however, that the CEA was moving away from being an organization of electrical engineers and becoming "an association for the benefit of electrical interests." The proposal was dropped and the hope was expressed that commerce and science could co-exist harmoniously.[33]

Inter-company tensions, on the other hand, surfaced almost immediately. The Committee on Legislation incurred a little over $600.00 in costs during its first year's efforts, for legal services, printed matter, postage, office assistance and so on. Committee members had paid their own expenses. Yule pointed out in his report that only fifteen companies had responded to requests for funds, in amounts ranging from $10 to $150. "It is quite evident to your committee," he said, "that if the work in hand is to be carried to a successful issue, a more general, liberal and hearty support will have to be accorded them."[34] The following year saw considerable improvement, which was fortunate since expenses more than tripled. Still, only fifty-one companies made contributions. Almost $2000 was collected, in subscriptions of $5 to $250. Included in this amount were two "unsolicited and substantial" contributions from the Royal Electric Company, a manufacturer in Montreal, and the Packard Electric Company, a manufacturer in St. Catharines. The Committee's annoyance with its tight-fisted colleagues was tempered this time by the satisfaction of success, and it contented itself with proposing that the companies agree to pay a small annual subscription to maintain a lookout for hostile amendments.[35] This attempt to regularize support failed, and the problem remained. The municipal ownership movement showed no signs of abatement and the protective legislation, financially beneficial to those companies under immediate threat of municipal competition, was subject to periodic attacks that required the Committee's attention. By 1901, Yule bitterly denounced those company owners who were prepared to reap where others had sown. "I am so much disgusted with the support we got from the companies that I feel like dropping the thing and letting them take care of themselves. . . ."[36] Two years later, the Committee drew on the Association's general revenues for the first time.[37]

The suspicions harboured by many producers toward the electrical supply men also emerged at an early stage. At the 1898 convention a wide-ranging discussion followed the Committee on Legislation's report. Stephen Noxon of Ingersoll wondered at one point how much responsibility for "this idea of municipal lighting" rested with the manufacturers. "It occurred to me that if the supply men would not encourage municipalities in this thing, it would go a long way towards getting rid of the difficulties." One of the suppliers responded by describing an occasion on which a number of manufacturers had agreed not to tender for a certain municipal plant until a definite decision had been made by the town, but the news had leaked out and the arrangement had fallen through. The delegate from Barrie, whose company was then under municipal siege, judged the manufacturers blameless in his case.[38] Then, following a general expression of loyalty to the "electrical fraternity" by another supplier, Yule revealed a defensiveness that belied his confident assurance of the previous year: "In regard to the supply men we know who are our friends and who are our foes. We know a great deal more than they give us credit for sometimes."

A.A. Wright said he would not soon forget how the rival company in Renfrew had been promoted by a manufacturer, but he warned that any outright alliance between operators and suppliers would be pounced on by their opponents. By telling "half the truth" they would "make the people believe" that an arrangement had been made not to sell plant or supplies to the municipalities. It would be best, he thought, if the supply men would simply recognize that it was in their own interest, since it was the utilities who bought their products, to be "very careful and throw all reasonable cold water" on municipal schemes. To this, one supplier bristled in reply that if operators in certain towns would buy in Canada, rather than across the border, the manufacturers would not have to approach municipal authorities to expand their trade into those towns. The discussion ended inconclusively, and would arise again, with similar result.[39]

Despite these tensions the major goal of the campaign was achieved. At the close of 1897 a bill was prepared that would prohibit a municipality from operating either an electric plant or a gas works until it had completed arrangements to purchase any privately owned plant that already offered the service. Gas works were included in order to secure the support of the gas companies and because a number of companies, such as the one in Guelph, combined the two operations. A board of arbitration would be appointed to resolve any difference that arose as to price. Provision was made as well for the resolution of disputes between a municipality and a company over lighting rates by means of arbitration. Donald Guthrie argued that this would deprive the municipality of an "excuse" for getting into the gas or electric business.[40] The bill proceeded as far as the Municipal Committee, where it came to a temporary halt. Probably with an eye on the approaching election, the chairman, Premier A.S. Hardy, suggested that the bill be allowed to stand over for a year to enable the municipalities to give it further consideration.[41]

The outlook was nevertheless encouraging for the companies. Both Hardy and Conservative Opposition Leader J.P. Whitney had approved of the bill in principle. And while municipal ownership was spreading, this very growth, according to the *Electrical News*, was stimulating interest in the CEA: "Electric light companies have become convinced of the necessity of organization in order to protect their property."[42] The Committee on Legislation presented an optimistic report to the 1898 convention.

The electrical men emphasized in their argument that their intention was not to prevent municipalities from owning their own utilities. It was only to ensure fair treatment to people who had originally risked capital in the lighting business, often with the express sanction or encouragement of municipal authorities. The proposed legislation in fact safeguarded municipalities since it not only provided for arbitration of their lighting rates but also prevented them from entering a potentially unprofitable competition, a point which at this stage might fairly be called whistling in the dark. To meet the objection that some towns might wish only to light their streets and public buildings and not to get involved in the supply of commercial light and power, the companies agreed reluctantly to provide for separation of plant and to allow the arbitrators to evaluate the effect of this on the business of the firm concerned.

The proposed legislation, it was argued, had at least two important precedents. One was the law already in effect in Ontario which protected the property of water supply companies from municipal competition.[43] The gas and electric utilities asked only for the extension of that law to cover themselves. Equally important, there was clear precedent for their request in British legislation. This, "the fact of a law having been passed in Britain, where they have had more experience probably than we have had in this country," was, in Stephen Noxon's view, a strong argument in favour of the bill.[44]

Above all, the point to which the companies returned again and again was the need for protection against municipal competition. Duplication of plant was wasteful and in itself to be avoided. When, in addition, one plant was owned municipally and the other privately, it was "a case of a whole community going into competition with private individuals who are the shareholders of the existing gas and electric light company." The effect was confiscatory.[45]

In 1899, James Conmee, the Liberal Member for West Algoma, agreed to guide the Association's bill through the Assembly. He did so with what one central station man later called "the enthusiasm of a man with a large amount of money invested in electrical interests."[46] Conmee presented the bill, which had been drafted by Donald Guthrie, as a measure of municipal reform. The Toronto *Globe*, under the sub-headline "A Bill to Enable Municipalities to Acquire Electric Light Plants," reported that one provision gave towns the same "right" to buy gas and electric companies as they already had to buy waterworks![47] Arguing against the bill with characteristic vehemence, the Toronto *Telegram* responded that the protection accorded water companies should be removed rather than extended to include gas and electricity.[48] Opposition to the bill focused on three specific areas. Arbitration was seen as a cumbersome process which would involve municipalities in an expense they could ill afford. Also, the larger cities especially might wish to establish plants for public purposes only, such as street lighting, and leave the commercial supply of light and power in the hands of a private company. Finally, concern was expressed that, under the conditions of arbitration, companies would be evaluated as "going concerns," that is, the purchase price would take into account prospective profits lost and the value of the franchise itself.[49] Conmee responded in the Municipal Committee to each of these objections: the arbitration process was streamlined, provision was made, as noted above, for separation of plant, and a clause was added specifying that value be determined on a basis of the plant alone.[50]

He was unable, however, to meet the more general opposition, which was to the constraints imposed by the bill on municipal freedom of action. Try as he might to describe the legislation as in the "line" of municipal reform, he insisted that municipal competition was "practical confiscation" and had to be prevented.[51] In a similar vein, Guthrie summed up the bill's purpose for the Municipal Committee of the Legislature as aiding private enterprise while not discouraging public enterprise.[52] That the bill did discourage public enterprise, however, by infringing on municipal rights, was the fundamental point of its opponents. Its effect, claimed the *Telegram*, was "to tie every municipality in Ontario up neck and heels to the electric light and gas companies."[53] The role of the legislature, in the view of Henry Carscallen, Conservative Member from Hamilton, was to protect the public; the corporations could take care of themselves.[54]

Despite these objections, the bill did not provoke strong resistance from the Conservative Opposition, and on the Liberal side Guthrie's connections were undoubtedly of some assistance, since Hardy appointed him to sit on the sub-committee which drafted the bill in final form.[55] It was incorporated in the Municipal Amendment Act and passed in the closing hours of the session on March 31.

The new law, which was linked ever after with its sponsor's name, outraged advocates of state ownership, for it forced municipalities, if they wished to enter the lighting business, in some cases to expend money on obsolete equipment, in others to buy a plant which had never been profitable since originally constructed, and, where competition already existed between private companies, to buy more than one plant.[56] Moreover, it removed some of their bargaining power, for unless they could secure special legislation granting exemption from its terms, they now had no recourse if, as a last resort in negotiation, a company simply cut off its service. The companies, on the other hand, were elated by their success. Three months after the bill's passage the CEA President was claiming that already the privately owned utilities were responding to their new-found security by extending their business and enlarging and improving their plants.[57] The value of the Association was now established beyond any doubt.[58]

At the same time, no one suggested the industry's troubles were over. The Committee on Legislation predicted, accurately, that attempts would be made to amend the Conmee clauses. It hoped for funds to maintain a watching brief, a hope which, as indicated earlier, soon became an angry plea.[59] It was important, too, that companies not abuse their legal protection; that would only prompt further antagonism. When in 1900 the association thanked John Yule for his leadership in the previous two or three years he included in his own remarks a piece of cautionary advice.

> If I were to give a word of warning to the companies throughout the province, I would say that they had better not be too aggressive in their dealings with corporations [i.e., municipal]. Meet the corporations as soon as any advance is made, and fairly and squarely deal with them as they would deal with any other item of business. It appears to me this movement is going to grow; it will grow for a time, and then I think it will die out after they have had a little experience.[60]

Even the subdued optimism of this forecast was not borne out by events. By 1903, in commenting on the financial problems of resisting the municipalities at Queen's Park, Yule's description of the situation was bleak. "Another thing that has weakened us, gentlemen, is that the companies are gradually going over to the municipalities; they are being gradually bought out; we are being weakened in that way; some of our strongest supporters have gone over, Berlin, Brockville, Owen Sound, Guelph and Kingston, etc."[61] The year previously, moreover, a new factor had required comment:

> The Socialistic candidates in the election campaign last month all advocated the policy of the Provincial Government generating electricity at the Falls [Niagara], transmitting and selling at cost to the different Municipalities. Whether this movement will grow or not the future will determine. We point this out for the purpose of showing the different lines of attack made upon our interests and the necessity of continued wakefulness on the part of the Companies.[62]

The passage of the Conmee clauses, indeed, was only one episode in a longer struggle.

The electrical men can scarcely be criticized for failing in 1899 to divine a future whose outline was only beginning to take definite shape in 1902 and 1903. For the moment, they had achieved formal recognition of what they regarded as an important claim on the resources of the state. In doing so, they had moved with ease from their private sphere to the public one. In Donald Guthrie they had had at their service a man of some substance in Liberal politics, who, though a private citizen, had played an active role in framing the amendment in committee. No serious opposition had been met in the legislature. The strength of their opponents, as yet only poorly organized, lay in individual towns and cities. More importantly, municipal ownership had not yet acquired the following among the provincial bourgeoisie that it would later attract when the value of electricity for motive power in manufacturing became apparent. In obtaining from the provincial government an amendment to the Municipal Act, the companies had successfully brought the restraining hand of a senior government to bear against the reformist tendencies of a junior one, just as, ten years later, private interests attempted unsuccessfully to persuade the Dominion government to disallow legislation pertaining to the province's new Hydro Commission.[63] In both cases, the appeal was made not so much against the reform itself as against the apparent lapse of the junior government in performing its protective duty toward business.

Notes

1. See John C. Weaver, *Shaping the Canadian City: Essays on Urban Politics and Policy, 1890–1920* (Toronto, 1977). For the place of this dispute in the history of Hydro, see Kenneth C. Dewar, "State Ownership in Canada: The Origins of Ontario Hydro" (Ph.D. thesis, University of Toronto, 1975).

2. *Canadian Electrical News*, Mar. 1892, 39; Aug. 1892, 96, 108. (Hereafter cited as *CEN*. Unless otherwise indicated, the footnotes in this paper are to the *News*.)

3. Oct. 1891, 143; Feb. 1892, 24.

4. The Guelph company is described in the Nov. 1892 issue of *CEN*, 155–56.

5. June 1897, 99–101. Yule offered parenthetical justification for his regional focus—"(I mention Ontario because it is the storm centre of the present agitation)"—presumably in deference to the feelings of those six delegates from Quebec and Nova Scotia. Fifty-seven people were listed from Ontario and five from the United States.

6. Mar. 1894, 31.

7. Jan. 1895, 10–11; June 1895, 101–3; Apr. 1897, 69–70.

8. July 1894, 82.

9. May 1895, 79.

10. June 1895, 90. On this point see also the paper by E. Carl Breithaupt, "Municipal Electrical Lighting," Oct. 1894, 140.

11. Oct. 1898, 198. A similar point is made in Mar. 1894, 26; Mar. 1898, 45; Sept. 1901, 171.

12. The *News* published extensive reports of convention discussions.

13. Jan. 1894, 8.

14. Apr. 1894, 37; also Apr. 1895, 61.

15. May 1894, 50.

16. Jan. 1896, 15.

17. June 1898, 111; J.K. Johnson, ed., *The Canadian Directory of Parliament, 1867–1967* (Ottawa, 1968).

18. July 1898, 143.

19. Ibid., 122–23.

20. June 1897, 99.

21. Dec. 1894, 167.

22. June 1894, 67. The editorial's confidence regarding the competitive threat to municipal ownership reflected the early stage of the movement.

23. Oct. 1894, 139–40.

24. In Oct. 1900, 195 the *News* criticized the financial statistics of municipal lighting plants for understating costs. Often they were adjuncts of other departments, which lowered an item such as salaries. For the reformers, this was simply one advantage of municipal ownership.

25. Dec. 1901, 20.

26. Nov. 1898, 217–18.

27. Oct. 1894, 140.

28. Apr. 1897, 68–69 and May 1897, 79–80.

29. Guthrie sat federally for Wellington South, 1876–82 and provincially for the same constituency, 1886–94. (Henry James Morgan, *The Canadian Men and Women of the Time: A Hand-Book of Canadian Biography of Living Characters*, 2nd ed. (Toronto, 1912)).

30. June 1897, 101, 105; Report of the Committee on Legislation, July 1898, 128–30.

31. On this point see also Dec. 1891, 165; Aug. 1892, 4; May 1897, 79–80.

32. June 1897, 100–1.

33. Sept. 1900, 159–61.

34. July 1898, 128–29. Help came from companies in Brockville, St. Thomas, London, Ottawa, Waterloo, Brantford, Carleton Place, Guelph, Lindsay, Galt, Barrie, Owne Sound, Cornwall, Strathroy and Cobourg.

35. Report of the Committee on Legislation, July 1899, 127–28. A list of contributors is appended to the report, as is a list of contributions by number and amount.

36. July 1901, 110.

37. July 1903, 137–38.

38. Reformers and companies alike drew on the Barrie dispute for ammunition (Toronto *Telegram*, 29 Mar. 1899).

39. July 1898, 131–33; July 1899, 145–47. Royal's and Packard's subsequent contributions to the Legislation Committee no doubt were made to demonstrate their goodwill.

40. July 1898, 129.

41. Ibid., 128–30; Toronto *Telegram*, 12 Jan. 1898.

42. June 1898, 100.

43. Section 507 of the Consolidated Municipal Act (1892).

44. July 1898, 131. A *News* editorial of Apr. 1898, 61 referred also to a Pennsylvania legal decision and legislation before the New York legislature.

45. The case was summarized in the *News* editorial of Mar. 1899, 41.

46. The compliment came from H.R. Leyden, manager of the Cataract Power Company in Hamilton (July 1899, 128). C.W. Chadwick of Rat Portage, who had run against Conmee in the 1898 provincial election, wrote J.P. Whitney that he suspected the bill was introduced in the interests of the local Citizens Electric Light and Power Company (Public Archives of Ontario, Mar. 8 Whitney Papers, 1899).

47. Toronto *Globe*, 4 Mar. 1899.

48. Toronto *Telegram*, 4 Mar. 1899.

49. Toronto *Globe*, 4 Mar. 1899.

50. Toronto *Evening Star*, 23 Mar. and 28 Mar. 1899.

51. Toronto *World*, 18 Mar. 1899.

52. Toronto *Telegram*, 23 Mar. 1899.

53. Ibid., 7 Mar. 1899.

54. Toronto *Evening Star*, 28 Mar. 1899.

55. The *Telegram* criticized the appointment (29 Mar.).

56. This was the case made in Municipal Committee by the City Solicitors of Toronto and Hamilton and the Town Solicitor of Prescott (Toronto *Evening Star*, 23 Mar. 1899).

57. July 1899, 126.

58. May 1899, 85.

59. Report of the Committee on Legislation, July 1897, 127–28. See Reports in Sept. 1900 and succeeding July issues of the *News*.

60. Sept. 1900, 169. See also the editorial of May 1900, 76–7.

61. July 1903, 137. Yule continued to manage the Guelph plant under municipal ownership until his retirement in 1907. (Greta M. Shutt, *History of Board of Light and Heat Commissioners of Guelph* (Municipal Electrical Histories; Ontario Hydro, n.d.)).

62. Report of the Committee on Legislation, July 1902, 108.

63. Cf. Christopher Armstrong and H.V. Nelles, "Private Property in Peril: Ontario Businessmen and the Federal System, 1898–1911," in *Enterprise and National Development: Essays in Canadian Business and Economic History*, edited by Glenn Porter and Robert Cuff (Toronto, 1973), 20–38.

THE CRISIS OF THE CRAFTSMAN: HAMILTON'S METAL WORKERS IN THE EARLY TWENTIETH CENTURY†

CRAIG HERON

"When you speak of 'skill,' do you mean 'ability'? What you term 'skill' or 'ability' might in reality be only dexterity." It was spring of 1916, and a panel of royal commissioners was seated in Hamilton's court house to hear evidence on unrest in the city's munitions industry. An unidentified machinist in the audience had just disrupted the proceedings by requesting permission to question his employer, who was on the witness stand. "Let us presume," the worker went on, "that a man comes into your employ who soon becomes proficient in operating a machine, from the fact that he is very bright, and becomes a piece worker, earning even more than your skilled men, such as toolmakers, would you call him a 'skilled' man?" Without waiting for a reply, the angry machinist turned to address the whole court room:

> I have seen men right in this shop who, by reason of doing the one thing day after day and week after week, the operation has become a part and parcel of their lives. . . . I have seen these piece workers move with the automatic precision and perform a certain operation with unerring facility. Yet you term these men 'skilled.' They are not skilled, . . . they have become automatons. Their work requires no brain power, whereas the toolmaker requires both brain and brawn. He must have constructive ability. And you, sir (he continued with a wave of his arms towards the witness), know nothing about that.

The worker sat down to loud applause from "many tool-hardened hands." The voice of Hamilton's beleaguered craftsmen had been heard.[1]

In recent years labour historians have been increasingly fascinated with the lively history of the skilled stratum of the nineteenth-century working class, the artisans. Often colourful, articulate, tough-minded men, these craftsmen were not only leading actors in the emergence of a working class in the early years of

†*Labour/Le Travailleur* 6 (Autumn 1980): 7–48. The author is grateful to Greg Kealey, Ian McKay, Bryan Palmer, and members of the Dalhousie History Department's North American seminar for useful criticism of earlier drafts of this article.

the century; when they gave up their self-employed status and entered the "manufactory" to practise their craft under one employer's roof, they brought with them the accumulated traditions, values, and institutions of the pre-industrial era. A vibrant artisanal culture therefore continued to thrive in late nineteenth-century industry, where the skills of these men were indispensable to many sectors of production.

Artisanal culture had much broader dimensions than life in the workshops where the craftsmen toiled. They were confident of the social worth their skills bestowed upon them and expected to lead dignified, respectable lives. Central to their outlook on the world was a gritty spirit of independence and determination to resist subordination. In the workshops, and in society generally, they demanded for all men and women the maximum of personal liberty and freedom from coercion and patronage, and politically they became the staunchest proponents of egalitarian democracy. From employers they expected no interference with their traditional craft practices, which controlled the form and pace of production. Their "manhood," they insisted, demanded such treatment. The principal institutions of collective self-help which promoted and defended this artisanal life were, of course, their craft unions.

All of these social and ideological phenomena, however, rested on the craftsmen's continuing shop-floor power, and by the end of the nineteenth century that power was being challenged by employers who saw these men and their mode of work as serious obstacles to larger corporate strategies. This essay will concentrate simply on the workplace crisis facing these craftsmen, without further reference to its implications for working-class ideology, politics, and social life. It will deal with the skilled men in one Canadian city, Hamilton, Ontario, and, more specifically, with that city's largest group of craftsmen at the turn of the century, the metal workers. An analysis of the clash between artisanal culture and industrial capitalist rationality will bring into focus the ambivalence of the artisanal legacy for the working class in the early twentieth century. On the one hand, these workingmen battled valiantly against the more dehumanizing, authoritarian tendencies of modernizing industry; they levelled an intelligent and impassioned critique at the process of change in Canadian industrial life. On the other, in fighting back they failed to transcend the sense of proud exclusiveness which their traditionally privileged position in the workplace engendered. For the most part, the response of these workers to the industrial age ushered in with the rise of corporate capitalism in Canada was an attempt to defend their shop-floor prerogatives, not to lead a broader working-class revolt. Craft pride tended to override class solidarity.

This essay will move from a description of the state of the two largest metal-working crafts at the end of the nineteenth century, the moulders and the machinists, to a discussion of the efforts of employers to transform their factories into more efficient, centrally managed workplaces, and finally to an assessment of the response of the craftsmen to these new conditions.

Metal working shops, especially foundries, machine shops, and agricultural implement works, had predominated in Hamilton's industrial structure since the mid-nineteenth century. According to one study, 50 metal-working firms employed 2634 workers, or 38 percent of the city's workforce, in 1891.[2] Particularly important were the stove-manufacturing shops, whose size and production made the city a national leader in the industry. The leading stove foundry, the Gurney-Tilden Company, was described in 1892 as "the largest industry of their kind in the Dominion."[3] It was in this industrial setting that Hamilton's artisans worked the metal into the wide range of products that won for Hamilton the epithet "The Birmingham of Canada."

Of the two most prominent groups of craftsmen in the city, the moulders could lay claim to the deepest roots in pre-industrial society. In fact, moulders liked to trace their ancient traditions to the biblical figure Tubal Cain. From their skilled hands came metal castings as diverse as stoves, machinery casings, and ornamental iron and brass work. Technological change had almost completely bypassed the foundry, which remained down to end of the nineteenth century a classic "manufactory" of highly skilled craftsmen working in one employer's shop. A turn-of-the-century article in *Iron Age* emphasized that the craft "is learned almost entirely by the sense of feeling, a sense that cannot be transferred to paper. It is something that must be acquired by actual practice. A sense of touch plays such an important part in the construction of a mold that without it it is impossible to construct a mold with any reasonable expectation of success."[4] This sense was what craftsmen liked to call the "mystery" of their trade. With a few tools and the knowledge under his cap, the moulder prepared the moulds to receive the molten iron or brass. A mould began with a "pattern," usually wooden, in the shape of the finished casting, which was imbedded in sand. Preparing and "ramming" the sand (that is, pounding it firmly with iron-shod poles) required great care and precision so that when the pattern was drawn out a perfect mould remained to hold the molten metal. If a cast product was to have a hollow space, the moulder inserted a "core," a lump of specially prepared sand that had been carefully shaped and baked hard at the coremaker's bench (originally moulders made their own cores, but gradually a division of labour emerged). Once cool, the casting was shaken out of the sand and cleaned, to be ready for any finishing processes. The size of the objects to be cast ranged so widely that the moulder might work on a bench or prepare his moulds in great stretches of sand on the foundry floor.[5] "The jobs he undertook," recalled one observer of Canadian foundries, "were varied in the extreme, a single job sometimes entailing days of careful labor, and the work being given a finish in which the maker took pride."[6]

That pride also fed on the physical demands of the work, which was notoriously heavy, dirty, and unhealthy. One Hamilton moulder described the city's foundries as "the darkest and rottenest places in Hamilton, and so stuffy that you can hardly breathe." He claimed the shop he was working in was so dark "that he had had to use a torch to see what he was doing." Ontario's factory inspectors repeatedly criticized foundry working conditions for the thick, smoky air, the extremes of heat and cold, and the heavy, dangerous tasks required. An American study also found abnormally high rates of death by respiratory diseases among foundry workers.[7]

Passing from the foundry to the machine shop in, say, the Sawyer-Massey agricultural implement works was to cross the great divide of the Industrial Revolution, from the more primitive methods of handicraft to the clatter of complex machinery. Machinists were a much newer group of craftsmen, whose role in industry was little more than a century old by 1900; yet, despite their position at the centre of the machine age, they too had developed a workplace culture in the artisanal mode. When the peripatetic Royal Commission on the Relations of Capital and Labour opened its hearings in Hamilton early in 1888, an elderly machinist named William Collins appeared. A retired artisan with British training, Collins described himself as "a general workman": "I learned the whole art or mystery of mechanics — that is, so far as human skill, I suppose, could accomplish it, either wood, iron, brass, blacksmithing, or anything; I am one of the old school."[8] He was, in fact, a relic of that period in the late eighteenth and early nineteenth centuries when a millwright, as he was then known, was a highly valued mechanic whose manual skills and ingenuity in the construction of machinery made possible the mechanical innovations of the Industrial Revolution in Britain. By mid-century, however, the typical British machine-builder was less in the Collins mould and more often a skilled operator of metalworking machinery. The introduction of steam-powered devices, especially lathes and planers, had brought the old craft into a new, technically more sophisticated phase,[9] where an engineer or machinist would use a mechanized cutting tool to shape metal objects — anything from machinery parts to gun barrels — usually in manufacturing firms or railway shops. The tools of the trade might be any number of simple lathes, drills, planers, shapers, or slotters, as well as various devices for careful measurement of the cut.

Although William Collins might regret that mechanization had been "detrimental to the interest of the employé, inasmuch as the introduction of machinery reduced the labour required."[10] individual manual skill did not disappear since most machine shop work still required the careful, trained hands of the craftsmen. Machine tools simply facilitated precision.[11] Another Hamilton machinist, Joseph James Whiteley, emphasized before the same royal commission that running his planer demanded expertise: "There is no man who can run a machine properly after three years apprenticeship. I served my time seven years at Whitworth's, of Manchester, the finest shop in the world, and I found I had something else to learn."[12] Craft pride, in fact, was nurtured by the confidence that "the industrial world depended for its success largely on the skill and technical knowledge of the machinist."[13]

The indispensable skills of these craftsmen in the metal trades gave them a functional autonomy on the shop floor that curbed employer interference with their established work routines. But their craft unions were the effective bastions protecting their workplace traditions. Both the moulders and the machinists constructed elaborate trade-union constitutions that stipulated all rules and procedures covering recruitment into the craft through apprenticeship, wage or piece rates, hours of work, and daily work load. The moulders' "set," for example, was a regulation of output, established by the local union, as an attempt to prevent reductions in piece rates and to maintain a humane pace of work. "Under unrestricted output," one study noted, "they had seen the vigorous molder, in the full enjoyment of health and strength, set a pace on certain work, which other molders of less bodily strength or of advanced years were expected to follow. When unable to do so they were subject to constant nagging by the foreman, and the output of the strongest and most active was continually held up to them as an example."[14] Similarly the machinists set collective restraints on the labour process. A 1903 article in the *Canadian Engineer* gives a glimpse of the ways in which these men modulated the rhythms of machine shop work:

> . . . if a certain piece of work was to be done, a drawing showing the essential dimensions accompanied the stock which went to the machinist, who followed his own way in (a) setting the work; (b) selecting the cutting tool and grinding it as he knew best; (c) choosing the running speed; (d) determining the cut; (e) and adjusting the feed. The completion of the work was, (1) limited by his intelligence; (2) restricted by his experience; (3) governed by his inclination; (4) and was subject to the limiting conditions laid down by that despot, the walking delegate. Result: Four hours taken to do what could be accomplished in less than one, and with a greater degree of accuracy.[15]

The much maligned "walking delegates" who enforced the customary practices of the craft were in the service of one of the craft unions which were taking a new lease on life with the return of prosperity in the late 1890s. In the arms of the more centralized unions affiliated with the American Federation of Labor, with its growing army of full-time organizers, craft unionists were setting about to consolidate their workplace prerogatives into powerful continental organizations.[16] Hamilton's moulders had first organized to defend their workplace customs in 1860 and had affiliated with the Iron Molders' Union the following year.[17] By the turn of the century IMU Local 26 was recognized as one of the strongest labour organizations in the city. Hamilton moulders enjoyed a rich associational life of parades, "smokers," and outings and were one of only two groups of craftsmen in the city with their own hall. The machinists in Hamilton had two unions: the British-based Amalgamated Society of Engineers, dating back to 1851, and the International Association of Machinists, successor to a number of earlier North American unionizing experiments, which organized Hamilton Lodge 414 in 1900.[18] These artisans of the machine shop, however, had a much spottier record of organizational success; the IAM Lodge, in fact, had to be re-organized in 1902.[19] As we shall see, their craft was more vulnerable to further subdivision, mechanization, and invasion by less skilled non-unionists.

These then were the two main groups of artisans comprising Hamilton's skilled metal workers. In the last half of the nineteenth century, the moulders and machinists were quite often employees of different firms, but by the turn of the century they more frequently worked in separate departments of larger corporations, where artisanal customs soon came into sharp conflict with the new imperatives of modern industry.

The 1890s marked a turning point in the work world of moulders and machinists. Over the next 30 years a transformation within metal-working factories swept away the artisanal culture of these workers which had flourished in the preceding decades. Technological and managerial innovations undermined and ultimately destroyed a work environment in which skilled craftsmen with indispensable expertise had presided over the pace and organization of the labour process.

The driving force behind this process of change sprang from the new shape of economic life in Canada. By the 1890s Hamilton's industrial life was being integrated into national and international markets which involved stiffer competition for the city's firms and the rise of increasingly large corporate enterprises. Hamilton not only participated in the Canadian merger movement in the pre-war decade, with the creation of such firms as the Steel Company of Canada and the Canadian Iron Corporation; it also opened its floodgates to branch plants of American giants like International Harvester and Canadian Westinghouse. These developments certainly increased both the scale of the average workplace in the city and the economic clout of employers and, perhaps more important, generated a sharpened concern about protecting profits against more powerful competition. Some of the city's oldest metal shops, especially the stove foundries, were particularly hard pressed in this new environment.

With their eyes fixed on profit margins, corporate managers in Hamilton attacked labour costs on two fronts. The first, aggressive anti-unionism, was ultimately the prerequisite for the second, the restructuring of the work process. The shop-floor power of craftsmen that was consolidated in their unions was a constant threat to corporate planning of production. Before 1900 individual employers, and occasionally groups of them, challenged unions in the city with varying degrees of success, but after the turn of the century anti-unionism became a cornerstone of labour relations for the largest Hamilton firms. The city's two largest employers of skilled metalworkers, in particular, had well-established reputations as union-busters before their arrival in Hamilton. International Harvester's predecessor companies had such an anti-labour record, dating from the 1880s, that the Hamilton labour movement mounted a vigorous and utlimately successful campaign to prevent the city fathers from granting the Deering company a bonus to locate in Hamilton.[20] Similarly in 1903 George Westinghouse, president of both the Canadian and American companies, engaged in a much publicized exchange with the American Federation of Labour President Samuel Gompers over the question of unionizing his staff; he made it quite clear that this was one corporation which would tolerate no workers' organizations in its plants.[21] The Westinghouse management in Hamilton never departed from that position.

The strikes in Hamilton's metalworking plants over the three decades from the 1890s to the 1920s fell into a pattern of union resurgence and employers' counterattack, in three periods of peak prosperity: 1899 to 1906, 1911 to 1913, and 1916 to 1919; and in most cases employers sought to use a strike as an occasion to drive out the union. Hamilton industrialists also participated in schemes to weaken the negotiating power of unions, like legislative restraints and promotion of immigration;[22] but probably more energy was directed to weakening the appeal of trade unionism through company-sponsored welfare programmes, which not only weaned workers away from reliance on the benefit schemes of the unions but also promoted loyalty to the corporation. Profit-sharing, benefit and pension schemes, and recreation programmes were introduced at the Steel Company of Canada, International Harvester, Canadian Westinghouse, Sawyer-Massey, and other large firms in the city before World War I and with new enthusiasm immediately after the war. In 1912 International Harvester and Canadian

Westinghouse even undertook to pre-empt the social functions of trade unions and to promote craft pride within the confines of the company by inaugurating banquets for their most skilled machinists, the toolmakers. Seven years later International Harvester went so far as to launch an industrial council as an alternative form of "industrial democracy" to trade unionism. These corporations evidently saw themselves locked in a battle for the allegiance of their workers.[23]

Only the stove foundries provided a significant exception to this pattern of anti-unionism in Hamilton's metalworking industries. By the 1890s two distinct branches within the foundry industry had emerged, each with its own distinct set of economic imperatives and pattern of labour relations. Moulders were employed either by one of several stove foundries or by one of the machinery or jobbing foundries and as a result did not share a single unifying experience.[24] By the early twentieth century stove manufacturers in southern Ontario and Maritime cities were struggling to get a toe-hold in the western Canadian market, where thousands of new farm homes would require stoves. The competition increased noticeably after 1900 when American manufacturers began to penetrate the same territory.[25]

The similarity of the production process in each shop encouraged the stove founders to standardize their employment policies through a common front in their relations with their workers. After a long history of collective aggression against any combination of workers that threatened the manufacturers' right to control production,[26] the Hamilton foundrymen began at the turn of the century to accept joint negotiations with the International Molders' Union to produce common labour practices and wage rates in all shops. Between 1902 and 1908 the union introduced a system of centralized bargaining with a large number of the provinces foundrymen, who in the latter year formally organized themselves into the Dominion Iron Founders' Defense Association, with Hamilton's John Tilden as its first president.[27] The economic slump of 1907–09, however, encouraged the founders to turn back to the older, antagonistic strategy, in order to force down wages in the face of even stiffer American competition. The *Industrial Banner*, Ontario's province-wide labour newspaper, later denounced this turn as "a manifest attempt to use the business depression as a lever to smash the labor organizations and put them out of business."[28]

In February 1909 the Hamilton founders wiped out ten years of wage increases for the moulders by instituting a 20 percent wage cut and declaring an "open" shop. By 1 March 170 moulders from the city's four stove shops had walked out. The strike dragged on for over two years, with the union moulders refusing to return at the new wage rates. The Hamilton *Herald* described it as "one of the most stubborn fights that was ever put up by a union in this city, as rather than give in, union moulders left homes and families and went to work in other places. Some even removed their families from the city."[29]

The continuing need for skilled moulders, however, weakened such an antagonistic approach to the stove founders' labour problems. With a general scarcity of labour and renewed consumer spending during World War I, the union seems to have reasserted itself in the stove shops. A new working arrangement with the stove foundrymen's association appears to have evolved by 1919, and, despite some conflict over a wage reduction in the early 1920s, negotiations on the old province-wide basis continued. This branch of moulding, however, was obsolescent, as sheet metal increasingly replaced cast iron in household stoves. Slowly this pocket of strength for the unionized craftsman in the foundry trade dwindled into insignificance.[30]

The stove foundrymen's fluctuating labour policies, which made room for accommodation with the union, conformed to a pattern evident among a variety of domestic consumer-goods industries at the turn of the century. In the Hamilton boot and shoe and tobacco plants, for example, local industrialists had similar collective bargaining arrangements with their employee's unions. Generally, however, this approach to management was declining, and, outside of the stove shops, employers in the city's metalworking factories made eradication of craft unionism among their workers the bulwark of their management strategies.

Employers were not simply attempting to eliminate unions in order to push their workers harder; they were equally concerned about having the flexibility to re-organize the work process in order to rid themselves of their reliance on testy, independent-minded craftsmen whose union regulations kept the supply of new men and the pace of work strictly under control. After 1900 Hamilton employers' strategies fit into an emerging consensus about factory management in Canada. During the decade before World War I Canadian companies succumbed to the North American mania for more "system" in industrial organization.[31] At first the emphasis was on precise cost accounting as a means of determining the actual production cost of an item and of isolating areas in the entire manufacturing operation where costs needed to be reduced. "Broadly speaking," wrote accountant H.L.C. Hall in *Industrial Canada*, organ of the Canadian Manufacturers' Association, "factory economy means the production of your output for less money. . . ." He suggested a two-fold purpose for a costing system: "First to induce economy by elimination of waste and second to induce economy by intensifying production." The manager could expect the "system" to tell him "the efficiency of every man and every machine per labour hour and machine hour," as well as informing him of "all delays and the reasons for the failure to arrive at the maximum." Often tied to these new cost-accounting plans were special wage-incentive schemes which encouraged each worker to attempt to increase his output in return for a bonus or premium in addition to his regular wages.[32]

The fascination with "systematic" management began to reach full flower in Canada after 1911, when American writers, notably Frederick W. Taylor and his school of "scientific management," were catching great public attention. These new management specialists advocated complex procedures for establishing "scientific" norms for the speed of work based on stop-watch measurement, along with incentive wage payment systems that both rewarded the fast worker and punished the laggard. A key tenet of the Taylor system was the centralization of all control over the production process in the hands of the managers through planning, routing, scheduling, and standardization.[33] The Canadian business press generally applauded these new plans. *Canadian Machinery*, metal-trades journal of the Maclean publishing empire, declared that "The principles are general in their application and where applied, valuable results will be obtained," and

Industrial Canada concluded in 1914: "The experience of manufacturers seems to be that scientific management decreases a staff while it increases its efficiency. . . . Reports from firms on this continent show that scientific management has become practical."[34] Clearly new ideas were in the air about how to run a factory.

Managers in Hamilton's metalworking industries used three related tactics to pursue their goals of tightening their grip on the labour process, speeding up production, and reducing labour costs. Wherever possible the chief elements in a re-organization of production in the city's foundries and machine shops became narrowing the work of the skilled, upgrading labourers to become "handymen" who specialized in only one fragment of the process, and introducing new machinery. "If skilled labor is necessary," argued one foundry expert, "means must be used to apply the skill only to those operations in which it is needed, subdivision of labor and the use of mechanical appliances and power being applied wherever this can be profitably done."[35] As the subdivision of labour and co-ordination of production progressed, primitive notions of assembly-line production began to appear. A Hamilton *Herald* reporter spotted this trend on a tour through the new Westinghouse plant in 1905:

> The thing that strikes the notice of the observer before all else is the manner in which everything is planned out so that everything that is being made makes a direct progression through the works. Economy is seen everywhere. The raw materials are delivered to the spot where they will be used . . . . And the machines are situated so that each piece passes right down the line to where the parts are assembled and put together ready for testing and shipping. Nothing is handled twice. . . . Everything works like clock-work, and all are truly "parts of one stupendous whole."[36]

Innovation in Canadian factories tended to be slower than in the United States, since with a much smaller market the work tended to be less specialized. In 1905 *Canadian Machinery* lamented that "the demand for a large class of machinery is still quite limited or orders for such machinery are often a year or more apart. . . ."[37] But Hamilton's large American-owned operations with specialty lines were able to introduce the latest technology and management and were frequently cited as models of technical and organizational sophistication.[38] Even smaller, Canadian-owned firms in Hamilton, like the London Machine Tool Company and the Ford-Smith Machine Company, were cited by business journals as innovative leaders in their field.[39]

Since the restructuring of the labour process moved at different paces in the foundries and the machine shops, we will consider each in turn. Foundrymen were well aware that skilled moulders could not be completely eliminated from the foundry. The machinery and jobbing shops in particular still needed the well-rounded craftsman who could prepare enormous castings for hydro-electric generators or any number of other diverse products. Wherever possible, especially in the stove foundries, the moulders' tasks were specialized. By the 1890s nine-tenths of North America's stove-plate moulders were reputedly engaged on piece-work, a system where "few molders make the castings for an entire stove and range," and "where it becomes necessary to make it quickly if you desire to make fair wages and keep your end up."[40] A moulder's work could also be rigidly confined to the specific tasks requiring his expertise, while other repetitive or purely physical labour could be divided up amongst less skilled, lower-paid workers. Foundry work had always involved sundry unskilled labourers and moulders' helpers, at one time known as "bucks" or "berkshires," as well as a small stock of men whose experience was in small, non-union shops and who never served a proper union apprenticeship. All of these men would develop some familiarity with foundry practice without ever attaining full craftsmanship. One writer in the trade press explained how to draw on this pool of unskilled men to create handymen:

> There are in nearly every foundry, certain labourers who, either through lack of opportunity or neglect have not in their boyhood days acquired a trade. They have now passed their early youth and look grimly into a sordid future at laborer's wages. This class of men respond readily to the foundryman who is endeavoring to develop molders by rapid stages.[41]

International Harvester's Hamilton operation made full use of such unskilled help, especially new European immigrants, by organizing them into "gangs," each of which would perform one step in the moulding process. "The usual system," explained the *Canadian Foundryman*, "is to divide the help in the foundry into ramming, finishing and coring gangs." The gangs could also be organized side by side to stimulate increased production through competition. "Each man made part of a machine," reported the local union president, James W. Ripley, in 1910, "and they had to work like Trojans to keep up. No ordinary mechanic could work that way, because he could not stand the pace . . . . The foreigners were rugged men, but even they did not last long." The company also hired women to work as coremakers. A reporter who visited their workroom in 1907 was struck by the accelerated pace of production: "the girls were working apparently for dear life."[42] Both immigrants and female labourers came to their jobs without any well-established customs of what constituted a "fair day's work" in the foundry, and both groups tended to leave the workforce quickly.

This kind of subdivision of the moulders' tasks, however, was really only made possible by increased mechanization of foundry work. In particular, it required the introduction of the moulding machine. A 1908 article in *Canadian Machinery* described the advantages of this new device over the foibles of human producers:

> The molding machine is purely and simply a mechanical molder and differing from its human competitor can work the whole twenty-four hours without stopping, knows no distinctions between Sundays, holidays and any ordinary day, requires as its only lubricant a little oil, being in fact abstinent in all other matters, has no near relatives dying at awkward moments, has no athletic propensities, belongs to no labor organizations, knows nothing about limitation of output, never thinks of wasting its owner's time in conversation with its fellow machines. Wars, rumors of war and baseball scores, have no interest for it and its only ambition in life is to do the best possible work in the greatest possible quantity.[43]

Actually, there was no one single machine, but rather a range of machinery with different applications. The earliest were hand-operated devices: the "squeezer," which pressed or "rammed" the sand into the mould by the use of a lever, and the stripping plate, which was used to draw the pattern out of the mould. Experiments began in the late 1880s to apply power to these processes and to combine the ramming and pattern-drawing; a further refinement was known as "jolt ramming" whereby the mould was dropped sharply by pneumatic pressure to pack the sand. Each year the American Foundrymen's Association convention featured more and more complex equipment on display. As well as specific devices for preparing the mould, North American foundrymen were soon fitting up their shops with a host of new labour-saving equipment: mechanical sand-mixers, conveyors to move the sand around the shop, tumbling barrels and pneumatic hammers and chippers for cleaning the castings, pneumatic ramming devices, and electric travelling cranes which could carry the iron to the mould or move moulds or castings easily.[44] The impact of all these additional devices was to lighten some of the burdensome work in the foundry and to reduce the time necessary for many of the ancillary tasks to the main arena of moulding.

Mechanization might have meant lighter work, but it also resulted in more castings per day. An Ontario factory inspector found that the men who operated the new machines had "to go lively, as the machines are generally speeded up to the limit." Margaret Loomis Stecker, a contemporary American student of moulding machinery whose sympathies lay with mechanization, noted that

> molding machines, instead of being labor-saving devices in the sense that they made easier the work of the molder, often necessitated a material increase in effort by the man who operated them. Though time was actually saved in making any mold, the fact that more molds were produced meant that there was more sand to shovel, more molds to lift, more molds to pour, more castings to shake out.

She concluded that "the molding-machine operator became himself a mere machine, with none of the variety to his work which characterized the skilled handworker."[45]

Moulding machines were introduced into Canada relatively slowly. Canadian trade journals were passionate promoters of the new equipment and criticized Canadian foundrymen for their backwardness. The editor of the *Canadian Engineer* argued in 1906 that

> the moulding machine is destined to revolutionize the foundry business, for when . . . a simple power machine, operated by one laborer, another shovelling sand, and one to carry out the flask, can turn out one mould per minute; or on a union rule of seven hours moulding, pouring 140 moulds per man; being twice as much as a union moulder can do by hand, then no enlightened owner of a foundry will submit to the primitive hand moulding methods of making duplicate castings, which we find in so many foundries in Canada today.[46]

In April 1908 *Canadian Machinery* was able to announce that "During the last one or two years Canadian foundrymen have been realizing the value of molding machines and several installations have been made, which are doing good work"; and in June it published a detailed analysis of moulding machine practice in an unidentified Canadian machinery foundry, where the installation of the machines and the use of handymen had cut production costs considerably. The same month, at the American Foundrymen's Association's first convention in Toronto, the new machinery was exhibited and discussed extensively. Canadian membership in the association immediately leaped from 17 to 57.[47]

Hamilton's foundries were not slow to adapt. The two biggest, International Harvester and Canadian Westinghouse, were, in fact, pioneers in the field. Henry Pridmore, a leading manufacturer of moulding machines, had begun his experiments in 1886 in the McCormick Harvester works in Chicago where the company introduced the new machinery in a successful attempt to drive out the local moulders' union. A company executive later boasted: "Their great foundries and their novel molding machinery were the admiration of the iron world." Not surprisingly then, a visitor to the new Hamilton Harvester plant's foundry in 1904 discovered moulding machinery in each moulder's stall.[48] The Canadian Westinghouse plant was similarly in the vanguard of managerial innovation. The superintendent of its foundry was David Reid, "one of the most prominent foundrymen of America." His extensive American experience had included managing a foundry where he had been responsible for some major restructuring of the work process: "By introducing modern methods here, such as molding machines, and dividing labor, whereby the molder practised the art of molding and nothing else, the melt was increased from 12 or 15 tons daily to between 50 and 60 tons."[49] Reid's influence, however, was not restricted to the Westinghouse foundry; in 1905 he became the president of the Associated Foundry Foremen of America, a scion of the American Foundrymen's Association, and launched a Hamilton branch. The purpose of the organization was "education" for better foremanship, and its meetings were devoted to discussions of more efficient foundry practice.[50]

Mechanization in other machinery foundries in Hamilton seems to have proceeded quickly. Gartshore-Thompson and the Berlin Machine works had them as early as 1908, Bowes-Jamieson by 1911, and Brown-Boggs, Dominion Steel Castings, and the Hamilton Malleable Iron Company by 1913.[51] The stove foundries showed some interest in the new machinery as well. Although this was not an arena where the moulding machine had been expected to make much impact,[52] the committee of the American Stove Founders' Defense Association which investigated the new techology in 1908 concluded that "All stove patterns can be molded with some form of machine or device now in use."[53] These discussions coincided with the assault of the Dominion Iron Founders' Defense Association on the moulders' union in Ontario and the foundrymen's desire to root out all obstacles to increased production at lower costs. As the Hamilton dispute reached the boiling point, the *Spectator* reported that stove manufacturers wanted to determine the value of the moulding machines and that "if they cannot secure the co-operation of the molders in trying them out, they will have to use other labor." Within a few weeks the strike-bound Gurney-Tilden Company introduced its first mechanical devices — a compressed air moulding machine and several squeezers — along with Italian labourers, and by May precipitated a strike of their scab moulders, who promptly joined the union.[54]

Mechanization did not sweep relentlessly over the whole industry; in 1916, for example, the NFA's committee on foundry methods found that not more than 25 percent of its North American membership had taken advantage of the available mechanical appliances. But it was in the larger foundries, such as those that dominated the industrial landscape in Hamilton, that innovation was most advanced. By the 1920s most of the city's foundries had introduced a full range of mechanical devices. The machinery at the Hamilton Stove and Heater Company so impressed a foundry trade journalist in 1920 that he burbled, "Verily, the molding machine only requires to be taught to talk, when it will be perfect." By 1928 The *Canadian Foundryman* could gloat over the sweeping changes since the pre-war years:

> Twenty years ago an unskilled man in the foundry would not have been permitted to handle even a slick, being only allowed to assist in the ramming of big jobs perhaps, lifting or similar work. Now unskilled labor can step into an up-to-date foundry and within a few days perform a task equal to that of the skilled molder, due to present day equipment.[55]

There was, nonetheless, a continuing need for the manual skill of expert moulders. A 1925 study of management practices in 54 Canadian foundries, undertaken by the Policyholders' Service Bureau of the Metropolitan Life Insurance Company, noted that "A foundry's proportional expenditure for labor in respect of total output is much higher than the average manufacturing plant." And an article on the Otis-Fensom Elevator Company's Hamilton plant pointed out that "with in most cases only a few pieces being required at one time from one pattern, good mechanics and the old system of hand moulding seems [sic] preferable." As the depression began to lift in the mid-1920s foundrymen undertook extensive discussions about where to find the skilled help they required now that the apprenticeship system was in disarray. It seems, however, that skilled moulders were needed in relatively small numbers. Between 1900 and 1913 in the United States, the percentage of skilled moulders in NFA foundries declined from 75.7 to 51.8, a trend which no doubt continued in the next decade. Canadian foundry experience probably paralleled this pattern. In 1911 census-takers found 1015 moulders in Hamilton, but only 645 in 1921 and 695 in 1931.[56]

By the 1920s, therefore, the role of the artisan in the foundry had been reduced to only those few tasks which could not be turned over to machines and handymen. Skilled workers had certainly not been banished from the industry, and their union survived down to the end of World War I on the basis of their continuing importance in the production process, however much that may have been eroded and confined. But they no longer wielded their artisanal control mechanisms for setting the pace of production as they had 30 years before. As early as 1909, Josiah Beare, a young union moulder in Hamilton, told a workmate: "Jim, I have worked too hard in my time; the pace is set too fast for the average man to keep up, and I am a nervous wreck"; he died six weeks later of "heart trouble." Half a century later Joe Davidson, future leader of Canada's postal workers, arrived in Hamilton as an experienced Scottish moulder and discovered "the more intense style of working" at Canada Iron Foundries; in nearby Dundas, he found, "The motto was 'produce or else' and every day was a mad race, the men working like beasts."[57]

The technology and management of machine shops went through a similar, perhaps even more dramatic evolution. In the second half of the nineteenth century the arms and sewing machine industries had been in the forefront of technological experimentation in British and North American machine shop work. One of the most important developments had been the turret lathe, a machine mounted with a cluster of tools which could be applied to a piece of work in a sequence of operations without adjusting the material in the lathe (though until these processes were automated, the workman's manual skill was still required). The other great innovation was the milling machine, a device with a set of rotating cutting tools for planing, curving, or otherwise shaping the metal, which required less individual skill in the hands of the operator. From the 1890s onward, in response to the mass production demands of, first, bicycle manufacturers and, later, automobile makers, the tendency in mechanical innovation was for increasingly sophisticated, specialized tools with more automation in their operation. The introduction of electric motors also greatly increased flexibility in machine shop work, and, as in the foundry, mechanization came to include new cranes and overhead tracks to lighten and speed up handling. "In general," a historian of the industry has suggested, "the trend of machine tool development was toward reducing the amount of physical effort and skill required to control tools while at the same time making it possible to rapidly produce work of high quality."[58]

In the closing years of the last century the industry was presented with an opportunity for yet another technological leap which would revolutionize machine shop practice. Throughout its history the machine tool industry had advanced by the experimentation of isolated individuals, often highly skilled artisans, scattered throughout the industry. In the last quarter of the nineteenth century, however, industrial innovation in the United States was increasingly taking place through a marriage with science, consummated in corporate research laboratories. One of these vanguards of the so-called "Second" Industrial Revolution was Pennsylvania's Midvale Steel Works, where in 1880 a young mechanical engineer, Frederick W. Taylor, began a 26-year scientific study to develop a new stronger form of steel for machine cutting tools. After moving to Bethlehem Steel, Taylor had the assistance of a metallurgist, Maunsel White, and in 1900 they unveiled the first fruits of their discoveries at the Paris Exhibition. Six years later Taylor took the annual meeting of the American Society of Mechanical Engineers by storm with his paper, "On the Art of Cutting Metals" (reprinted the next month in *Canadian Machinery*).[59] The use of this so-called "high-speed steel" allowed cutting speeds to be increased enormously, resulting in higher rates of production ranging from 50 to 400 per cent.[60] As a Canadian business journalist explained in 1910, "All the radical changes in machine tool practice in the past few years have been the result of the introduction of high speed steel."[61]

The widespread adoption of the new cutting steel followed from the insistent demand for greater output per machine. It is not surprising, therefore, that at the same time the machine shop should have been a leading industrial laboratory for new managerial experiments to rationalize and intensify the work process. It was no accident that Taylor should have been responsible for both the new technology of high-speed steel and the new school of scientific management; both aimed at increasing the output of labour at a lower cost per product. "The modern machine tool, coupled with good management, is a great factor in present-day competition," said a Canadian journal in 1910, "and the shop that is up-to-date is the one that produces at a minimum cost."[62]

The use of unskilled labour was possible on machine tools which incorporated automatic features, but these mechanisms were installed only gradually. In 1905, for example, the Hamilton *Herald* found that in Canadian Westinghouse's modern machine shop automatics were not generally used.[63] A more common practice for reducing labour costs became subdivision of labour, using handymen as specialists on one simple machine that performed part of the work on a product. A 1913 survey of the industry in Canada indicated how far the process had advanced:

> Modern methods of manufacturing are responsible for limiting the employment of men to specific operations only, and pursuit of the plan is making it hard to secure all-round machinists. Young men come into the factory and soon acquire the necessary skill to become proficient drill press operators or milling machine operators. They are able to earn fairly good wages in a shorter space of time than if they served the necessary term of apprenticeship to become competent all-round machinists.

The trend was clear in Hamilton from the turn of the century. Information on 1901 wage rates in the city's machine shops reveals a range of specialized work for toolmakers, lathe hands, planer and shaper hands, vise hands and fitters, and drill hands, each with a different scale of wages. By 1908 specialization was so widespread that, surveying the sad state of unionism among the city's machinists, the union's Canadian vice-president concluded that the local lodge would "have to turn its attention soon to organizing the specialists' class before undertaking any important move in the machine trade."[64]

World War I accelerated this trend. Almost every metalworking plant in the city re-opened and converted all or part of its production to filling large munitions contracts with Allied governments, mostly for shells. Many thus came to be engaged for the first time in the mass production of identical products. In the face of a severe labour shortage, these firms began to subdivide labour more extensively, using workers with no machining experience to operate simple "single-purpose" equipment which made only one of the series of cuts required on the shell. By the end of the war nine-tenths of the country's shell plants were using this specialized machinery.[65] These simplified procedures facilitated the introduction of unskilled women workers into the shell shops, which the Imperial Munitions Board's Labour Department began to encourage toward the end of 1916. A special employment bureau for women was opened in Hamilton in January 1917 in order to funnel more labour into the factories.[66] The advantage of such a new workforce over the artisanal sensibilities of the machinist was soon evident; it was found that "men of this description could be relied upon to do more than mechanics who had been accustomed to perform their work in the variety form; the repetition style of single operation to these latter being too montonous for effective accomplishment."[67] While it was argued that the majority of shell workers were "illiterate help whose visible signs of intelligence are limited to the turning of a hand wheel in one direction till it stops, and then in the opposite direction," there was some sentiment that "the training that the army of shell workers are receiving at present time will fit large numbers for positions in the ranks of the 'skilled' mechanics, when the country settles down to peaceful pursuits," at least in those branches of the industry where high volume would be required.[68]

Automation and subdivision of labour, of course, did not sweep aside all skill requirements. Much work, especially of the less specialized kind, continued to be done on machinery that required the touch of the craftsman. And, as one writer stressed, "the use of automatically controlled machines increases the need of skilful supervision and of skilled men for their construction and repair." This latter group included the emerging elite of the machinists' trade, the toolmakers, who prepared the jigs and dies for use on machines handled by the less skilled. During the war a *Canadian Machinery* editorial claimed, with well-mixed metaphor, that "the keystone of the whole fabric has been the craft, skill, perseverance and painstaking effort of that tiny group of workers known as toolmakers."[69]

If some skill was still required, managers wanted to apply it as intensively as possible. One of the earliest tactics was doubling the workload by requiring a machinist to run two machines at once, a course which International Harvester followed in 1904. But the issue of operating two machines seems to have declined in importance for the machine-shop managers once high-speed steel had made its impact.[70]

Moreover, across North America the two-machine issue was being eclipsed by the ever more common wage-payment schemes based on piecework, which machine-shop owners and managers were installing from the 1890s onward.[71] Since the speed of work in the shop still depended largely on the speed of the individual machine operator, industrialists turned to payment by the piece as an incentive for each worker to produce more each day in the hopes of higher wages and as a goad to competitiveness between shopmates.

It is difficult to document specifically how extensively Hamilton industrialists adopted these new managerial practices, but in the years before World War I the city's machinists were certainly denouncing such plans. In February 1913 workers in the meter assembly department at Canadian Westinghouse objected to "a change in the method of giving out work and the consequent adjustment in the piece work prices," and simultaneously workers in the punch department denounced time-clocks installed to keep closer track of their work. The spontaneous strikes which resulted in both cases quickly petered out.[72] In his first report as the machinists' business agent in 1913 Richard Riley noted: "Mr. Taylor's system of scientific shop management is in use in some shops here. In one case, two cuts in piecework have taken place recently. A great many of the men don't know what they are getting until they get their pay envelope."[73] While it seems unlikely that pure and simple Taylorism was introduced in the city, at least some parts of the new management ideas were finding their way into the plants.

Opportunities quickly opened up during the war, under the pressure of munitions orders and labour shortages, for more managerial experimentation to speed up and rationalize production. A Hamilton employer of over 1000 munitions workers claimed in 1916 that "There is no industrial system which brings out individual value so well as the piece system"; and Richard Riley reported that almost all shell work used the system.[74] In fall 1915 *Canadian Machinery* revealed how one shrapnel shell factory had increased its daily output from 800 to 2700, largely as a result of "the efforts and ability of the company's executives in providing labor saving devices, improved machining methods, rebuilding machines, developing chute systems and otherwise keeping up every detail of the work to the last notch of efficiency." The following summer the same journal reported how another factory had adapted to the labour shortage and production demands: machinists were rearranged to allow one man to handle more machines; and machinists were discouraged from moving around the shop by using boys and labourers to perform all purely physical operations, to make rough cuts, to sweep up, and to bring tools and lubricants to the worker at his machines, and by installing several new drinking fountains and toilets ("this saved the time it took to walk 250 feet several times a day"). "The shortage of men," the journal happily concluded, "thus started what proved to be an efficiency campaign." Still another firm was cited in 1917 for having raised its daily capacity from 700 to 800 shells to 5000, without expanding their floor space appreciably.[75] Speed-up was under way in the machine shops as never before.

New technology and new schemes of management, therefore, set off what contemporaries called a "revolution" in the machine shop, and by the 1920s the machinists' craft had been fundamentally altered. G.L. Sprague, principal of the Hamilton Technical School, noted in 1921 what few opportunities remained for the highly skilled man:

> Modern manufacturing methods have broken down standards in the machinist trades. Only in the tool room and repair departments are found men who could classify as all-round machinists. The rank and file of men operating machines in what is known as the metal trades are merely machine tenders, operators, and specialists, according to the mastery they possess in producing on some particular machine.[76]

Outside of the toolrooms, repair departments, foremen's offices, and the small railway shops in the city, the day of the artisan in the machine shop was gone.

The profound changes of these years did not proceed smoothly or without resistance from the craftsmen who were being displaced. Through their craft organizations they voiced an eloquent critique of the major industrial trends of the age. In fact their all-round knowledge of the work process made them the most informed critics of the period. The editor of the *Iron Molders' Journal* had pointed out as early as 1897 how the benefits of the new metal-working machinery so often did not extend to the workers:

> In a properly constituted society these innovations and improvements would be hailed with pleasure, as according to mankind further immunity from arduous toil in supplying his wants, but under present conditions the worker has learned too well that progress in this direction means further degradation and poverty for him.[77]

The machinists' union was just as unhappy with the new techniques of workshop management; its constitution denounced the "pernicious" piecework system, which it saw as responsible for "cultivating man's selfish nature to the extent of losing sight of the rights of his brother workman." Similarly the IAM's Canadian vice-president, James Somerville, argued:

> When we say piece-work and task-work has [sic] the tendency to destroy the finer sensibilities in men, we know what we are talking about, and the world will yet give us credit for loftier motives than restriction of output. Touch the mainstring of the human heart and show an enlightened conscience where this accursed competitive system is leading to, and it is beyond you or I to conceive what the result will be.[78]

There was a general fear, here as in other trades, that increased output would result in cuts in piece rates, and widespread concern about speed-up. In 1903 the union made a last desperate attempt to halt the spread of the system by forbidding machinists to work "by the piece, premiums, task, merit or contract systems," under the penalty of expulsion, but much of the membership failed to conform. The union nonetheless continued to resist these innovations, and in 1909 the IAM president reported that at least 50 per cent of the strikes fought during the preceding year grew out of the employers' attempts to introduce piecework; "yet we can not credit ourselves with preventing the growth of this system, because, in my opinion, it is largely on the increase."[79] During a machinists' organizing drive, a front-page article in the Hamilton *Labor News* conveyed the local workers' indignation at how far these new managerial initiatives had gone: "The 'one man two machines,' the 'Taylor,' 'Scientific,' 'Premium,' 'piecework' and other systems introduced in the metal shops, are making of men what men are supposed to make of metals: machines."[80]

Perhaps the craftsmen's most strident critiques of modern industry percolated through their persistent campaign for shorter hours of work. Not only did skilled metal workers raise this issue in virtually every confrontation with their employers, culminating in the post-war demand for an eight-hour day; the question of shorter hours was also one of the few workplace issues injected into politics. Hamilton's Independent Labor Party stalwart in the Ontario legislature, Allan Studholme, repeatedly introduced bills to establish a legal eight-hour day, and the buoyant Ontario ILP which emerged in 1917 entrenched a shorter-hours plank in its platform.[81] In fact, the eight-hour day had become the leading concern of the entire Canadian labour movement by the time of the convening of the National Industrial Conference in Ottawa in September 1919.[82] In an age when employers were straining their imagination for new ways to increase the workload required each hour, in order to speed up production and cheapen labour costs, skilled workers in Hamilton, as elsewhere in Canada, fought to control how long they would have to labour at the new pace. As a union moulder asserted in 1921, "A working man appreciates life just as much as anyone else does and he should not be expected to slave so that others could have comfort."[83]

As an alternative to the rationalizing tendencies of corporate capitalism, these craftsmen asserted the less authoritarian, more decentralized, craft-dominated routines of the immediate past, which company managers were seeking to root out. Their strategy of oppositon, therefore, was to attempt to re-establish the control mechanisms of the crafts over the metal-working factories, by compelling employers to adopt their "schedules" setting out the conditions of employment. They clung tenaciously to their craft unionism and made no substantial efforts to broaden their membership base and draw in their less skilled workmates.

The moulders, of all the metal trades workers, probably had most to lose, since their union and its traditions were so well entrenched in Hamilton at the turn of the century. In the fifteen years after 1905, the stove moulders fought one major strike, which has already been described, and the machinery and jobbing moulders five more. There were three periods of renewed strength for this latter group: 1905–07, 1911–13, and 1917–19. In each instance, their value to employers in the booming local economy won for them verbal agreements for wage increases and tacit acceptance of the craftsmen's shop practices; but in each period employers promptly fought back against these union incursions. In all three periods it was a downturn in the economy which brought defeat for the moulders. By 1913 the union had signed up members in eleven large firms, established the nine-hour day, and won wage increases in eight of the largest companies.[84] Three others, however, refused to concede the union control of production. A Westinghouse official explained what was at stake: "In reality, it was an effort to make this Foundry a strict Union Shop with union committees and other union regulation of its operation." The ensuing strike severely disrupted production, costing the Westinghouse plant alone some $100 000, but it collapsed in the depression that began in the second half of the year.[85]

The general stimulus of the war economy eventually brought back full employment and renewed union activity in the machinery and jobbing foundries.[86] Early in 1918 the union's bold demand for an increase from $4.50 to $6 a day raised the hackles of the foundrymen, and a month-long strike of 250 to 300 men from eight shops was only ended through the intervention of Mark Irish of the Imperial Munitions Board.[87] In May 1919, with unemployment in the foundries mounting steadily, the foundrymen in Hamilton and other Canadian cities dug in their heels to resist the union's new demand for an eight-hour day and another wage hike. The Hamilton Employers' Association, formed in 1916, joined hands with Toronto employers to fight the metal trades unions. Once again their refusal to budge kept their shops "open" until depression, which settled in again in 1920, eroded the moulders' bargaining strength.[88] This time, however, the defeat seems to have been permanent; only two of the machinery firms gave in early in 1920, and one of these, the Hamilton Foundry Company, drove out the union in 1925.[89] Moreover, in 1920 the employers consolidated their strength in a large new open-shop organization, the Canadian Founders' Association (renamed the Canadian Founders' and Metal Trades' Association a few months later), whose commissioner, C.W. Burgess, kept up a belligerent anti-union campaign well into the 1920s.[90] A *Canadian Foundryman* editorial caught the tone of the employers' attempts to roll back the advances workers had made during the war: "What is more important . . . than the readjustment of wage rates is that the workmen agree to remove the restrictions upon output which have been a crying evil in the period now drawing to a close."[91]

Before World War I the machinists' organizations in Hamilton had considerably less success than the moulders in stemming the tide of change in their working lives. Their only major strike before the war was an unsuccessful confrontation with International Harvester in 1904 over the two-machine question.[92] Efforts to rally Hamilton's machinists again before the war had no lasting impact. In 1910 the union's Canadian vice-president scoffed that "the machinists of Hamilton are ignorant of the principles of unionism . . ." and that "they appear to have some hobby or other that seems to occupy their valuable time that should be devoted to improving their conditions." A year later he told the Hamilton lodge that "the wages paid in Hamilton would not do credit to the men who swept the city streets." In 1917 Hamilton business agent Richard Riley had to admit that "for the past fifteen years in the majority of shops in this city the machinists have not dared to admit they belonged to the IA of M, and employers did as they pleased with them."[93]

This record of failure was not always the result of inertia. A province-wide organizing campaign begun early in 1912 generated a spurt of local activity, including weekly mass meetings and home visitations. A new schedule was drafted to be presented to the city's employers, demanding a nine-hour day, higher wages, and re-establishment of craft controls. The men who undertook this initiative were not prepared to accept the undermining of their craft that had occurred during the previous two decades. In the first article of their new schedule they explicitly stated that "Helpers or handy men shall not be allowed to perform any work designated as machinists' work," and that a four-year apprenticeship system should be reintroduced, with no more than one apprentice for every five machinists employed in any one shop.[94] The impact of this organizing effort was quite limited, not least because some companies granted voluntary wage increases to head off unionization. By summer 1913, as some of Hamilton's largest firms began laying off staff in the first wave of the mass unemployment that was to ensue, Riley indicated how little headway the campaign had made:

> The average machinist who works ten hours per day, which is the rule in this district, and who during that ten hours has a speeder standing over him, or the man who has to work all day at top speed to make $3.25, has not energy enough left to drag his weary limbs to an open meeting or to discuss trades unionism if you call upon them [sic].[95]

The efforts of the machine-shop craftsmen to re-establish their craft hegemony in the industry had evidently failed.

The wartime boom in Hamilton's machine shops, however, shifted the advantage once again to the machinists. By April 1915 Riley could report that all IAM members in the city were back at work, and indeed before long a severe shortage of qualified machinists was attacting more craftsmen to the city.[96] The machinists' value to the industrial life of the city, and of the country, reached new heights. So too, however, did their discontent with their working conditions. For the craftsmen working in these munitions plants the wartime labour process was clearly an intensification of pre-war patterns. Initially they found that the new burst of productive activity had made little difference to the longstanding policy of low wages and long hours. "Some of the firms are taking advantage of the unorganized state of the machinists," Riley reported in 1915, "by paying them starvation wages and working them overtime and on Sundays for straight time," and justifying their actions with appeals to patriotism. One Hamilton machinist riled against this situation:

> The workers are by no means less loyal than the manufacturers, and if the capitalist were to contribute his industry and raw material absolutely free or at cost, the worker would be the first to follow, but since they are making fat profits out of the dire needs of the government, we workers should at least receive our share, a living wage.[97]

As more unskilled machine-tenders were hired, the wage question took on a new twist for the skilled machinist and toolmaker. Thanks to long hours at piece-work and the accelerated rate of production, many of these new workers were soon taking home enormous pay packets.[98] Many of the skilled men, often working at straight hourly rates, resented the erosion of the wage differential that had always symbolized their value to industry. When asked why he was dissatisfied with his working conditions, one Hamilton machinist told a royal commission in spring 1916: "Because, sir, there are other men on single operations who make a lot more than I do." Another complained: "Many men are running machines now who were farm laborers some time ago . . . and they make as much money as I do." The editor of *Canadian Machinery* reported that these newcomers to the machine shop "after a few days of preliminary training were receiving three, four and even five times what they earned before, while the mechanics and toolmakers about the shop who told these men what to do and set the machines in order that they could serve, were forced to work at less than half the wage." As tensions mounted in spring 1916, a Hamilton ASE official recalled bitterly that "the skilled workers in the factories greatly assisted their employers, and consequently their country, by instructing the unskilled . . . in the best ways of increasing their efficiency." The works engineer of International Harvester, T. Daly, also recognized how "This influx of unskilled labor in the mechanical field makes the machinist imagine his services to be underrated."[99]

The local IAM lodge and ASE branch lost no time in organizing regular mass meetings to sign up hundreds of disgruntled machinists,[100] and on 1 April 1916 the IAM circulated to all the city's metal shops a new schedule of wages, hours, and working conditions for machinists. This new document, like its 1912 predecessor, was a blueprint for reimposing rigid union policing of working procedures and reasserting the hegemony of the craftsman over the city's machine shops. An appeal to artisanal pride had been a keynote of the union's organizing campaign; in a speech to Hamilton machinists organizer McCallum said

> it was not to the credit of skilled machinists who had to spend years of apprenticeship and large sums of money for proper tools, to be working almost for laborers' wages and long hours. He declared that if printers, masons and bricklayers, and other building trades worked but eight hours a day, machinists at least should work no more.[101]

Hamilton's metal trades employers were soon alarmed at this resurrection of craft unionism in their midst. Individual skirmishes with union organizers gave way to a united front after the local branch of the Canadian Manufacturers' Association struck a special committee to co-ordinate a response.[102] As employer hostility stiffened and a showdown seemed imminent, the federal government intervened promptly by appointing a three-man royal commission to investigate munitions workers' grievances in Hamilton and Toronto. The commission's hearings held in early May gave the machinists the public forum they wanted to carry on their arguments with their bosses. Riley ushered in a parade of worker witnesses and was allowed to cross-examine company officials.[103] The sessions often turned into extended debates over the nature of work in the city's machine shops, including conflicting views on a worker's productivity in a nine-hour day. All the resentment against the previous decades' changes in their workplace experience bubbled up in the munitions workers' testimony.

It quickly became clear that, while most workers wanted higher wages to meet the rising cost of living, the union demand for a nine-hour day focussed on the crux of their discontent. A *Herald* report on the hearings highlighted this concern:

> The evidence of the employees was to the effect that the men are dissatisfied mainly because the hours of work are ten to the day; that the machines are run at a higher speed than they were in times of peace, and that the consequent strain on their constitutions was too great to permit them to work ten hours a day. Although the average machinist receives about 37½ cents per hour, a considerable advance compared with some years ago, still the men contend that owing to the strain of production with machines speeded up to the limit, a man's life as a machinist or munition worker contains few attractions aside from the weekly or monthly pay envelope.[104]

The employers nonetheless continued their resistance to a shorter working day, correctly fearing a precedent for post-war industry, and rejected the commission's final recommendation in favour of the nine-hour principle.[105] Early in June, 38 of the city's leading firms gave birth to the Employers' Association of Hamilton, which announced in a series of strident newspaper advertisements that its purpose was "to see that there shall be no improper restriction of output, and that no conditions shall arise to prevent any workman from earning a wage proportionate to his productive capacity." After several weeks of frantic lobbying by federal and municipal officials to head off the inevitable confrontation, some 1500 machinists and unskilled munitions workers walked out on 12 June, demanding implementation of the royal commission's recommendations. According to the *Spectator* the strike was "a contest of the open shop against the one operated under union regulations . . . [;] each is fighting for what it regards as principle."[106] The strike, however, had floundered by the end of the summer, in the face of government censorship and renewed rivalry between the IAM and ASE.[107]

Summer 1916 was thus a historic moment in the evolution of the machinists' craft in Hamilton. War conditions had given both the pressing need and the collective strength to protest changes in their working lives which, while more intense under war production, were simply the culmination of two decades of industrial practice. As ASE representative Fred Flatman argued during the strike,

"Matters only started to reach a head some eight weeks ago, but we have been fighting for this thing for years, have been fighting to get a nine-hour working day, fighting long before munitions were introduced in our factories."[108] These artisans of the machine shop were attempting to reassert their old craft control over the work process in which they were involved and in so doing met the combined resistance of Hamilton's manufacturers, who could not countenance such a rupture in the new work routines they had been developing. Never again were the Hamilton machinists able to mount such a challenge. While several firms in the city eventually did concede the shorter working day before the end of the war, it was in each case a gesture meant to pacify their workers without conceding any power to the craftsmen's union.[109] And when industrial unrest in Canada was reaching a peak in spring 1919, Hamilton's machinists were in no position to join the general strikes of metal trades workers in several other centres.[110]

The depression of the early 1920s left little chance for a quick recovery of union strength. But for the first time since the 1890s the return of prosperity in the late 1920s saw no revival of unionism in the machine shops in Hamilton, as elsewhere in Canada. Only in the railway shops was the IAM able to hold on to any significant membership. In 1927 IAM Canadian vice-president James Somerville indicated that organizing efforts had not yet "developed anything to create excitement or to write home about . . ." and a year later he declaimed: "The average wage paid machinists in Canada off the railways is a disgrace . . . ."[111] The failure of the machinists to rise phoenix-like from the depression did not simply indicate inertia or apathy. The craft had now been so thoroughly altered that there was no longer a basis on which to build a viable craft union movement in Hamilton's metalworking factories.

While the rhythm of change was quite different in the foundry and the machine shop, the cumulative effect was similar. What is remarkable is how little inclination the moulders and machinists showed to reorient their defensive strategies by uniting with other skilled metal workers or with their less skilled workmates. Within the ranks of the moulders, the men in the stove shops and those in the machinery and jobbing shops went their separate ways, with no hint of a sympathetic strike. In 1913 Hamilton's moulders made their first and only attempt to organize machine-tenders in the foundry and to set a fixed rate for their work — in effect, to extend the union's extensive work regulations to cover moulding-machinery work. At this point Canadian Westinghouse's concern about the contamination of its handymen by the unionized skilled workers became one of the factors in its decision to build its new foundry, designed for moulding machinery work, in the opposite end of the city from its existing plant. But the 1913 strike ended in defeat for the moulders, and they undertook no further efforts to organize the less skilled.[112]

Similarly the wartime experience of skill dilution did little to alter the traditional craft pride of Hamilton's machinists. By the 1916 strike the union had begun to include specialists in its membership but not the less skilled shell workers. The local business agent heaved a sigh of relief when the munitions industry shut down: "We say good-bye with great pleasure to the shell operators and hope they will never have another opportunity or excuse for being caught in a machine shop." In 1919 the only union members in International Harvester's huge staff were the cream of the craft, the toolmakers. And rather than turning to a new organizing strategy with a wider membership base, the union took up the cause of a new category of craftsmen outside the factories, the auto mechanics.[113]

There were some halting attempts towards metal trades solidarity, usually spearheaded by the machinists (whose international union after 1912 was committed, at least rhetorically, to socialism and to some form of craft amalgamation as a step toward industrial unionism[114]); but in Hamilton none of these efforts ever effectively broke the bounds of craft exclusivenss. A Metal Trades Council formed in 1910 perished in the pre-war depression, only to be revived again for a year in 1919–20. In each period of its existence the council seems to have been little more than a forum for the exchange of information and the clarification of jurisdictions, although in 1920 a joint organizing drive was undertaken under the council's sponsorship.[115] In 1913 the moulders' representatives in the AFL Metal Trades Department squelched an effort to use these local councils as general strike committees against one or more employers.[116] The *International Molders' Journal* thundered in 1915:

> Are the molders, who have maintained their union for fifty-six years, and who have made it one of the most effective trade-unions in the world, willing to surrender their organization and afterwards allow men of the other trades to determine what the laws shall be which will govern molders?[117]

True to form, the moulders' union in Hamilton refused to join the revived council in 1919.[118] A more overt effort at collective action among the city's metalworkers began in spring 1918 when the IAM and ASE formed an Amalgamation Committee. The committee's leading propagandist, Fred Flatman, campaigned vigorously among the other metal-working crafts to generate interest in the fusion idea, winning at least a lukewarm reception, but this initiative collapsed when Flatman and several other militants opted for the short-lived Metal Workers' Unit of the One Big Union.[119] In spring 1919 *Labor News* editor Walter Rollo reminded his readers that there were "thousands of handy men, specialists, grinders, helpers and laborers working in the big East End plants with no organization at all. . . ."[120] Perhaps the only significant departure from narrow craft lines was the insistent demand for shorter hours, which arguably would benefit all workers in an industry.

This reluctance of the craftsmen to embrace the unskilled was fed from two directions. The most evident was the nativist bias of the predominantly Anglo-Saxon skilled workers against the thousands of European immigrants who were swelling the ranks of the unskilled in Hamilton's factories in this period. In 1913, for example, a "foreigner" hired by Westinghouse to work in the coremaking department of this foundry was beaten up at quitting time by two English-speaking coremakers, and, when the pair was fired for the assault, their fellow-workers marched out in sympathy.[121] Ethnicity was certainly one of the most effective divisive factors in the Hamilton working class. The other source was a subtler strand in artisanal culture. Craftsmen placed a high value on the self-reliant, independent man of principle who stood by his craft organization. Appeals to non-unionists were usually exhortations to individual conscience and a sense of "manhood." In 1914 the local *Labor News* described "a sort of unwritten law in the Hamilton Trades and Labor Council not to waste much time in giving any aid to any class of wage earners who were persistent in refusing to aid themselves . . . who will not recognize the principle of self help and unite and maintain an organization."[122] The artisans' moral criteria for the independent, self-disciplined character of a good worker apparently blinded them to the concrete difficulties faced by the unskilled in organizing on the job.

The limitations of craft culture, however, do not seem to have been the only obstacle to class solidarity among these skilled men. By the early twentieth century the union's older notion of "brotherhood" in the workshop was competing with an increasingly potent alternative view of quick economic gain among the rank and file. Several factors intensified this more self-centred, instrumental approach to work. During these years great hordes of workers, especially young men, were setting out from Britain, the United States, or some Canadian town or city in search of work and high wages, always moving in a restless spirit of adventure. The machinists recognized a whole category of such craftsmen known as "boomers," who pursued new jobs and high pay across the continent. The 1916 royal commission heard several of these men; one from Buffalo hit the road from Hamilton "just for a change" and another arrived from Detroit "just to see Hamilton."[123] Many of them were keen union activists who carried their union principles through many shop doors. But many, especially those recently off the boat from Britain, were far more interested in the comparatively higher wages they could suddenly earn. Hamilton moulder James Roberts roasted these Old Country freebooters in 1912, and Richard Riley similarly denounced them a year later:

> The majority of such men seem to think that they are dropping into a ready-made paradise of high wages and short hours, where such things as trade unions are unnecesary because of the great benevolence of the employers. They are intoxicated with the difference of the wages they now receive and what they used to get "at home."

Hamilton, he later claimed, was a "mecca for all the Old Country machinists coming to Canada."[124]

Of course, none of this behaviour was entirely new in the early twentieth century; a great migration of workers around the North American continent was a familiar pattern in the nineteenth century. But two factors combined to make the pattern more compelling after 1900. Both the soaring cost of living and the boom-and-bust cycles of the Canadian economy in this period, with three severe depressions over 30 years, no doubt contributed to a mentality of making hay while the sun shone. Many metalworkers probably welcomed the opportunity to swell their pay packets through the new wage-incentive plans. With quiet consternation a contributor to the machinists' *Bulletin* in 1916 surveyed the boost that wartime production practices had given to this more materialistic view of work:

> The lust for gain has defeated all reason, and with little or no obstruction in the path of the producer it develops into the survival of the fittest. To excuse

the situation on the ground that the times are exceptional and everybody should do his uttermost during the crisis may be acceptable, but the fact remains that the contract or piece work system has received an impetus that a hundred years of oration on its evils will not eliminate.

. . . [A]s long as it is possible for men to increase their daily earnings by the adoption of any system whatsoever that system is likely to remain.[125]

Feeling the double pinch of inflation and uncertain employment, and offered the chance to earn more money, the proud artisan with workplace traditions to defend could all too easily become the hustler in search of a fast buck. There is, of course, no way to gauge how widespread such an attitude became, but craft unionists certainly recognized it as a crippling factor in defending their principles.

It seems unlikely, however, that this instrumental attitude would have been appreciably stronger in Hamilton than in other Canadian cities. How then can we explain the relatively limp response of Hamilton's craftsmen to the reorganization of their workplace? Why were Hamilton's machinists in such a weak position before 1916? Why, with the exception of the moulders' strike in May 1919, did the city avoid the great labour upsurge that hit metal shops in Winnipeg, Toronto, Montreal, Amherst, and other centres that spring? A full explanation would undoubtedly require a broader study of working-class life in Hamilton than is possible here, including in particular ideological currents. But three related aspects of the city's industrial structure and evolution might provide part of an explanation for Hamilton's apparently unique experience.

In the first place, Hamilton lacked the large railway shops that harboured scores of machinists in cities like Winnipeg, Toronto, and Montreal. Work in these shops demanded men of all-round abilities, unlike the more specialized requirements of Hamilton firms like International Harvester or Canadian Westinghouse. Perhaps this gap in the city's industrial structure left the workforce with relatively more handymen-specialists than artisanal machinists.

Secondly, we can point to the remarkable hostility and strength of Hamilton industrialists. International Harvester and Canadian Westinghouse have already been described as two giant union-baiters in the city, but we should not overlook the importance of the local steel industry in helping to set the tone of corporate labour policies. Hamilton Steel and Iron Company and later the Steel Company of Canada shared the North American steel industry's intense opposition to craftsmen and their unions that David Brody has described in his study of American steelworkers.[126] In a tightly knit local business community the executive officers of that company, especially vice-president and general manager Robert Hobson, were often the spokesmen of the manufacturers, notably in the 1916 machinists' strike where federal officials recognized Hobson as the leader of the employers' counter-offensive. Hamilton's skilled metal workers may, therefore, have faced a much stiffer opposition than workers in other Canadian cities where steel was less prominent in the industrial structure.

Thirdly, we might turn to the unique pattern of industrial conflict which emerged in Hamilton, especially during World War I and principally as a result of employer hostility. The years between 1917 and 1919 saw industrial militancy in Canada increasingly mingled with a political radicalism that was forged in the heat of government insensitivity and repression. Hamilton's labour movement, however, was unlikely to evolve as fully in this direction after the thorough defeat of the machinists in 1916, well before the new, more radical political spirit had coalesced in the country. Elsewhere the machinists would be important leaven in the rise of post-war working-class dissent. In Hamilton that role fell to the more cautious craftsmen of the foundry, the moulders. A more militant posture and a wider solidarity seemed unlikely under such circumstances.

> Twenty years ago a molder was at home with his slick and trowel, but place the good mechanic of those years in the modern foundry and he would feel like a "fish out of water."[127]

In 1927 most observers would have agreed with this Canadian business journalist that the heyday of the craft worker in Canada's metalworking industries had passed. A new, rationalized, more highly mechanized mode of work had emerged to confine the skilled metal worker to small, unspecialized shops on the periphery of modern industry or to a sharply limited role in the process of mass production. On the one hand, in the case of both the moulders and the machinists, the craftsmen found large areas of their traditional work mechanized and divided up among less skilled labourers. On the other, a few "well-rounded mechanics" survived inside large-scale industry, but these craftsmen found their work narrowed, circumscribed, and intensified. In this new role in production there was increased pressure on the skilled men to apply themselves strictly to work that required their technical know-how. The old artisanal sense of working a product through all or most of its stages of production to completion was lost. And the pace of work, formerly so carefully regulated by custom and entrenched in union regulations was now set by corporate administrators.[128] The skilled metal workers who hung on in the context of mass production became simply a part of a complex continuum of industrial workers under the detailed supervision of efficiency-conscious managers. The artisan of the 1890s gave way to the skilled production worker whose overall status in the workplace had undoubtedly declined.

If some craftsmen survived in the workplace, artisanal *culture* did not. The mode of work in the foundries and machine shops of the late nineteenth century had involved a commanding role for the artisans in determining the rhythms of the total production process. These men had nurtured an intense craft pride that fed on their indispensability to industry. Structurally the craftsmen's trade unions had been the repositories of both the mechanisms of job control and the ideology of craft superiority. Thirty years of conflict with employers who saw the manifestation of this culture in their factories as an obstacle to their larger corporate strategies, however, resulted in final defeat for the craft unions and all they represented by the early 1920s.

The pattern of defeat was slightly different in each of the two crafts discussed above. The mechanization of the moulders' craft came late and was still incomplete by the 1920s; the all-round craftsman was never as thoroughly eliminated from the foundry as elsewhere in the metalworking factory. On the other hand, from the mid-nineteenth century onward the machinist used power-driven tools, which by the early 1900s were becoming sophisticated enough to reduce much more completely the manual skill requirements of machine-shop work. The machinists' craft was also more fundamentally affected by World War I munitions production, which did not incorporate moulding work. On the whole, however, the *predominant* response of Hamilton's metal-working craftsmen to this prolonged crisis threatening their shopfloor power and prestige was craft exclusiveness, that is, a strategy of defending those parts of their trades with continuing high skill content and attempting to reimpose craft control over wider industrial territory in times of full employment. There was no evidence of a transformation of their consciousness towards a broader solidarity with the less skilled.

Artisanal culture was thus highly ambivalent. It was often a reservoir of creative criticism of modernizing industrial practices, but its structure was still fundamentally a defence of craft privilege — "the clinging dross of exclusivism," to use James Hinton's apt phrase.[129] Yet, at the same time, it would be too easy to embrace a theory of an aristocracy of labour in the Hamilton working class. An examination of workplace behaviour alone would be insufficient to confirm such a theory; for as the most sensitive British studies have emphasized,[130] we would need a fuller portrait of artisanal culture that took into account social and political associations outside the workplace. It was many of these same men, for example, who were prominent in the leadership of the city's working-class political organization, the Independent Labor Party, which promoted class unity at the polls. The evidence presented here, in any case, should certainly raise doubts about any suggestion that these skilled workers were enjoying any special favours from capital; they were, in fact, being persistently harassed by belligerent employers.

Clearly specific responses of Canadian workers to the great industrial transformations of the age must be studied in local settings, in order to capture the unevenness and the variety of experience. But more detailed research into the history of skilled workers in other Canadian communities may well reveal that the ambivalence of artisanal culture in the workplace that characterized Hamilton's metal workers was more common than historians of the Canadian working class have so far suggested. The failure to transcend that worldview probably meant that the sweeping changes in the work process that accompanied the rise of monopoly capitalism in Canada prompted a highly fragmented response from the working class.

Notes

1. *Herald* (Hamilton), 4 May 1916. The literature on craftsmen has become voluminous. A few of the more insightful works which have influenced the ensuing discussion include the following: on Canada, Gregory S. Kealey, " 'The Honest Workingman' and Workers' Control: The Experience of Toronto Skilled Workers, 1860–1892," *Labour/Le Travailleur* 1 (1976): 32–68; Ian McKay, "Capital and Labour in the Halifax Baking and Confectionery Industry During the Last Half of the Nineteenth Century," ibid., 3 (1978): 63–108; Bryan D. Palmer, "Most Uncommon Common Men: Craft and Culture in Historical Perspective," ibid., 1 (1976): 5–31; Wayne Roberts, "The Last Artisans: Toronto Printers, 1896–1914," in *Essays in Canadian Working Class History*, edited by Gregory Kealey and Peter Warrian (Toronto, 1976), 125–42; on Britain, Geoffrey Crossick, "The Labour Aristocracy and Its Values: A Study of Mid-Victorian Kentish London," *Victorian Studies* 19 (1976): 301–28; R.Q. Gray, "Styles of Life, the 'Labour Aristocracy,' and

Class relations in Later Nineteenth Century Edinburgh," *International Review of Social History* 17 (1973): 428–52; James Hinton, *The First Shop Stewards' Movement* (London, 1973): 56–100; E.P. Thompson, *The Making of the English Working Class* (Harmondsworth, 1968), 259–96; on the United States, Paul Faler, "Cultural Aspects of the Industrial Revolution: Lynn, Massachusetts, Shoemakers and Industrial Morality, 1826–1860," *Labor History* 15 (1974): 367–94; Herbert Gutman, *Work, Culture and Society in Industrializing America* (New York, 1976), 32–54; Bruce Laurie, " 'Nothing on Compulsion': Life Styles of Philadelphia Artisans, 1820–1850," *Labor History* 15 (1974): 337–66; David Montgomery, "Workers' Control of Machine Production in the Nineteenth Century," ibid., 17 (1976): 485–509.

2. R.D. Roberts, "The Changing Patterns in Distribution and Composition of Manufacturing Activity in Hamilton Between 1861 and 1921" (M.A. thesis, McMaster University, 1964), 78.

3. *Hamilton: The Birmingham of Canada* (Hamilton, 1892). The E.C. Gurney Company became Gurney-Tilden during the 1890s when John H. Tilden moved into control. The Toronto branch of the firm became independent and retained the Gurney name. Stoves were Canada's most important foundry products at the turn of the century; in 1902 there were 297 stove foundries in Canada out of a total of 527. Clyde A. Saunders and Dudley C. Gould, *History Cast in Metal: The Founders of North America* (n.p., 1976), 15. On the growth of industry in Hamilton see, in particular, Marjorie Freeman Campbell, *A Mountain and a City: The Story of Hamilton* (Toronto, 1966); C.M. Johnston, *The Head of the Lake: A History of Wentworth County*, rev. ed. (Hamilton, 1967); Bryan D. Palmer, "Most Uncommon Common Men: Craft, Culture and Conflict in a Canadian Community, 1860–1914" (Ph.D. thesis, State University of New York at Binghamton, 1977); Roberts, "Manufacturing Activity"; Robert H. Storey, "Industrialization in Canada: The Emergence of the Hamilton Working Class, 1850–1870s" (M.A. thesis, Dalhousie University, 1975).

4. John Sadlier, "The Problem of the Molder," *Iron Age*, 6 June 1901, 26b.

5. Benjamin Brooks, "The Molders," reprinted from *Scribner's* in *Iron Molders' Journal* (hereafter *IMJ* XLII, 11 (Nov. 1906): 801–8; Margaret Loomis Stecker, "The Founders, the Molders, and the Molding Machine," in *Trade Unionism and Labor Problems*, edited by J.R. Commons, 2nd ed. (Boston, 1921), 343–45.

6. *Canadian Foundryman* (hereafter *CF*) XIX, 5 (May 1928): 39.

7. *Herald*, 8 Oct. 1910; Ontario, Factory Inspectors, *Report, 1908* (Toronto, 1909), 34; *IMJ* XLV, 5 (May 1909): 302–4.

8. Canada, Royal Commission on the Relations of Capital and Labour, *Report: Evidence—Ontario* (Ottawa, 1889), 826. See also Sir Alexander Bertram, "Development of the Machine Tool Industry," *CM* XXVI, 26 (29 Dec. 1921): 153, for similar comments on the skills of his late father, John Bertram, an artisanal entrepreneur in nearby Dundas.

9. L.T.C. Rolt, *Tools for the Job: A Short History of Machine Tools* (London, 1965), 122–91; James B. Jefferys, *The Story of the Engineers, 1800–1945* (London, 1945), 9–14. These craftsmen were known as engineers in Britain and machinists in North America.

10. Royal Commission on Capital and Labour, *Report: Ontario*, 827–28.

11. Raphael Samuel, "Workshop of the World: Steam Power and Hand Technology in Mid-Victorian Britain," *History Workshop Journal* 3 (1977): 6–72.

12. Royal Commission on Capital and Labour, *Report: Ontario* 881.

13. *Herald*, 23 Mar. 1912.

14. John P. Frey and John R. Commons, "Conciliation in the Stove Industry," United States, Bureau of Labor, *Bulletin* XII, 1 (Jan. 1906): 177. On the moulders' workplace customs see Kealey, "The Honest Workingman," 40–43.

15. Robert T. Lozier, "Variable Motor Speeds and Their Relation to New Shop Methods," *Canadian Engineer* (hereafter *CE*) X, 7 (July 1903): 189.

16. Robert H. Babcock, *Gompers in Canada: A Study in American Continentalism Before the First World War* (Toronto, 1974), 38–54.

17. Storey, "Industrialization in Canada," 123; Frank T. Stockton, *International Molders' Union of North American* (Baltimore, 1921), 20. The union's name was changed to the International Molders' Union in 1907.

18. *Labour Gazette* (hereafter *LG*) II, 4 (Oct. 1901): 250; Mark Perlman, *The Machinists: A New Study in American Trade Unionism* (Cambridge, Mass. 1961), 7; Palmer, "Most Uncommon Common Men," 435–36.

19. *Machinists' Monthly Journal* (hereafter *MMJ*) XIV, 11 (Nov. 1902): 739.

20. Hamilton Public Library, Hamilton Collection, International Harvester Scrapbook, 1.

21. *Pittsburgh Dispatch*, 3 May 1903 (clipping in Westinghouse Canada Archives, P.J. Myler Scrapbook).

22. See Craig Heron and Bryan D. Palmer, "Through the Prism of the Strike: Industrial Conflict in Southern Ontario, 1901–14," *Canadian Historical Review* 58 (1977): 446–56.

23. Public Archives of Ontario, RG 7, XV-4, vol. 3; *LG* IX, 4 (Oct. 1908): 378; ibid. 7 (Jan. 1909): 744–45; XIV, 2 (Aug. 1913): 117; Herald, 30 Jan., 22 Nov. 1912, 10 Feb. 1913; *Canadian Machinery* (hereafter *CM*) IX, 7 (6 Mar. 1913): 239; XI, 5 (29 Jan. 1914): 76.

24. Given their penchant for "tramping" about in search of work or broader experience moulders undoubtedly accumulated experience in both branches of the industry as well as in small-town foundries where they might work alone. See "Passing of the Small Foundry," *CM* XXI, 1 (Jan. 1925): 102; and the autobiographical articles of a Port Arthur foundryman, John Woodside, in *CE* VIII, 11 (Nov. 1917): 195–96; X, 12 (Dec. 1919): 360; XI, 1 (Jan. 1920): 15; XIII, 7 (July 1922): 36–37. And Stockton, *International Molders' Union*, 94. See also obituaries of Hamilton molders in *IMJ* XLIV, 7 (July 1908): 508; XLV, 5 (May 1909), 331–32; ibid., 7 (July 1909): 516; ibid., 11 (Nov. 1909): 779; 12 (Dec. 1914):914.

25. Like so many other Canadian businessmen faced with such a situation, Hamilton's stove foundrymen turned to the monopolistic alternative; between 1899 and 1901, and again in 1910, they undertook unsuccessful initiatives to consolidate all the major stove foundries in the province, along with a number south of the border. Their failure meant that the Canadian stove-founding industry was to remain an array of relatively small plants competing in a national market. *CE* VIII, 7 (July 1900): 62; *IMJ* XXXVI, 8 (Aug. 1900): 534; *Iron Age*, 3 May 1900, 27; 23 Aug. 1900, 16; 10 Jan. 1901, 22; *Herald*, 6 July 1910. On the Canadian business community's "flight from competition" in this period, see Michael Bliss, *A Living Profit: Studies in the Social History of Canadian Business, 1883–1911* (Toronto, 1974), 33–54.

26. Palmer, "Most Uncommon Common Men," 252–57, 267–71; Kealey, "Honest Workingman," 42–47; Storey, "Industrialization in Canada," 130; House of Commons, *Journals* XXII (1888), app. 3, 8–9, 391–97, 699–705; *Iron Age*, 23 Aug. 1900, 16.

27. The model for this centralized bargaining was the Stove Founders Defense Association in the United States, which had originally been a militantly anti-union organization but which began annual national conferences with the IMU in 1893. Frey and Commons, "Conciliation in the Stove Industry"; Stockton, *International Molders' Union*, 120–25; F.W. Hilbert, "Trade Union Agreements in the Iron Molders' Union," in *Studies in American Trade Unionism*, edited by Jacob H. Hollander and George E. Barnett (New York, 1907), 229–32. On the Canadian experience, see *IMJ* XXXVI, 3 (March 1900): 143; ibid., 8 (Aug. 1900): 534; XXXVIII, 6 (June 1902): 385; XLII, 3 (March 1906): 148; XLIV, 5 (May 1908): 351; *Spectator*, 16 Feb. 1909; *CF* I, 5 (Oct. 1910):18.

28. *IMJ* XLIV, 6 (June 1908): 437; *LG* VIII, 9 (March 1908): 1059; ibid., 10 (April): 1201. *Industrial Banner* (hereafter *IB*), April 1909.

29. The negotiations and the ensuing strike can be traced in PAC, RG 27, vol. 296, f. 1909–3124; *LG* IX, 9 (March 1909): 936–37; ibid., 10 (April 1909): 1146; and in the daily press early in 1909, especially *Spectator*, 15, 16, 18, 19, 23–26 Feb., 1, 3, 24, 27 March; and *Herald*, 24, 26 Feb., 15, 23 March. On the length of the strike see ibid, 5 May, 5 Aug., 20 Dec. 1910; *LG* 12 (June 1910): 1372.

30. *IMJ* LV, 2 (Feb. 1919): 140; LVI, 2 (Feb. 1920): 130; LVII, 2 (Feb. 1921): 99; ibid., 3 (March 1921): 157; LIX, 2 (Feb. 1923): 96; *LN*, 30 Jan. 1923; *New Democracy* (hereafter *ND*), 5 April 1923; Frey and Commons, "Conciliation in the Stove Industry," 125.

31. On the growing interest in "systematic" business management in the late nineteenth century, see Joseph A. Litterer, "Systematic Management: The Search for Order and Integration," *Business History Review* 35 (1961): 461–76; Daniel Nelson, *Managers and Workers: Origins of the New Factory System in the United States 1880–1920* (Madison, Wisc., 1975), 48–54. Canadian business journals directed their readers' attention to various management theories and experiments in North America. In 1905 the *Canadian Engineer* began a two-year series of articles by one A.J. Lavoie on system in business operation. The outpouring from other publications included: G.C. Keith, "The General Scheme of Cost Keeping," *CM* I, 4 (April 1905): 131–32; "Systematic Works Management," ibid. I, 10 (Oct. 1905): 403; G.C. Keith, "Is Piecework a Necessity?" ibid. III, 4 (April 1907): 122–23; D.B. Swinton, "Day Work vs. Piecework," ibid. II, 12 (Dec. 1906): 453; "The Art of Handling Men," ibid. III, 9 (Sept. 1907): 27–29; "Machine Shop Time and Cost System," ibid., 32–34. Also H.C.L. Hall, "Economy in Manufacturing," *Industrial Canada*

138 CRAIG HERON

(hereafter *IC*) VI, 7 (Feb. 1906): 430–31, ibid. 11 (June 1906): 732–35; VII, 2 (Sept. 1906): 103–5; "The Model Factory," ibid. VII, 7 (Feb. 1907): 586–88; ibid., 9 (April 1907): 723–25; C.R. Stevenson, "System Applied to Factories," ibid., 5 (Dec. 1907): 420; L.E. Bowerman, "What a Cost System Will Accomplish," ibid. VIII, 10 (May 1908): 774–75; Kenneth Falconer, "Cost Finding in the Factory," ibid. VIII, 8 (March 1908): 639–40.

32. Hall, "Economy in Manufacturing," 420, 430, 732–33. The increasing use of timeclocks in Canadian factories facilitated the computation of precise labour-time. See my "Punching the Clock," *Canadian Dimension* 14 (Dec. 1979): 26–29.

33. Harry Braverman, *Labor and Monopoly Capital: The Degradation of Work in the Twentieth Century* (New York, 1974), 85–138; Bryan Palmer, "Class, Conception and Conflict: The Thrust for Efficiency, Managerial Views of Labor and the Working Class Rebellion, 1903–22," *Review of Radical Political Economics* 7 (1975): 31–49; Nelson, *Managers and Workers*, 55–78; Samuel Haber, *Efficiency and Uplift: Scientific Management in the Progressive Era, 1890–1920* (Chicago, 1964), 52–55; Heron and Palmer, "Through the Prism of the Strike," 430–34; Graham S. Lowe, "The Rise of Modern Management in Canada" *Canadian Dimension* 14 (Dec. 1979): 32–38.

34. *CM* VII, 2 (Feb. 1911): 58; *IC* XIV, 4 (Nov., 1913): 423.

35. Arthur Smith, "Methods of Solving the Problem of Foundry Help," *CF* V, 5 (May 1914): 85.

36. *Herald*, 14 Oct. 1905 (clipping in Westinghouse Canada Archives, P.J. Myler Scrapbook).

37. *CM* I, 7 (July 1905): 273.

38. On International Harvester see *Iron Age*, 1 Sept. 1904, 1–9; 8 Sept. 1904, 7–12. On Westinghouse see *CE* XI, 6 (June 1904): 154–55; *Herald*, 14 Oct. 1905; *CM* I, 10 (Oct. 1905): 383–88. On the Berlin Machine works see ibid. IV, 12 (Dec. 1908): 29–32.

39. See, for example, *CM* II, 7 (July 1906): 249–51; XXXIII, 3 (15 Jan. 1925): 17–25.

40. Frey and Commons, "Conciliation in the Stove Industry," 126; "Squire," "Stove Plate: Hints on an Important Branch of the Molding Industry," *IMJ* XXXII, 2 (Feb. 1896): 63. See also ibid. XXXVII, 4 (April 1901): 225.

41. Arthur Smith, "Methods of Solving the Problem of Foundry Help," *CF* V, 5 (May 1914): 85.

42. *Spectator*, 20 April 1904; 16, 20 April 1907; Arthur Smith, "Moulding Machine Foundry Practice," *CF* V, 8 (Aug. 1914):143; *Herald*, 8 Oct. 1910.

43. "Moulding Machines: Principles Involved in Their Operation," *CM* IV, 4 (April 1908):53.

44. Victor S. Clark, *History of Manufactures in the United States*, vol. 3, *1893–1928* (New York, 1929), 85.

45. Ontario, Factory Inspectors, *Report, 1908* (Toronto, 1909), 22; Stecker, "Founders, Molders, and Molding Machines," 438. See also Thomas F. Kennedy, "Banishing Skill from the Foundry," *International Socialist Review* XI, 8 (Feb. 1911): 469–73; and "A Molderless Foundry," ibid., 10 (April 1911):610–12.

46. "The Coming of the Molding Machine," *CE* XIII, 7 (July 1906): 265. The journal urged foundrymen to attend the annual convention of the American Foundrymen's Association to learn more about the new machinery. Among the few Canadians who did attend were Hamiltonians David Reid of Canadian Westinghouse and A.H. Tallman of Tallman Brass, *CM* III, 6 (June 1907): 36–37.

47. "Molding Machines: Principles Involved in Their Operation," *CM* IV, 4 (April 1908): 53–56; "Molding Machine Practice in a Canadian Machine Foundry," ibid. IV, 6 (June 1908): 65–66; ibid., 7 (July 1908): 46–48, 52; *IC* VIII (July 1908): 1108. *Canadian Machinery* carried numerous descriptive articles and advertisements for the machinery, as did the *Canadian Foundrymen* when it was launched in 1910.

48. "Stripping Plate Machine: Inception and Development," *CF* IX, 6 (June 1918): 123; Robert Ozanne, *A Century of Labor-Management Relations at McCormick and International Harvester* (Madison, 1967), 20–28; Cyrus McCormick, *The Century of the Reaper: An Account of Cyrus Hall McCormick, the Inventor of the Reaper; of the McCormick Harvesting Machine Company, the Business He Created; and of the International Harvester Company, his Heir and Chief Memorial* (Boston, 1931), 131–250; *Iron Age*, 1 Sept. 1904, 3. This must have been one of the first installations of moulding equipment in Canada.

49. *CM* II, 4 (April 1906): 145–46.

50. Ibid., 145–46; *LG* V, 9 (April 1905): 1047; *CE* XIII, 8 (Aug. 1906): 303. The foundry foremen's association became the subject of considerable controversy in 1906, since the moulders' journal was convinced the new organization was yet another union-crushing apparatus of the foundrymen. David Reid vigorously denied the charge, but in some North American cities it did conform to the union's expectations.

See National Founders' Association, *Review*, Feb. 1906, 17–18; *IMJ* XL, 8 (Aug. 1904):608–9; XLII, 2 (Feb. 1906), 98; ibid., 3 (March 1906):181–84; ibid., 5 (May 1906):358–60; ibid., 7 (July 1906), 505–6; ibid., 9 (Sept. 1906):670.

51. *CM* IV, 2 (Feb. 1908):58; ibid., 12 (Dec. 1908), 32; IX, 1 (2 Jan. 1913), 23, 52, 59; X, 2 (10 July 1913):41; *CF* II, 9 (Sept. 1911):18.

52. Abraham C. Mott, "Molding Machines for Stove Plates," *IMJ* XXXV, 9 (Sept. 1899):456–58; Frey and Commons, "Conciliation in the Stove Industry," 129–30.

53. "Foundry Machinery — Molding Machines, Flasks, Mills, Etc.," *CM* V, 1 (Jan. 1909):63–64; ibid., 2 (Feb. 1909):59–60. The cities which the committee visited in its investigations included Toronto.

54. *Spectator*, 23 Feb. 1909; PAC, RG 27, vol. 296, f. 3148.

55. Stecker, "Founders, Molders, and Molding Machine," 435; *CF* X, 3 (March 1919):58–59; XI, 4 (April 1920):115, XIV, 10 (Oct. 1923):30; XVIII, 5 (May 1927):6–9; ibid., 7 (July 1927):6; ibid., 10 (Oct. 1927):8–10; XIX, 5 (May 1928): 17–18, 39.

56. *CF* XVI, 8 (Aug. 1925): 9; XVII, 7 (July 1927): 6; XIV, 5 (May 1923):33–37, 40; ibid., 7 (July 1923):17; Stecker, "Founders, Molders, and Molding Machine," 455; Canada, *Census, 1911*, VI:310; *1921*, IV:402; *1931*; VII:184.

57. *IMJ* XLV, 9 (Sept. 1909), 647; Joe Davidson and John Deverell, *Joe Davidson* (Toronto, 1978), 39–40.

58. Harless D. Wagoner, *The U.S. Machine Tool Industry from 1900 to 1950* (Cambridge, Mass., 1968), 18. See also Roderick Floud, *The British Machine Tool Industry, 1850–1914* (London, 1976); Rolt, *Tools for the Job*; Nathan Rosenberg, "Technological Change in the Machine Tool Industry, 1840–1910," *Journal of Economic History* 23 (1963):414–43; *CE* VII (April 1900):321; *CM* I, 2 (Feb. 1905):53; *Canadian Manufacturer* XXX, 1 (28 Jan. 1910):84.

59. Rolt, *Tools for the Job*, 197–201; *CM* III, 1 (Jan. 1907):18–21; ibid., 2 (Feb. 1907):50–51; E.R. Norris, "Machine Shop Equipment, Methods and Processes," ibid., XVI, 15 (12 Oct. 1916):393–95.

60. *Canadian Manufacturer* XXX, 1 (28 Jan. 1910), 84.

61. Ibid. See also G.S. Keith, "Five Years' Development of Machine Tools in Canada," *CM* VI, 1 (Jan. 1910):27–32.

62. Ibid. VI, 3 (March 1910):51.

63. *Herald*, 14 Oct. 1905. The novelty of automatics was also evident in an amusing short story published in *Canadian Machinery* in 1908, in which a machine-shop apprentice had a nightmare about having to operate one of "them new-fangled autermatic marchines." See "Onlooker," "Tommy Fairfield's Experience With an Automatic Machine," *CM* 3 (March 1908):42–43.

64. "Developments in Machine Shop Practice During a Decade," *CM* IX, 10 (20 March 1913):282; *LG* I, 9 (March 1901):356–57; *MMJ* XX, 4 (April 1908):319.

65. "A Post-War Problem of Labor," *CM* XVII, 15 (12 April 1917):381; Rodgers, "Evolution and Revolution," 677–82; "Tendency in Machine Tool Development," *CM* XVIII, 23 (6 Dec. 1917):630; J.H. Rodgers, "There Should Be No Post-War Slump in Machine Tools," ibid. XX, 7 (22 Aug. 1918):240–41; Rodgers, "More Efficient Methods Follow War Work," ibid., 26 (26 Dec. 1918):750–53. Throughout the war *Canadian Machinery* provided extensive reports and commentary on developments in munitions plants. Censorship regulations, however, prevented the journal from identifying the location of companies under discussion.

66. Mark H. Irish, " 'Dilution' of Labor in Canadian Munition Plants," *CM* XVI, 26 (28 Dec. 1916):717–19; *LN*, 12, 19 Jan. 23, 26 Feb. 1917; *LG* XVII, 2 (Feb. 1917):97; *Herald*, 30 Nov. 1916.

67. Rodgers, "Evolution and Revolution," 680.

68. "Developing Present Help," *CM* XVI, 14 (5 Oct. 1916):372; "Machines and the New Mechanic," ibid., 19 (9 Nov. 1916):496; XX, 26 (26 Dec. 1918):751.

69. L.D. Burlingame, "Lathe and Screw Machine Automatic Control," ibid. XV, 8 (24 Feb. 1916):171–75; "The Pre-eminence of the Toolmaker's Craft," ibid. XVIII, 15 (11 Oct. 1917), 422.

70. "Multi-Machine Operation," *CM* XIX, 2 (10 Jan. 1918):64.

71. The IAM president claimed in 1895 that "it has become an established system in nearly every section under the jurisdiction of our order. . . ." *IAM Proceedings* (1895).

72. *Herald*, 19–20 Feb. 1913; PAC, RG 27, vol. 301, f.13(11); f.13(15).

73. *MMJ* XXV, 6 (June 1913): 588.

74. *MMJ* XXVII, 9 (Sept. 1915):840; *Spectator*, 4 May 1916.

75. *CM* XIV, 17 (21 Oct. 1915):384; D.A. Hampson, "Machine Shop Adaptation to Labor Shortage," ibid. XVI, 9 (31 Aug. 1916):225–26; J.H. Rodgers, "Evolution and Revolution in Machine Shop Practice," ibid. XVII, 26 (28 June 1917):679.

76. G.L Sprague, "Interest in Your Work an Absolute Necessity," *CM* XXV, 2 (13 Jan. 1921):39. See also T. Daley, "Machinists Should Be Given a Variety of Work," *CM* XXIV, 19 (4 Nov. 1920):427. Daley was works engineer at International Harvester.

77. *IMJ* XXXIII, 5 (May 1897):222.

78. *MMJ* IX, 3 (March 1897):218; XX, 9 (Sept. 1908):808. The Winnipeg machinists' *Bulletin* lamented that "Overtime and piece work are twin devices by which individual greed is used to degrade the mass" (IV, 2 (Feb. 1915):1).

79. Perlman, *Machinists*, 29; *MMJ* XXI, 9 (Sept. 1909):928.

80. *LN*, 1 March 1912.

81. *Herald*, 18 March 1910; Canada, Department of Labour, *Labour Organization in Canada, 1919* (Ottawa, 1920), 57.

82. See Canada, National Industrial Conference . . . , *Official Report of Proceedings and Discussions . . .* (Ottawa, 1919).

83. *CF* XII, 3 (March 1921):41.

84. *LG* XI, 11 (May 1911):1355; XII, 12 (June 1912): 1175–76; *Herald*, 18 April, 9 May 1912; *LN* 10 May 1912; *IMJ* XLVIII, 6 (June 1912):45; PAC, RG 27, vol. 299, f. 3492.

85. *IMJ* XLIX, 4 (April 1913):315; *LG* XIII, 10 (April 1913):1060, 1139; XIV, 1 (July 1913):87, 91; ibid., 3 (Sept. 1913):355; Hamilton Trades and Labour Council, Minutes, 18 April 1913, 257, 261; 2 May 1913, 263, 267; 16 May 1913, 274–75; 6 June 1913, 280; PAC, RG 27, vol. 301, f. 13(27); *Herald*, 31 Jan., 17 Feb., 26 March, 11, 21, 22–26 April, 5 June 1913.

86. *IMJ* LII, 4 (April 1916): 343; ibid., 6 (June 1916): 466; *LN*, 8 Sept., 8, 29 Dec. 1916; 12 Jan., 18 May 1917.

87. *LG* XVIII, 12 (June 1918):408; PAC, RG 27, vol. 303, f. 18(80); *LN*, 3, 10 May 1918; *Herald*, 3, 6 May; 1 June 1918; *IMJ* LIV, 6 (June 1918):448; ibid., 7 (July 1918):542.

88. PAC, RG 27, vol. 312, f. 19(104); *LN*, 9, 16 May; 20 June; 8 Aug.; 12 Sept.; 7 Nov.; 25 Dec. 1919; 13 Feb.; 7 May; 5 June 1920; 29 July 1921; *ND*, 14 Jan. 1920; *CF* XI, 1 (Jan. 1920):28; *Herald*, 29–30 April; 3, 6–8, 12 May 1919; 17–18 Feb. 1920; *Spectator*, 28 May 1919; PAC, MG 28, I, 230, vol. 17, f. 1918–19, 11 April 1919.

89. PAC, RG 27, vol. 334, f. 25(10).

90. Canada, Department of Labour, *Report on Organization in Industry, Commerce, and the Professions in Canada* (Ottawa, 1923). For Burgess' attacks see, for example, *CF* XIV, 6 (June 1923):32–34; *MMJ* XXXVII, 1 (Jan. 1925):25; *Canadian Congress Journal* III, 12 (Dec. 1924):37.

91. *CF* XII, 1 (Jan. 1921):37.

92. *MMJ* XVI, 3 (March 1904):226; ibid., 7 (July 1904):603–4; *Spectator*, 27, 30 May; 3, 10, 14 June; 3, 12, 15 Aug. 1904; *LG* IV, 12 (June 1904):1209; V, 1 (July 1904):84; ibid., 3 (Sept. 1904):240, 294.

93. *MMJ* XXII, 3 (March 1910):244; ibid., 5 (May 1910):441; XXIII, 3 (March 1911):230; XXIX, 2 (Feb. 1917):158; *IB*, April 1911.

94. *IB*, April 11; *MMJ* XXIV, 2 (Feb. 1912):140, 150; ibid., 3 (March 1912):225, 247; ibid., 4 (April 1912):324, 256; ibid., 5 (May 1912):442, 449; ibid., 6 (June 1912):518; ibid., 7 (July 1912):634; ibid., 8 (Aug. 1912):730; ibid., 12 (Dec. 1912):1125; XXV, 3 (March 1913):254; *LN*, 2, 9 Feb., 8 March, 19 April 1912; *Herald*, 23 March 1912.

95. *MMJ* XXV, 6 (June 1913): 588; ibid., 9 (Sept. 1913):910. By Sept. 1914 well over half of Hamilton's machinists were out of work. *LN*, 4 Sept. 1914.

96. *CM* XIII, 13 (18 March 1915):227; Hamilton *Times*, 18 March, 28 June 1915; *MMJ* XXVII, 5 (May 1915):448; ibid., 11 (Nov. 1915):1021.

97. *MMJ* XXVII, 5 (May 1915):448; ibid., 9 (Sept. 1915):840; *LN*, 26 March 1915.

98. *MMJ* XXVII, 9 (Sept. 1915):840.

99. *Herald*, 3, 4 May 1916; Rodgers, "Evolution and Revolution," 680; see also "Man-Power Demands and the Supply," *CM* XIX, 17 (25 April 1918):436; *Spectator*, 22 May 1916; *CM* XXIV, 19 (4 Nov. 1920), 427.

100. Nationally the machinists' leaders worked with the Executive of the Trades and Labour Congress of Canada to pressure the Borden government into guaranteeing a fair wage clause in munitions contracts. See D.J. Bercuson, "Organized Labour and the Imperial Munitions Board," *Relations industrielles* 28 (1973):602–16; Peter Edward Rider, "The Imperial Munitions Board and its Relationship to Government, Business, and Labour" (Ph.D. thesis, University of Toronto, 1974), ch. 9; Myer Siemiatycki, "Munitions and Labour Militancy: The 1916 Hamilton Machinists' Strike," *Labour/Le Travailleur* 3 (1978):134–37.

101. *LN*, 7 April 1916; 28 Jan. 1916.

102. PAC, MG 28, I, 230, vol. 17, f. 1915–16, 5 April 1916.

103. *Spectator*, 2, 4–5 May 1916; *Herald*, 3–5 May 1916.

104. Ibid., 5 May 1916.

105. PAC, MG 30, A, Ib, vol. 2, f. 11 (Department of Labour, 1916). The report was printed in *LG* XVI, 12 (June 1916): 1295–97.

106. *Times*, 10 June 1916; *Spectator*, 9, 12 June 1916.

107. For a thorough discussion of the evolution of the strike and its demise see Siemiatycki, "Munitions and Labour Militancy," 137–51. A similar, though less dramatic strike was waged that spring against the Toronto, Hamilton, and Buffalo Railway by the machinists, boilermakers, blacksmiths, and carmen in a short-lived system federation. It was equally unsuccessful and destroyed the federation. See PAC, RG 27, vol. 557, f. 1916–49B.

108. *Times*, 12 June 1916.

109. *LN*, 11 May 1917; 27 March 1918; *MMJ* XXIX, 4 (April 1917):438.

110. *Herald*, 30 April 1919; *LN*, 23 May 1919; Canada, Royal Commission on Industrial Relations, "Evidence" (typescript at Department of Labour Library), III:2267. A new schedule from the local machinists' union submitted to Hamilton employers in the spring of 1919 was completely ignored. Ibid., 2265.

111. *MMJ* XXXIX, 3 (March 1927):169; XL, 5 (May 1928):301.

112. PAC, RG 27, vol. 301, f. 13(27). This dispute involved only 38 machine tenders out of 276 strikers. The union was attempting to establish a minimum wage of $2.50 per day for these workers, compared with $3.25 for skilled moulders. Westinghouse Canada Archives, F.A. Merrick, "Report on Plant and Operation Year 1912" (typescript), 9–10.

113. Royal Commission on Industrial Relations, "Evidence," 2278; *MMJ* XXXI, 1 (Jan. 1919), 58; ibid., 12 (Dec. 1919), 1127.

114. Perlman, *Machinists*, 39–56; John H.M. Laslett, *Labor and the Left: A Study of Socialist and Radical Influences in the American Labor Movement, 1881–1924* (New York, 1970), 144–79.

115. *Herald*, 16 April 1910; Canada, Department of Labour, *Labour Organization in Canada*, 1911–14, 1919–20; *ND*, 14, 28 Jan., 5 Feb. 1920; *LN*, 22 Jan., 13 Feb., 5 March, 20 Aug. 1920.

116. Albert Theodore Helbing, *The Departments of the American Federation of Labor* (Baltimore, 1931), 48–51; Stockton, *International Molders' Union*, 112–13; Bruno Ramirez, "Collective Bargaining and the Politics of Industrial Relations, 1896–1916" (Ph.D. thesis, University of Toronto, 1975), 197–99.

117. *IMJ* LI, 7 (July 1915):517.

118. *LN*, 2 May 1919.

119. Ibid., 1 March; 12, 19 April; 5 July 1918; *Labour Organizations in Canada*, 1919, 35. The amalgamation idea was revived under left-wing sponsorship again in 1923. *LN*, 28 Aug. 1923.

120. Ibid., 23 May 1919.

121. PAC, RG 27, vol. 301, f. 13(15); *Herald*, 26 Feb. 1913. This question of ethnicity will be discussed further in my forthcoming thesis on Hamilton workers between 1895 and 1930.

122. *LN*, 25 Sept. 1914. See also Crossick, "Labour Aristocracy," 317–18.

123. *Herald*, 4 May 1916.

124. *IMJ* XLVIII, 9 (Sept. 1912):733–34; *MMJ* XXV, 6 (June 1913):588; XXXII, 11 (Nov. 1920):1014. One writer in the business press compared the cost of living and wages in Hamilton and Birmingham, England, and concluded that Hamilton workers were much better off. W.A. Craik, "British and Canadian Workmen," *IC* XII, 9 (April 1912):1054–55.

125. IAM *Bulletin* V, 1 (Jan. 1916):2.

126. David Brody, *Steelworkers in America: The Nonunion Era* (New York, 1960).

127. *CF* XIX, 5 (May 1928):39

128. Of course, while formal trade union controls disappeared, we should not ignore informal techniques that workers used to regulate the pace of work in North American industry for years to come. See Stanley B. Mathewson, *Restriction of Output Among Unorganized Workers* (New York, 1931); Donald Roy, "Quota Restriction and Goldbricking in a Machine Shop," *American Journal of Sociology* 57 (March 1952):427–42; Bill Watson, "Counter-Planning on the Shop Floor," *Radical America* 5 (May–June 1971):77–85.

129. Hinton, *First Shop Stewards' Movement*, 337. The evidence presented in this paper, therefore, suggests that a wholesale application of David Montgomery's influential conceptualization of American working-class history in this period would be unwise, at least in the southern Ontario context. While his emphasis on struggles for control in the workplace is crucial for an understanding of craftsmen's activity, his suggestion that the workplace struggles of the skilled and unskilled tended to fuse during and after World War I is not sustained by the behaviour of Hamilton workers during these years. See David Montgomery, "The 'New Unionism' and the Transformation of Workers' Consciousness in America, 1902–22," *Journal of Social History* VII (1973):519–20.

130. Gray, "Styles of Life"; Crossick, "Labour Aristocracy." For a discussion of the usefulness of a labour-artistocracy theory in a Canadian context, see Ian McKay, "Capital and Labour in the Halifax Baking and Confectionery Industry."

THE WOMEN ONTARIO WELCOMED: IMMIGRANT DOMESTICS FOR ONTARIO HOMES, 1870–1930†

MARILYN BARBER

"Female Domestics Wanted for Ontario, Canada: Situations Guaranteed at Good Wages." Such was the message of an Ontario advertising poster used in Britain in the 1920s, but the appeal was an old one, unchanged from the 1870s. Throughout the period from 1870 to 1930, domestic servants were actively recruited for Ontario by both the federal and the provincial government. Domestics were the only unaccompanied female immigrants so solicited and they were treated as preferred immigrants along with farm families and single male farm labourers. The number of women who responded to the appeal and came specifically to the province of Ontario cannot be accurately tabulated. However, between Confederation and the depression of the 1930s, over 250 000 women immigrated to Canada stating their intended occupation as domestic service. For those from the British Isles, Ontario was the favoured destination although Montreal and the western provinces also attracted many. In addition, in the 1920s, Ontario began to receive an increasing number of women from continental Europe. Domestic service played a vital role in enabling single women to immigrate to Ontario and to begin life in a new country. And, conversely, immigrant domestics formed a significant proportion of the women working in Ontario homes and helped shape the character of domestic service in the province.

The servant girl problem, as it was called in the periodicals and newspapers of the day, was a dominant concern of many Ontario women because the province suffered from a chronic shortage of domestic servants. Servants were employed not simply by the rich, but also by the wives of professional and small business men in towns and villages as well as cities. In addition, there was a strong unsatisfied demand for household help on the farms of the province. The majority of domestics in Ontario, therefore, were not engaged in homes with a large staff of the Upstairs-Downstairs variety, but rather worked in one-servant households as generals or cook-generals.

†*Ontario History* 72 (1980): 148–73.

In part, servants were employed as a symbol of status. A *lady* did not do her own work, or at least not all of it. If she could not afford the luxury of complete leisure from household duties, employing a servant to assist her maintained her standing in the community. Attitudes were changing regarding the social accept-ability of doing one's own work, but slowly. In 1878, a columnist in *The Farmer's Advocate*, published in London, Ontario, commented:

> Does Her Own Work. Does she? What of it? Is it a disgrace to her? Is she less a true woman, less worthy of respect than she who sits in silk and satin and is vain of fingers who never knew labor? . . . In matter of fact, is it more dishonorable for the merchant's wife to do her own work than for the merchant to do his? For her to look after her house than for him to look after his store?[1]

The very protest, however, showed that contrary ideas persisted. Indeed, almost thirty years later, the president of the Ontario Women's Institutes, was still emphasizing the recent acceptance of doing one's own work. In her words:

> Of late years, since domestic help has been so hard to procure, and wages have advanced so rapidly, many housewives have been compelled to do all their own work, and when one would enquire of a friend as to how she was getting along, she would perhaps acknowledge with reluctance that she was doing "all her own work," and in a tone that would indicate that she was owning up to poverty or something of the kind. But now a lady will announce with pride to her friends, without even being asked, "I am doing all my own work," and we never give the condition or circumstances a second thought.[2]

Many women, however, had to give the circumstances a second thought, because they desperately needed help simply to accomplish their work. Without electricity or many labour-saving devices, household work was both strenuous and time-consuming. A servant could greatly ease the burden of laundry day with its tubs of boiling water to be heated early and tended by hand, of ironing day with the heavy flat irons, and of cleaning, baking, and cooking. Especially was a servant a necessity rather than a luxury in homes with a young family where the wife might well be expecting another child, or in farm homes where the wife helped with outside chores — the dairy, the poultry, and the garden — in addition to coping with her inside housework. Modernization and improved technology, which came earlier to city homes than to rural districts, eased somewhat the burden of woman's work within the home, but do not seem to have significantly reduced the demand for domestic servants. As a countervailing influence, the growth in affluence of the middle class, which accompanied industrialization, meant that more families could readily afford to hire domestic help. In addition, any decrease in the burden of housework was offset by the increasing activity of women in affairs outside the home, often through the churches or organizations such as the W.C.T.U., the Local Councils of Women, or the farm women's associations. Women were told that it was their responsibility to be concerned with issues such as prohibition, child welfare, or farm co-operation, and that they must organize their work to allow themselves time for these activities. Therefore, the demand for domestic servants, whether as a status symbol or as essential assistance, constantly exceeded the supply in Ontario, as in the rest of the country, throughout the period from 1870 to 1930.

The servant girl problem existed because women in Canada entering the labour force shunned domestic service if possible. Thus, while the proportion of women in the paid labour force relative to the female population increased in the twentieth century, the percentage of the female labour force in domestic servce decreased. In 1891, approximately 40 percent of working women in Canada were domestic servants, but the number declined to less than 20 percent after World War I, and had only increased slightly at the time of the 1931 census. In Ontario, the proportion of the female labour force in domestic service was similar to, but slightly lower than the national average, probably because of the greater opportunities for women in Ontario in other occupations.[3] Unfortunately, the division between live-in and live-out or daily domestics is not revealed in the census statistics. In the United States, domestic service in the early twentieth century was in the process of changing from predominantly live-in to predominantly live-out work. By the 1920s, live-in service was dying out and the modern system of day work had become entrenched.[4] The same trend was taking place in Canada, but at a slower pace, because Canada did not have the black married domestics who were the first and most substantial basis of live-out domestic service of the United States. In Canada, to the end of the 1920s, live-in domestic service was still very important, but it was definitely not popular with Canadian women seeking work.

Objections to domestic service centred on the lack of freedom, the isolation or loneliness, and the low status of the occupation. Canadian women prefered clerical, shop, or factory work, even at lower net wages than domestic work, because of the greater freedom and independence. They had every evening off instead of one or two a week, and, as their home environment was separate from their work environment, they were not always under the direct supervision and authority of their employer. Young women working outside the home also had more opportunity of making social contact with others of their own age, whereas those in domestic service complained of being ostracized as "only a servant" by other young people on the rare opportunities when they were free for social activities. Employers were aware of the problem and throughout the period discussed means of elevating the status of housework, but with little success. In 1900 *The Farmer's Advocate* accurately described "The Problem of Domestic Service":

> From one side comes the cry of the worried and harrassed housekeeper: "Where, and oh! where are our household helpers gone?" And from the other side comes the reply: "To the factories and to the stores, where, if our positions are not always of certain tenure, and our salaries leave something to be desired by way of margin after our board bills are paid, yet oh! glorious privilege, we are, after business hours, our own mistresses, and we can go to the theatres and band concerts, to big balls and little 'hops,' with Jack to-day and Tom tomorrow, and who shall say us 'nay.' "[5]

The Advocate believed that the problem soon would be solved because:

The trend of present-day teaching being to elevate domestic service and to remove from it the old mistaken idea that it is a step lower in the social scale than employment on other lines — a mistake which is at the bottom of nearly all the trouble — we can afford to leave the future to take care of itself.[6]

The introduction of domestic science in Ontario elementary schools at the turn of the century, the development of the Macdonald Institute at Guelph for the professional teaching of domestic science, and the recommendations of the Royal Commission on Industrial Training and Technical Education in 1913 that women be trained for housework all were intended to elevate the status of household work in the province. Ontario women, however, remained unconvinced by the argument that household work was the best preparation for their ultimate careers as wives and mothers. The attempted change in terminology in the 1920s from "domestic servants" or "maids" to "houseworkers" or "household workers" also failed to change the common view of the occupation. In 1928, an article in *Chatelaine*, titled "What's the Matter with Housework?" continued to point to the lower social status of housework. At the end of the 1920s, as at the turn of the century, the reply to the question why young people did not respect housework as much as other occupations remained:

Simply because of the old feudal conditions generally attached to it — because the worker's life and time is not her own. To them she is not an adult of free will, to live as they do and share their recreations and social life. She is to them a chattel, a shut-in.[7]

Because Canadian women did not enter domestic service in sufficient numbers, employers and governments turned to immigration to find the solution to the servant girl problem. All those influential in the formation of immigration policy agreed that the immigration of domestic servants should be actively encouraged. As one Member of Parliament commented, nothing else he could do pleased his constituents as much as obtaining maids for their wives.[8] Cabinet ministers, leading members of the civil service including those in the Immigration Branch, important business men, and socially prominent women had a personal as well as a community interest in the importation of domestic servants. From an 1898 party of Scottish domestic servants specially selected for western Canada, one was left in Montreal for Sydney Fisher, Minister of Agriculture, and two were left in Ottawa for Clifford Sifton, Minister of the Interior, and James Smart, Deputy Minister of the Interior. Similarly, the resources of the Immigration Branch were used to secure Scottish servants for Mackenzie King's mother in Toronto; Mr. Harvey, manager of the Bank of British North America in Ottawa; Dr. King, director and chief astronomer of the Dominion Observatory; Mr. White, inspector of U.S. agencies for the Immigration Branch; and many others.[9] Against this interest in procuring domestic servants, there was no opposition. The demand was so great there was little danger that the market might be flooded. In addition, Canadian domestic servants were unorganized, had no union to represent their interests or to protest that large-scale immigration might lower the wages of native workers. Hence, female domestic servants joined farmers and farm labourers as the only class of immigrant which the government openly and actively recruited throughout the period.

Since immigration is a joint responsibility of the Dominion and the provinces under section 95 of the B.N.A. Act, the Ontario government as well as the federal government worked to promote the immigration of domestic servants. From 1874 to 1899, Ontario maintained a separate Department of Immigration whose work was then taken over in the twentieth century by the Bureau of Colonization and the Department of Agriculture. In its recruitment efforts throughout the period, the Ontario government concentrated on the British Isles, as British domestic servants were preferred. Ontario agents were stationed in Britain to advertise the advantages of the province, and at the port of Quebec to oversee the forwarding of immigrants for Ontario and to protect Ontario parties against the raids of Quebec agents.[10] While the Dominion government for much of the nineteenth century offered special low fares to domestic servants to attract them to Canada, Ontario gave its own additional bonus to domestics to entice them to make Ontario their Canadian destination.[11] Immigrant domestics coming to Ontario were placed in employment by government immigration agents at Ottawa, Kingston, Toronto, Hamilton, and London. The supply was never equal to the demand, and, year after year, agents reported that applications could not be filled. In particular, it was difficult to persuade servants to accept situations in rural districts or to travel west of Toronto. For example, the unequal regional distribution is shown by statistics for 1882 when the Ontario agent at Quebec sent 1087 domestics to Toronto, 404 to places east of Toronto, but only 75 to the region west of Toronto, including Hamilton, London, and Stratford.[12]

The competition for immigrant domestics was strong. Most prospective employers visited the district immigration offices — the Toronto agent reported in 1887 that as many as thirty a day called at the office and had to go away disappointed[13] — or wrote letters of varying degrees of literacy to the Toronto headquarters. They specified their requirements or preferences, and the inducements which they offered. A women near Chatsworth wrote:

> I want a girl Scotch or Irish Protestant if you have one must be able to milk and wash and shall have a good home and as high wages as are going in this part of the country.[14]

A farmer near Armow was even more detailed in his instructions:

> I am a farmer and want a girl to help do house work and cook. I want a good strong healthy good looking English speaking girl to such a girl I would give good wages steady employment and a good home.[15]

However, the Rev. W.J. Smith at Uxbridge was prepared to be flexible, within certain limits, if necessary:

> I would be glad if you could [send] me a servant girl from among the Immigrants. One about 16 or 17 would suit us — but it would not matter about the age if we got a good trusty girl. If such could not be got a trusty and respectable old lady would do us.[16]

Some, however, were not content with the official channels of application. In order to prevent girls being spirited off the immigrant train before they reached their destination, the department arranged with the Grand Trunk Railway in 1884 that the baggage of assisted immigrants was not to be given up except at the station to which it was checked.[17] The Ontario agent at Quebec carried the supervision of assisted domestics even further on at least one occasion. In his words:

> I have some difficulty occasionally keeping girls from sailors and cattle men as an instance by last mail steamer, were three pretty girls with their mother — after giving them passes (3) for Toronto I had occasion to go over to the hotel at noon and to my astonishment, I saw these same girls drinking beer with two sailors. I waited for nearly an hour and counted 8 glasses of beer. Barkeeper stated they had in all 12 glasses each. I lost patience and had the two sailors locked up and took the passes from the three girls who bought their own tickets to Montreal.[18]

Concern for women travelling unaccompanied, together with the problems of women in both Britain and Canada, led women's organizations on both sides of the Atlantic to join the government in promoting female immigration. The most important of these organizations was not Canadian but British, the British Women's Emigration Association, formed in 1884. The founders of the B.W.E.A. wished to solve the problems of surplus or unemployed British women in the context of Imperial development. The imbalance of the sexes in both Britain and the colonies — too many women in Britain, not enough women in the colonies — might be solved by encouraging more women to emigrate. In addition, the Association emphasized careful selection of the women to be sponsored for "the requirements of the Empire must come before the needs of the individual," and "only the best were good enough to carry on overseas the finest of British traditions."[19] With these principles, Canadian women would heartily agree. British and Canadian interests, however, were not so easily reconciled when it came to deciding more specifically which women should be encouraged to move across the Atlantic. Good experienced domestic servants were scarce in the British Isles too, as was noted by Ontario immigration agents as early as 1868.[20] The class of female immigrant which Canadian women's organizations most wanted to attract, therefore, was the class which British women definitely did not want to see depart. The B.W.E.A. was quite willing to encourage British women to take work in Canadian homes, provided the prospective emigrants were not already in domestic service in Britain. Hence, when the B.W.E.A. established a loan fund to assist women with passage fares, loans were not granted to British domestic servants, but only to factory workers who would agree to enter domestic service in Canada. Similarly, the Association made loans available to educated gentlewomen who wished to emigrate to Canada as home-helps. In addition, the B.W.E.A. advised British women that Canada offered a wide range of employment possibilities for women. The Association co-operated with factory owners in Canada who wanted to obtain female workers for their mills, and also sponsored educated women seeking opportunities in Canada in teaching, nursing, or secretarial work. However, the majority of women who emigrated with the Association's parties were destined to domestic service, and many had already been in service in Britain.[21]

The British Women's Emigration Association insisted on careful protection for the women whom it sponsored, sending them overseas in escorted parties. The Association provided hostels for the initial assembly of its parties at London and Liverpool, and employed matrons to supervise the journey. In addition, parties were sent only to Canadian centres where satisfactory reception and placement arrangements had been made by local correspondents. The B.W.E.A. first sent the majority of their immigrants to Montreal, where a hostel had been begun in 1881, and later included Winnipeg, when Octavia Fowler founded the Girls' Home of Welcome there in 1896. Toronto ladies were anxious to receive domestics from the Association, and the B.W.E.A. equally wished to send women to Toronto. Consequently, Agnes FitzGibbon, a committed Imperialist and president of the Toronto Local Council of Women, became, in her words, the "instrument through the use of which the work has been done."[22] While in England in 1902 for the Coronation, FitzGibbon became actively interested in women's immigration, writing on the topic. At the request of Lady Aberdeen, she addressed an Edinburgh meeting of the National Union of Women Workers of Great Britain and Ireland, and she was urged to become a correspondent of the B.W.E.A. Upon her return to Toronto, FitzGibbon organized a small committee of the Local Council of Women to meet and place B.W.E.A. parties, but, in effect, did nearly all the work herself. Because of the difficulty of procuring suitable temporary quarters for housing the women, FitzGibbon again took the lead in insisting that the work could not continue unless a Receiving Home be established. Largely as a result of her initiative and pressure, the Women's Welcome Hostel was opened in 1905 at 66 Wellesley Street, where it remained until larger quarters were secured in 1911 at 52 St. Alban's Street.[23] Agnes FitzGibbon's contacts with influential Torontonians assisted her greatly in her work. She was well known in Toronto circles, not only as the president of the Local Council of Women and founder of the Women's Canadian Historical Society of Toronto, but also as a popular writer descended from the Strickland family. She was the granddaughter of Susanna Moodie, an English immigrant of the 1830s, who in her best known book, *Roughing It in the Bush*, made some rather acerbic remarks about the character of domestic servants in Upper Canada. Her grandmother undoubtedly would have been interested in the work which Agnes FitzGibbon directed as secretary-manager of the Women's Welcome Hostel until her death in 1915.[24]

Begun with a provincial government grant and private subscription, the Toronto Hostel offered 24 hours' free board and lodging to immigrant domestics so that they might have a chance to rest — one day — before being sent to work. Because the Hostel was supported by a provincial grant, a deliberate effort was made to distribute the maids around the province. After 1907, the Hostel also received a federal grant in recognition of the national importance of its work with immigrant women. The Hostel kept complete records of the women it received, collected loans, and corresponded with both prospective immigrants and employers.[25] In the 1906 Hostel report, FitzGibbon noted that:

A book with a full entry of the history of the immigration is kept, giving name, nationality, age, calling, religion, date of arrival, destination, name and address of employer, wages received, whether the immigrant has received a loan and the amount returned by her from time to time. Many of these girls are only enabled to emigrate because of loans made them by organizations in Great Britain and these loans are repaid by the girls through our agency.[26]

Such records, unfortunately, do not seem to have survived. The largest parties at the Hostel came from the British Women's Emigration Association, but women sent by other agencies, including booking agents in the British Isles, were also received. In addition to being a control agency, the Hostel was intended as a social centre where domestics could come during their afternoons off or between placements. For many immigrant domestics the Hostel thus served as a home away from home and it received high praise from the chairman of the British Emigrants' Information Office when he visited Canada in 1909. In his view:

The hostel is most comfortable and evidently well managed and appears to be conducted on the most highly commendable lines. Miss FitzGibbon herself is a lady of great force of intellect and of high character.[27]

While the British Women's Emigration Association and its Canadian associates, the Local Councils of Women and the Y.W.C.A., emphasized care in the selection and placement of domestics, all agencies were not so scrupulous. Because many prospective immigrant domestics could not afford the expense of the journey to Canada, a number of practices developed to overcome the difficulty. Sometimes the Canadian employer advanced the fare to an agent and then deducted a set amount monthly from the servant's wages until the advance had been repaid. More frequently, the fare was advanced by one of the numerous societies or agencies which sprang up to deal with the trade in female domestic servants. The system was unorganized, chaotic, and open to abuse by both the immigrants and the agencies. Servants left their employers before repaying their passage advance, and employers found themselves not only out of pocket but also with no servant. Few employers were able to follow the example of Peter Bryce, chief medical inspector of the Department of the Interior, who tracked down his servant when she left after five days, and, as she seemed "utterly callous as to her responsibility to the extent of £5.7.9" brought her before a police magistrate to ensure that the money would be repaid.[28] On the other hand, some agencies were in the business solely for the object of gain as it was possible in the immediate pre-war period to earn a bonus of $5 from the federal government, a similar bonus from the Ontario government, a $2 commission from the federal government for placing the domestic, a sum from the immigrant herself for the advance of passage money, and a fee from the employer for providing her with a servant. Agencies primarily interested in financial rewards wanted to bring as many domestics as possible and gave little attention to either careful selection overseas or proper placement in Canada.[29] The situation before the First World War thus often exacerbated the difficulty of reconciling the personality and interests of the newly arrived domestics and the Canadian employers.

The First World War essentially cut off overseas immigration to Canada and gave the government a chance to assess old policies and work out new policies. In 1914 and 1915, as a result of the recession and unemployment, the demand for domestic servants was at a low ebb in Canada. In Ontario, it was reported that while there was still a need for domestics in the rural areas, there were women idle in the cities who were willing to take domestic work.[30] Therefore, for the first time, the immigration of domestic servants was not encouraged. The government withdrew the bonus for domestic servants from Canadian agencies, and paid it to British booking agents only on experienced domestics who could show by references that they had been at least one year in service.[31] As the war brought full employment, the demand soon fully revived. Canadian women, like British women, left domestic service to take up war work, and new recruits were not available. However, immigration could not be revived because the British government in 1917 forbade, for the duration of the war, the departure of women capable of war work.[32] The war, accompanied by a reform sentiment that a new and better society must emerge in Canada to justify the war, thus gave both the opportunity and the impetus for change in women's immigration.

At the end of the war, the Canadian government expected and prepared for a sudden mass influx of pent-up British immigrants. The most immediate concern was to protect the country against undesirable immigrants. The Women's Advisory Committee of the Repatriation Committee, formed to look after the interests of returning soldiers and their dependants, feared that women of questionable character would come to Canada following the soldiers.[33] Even leaving aside the question of female army followers, reformers and social workers believed that much more care needed to be taken in the selection of domestic servants in order to safeguard Canadian society from mental and moral misfits, especially of the factory worker class. Helen Reid, a member of the Repatriation Committee and the Dominion Council of Health, wrote:

> stricter measures must be taken to encourage the admission of the best class of household worker and to prevent the entry of unqualified women from British mill and factory, who, in addition to their lack of training for domestic service, bring with them only too often, serious mental and moral disabilities. These women either glut the labour market here, reducing the wages of working men, or end up, alas! too frequently, in our jails, hospitals and asylums.[34]

The anticipated influx, however, did not occur, in spite of the free ocean passages offered by the British government to ex-service men and women. Attention in Canada, therefore, soon was forced to focus, not on careful selection from large numbers available, but on the increasing more difficult task of combining careful selection with the need to attract scarce domestic servants. The shortage of domestic servants in Britain in the 1920s was even more acute than in the pre-war years. As reported to the Canadian government:

> 400,000 women left domestic service during the war. Girls of 14, who in ordinary times would have started in as scullery maids, started clerical and other work at 30s a week, and having tasted blood, as it were, refused to enter housework.[35]

At the same time, Canada had to continue to compete for British domestic servants with other Dominions, especially Australia, which offered free passages.

To promote more effective recruiting, as well as to ensure both careful selection and protection of immigrant domestic servants, a new and much more extensive government organization dealing with women's immigration developed. The Women's Division of the Immigration Department resulted from the belief that the immigration of women was best supervised by women.[36] In the 1920s, it expanded to include not only a permanent supervisor in Ottawa, but also a staff of women officers in both the United Kingdom and Canada. The Women's Branch undertook the control and supervision of British domestics from the point of initial investigation in the British Isles to the provision of follow-up services after placement in Canada. A British woman who wished to come to Canada to engage in domestic service, first was interviewed by a Canadian woman officer, and, in addition, had to pass a medical examination. The medical examination was a source of controversy, because not only was the giving of a medical exam overseas a new procedure, but also it was initially required only for unaccompanied women. By the end of the 1920s, the examination overseas was made compulsory for all immigrants, replacing the examination at Canadian ports, and eliminating the expense and heartache of rejection after a long ocean journey. In the early 1920s, however, the implementation in Britain of a medical examination only for unaccompanied women seemed to discriminate against those women as much as it favoured them. The implication seemed clear that not only were women with medical problems, or those assisting them, to be spared the expense of the ocean journey, but also that the medical examination could be used to ensure more careful selection of unaccompanied women than of other groups. The latter concern is evident in a 1920 memorandum from the supervisor of the Women's Division, who wished to have included the question, "Has the applicant ever suffered from a loathsome disease," noting that "undoubtedly this latter question, although the most important to us, will raise considerable question in England."[37] The applicant who successfully passed the medical exam and the interview was issued a sailing permit and came to Canada in a conducted party, supervised on board ship by a woman conductress appointed by the shipping company, and on the train journey by a travelling conductress of the Immigration Department. Her destination most often was one of a chain of Canadian Women's Hostels established across the country to receive immigrant domestics. The Women's Welcome Hostel at Toronto, taken over by the government in the 1920s, provided the Ontario link in the chain, and women taken there were placed in situations by the women's branch of the government employment service, another development of the 1920s. Toronto was fortunate in having a very competent woman, Jessie Duff, at the head of its women's employment service, and thus avoided some of the problems which arose elsewhere in the country.

The establishment of such a government network for the selection and placement of British domestics reflected both the more restrictive immigration practices of the 1920s and the increasing involvement of government in social services in co-operation with voluntary agencies. In part, the protection seems to have been an outgrowth of the social purity movement, of the concern that women as the centre of the family must be kept pure to safeguard the values of the nation, and of the fear that lower class women were only too prone to stray. However, the authorities also definitely viewed the system as encouraging rather than discouraging unaccompanied female immigrants. A better class might be induced to immigrate if they and their relatives knew that they would be well cared for on the journey and placed in satisfactory situations in Canada. The old adage that a satisfied immigrant made the best immigration agent was always kept firmly in mind.

The emphasis on quality, however, always had to be balanced against the need for domestic servants. A joke from Toronto which circulated in the Immigration Department in the mid-1920s illustrated the problem:

> A Magistrate remarked to a man brought up before him for speeding. "The Officer tells me that you were going forty miles an hour." "Yes Sir, your honor" the culprit admitted, "I was. I had just received word from the Employment Office that they had found a COOK who would agree to come to our house in the suburbs and stay at least a week." Fortunately the magistrate, too, lived in the suburbs. "Officer," he ordered, "Get my car for this man at once. It does at least sixty miles an hour easily."[38]

Competition among the Canadian provinces for domestics was almost as great as competition between Canada and other countries. To attract experienced domestics to Ontario, the Ontario government in 1920 renewed its pre-war offer of passage assistance to be repaid out of wages. The most significant measure of assistance to British immigrant domestics in the 1920s, however, was the Empire Settlement Act, a British Act passed to promote migration within the Empire. Under the Empire Settlement Act, the Ontario government as well as the federal government entered into agreements with the United Kingdom government to assist on a fifty-fifty basis the immigration of British domestics to Canada first by passage loans and later by drastically reduced ocean fares.[39] By entering into a separate agreement, the Ontario government was able to continue its own work of recruiting domestics specifically for the province, as well as share in the proceeds of the Dominion government's activities. The province, indeed, received more than its fair share of British domestics, as Toronto especially became the mecca for British immigrant domestics in the 1920s, much to the distress of non-Torontonians.

The dominance of Toronto became a problem for the Ontario government as well as for other provinces. Many immigrant domestics chose to go to Toronto because relatives or friends had preceded them to the city, because Toronto seemed to offer more opportunities, or simply because the name became known to them through government advertising overseas. The presence in Toronto of the main Ontario distribution centre for domestics, the Women's Welcome Hostel, also served to channel British domestics into that city, and, once there, they refused to leave. Working near the Hostel could, in itself, be an attraction. As one Irish immigrant recollected, "It was home. The Hostel was home and you always met your friends there. It was great."[40] In an attempt to achieve a more equal distribution of immigrant domestics around the province, the Ontario government reduced the prominence of Toronto in Ontario publicity overseas. In addition, instructions were given to the Ontario agent in London, England, to send women directly to Ottawa, London, Hamilton, and Kingston to be accommodated at the Y.W.C.A. on arrival and placed through the government employment bureaus in those cities.[41] Such efforts did direct some immigrant domestics away from Toronto, but, at a time of scarcity of domestic servants, did not significantly alter Toronto's position as the main receiving centre.

Even the low passage fare and guaranteed employment offered by the Empire Settlement Act did not procure enough British houseworkers to fill the demand, and Ontario was forced to turn to other expedients. In 1928, Ontario, along with Manitoba, Saskatchewan, and Alberta, agreed to co-operate with the Canadian government in providing financial assistance to inexperienced girls who trained for Canadian domestic service in British hostels. Previously, only those with satisfactory domestic experience in service or in their own homes had been eligible for assistance under the Empire Settlement Act. The training hostel experiment was designed to extend this assistance to factory and shop women who showed a willingness and ability to enter domestic service by taking an eight-week course of training in Canadian household methods, including cooking, laundry, ironing, and cleaning. British authorities ran the training hostels which were established at Lenzie (near Glasgow), Newcastle, Cardiff, and London, but the Canadian government paid half the cost of the Canadian equipment installed in the hostels, and provided a woman officer to screen applicants and give final approval to each trainee before emigration. The Canadian government also paid $20 towards the passage of each trainee, and each participating province contributed $5 of the $20 for each trainee it received.[42]

The training experiment was cut off in 1930 because of the depression, but it was not considered a success during its short period of operation. The scheme did not greatly increase the number of immigrant domestics coming to Canada. Ontario both requested and received more trainees than the other participating provinces, but the total number of trainees who came to Canada was only 507. More importantly, Canadian authorities reported an abnormally high number of problem cases among the trainees.[43] The high failure rate was attributed to the background of the women and to the inadequacy of the short training course. The British government, which took the initiative in urging the hostel training programme, was most concerned to aid those in depressed areas by enabling them to emigrate. Canada chose to co-operate with the local training programme of the British Ministry of Labour because the cost to the Canadian government was minimal. Hence, three of the hostels — Lenzie, Newcastle, and Cardiff — were established near districts experiencing a mining slump and preference was given to girls from the depressed areas. Although the Canadian woman officer sought to approve only "girls over seventeen with good tonsils, sound teeth, and of refined appearance," she stressed their ignorance of "decent home life."[44] In her words:

> The girls were recruited from Pit-Head workers, Mill hands, Factory workers, Shop assistants, a very few Out-door workers and still fewer girls from their own homes. With few exceptions these girls came from one and

two-roomed homes where there would be a family of possibly 6, 8, or 10 people. They, therefore, had little or no opportunity of learning routine house work and cooking, in fact many of them did not know how to keep themselves clean.[45]

For such inexperienced girls, an eight-week course hardly provided an introduction to even the rudiments of housework in Canadian homes. Yet the first trainees were placed in Ontario as trained domestic servants with resulting frustration for both employer and employee. As a result of complaints, the Ontario employment service later tried to take great care in placing the trainees as inexperienced workers in specially selected homes, mainly in Hamilton, Toronto, and Ottawa. Nevertheless, as the supervisor of the Women's Division reported, the Canadian centres which took the trainees came to regard them "as about the most troublesome and inexperienced type of women workers that we get from the Mother Country."[46] The training hostel experiment seemed to create more problems than it solved, and Canadian officials were not sorry when changed economic conditions brought it to an end.

Another solution to the inadequate supply of domestic servants in the latter 1920s was the recruitment of women from continental Europe. As the Agent General for Ontario in London reported in 1923:

> I am still of the opinion that sooner or later should we wish to increase the supply of domestic workers in Canada, especially the Eastern portion, that we will have to go further abroad than English-speaking people. All our large industries have required to bring in certain nationalities to do certain classes of work, and it seems to me that sooner or later our household demands cannot be filled excepting they are willing to take on certain other domestic workers than English-speaking.[47]

In 1925 his advice was followed as continental Europe was opened up to Canadian immigration activity by the Railways Agreement negotiated by the Department of Immigration and the Colonization Branches of the C.P.R. and the C.N.R. The Railways Agreement authorized the railways to recruit, transport, and place in Canada farmers, farm workers and domestic servants from what were called the "non-preferred" countries of central and eastern Europe, such as Poland, Russia, Hungary, and Romania. Domestics could be brought to Ontario only if they were directly nominated by name by someone in the province who guaranteed to ensure employment for them. For the prairie provinces, however, the railways could also bring forward what were called "bulk orders" of domestics to be placed in rural homes, and once in Canada a number of these women found their way back to friends or relatives in Ontario.[48] A 1928 letter from a woman in Banff to the Calgary placement office of the C.P.R. is illustrative:

> Here I am in trouble again. This Mary Virgolova whom you sent me July 19 has been quite bright and satisfactory with her work and apparently happy. At first she was specially dumb — but she responded nicely to teaching. She has been corresponding a little and claims to have a brother in Toronto. Yesterday she received a registered letter from him — containing $50 and she says he wants her to go there. . . . Had I ever thought that she would leave so soon, of course we wouldn't have undertaken the nerve-wrecking job of training her. . . . I wish we could take steps to have Toronto taken off the map.[49]

With the Railways Agreement, and with restrictive American laws which turned European immigrants to Canada, the proportion of Ontario domestic servants born in continental Europe increased in the 1920s.[50]

From 1870 to 1930, the women Ontario wished to welcome were experienced domestics from the British Isles. However, because of the scarcity of domestic servants in Britain, inexperienced women from Britain or women from continental Europe who agreed to enter domestic service in Canada were also welcomed, although not always by their first employer. Those engaging immigrant women included both employers who believed that experienced domestics from the British Isles were superior to others, and employers who believed that immigrant meant cheap labour. In general, though, with the scarcity of domestic servants, those who hired immigrant domestics were those who could obtain them. Immigrant domestics were concentrated in urban areas in Ontario, but that was a result of immigrant preference, not employer choice. The 1911 census, the one published census which tabulates domestic servants by city and birthplace, shows half of the immigrant domestics in Ontario were in cities with a population of 15 000 or more. The distribution is more striking when it is noted that in Ontario cities 15 000 and over, domestic servants were divided evenly between Canadian-born and immigrant, whereas outside the larger cities 70 percent of domestic servants were Canadian-born and only 30 percent immigrants. Even the urban concentration of domestic servants was largely accounted for by the cities of Toronto and Hamilton, while in Ottawa, the second largest city in Ontario in 1911, only 30 percent of domestic servants were classified as immigrant.[51]

The interests and aims of governments, agencies, and employers are much clearer in the literature than are those of the immigrants themselves. Who were these women and why did they choose to come to Canada? What were their hopes and fears, successes and failures? How did they view domestic service in Canada? For both British and continental European women, beyond providing an entry to the country, the main attraction of domestic service was economic. It offered them the certainty of immediate employment, and, with board and room provided, the opportunity to save more money than was possible in factory or shop work. Many of the women were acutely aware of the need to earn money beyond their immediate expenses because they usually had to pay back their passage fare, and also often were sending money home or were saving to bring relatives to Canada. Hence, they looked for the position which paid the highest wage, one of the reasons for the reluctance to go to the lower-paying rural areas. Disputes between mistress and maid frequently centred on the question of wages, the employer insisting that the girl should accept a low wage because of her inexperience in Canadian ways, or complaining that as soon as she acquired some training the girl left for a better paying position.

Many immigrant women regarded domestic service as a temporary occupation, as the bridge which enabled them to cross to the opportunities of the new world, of America, where freedom, money, marriage or other careers awaited them. They came with a spirit of adventure, seeking to build new lives for themselves, and in the process contributed to their new country. Nearly all suffered initial problems of adjustment. Most were placed alone as cook-generals in middle-class households where, in urban areas, uniforms, servants' quarters, and a formality of manner distanced servant from employer. For those who had expected greater equality, more free time, or higher wages, the reality was a shock. The loneliness of being in a strange household was accentuated by the strain of learning new ways, and, for European domestics, a new language. Many minor irritants could lead to major dissatisfaction, and help to explain the frequent movement of domestics from one position to another. Cooking, in particular, required adjusting to new equipment and new foods, especially for women from poorer homes. Complaints that supposedly experienced domestics from Ireland could not cook resulted in the 1924 report that their experience had been with cooking over a turf fire made on the floor of the house and that therefore they would be entirely lost if asked to do cooking on a gas range or an electric stove.[52] Health problems could be even more serious than work problems. While some employers were very kind, others refused to allow a domestic to remain in their house if she became ill. There are frequent reports from the Toronto Hostel of domestics returning to the Hostel because they had bad colds, asthma, eczema, mumps, tonsillitis, ulcers, and even brain tumour.[53] Such illness not only caused physical problems, but also was a heavy drain on the slender finances of a recently arrived domestic. For most immigrant women, pride and determination led to overcoming the obstacles. Others, because of circumstance or character, were not so fortunate, and there are Hostel or deportation records of domestics who were considered major problems for reasons of illegitimacy, immorality, bad conduct, or mental deficiency.[54] However, the lives of the immigrant domestics, for the most part, remain obscure, and it is impossible to determine how many married, went into other employment, or returned to their country of origin.

As the decade of the 1920s ended, an era in the immigration of domestic servants for Ontario homes also drew to a close. From 1870 to 1930, Ontario employers relied upon governments, women's associations, and private agents to recruit immigrant domestics for their homes. Throughout the period, the British Isles remained the preferred and dominant source of supply. However, by December 1929, the Toronto bureau of the Ontario employment service was reporting that there were "a great many industrial and clerical workers who are unfortunate in finding employment trying for domestic positions. The local supply of inexperienced help more than equals the demand."[55] With the unemployment crisis of the 1930s, attention shifted from recruiting immigrants to training Canadians for household work. By the time immigration resumed after World War II, immigrant domestic servants from the British Isles no longer figured prominently among the women Ontario welcomed.

Notes

1. *The Farmer's Advocate*, Oct. 1878, 237.

2. *Report of the Women's Institutes of the Province of Ontario, 1906*, Ontario, *Sessional Papers*, 1907, Vol. XXXIX, Part VI, No. 24, 21–22.

3. *Sixth Census of Canada*, 1921, Vol. IV, *Occupations*, 2–3; *Seventh Census of Canada*, 1931, Vol. III, *Occupations*. According to the 1921 Census, female servants were 41 percent of the female work force in 1891, 34 percent in 1901, 27 percent in 1911, and 18 percent in 1921. In 1931 the specific domestic servant

category (excluding cooks and housekeepers) was 20 percent of the female labour force. While the exact percentage can very slightly depending on how the category of domestic servant is defined, the trend is clear.

4. David M. Katzman, *Seven Days a Week* (New York, 1978), 87, 94.

5. *The Farmer's Advocate*, 20 Nov. 1900, 639.

6. Ibid.

7. Maude Petitt Hill, "What's the Matter with Housework?" *The Chatelaine*, March 1928, 57.

8. PAC, R.G. 76, Records of the Immigration Branch, File 356358-2, M. Agnes FitzGibbon to Scott, 31 Aug. 1908. FitzGibbon cites the member to reinforce her appeal for payment of the government grant to the Toronto Hostel.

9. Ibid., File 22787-1, 3.

10. PAO, R.G. 11, Department of Immigration, Correspondence, R.M. Persse, Ontario Immigration Agent, Quebec, to David Spence, 17 Sept. 1881, 10 Oct. 1881.

11. The exact amount of assistance fluctuated during the period. For example in the mid-1870s British domestics going to Ontario were offered a special low passage fare of £2.5.0, including provisions, but not bedding or mess utensils, and an Ontario refund of $6, in addition to a free railway pass from Quebec provided by the Ontario government. See *Report of the Immigration Department for Ontario*, Ontario, *Sessional Papers*, for details.

12. *Report of the Department of Immigration for the Province of Ontario, 1882–83*, Ontario, *Sessional Papers*, 1883, No. 6, p. 5.

13. Ibid., 1887, Ontario, *Sessional Papers*, 1888, No. 19, 8.

14. PAO, R.G. 11, Immigration, Mrs. Duncan Matheson to Spence, 18 June 1878.

15. Ibid., John Shier to Spence, 8 July 1885.

16. Ibid., Rev. W.J. Smyth to Spence, 26 April 1878.

17. Ibid., J. Stephenson, Grand Trunk Railway of Canada to Spence, 10 July 1884.

18. Ibid., R.M. Persse to Spence, 12 July 1883.

19. *The Imperial Colonist*, Oct. 1909, 147; Una Monk, *New Horizons* (London, 1963), 16.

20. *Annual Report of the Commissioner of Agriculture and Public Works for the Province of Ontario and Immigration*, Ontario, *Sessional Papers*, No. 45, 9.

21. *The Imperial Colonist*, 1902–14; James Hammerton, *Emigrant Gentlewomen* (London, 1979), ch. 6.

22. PAC, R.G. 76, File 356358, *Annual Report of the Women's Welcome Hostel for 1912*, 16.

23. Ibid., *Annual Report of the Women's Welcome Hostel for 1912*, M. Agnes FitzGibbon to Minister of the Interior, n.d. (received 19 Jan. 1905).

24. H.J. Morgan, *The Canadian Men and Women of the Time*, 2nd ed. (Toronto, 1912), 400.

25. PAC, R.G. 76, File 356358, *Annual Report of the Women's Welcome Hostel, 1906–13*. The federal grant was given particularly because of the number of maids who went West after a year or two in Ontario. *Report*, 1908, 11.

26. Ibid., 1906.

27. Public Records Office, C.O. 721, Overseas Settlement, Vol. 67, 1923, Reports on Visits to Canada.

28. PAC, R.G. 76, File 22787, P.H. Bryce to Walker, 17 Sept. 1906.

29. Ibid., Report by Miss MacFarlane to Mr. Jolliff on the establishment and work of the women's division, 3 Aug. 1944, 1–2.

30. Ibid., W.D. Scott to Cory, Memorandum, 23 Nov. 1914.

31. Ibid., Scott to Canadian agencies, 26 Nov. 1914; Scott to J. Obed Smith, Assistant Superintendent of Emigration, London, 10 Dec. 1914.

32. Ibid., J. Obed Smith to Scott, 1 Feb. 1917.

33. Ibid., Report by Miss MacFarlane to Mr. Jolliff on women's division, 3 Aug. 1944, 2.

34. Ibid., Helen R.Y. Reid, Canadian Patriotic Fund, Montreal, to Calder, 16 July 1919.

35. Ibid., J. Robson, Women's Branch, to Calder, 29 April 1920.

36. Ibid., Conference on Immigration, 28 March 1919.

37. Ibid., Memorandum, J.S. Robson to F.C. Blair, 27 Jan. 1920.

38. Ibid., Jessie Duff to Burnham, 16 April 1925.

39. In order to remove the burden of a large loan to be repaid from wages in Canada, the Empire Settlement ocean passage fare for houseworkers was set at £3 in 1926 and £2 in 1927. The regular fare in 1926 was £18.15.0.

40. Interview with a 1923 Empire Settlement Act immigrant, Victoria B.C., 25 Oct. 1979.

41. PAC, R.G. 76, File 990380, Burnham to Duff, 15 March 1923; Duff to Burnham, 4 June 1923. In addition Catholic women were sent to the Catholic Women's League Hostel in Toronto and Rosary Hall in Ottawa.

42. Ibid., File 359252, Blair to Walker, 4 Feb. 1929.

43. Ibid., File 22787, Report by Miss MacFarlane to Mr. Jolliff on the establishment and work of the women's division, 3 Aug. 1944, 35–40.

44. Ibid., File 359252, Charlesworth to Walker, 25 July 1929.

45. Ibid., Report of Charlesworth attached to Burnham memo, 23 Aug. 1929.

46. Ibid., Blair to Little, 22 Jan. 1930.

47. Ibid., File 990380, Noxon to Burnham, 2 May 1923.

48. Ibid., File 216882, Railways Agreement.

49. Glenbow Archives, C.P.R. Records, Box 149, Edith Robinson to Elsa Wares, Secretary, Central Women's Colonisation Board, 17 Sept. 1928.

50. In 1921, 2.25 percent of Ontario domestic servants were born in continental Europe whereas in 1931 the number had risen to 10.4 percent. Immigrant domestic servants in Ontario were 89 percent British and 6 percent European in 1921, but 72.5 percent British and 24.5 percent European in 1931. (Statistics calculated from the 1921 and 1931 Census.)

51. *Fifth Census of Canada*, 1911, Vol. VI, *Occupations*, table VI.

52. PAC, R.G. 76, File 22787, Little to Blair, 15 April 1924.

53. Ibid., File 356358.

54. Ibid., File 22787, Report by Miss MacFarlane to Mr. Jolliff on women's division, 3 Aug. 1944, 33–35.

55. Ibid., File 359252, Kennedy to Burnham, 27 Dec. 1929.

THE NEW EDUCATION MOVEMENT — THOSE "YANKEE FRILLS"†

ROBERT M. STAMP

Ontario teachers were formally introduced to an alternative educational approach in 1886, when J.E. Wetherell, principal of Strathroy Collegiate, addressed the Ontario Teachers' Association on "Conservatism and Reform in Education Methods." Wetherell went to great lengths to distinguish between what he called the "Old Education" and the "New Education." The former "stored the mind with knowledge, useful and useless, and only incidentally trained the mind," while the latter "puts training in the first place and makes the acquisition of knowledge incidental." The Old Education was devoted to the study of books while the New Education "is devoted more to things than books." The old approach "was eminently subjective, dealing largely in abstractions" while the new "employs objective methods, preferring the presentation of truth in the concrete." Rather than beginning with "the unseen and the unfamiliar," the New Education "begins with the seen and the common and gradually develops the reflective faculties by reference to knowledge already obtained . . . by the child." Finally, while the Old Education was too one-sided, the New Education promised to develop "the whole being, the mental, the moral, the physical."[1]

The end-of-the-century reform movement that took the name "New Education" could trace its roots to earlier nineteenth-century European education reformers like Johann Pestalozzi and Friedrich Froebel. Inspector James Hughes of Toronto once proclaimed that "if all the work of all the great educators of the past were destroyed, all that is vital in modern education" would be found in the writings of these two men.[2] Teaching and writing in early nineteenth-century Switzerland, Pestalozzi had advocated a complete change in the purpose of the school: it should develop the child's own powers and faculties rather than impart facts, show not so much what to learn as how to learn. In mid-century Germany, Froebel had extended Pestalozzian ideas with his pioneer work in kindergarten education. Froebel placed even greater emphasis on the activity of the child, on "learning by doing," and on the overriding importance of play and physical activity in the education of the young child. By the end of the nineteenth century the ideas of both these men were well known to North American educators, through a

†From Robert M. Stamp, *The Schools of Ontario, 1876–1976*, Ontario Historical Studies Series (Toronto: University of Toronto Press, 1982), 51–73.

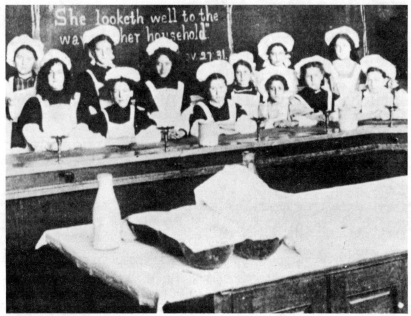

Household Science and Manual Training, c. 1903.

proliferation of books and an endless number of convention addresses. One book that attracted more than its share of attention was Hughes's *Froebel's Educational Laws for All Teachers*; an American kindergarten leader claimed it did the most to emphasize "the universal character of Froebel's principles."[3]

But the United States, not Europe, provided the immediate source of inspiration for Ontario school reformers. J.H. Putman identified psychologist G. Stanley Hall and educational philosopher John Dewey as the two greatest influences on him at the time of his appointment to the Ottawa Model School staff in 1894. Hall's 1880 article, "The Contents of Children's Minds upon Entering School," moved child study away from the speculative inquiry of pioneers like Froebel and helped give it a scientific base. Hall's central thesis was that young children have special characteristics which must be studied and appreciated before effective teaching and learning can take place. In 1894 he delivered a series of lectures on child study in Toronto, and the following year a child study section was formed within the Ontario Education Association. Although Ontario teachers had to wait till 1917 for a personal visit from John Dewey, they were as familiar with his ideas as with those of Hall. As early as 1889 high school inspector James McLellan had co-authored with Dewey a major textbook, *Applied Psychology*, which introduced Ontario normal school students to scientific psychology and child-centred teaching methods. F.W. Merchant journeyed to Chicago "to sit at Dewey's feet" just prior to assuming his new duties as principal of London Normal School in 1900.[4] Ontario disciples were familiar, not only with Dewey's principles, but also with his picturesque turn of phrase. "The child is the centre

of the educational system, as the sun is the centre of the planetary system,"
parrotted Frederick Tracy,[5] a University of Toronto philosophy professor.

Putman, McLellan, Merchant, and Tracy were representative of a growing
number of Ontarians reacting against traditional nineteenth-century curriculum
and teaching methods and willing to embrace the more child-centred pedagogy
offered by the New Education movement. They were joined by Adelaide
Hoodless, the promoter of domestic science education; James Robertson, the
federal agricultural commissioner who campaigned for rural school improvement;
and J.J. Kelso, the Toronto humanitarian crusader who provided the link with
the related child-saving and urban-reform movements. Within the Ontario cabinet,
pedagogical reform found support from J.M. Gibson, provincial secretary in the
1890s; Richard Harcourt, Ross's successor as education minister in 1899; and
W.J. Hanna, provincial secretary in the later Whitney administration. But the
foremost Canadian advocates of the New Education were the husband-and-wife
team of James and Ada Hughes. As inspector of Toronto schools since 1874 and
promoter of the kindergarten, James was the earliest champion and acknowledged philosopher of the movement. The New Education was "more of a revolution than an evolution," he declared, arguing that new aims, new methods,
and new principles must be substituted for old.[6] As Toronto's first public
kindergarten teacher, his wife Ada came to see social as well as pedagogic
dimensions to the reform movement. "The traditional methods of the old
education are not equal to the demands of the new conditions and modern needs,"
she declared. The New Education was crucial for wider social reform. "The
possibilities for the uplift of society," could only come "through the better
understanding and more intelligent training of child life."[7]

Under the leadership of people such as J.J. Kelso and James Hughes, there
developed in Toronto and other Ontario centres by the end of the century a
loosely knit "child saving" movement which focused its attention on a variety of
interconnected school and school-related reforms. To improve the quality of
childhood and the nature of family life, reformers stressed infant care and child-
rearing practices, child psychology, improved housing, day nurseries for working
mothers, supervised playgrounds, and sex- and family-life education in home
and school. In the area of child and family welfare, they worked for factory
legislation for women and children, proper care and placement of neglected
children, detention homes, industrial schools and juvenile courts for delinquent
children, and changes in legislation affecting desertion, divorce, support, and
child custody. Out of their concern for child and family health they campaigned
for the reduction of infant and child mortality, for maternity and children's
hospitals, pure water and pure milk supplies, compulsory vaccination and
immunization, medical and dental inspection in the schools, fresh-air camps for
slum children, and special care and education for mentally and physically
handicapped children. The child savers viewed themselves as altruists and
humanitarians, dedicated to rescuing those who were less fortunately placed in
the social order. But like most moral crusades, the child-saving movement
reaffirmed faith in traditional values and stressed the positive capacities of traditional institutions. Thus two of their earliest successes in protecting the youth

from social ills — the temperance curriculum of 1887 and the compulsory atten-dance legislation of 1891 — established the pattern of using the institutional school to regulate youthful behaviour.

The transformation of the school via the New Education movement was central to the child-saving crusade. New methods of instruction stressed learning by activity rather than memorization; correlation of the subject matter around the child's own widening experience; enrichment of class-room study with material drawn from the school's immediate neighbourhood; and the substitution of love for fear, and of interest for authority, in class-room discipline. The purpose of these child-centred methods was not to preach permissiveness, but rather to lead the child to his own acceptance of traditional moral values that had once been externally imposed by adult society. The end had not changed — despite James Hughes's talk of revolution — only the means to that end. Likewise the curriculum was broadened, not to introduce the principle of free choice, but to encompass the occupational, civic, and moral training which the family in the new urban environment seemed no longer able to provide. The new subjects were the mechan-ical, agricultural, and household arts; social studies, especially civics; hygiene and physical instruction; and moral education, grounded in religious faith but executed in practice in ethical decision making. The New Education reformers also sought to improve rural schools, partially under the guise of equality of educational oppor-tunity, but also to strengthen rural life and stop the drift of country children to the wicked and materialistic cities.

The kindergarten was an early example of the link between the curricular reforms of the New Education and the social and moral crusades of the child-saving and urban-reform movements. Shortly after his 1874 appointment as Toronto's public school inspector, James Hughes spent what he later described as an "epoch-making morning" visiting a private kindergarten in Boston. "I saw an educational process that was intended to develop vital centres of power and skill and character, instead of merely storing the memory and giving an abstract training in reasoning." Fired with enthusiasm, Hughes at once set about learning all he could of the Froebelian kindergarten movement that was exciting American urban school reformers. "I shall be the first man in Canada to establish a kindergarten," he boasted.[8] Every year he concluded his annual report to his trustees with the same words: "It must ultimately become part of our system, and I trust it may soon." With the backing of Toronto's two leading morning newspapers, and the support of education minister Adam Crooks, Hughes began convincing a sceptical public. Finally, in September 1883 Canada's first public kindergarten began in Toron-to's Niagara Street School with seventy children under the direction of Ada Marean — the future Mrs. James Hughes. London, Hamilton, and Ottawa followed suit, and by the end of the 1880s, the province offered financial grants and teacher-training classes, and at least one commercial firm in Toronto specialized in the sale of kindergarten materials.

The kindergarten meant different things to different people. To some humani-tarians, it suggested the emancipation of the child from traditional and insensitive restrictions, the enhancement of spontaneity and creativity. When carried too far, this view led some critics to consider the kindergarten "in the light of a new kind of play, for the conduct of which little or no training is required — or of a nursery where babies are taken in charge — in order that their mothers may have more leisure for running about." Such was the complaint of a London kindergarten teacher in 1894. "The very last thing to be appreciated is the educational value."[9] But schoolmen did note the educational value of the kindergarten. It engaged in what later came to be called reading readiness, or as a contemporary inspector put it, "preparing the pupils for the prosecution of their studies in more advanced classes."[10] It was a new bottom rung on the educational ladder! But its advocates hoped that the methods of the kindergarten would have some effect on improving primary-grade teaching methods. One inspector did note such an improvement in 1889, and attributed the change "to the diffusion of a knowledge of the principles and methods peculiar to the Kindergarten system."[11] George Ross agreed that kindergarten methods lay at the foundation of all successful primary work. He argued that "anything done to improve primary education would be of great advantage to our Public Schools."[12]

Yet if kindergarten instruction suggested freedom and creativity to some critics, and improved primary teaching methods to some supporters, it also suggested uniformity and control. Kindergarten teachers evolved a complex and highly structured methodology of play activities which channelled childhood spontaneity into a desired social behaviour. All play activities, however, were not equally valid. Music, games, and marching were most important; while calling for great activity, they kept children within a highly structured program and prevented "disagreeable romping." Proponents of this social function of schooling claimed for the kindergarten almost the entire gamut of social improvement — from the prevention of pauperism to the salvation of man. Rev. Alexander Jackson catalogued the benefits in an 1896 address to the OEA. Kindergarten training, he argued, "would supply our country with intelligent, tactful and capable mothers . . . improve the quality of the citizens which it would turn out of the public schools . . . [and] materially lessen the number of criminals and the cost of their care." Finally, as national economic growth became a topic of public concern, "the kindergarten system would save children for their usefulness to the nation."[13]

While not denying the benefits of this structured pre-school experience for middle- and upper-class children, reformers above all emphasized the necessity of the kindergarten for the children of the poor. J.J. Kelso promoted the "mission kindergarten" as second only to a "mother's own good teaching" among preventive social-service agencies. Here, the "little ones are gathered from the streets and alleys" and "they are saved from acquiring evil and untidy habits."[14] Advocates of charity and public kindergartens insisted that the child continually learned things before he entered the formal school. He could learn vice, crime, intemperance, and despair in the slum; however, he could learn desired social relationships and moral values in the kindergarten. Although the ideal was never fully attained in Ontario, the kindergarten movement also proposed to reach out beyond the class-room and influence the lower-class child in his poverty-stricken home environment. In some centres, kindergarten teachers were at first placed on half-day teaching schedules, leaving time for both mothers' meetings and home visitations. Through these meetings the teacher tried to bring the mothers into closer contact with the school program and discuss general domestic questions of mutual interest. Home visitations personalized this contact, with the teacher tactfully discussing issues of nutrition, hygiene, and child development.

Hughes's enthusiastic campaign for the kindergarten, similar to his later crusades for other aspects of the New Education movement, was a manifestation of his developing philosophy of education and his concern for social cohesion in an urban environment. He argued that the kindergarten provided a "bridge from the nursery to the school," between the play activities of childhood and the work activities of the class-room. "Play is the work of childhood," wrote Hughes in recalling his own boyhood in Durham County. "It develops a tendency to work, and cultivates in the energetic player the physical force and the characteristic aggressive spirit that enjoys work and accomplishes mighty deeds."[15] Hughes envisaged the kindergarten as a miniature community within which the child learned the skills and moral values of responsibility and co-operation, so necessary for social living. The process of moral growth involved the "transference of the child's interest from evil to good in so natural a way that the child is not conscious of the external, guiding influence in making the change."[16] He saw the kindergarten as especially valuable for Toronto urban schools. More and more children were attending from slum dwellings and lower-class backgrounds, where school readiness and acceptable middle-class social and moral attitudes were not stressed. As with so many educational innovations, the kindergarten was proposed, not solely to open wider horizons for under-privileged children, but also to channel these youngsters into socially desirable patterns of behaviour.

By 1902, almost twenty years after introducing the first public-school kindergarten, James Hughes could feel justifiably proud of his creation. That year there were some 120 kindergarten class-rooms in the province, where 247 trained teachers taught more than 11 000 five-year-olds. Hughes could take satisfaction in the fact that his educational rival and arch political enemy, George Ross, admitted that "there is no department of our school work more useful than the course of instruction in our Kindergarten schools."[17] In April 1902 Hughes was at his poetic and prophetic best in an article on "The Future Evolution of the Kindergarten." To Hughes, the kindergarten was not just "a system adapted to any special stage of human development . . . not a philosophy designed for an epoch in human progress . . . not a process through which the race must pass, and which will cease to be of value, when the race has grown beyond it." No, the kindergarten was a "universal ideal," "broad enough to make it the true basis of growth to higher stages of consciousness for every existing condition of humanity" and "deep enough to be the vital principle that must guide mankind in its advances through clearer insights and grander achievements to higher and higher conditions in its definite and conscious growth toward the infinite."[18]

Hughes was not prepared to admit that Froebelian principles ended at the kindergarten level. "Froebel wrote a philosophy for the university as well as the kindergarten," he maintained. "The application of principles should change as the child ascends through the advancing periods of its growth, but the laws of true educational development apply universally."[19] Hughes believed that the subject of manual training or industrial arts provided the natural extension for Froebelian ideas to influence the entire school curriculum. He saw it as a logical development from the controlled play activities of the kindergarten, as both the starting point and the perpetual means of all other educational development. "You cannot kindle all children by literature," Hughes argued. "A very large proportion were not meant to be deep lovers of book learning." Other subjects had their place, but more could be kindled with art and manual training "than by all the others put together." Why? "Because God meant men and women to be productive."[20]

Hughes envisaged an integrated and comprehensive manual training program that would permeate the entire elementary school curriculum. It would begin in the kindergarten, since "all kindergarten occupations and clay modelling exercises are perfect types of manual training for young children." Youngsters in First and Second Book classes would take up pencil drawing and cardboard construction. In Third Book classes, sewing would be available to the girls while the boys moved on to knife work with soft wood. Up to this point the manual training activities could be handled by the regular class-room teacher and, it was hoped, be integrated with the other subjects of the curriculum. But special rooms and specially trained teachers would be needed for Fourth and Fifth Book classes. Here, the girls would concentrate on sewing and cooking, while the boys followed a standard curriculum, based on English and Swedish models, that combined drafting, the introduction of hand tools, and the making of such "useful" wooden articles as sock darners, corner shelves, and towel rollers.[21]

As with other elements of the New Education, manual training was in part an attempt to preserve the traditional values of a society threatened by urban-industrial growth. Hughes looked back on his early years in Durham County with fond memories. "The boy whose childhood is spent in the country has better opportunities for the natural development of mind and body than the boy who is brought up in city or town." Problems encountered in doing chores or investigating the natural environment of the farm "gave me the best possible training for the recognition and solution of the problems of life."[22] Unfortunately, this ideal rural environment was not possible for the many thousands of young children growing up in crowded cities. But manual training — an institutional re-creation of the challenges of earlier days — offered possibilities for both mental training and character development.

Beginning in 1886, Hughes's yearly reports to the Toronto Public School Board included a strong plea for the new subject. The aim of the movement, he wrote, "is not to make mechanics or expert manufacturers, but to train a race of skilful and intelligent men." He was careful to preserve a balance among educational, social, and practical benefits. Manual training would develop the observant powers, provide for the application of knowledge, allow opportunities for the child to observe his success and progress, create a higher respect for labour, increase the earning potential of the individual, and benefit the nation industrially.[23] By 1897, Hughes was emphasizing the social and moral potential of manual training. It made pupils constructive rather than destructive, contributed to the nation's moral development, preserved the taste for work, increased respect for honest labour, led to more originality in the products of labour, and provided a great moral force for combatting the vices of drunkenness and lack of thrift.[24]

There were vigorous objections to manual training at the time. Many middle-class parents regarded it as something menial and decidedly inferior to book learning, associating it with the training schools for poor and delinquent children. Teachers complained that the elementary school curriculum was already over-loaded. "In the present crowded state of the programme of studies," resolved the staff of Toronto's Wellesley Street School in 1895, "it would be impossible to give one half day each week to the subject."[25] Strenuous opposition came also from trade union leaders. In part, the unions objected on economic grounds; they feared manual training would undercut the apprenticeship system, take work away from properly qualified tradesmen, and produce second-rate workers — "botch carpenters" was the term used. Labour spokesmen also feared that man-ual training would trap working-class children by denying them the type of education that would increase their chances of upward social mobility. "Manual training would be prejudicial to the interest and welfare of mechanics generally," Robert Glocking told the 1888 meeting of the Trades and Labour Congress.[26] Yet manual training gradually won additional converts. At their annual meet-ings, Ontario teachers listened regularly to spokesmen such as W.H. Huston proclaim that "shopwork disciplined the mind and trained the student in order and method," or J.H. Putman argue that young people should have something useful to do, otherwise they would "become somewhat listless, and pass through a period when they are in a kind of comatose, stand-still, won't-be-interested-in-anything condition."[27] Regular manual-training classes were established in 1889 at Woodstock College, a private boys' school, and in 1896 in Kingston's public elementary schools.

The Macdonald Education Movement provided the much-needed funds for urban school-boards to initiate the new subject. Federal agricultural commissioner James Robertson persuaded tobacco millionaire William Macdonald to donate large sums of money to a number of innovative projects associated with the New Education — manual training, domestic science, school gardens, and rural school consolidation. Although the improvement of rural schools was the ultimate aim of Macdonald and Robertson, their first project was the establishment in 1899 of the Macdonald Manual Training Fund. Robertson later claimed this was a necess-ary first step in helping rural education; since country people were accustomed to following an urban lead, successful practical work in city schools would create a demand for comparable improvements in rural schools.[28] Despite this political ploy, Robertson was as convinced as Hughes of the cultural and moral values of the subject; he saw it "as an educational means for developing intellectual and moral qualities of high value in all children."[29] Under Robertson's direction, Macdonald Manual Training Centres were guaranteed staff and maintenance for three years, at no cost to local school-boards. At the end of this three-year demonstration period, it was hoped that local and provincial authorities would be so convinced of the subject's value that they would take over the centres and extend the work. The first centre in Ontario opened in Brockville in April 1900; during the next school year additional centres were opened in Ottawa and, to Hughes's satisfaction, Toronto. Within three years the Macdonald fund was maintaining centres in twenty-one Canadian cities, paying the salaries of forty-five teachers at a monthly cost of $3600 and offering manual training to some 7000 boys.

While Hughes and his colleagues sought to adjust male schooling to the demands of the new urban-industrial order, a growing number of women in late nineteenth-century Canada attempted similar reforms in the education of girls. Foremost among these was Adelaide Hoodless, the country's leading promoter of domestic science or home economics. Hoodless saw the growing independence of women as a mixed blessing—the advantages of the new freedom had to be weighed against potential personal and societal disaster. Young women working in factories, shops, and offices had too little time to devote to domestic concerns, were exposed to "too much of the seamy side of life," and were deprived "of the refining and protecting influences of home life at a time when the character was being formed."[30] The home, in contrast, constituted "a second heredity, a moral shaping by suggestion, example and influence."[31] The management of the home, she believed, "has more to do in the moulding of character than any other influence, owing to the large place it fills in the early life of the individual during the most plastic stage of development."[32] But the new urban-industrial world created opportunities for women to neglect their role in the home. "Instead of finding the chief pleasures and duties of life in the Home circle, our young women seek a career. Inventions and changed conditions have altered the whole structure."[33] The result, she concluded, was contrary to natural law and a threat to domestic life. "The subversion of natural law," she told the National Council of Women in 1902, "which makes man the bread-winner and woman the home-maker, cannot fail to have injurious effect on social conditions, both morally and physically."[34]

Hoodless believed that the school system of the day compounded the problem, through its failure to adjust to the demands of the new society. When the home was the manufacturing centre "from which the necessities of life were produced," little was demanded of the elementary school except the three Rs. But "changes in industrial conditions demand a readjustment of educational methods and courses of study."[35] Yet theoretical questions still took precedence over practical problems in the school curriculum, with unfortunate results for home-making. "If practical knowledge formed part of the education of every girl we would not see so many domestic shipwrecks."[36] The answer seemed to lie in the New Education which "aims to affiliate school with life, to correlate all subjects into a unity of physical, mental, moral and spiritual action."[37] In particular, the answer was domestic science in the elementary school. Hoodless saw the new subject as fulfilling the twin aims of integrating school life with desired home life, and preparing women for their all-important role at the centre of that home life. "Girls should be educated to fit them for the sphere of life for which they were destined — that of the homemaker."[38]

Like Hughes, Adelaide Hoodless pictured a comprehensive elementary school curriculum in domestic science that began in the kindergarten. "Small tables are set with all the necessary dishes, cutlery, napkins, etc., and real dinners are eaten by the little ones." The youngsters would also engage in bed-making, laundry-folding, knitting, and stocking-darning. Graduated exercises in sewing and cooking would continue through First Book to Fifth Book classes. The teaching of "cookery" would include far more than "simply imparting a knowledge of the preparation of certain dishes." It would also entail "instruction on the nature of food and the art of choosing suitable, nourishing and at the same time economical articles of diet in order that the smallest incomes may be made to serve the needs of even large families."[39] Hoodless's 1898 textbook, *Public School Domestic Science*, included calorie charts and chemical analyses of different types of foods, and chapters dealing with the parts of the body, the relation of food to the body, infants' diets, and household management.

In 1897 Stratford became the first city in the province to make domestic science an integral part of its public school curriculum. Again, it was the Macdonald Manual Training Fund, rather than support from the provincial department of education, that helped the new subject gain a foothold in urban centres. Although the Macdonald Fund provided no direct money for domestic science, it challenged local boards to provide some activity for the girls while the boys were in manual training classes. Ultimately, domestic science was accepted, not solely for its limited educational purposes, but for its more sweeping social and moral promises. "There are tremendous possibilities involved in this new movement," wrote Hoodless, "not only as an educational factor, but as a social power." In the city, domestic science would help alleviate the social problems of slum housing by instilling into girls the desire and the "executive ability" to turn "hovels into homes."[40] In the country it would attack a main source of social dislocation — rural depopulation — by imparting to country girls a fitting appreciation for rural life, by training "proper farm wives" to create and maintain an agreeable home life.[41] Above all were the ethical considerations. "Character is formed in the home, and largely under the influence of the mother," Hoodless argued, "and unless women are educated so as to realize and faithfully perform the duties and responsibilities of homemakers, we cannot expect a higher type of citizen." There was no branch of education so conducive to ethical instruction as domestic science, "dealing as it does directly with the home and the occupations carried on there."[42] Finally, the new subject might stem the tide of women leaving the home. "Girls should have special opportunities for acquiring a knowledge which not only develops character but fits them for their God-given place in life."[43]

While James Hughes and Adelaide Hoodless sought to make city schools more relevant to the social needs of the turn-of-the-century urban environment, other reformers concentrated their attention on the rural schools. "The rural school problem is the most important question before the people of Ontario today," journalist W.R. Parkinson told the 1903 OEA meeting. Lamenting the "growing tendency towards urban life," Parkinson concluded that the rural school and the provincial education system were not doing enough "to keep the boy on the farm." Rather, "the whole trend of his training" was "calculated to fix his attention on the High School, then on the University, and finally to induce him to enter professional life." Even the unsuccessful young man was likely to "come back filled with the idea that his father and mother are slow, and that he is too clever to earn his living by soiling his hands at the plough."[44] Parkinson took for granted a basic assumption that found wide support at the time: a reformed rural school would halt the decline in rural population and restore the idyllic virtues of country life.

Reformers could point with pride to a few rural schools in the province that seemed to relate to their immediate communities and serve the larger needs of agrarian society. One such institution was the Rittenhouse School, located near the village of Jordan Station in the heart of the Niagara Peninsula fruitlands. Moses Franklin Rittenhouse was the personal benefactor of this school; his was a classic Horatio Alger story, as he rose from Lincoln County farm boy to prosperous Chicago lumber baron. Local trustees in 1890 accepted Rittenhouse's offer to bear half the costs of a new schoolhouse on the site where young Moses had been educated back in the 1850s. The result was a handsome two-room, brick structure, well endowed with the latest in teaching aids and library books, electricity, and indoor plumbing. But that was not the end of Rittenhouse's beneficence; in due course he provided money for domestic-science and manual-training rooms in the basement, and for an adjacent music and lecture theatre which made the school the centre for community activities. He also employed a landscape gardener to beautify the grounds with a variety of shrubs, trees, and hedges, "making it not only a paradise for the children but also a beauty spot from which other sections might receive inspiration."[45] But other school districts lacked a philanthropist of comparable wealth and generosity. The Rittenhouse School remained the exception to the rule; local effort was not sufficient to provide the ideal rural schooling demanded by the agrarian visionaries.

At the secondary level, turn-of-the-century agrarian reformers initially put their hopes on the continuation schools. Beginning in 1896, these were formed around Fifth Book or First Form classes that had sprung up in many village and rural elementary schools. Within three years, many of these schools added the Second Form, and by 1906 some offered the entire high school program. Continuation schools were especially successful in Carleton, where Inspector R.H. Cowley soon had the county blanketed. They provided a preferred alternative to the cost of erecting a central county high school or to the high non-resident fees charged by Ottawa Collegiate. As a local member of the legislature remarked, "these classes relieve us from the necessity of sending our children from the good, innocent farm life to the cities and towns for high school education."[46] Farsighted educators cherished the hope that the continuation schools would provide a type of secondary education particularly suited to rural, agricultural needs. But the majority of country dwellers cherished no such desire. They wanted the new schools to be miniature reproductions of traditional town high schools. Cowley himself observed with amazement that the farmers were intensely interested in their sons learning Latin. "There appeared to be a glamour about it that pleased them. They would speak with pride to their neighbours, while their eyes brightened up."[47] As early as 1899, the department of education admitted that the objectives of the continuation schools were identical to those of the town high schools. "A different course of study . . . could not be thought of."[48]

While the continuation school provided a partial answer to the problem of rural secondary education, it was educator James Robertson and philanthropist William Macdonald, working together in the Macdonald Education Movement, who provided the most concerted attack on the problems of rural elementary education. "In our educational progress not much has been done for the girls and boys in rural schools compared with what has been given to and made possible for the children in towns and cities," Robertson wrote to Premier Ross in 1902.[49] But once manual training had gained a foothold in urban schools, Robertson and Macdonald could turn their attention to their original concern — the rural school. Their reform thrust was essentially conservative. Robertson claimed that its aim was not to destroy anything that existed in rural districts — "except weeds" — but rather to "build up something better than is now known and done, and thereby replace what is poor." Its vocational aim was to provide more competent leaders for the horticultural and agricultural population while its social aim was to "help the rural population to understand better what education is and what it aims at for them and their children."[50] Rural discontent and unrest could be defused through greater support for and confidence in the country school.

The first Macdonald-Robertson venture in country education was the Macdonald Rural Schools Fund, which saw school gardens established at five rural schools in each of the five eastern provinces in 1904. The designated Ontario schools were all in Carleton County, largely due to the efforts of Inspector Cowley. As with the manual training fund, Macdonald bore the costs of establishing the gardens and maintaining supervisory personnel for three years. The pupils were shown the value of seed selection, crop rotation, and protection against weed, insects, and disease. Supporters claimed both practical and social values for the school gardens. Robertson maintained they could be used "for the training of children to habits of close observation, of thoughtfulness," with the result that the child "becomes a better pupil and the promise of a better citizen in every sense."[51] The department of education saw them as bringing school life closer to social life and giving children "brighter impressions of the work of the farmer."[52] Cowley was the most starry-eyed supporter. He claimed the gardens would "cultivate the sense of ownership and a social spirit of co-operation and mutual respect for one another's rights" and "provide an avenue of communication between school and home, thereby strengthening public interest in the school as a national institution."[53] As school gardens spread from Carleton County to other parts of the province, their success led to the very popular school agricultural fairs, which began in North Dumfries Township (Waterloo County) in 1909. Like the gardens, the rural school fairs were seen as conservative social force. They would "prepare the boys and girls for the farm, create in them a greater love for farm life, make them more efficient workers, more practical thinkers, and more intelligent citizens."[54]

Initial enthusiasm for school gardens led to an even bolder scheme for the regeneration of rural education and rural life — the Macdonald Consolidated School Project. This plan sought to extend the benefits of the gardens and add those of manual training and domestic science by amalgamating several small rural school districts and building one large, consolidated school. "It has not been difficult in Canada to arrange routes for the collecting of milk or cream to one central place," argued Robertson. "It would not be more difficult to arrange for the collection of children on various roads to one central school."[55] Macdonald money again provided for the construction of a new building and part of the extra operating costs over a three-year period. Interest was keen throughout the province, as correspondents from several counties wrote education minister Richard Harcourt begging that the one Macdonald demonstration school allotted to Ontario be established in their locality. Finally, a site near Guelph was chosen, to give the school close proximity to the Ontario Agricultural College. Robertson saw several immediate practical advantages of consolidation: better buildings and equipment, higher qualified staff, better classification of pupils, improved attendance, an enriched program, and the opportunity of obtaining a high school education close to home.[56] But again there were important social aims. Journalist W.R. Parkinson believed consolidation the best possible solution to the problem of rural depopulation. It would "keep boys and girls at home, save them from the bedizening influences of city life, and turn them into an intelligent rural constituency."[57] Education minister Richard Harcourt confided to Macdonald that he knew of "nothing which would tend to make our farmers' sons and daughters more contented with rural life."[58]

Harcourt's enthusiasm for consolidation was consistent with the support he gave to all facets of the New Education movement during his years as education minister from 1899 to 1905. A new tone is evident in the department's annual reports during the Harcourt years — the challenge of scientific and industrial development. "The progress of science, in this latter part of the nineteenth century, has revolutionized all our industries," Harcourt prefaced his 1899 report. "The curriculum of fifty years ago will not do today."[59] His annual remarks to the OEA were less defensive and more conducive to change than those of Ross had been. "We have reached the time when our course of study should be remodelled," he told the teachers in 1903. "The needs, the conditions, the circumstances of today must dominate the situation."[60] Those circumstances demanded that the schools address themselves to practical preparation for the industrial world. "The training given in our High and Public Schools should be as practical as possible," he declared, "and the subjects taken up should have in view the pursuits that will necessarily be followed by the great majority of our citizens." Practical training had the potential for making the pupil intelligent, industrious, and law-abiding. And the subjects promoted by the New Education reformers seemed to fill the bill. To Harcourt, manual training was essential "if we are to have well-trained mechanics, farmers, and merchants"; it would furnish effective relief from an altogether too bookish curriculum; help co-ordinate "the training of hand and eye" so vital for young children; and give "a due regard to the dignity of labour."[61]

Harcourt at once began corresponding with local school-board chairmen, principals, and other educators, urging them to introduce the new subjects. "The change will come, must come. Why delay it?" he asked a Lindsay school principal. "You would popularize your schools immensely by making the change." He implored James Mills, president of the Ontario Agricultural College, to preach the virtues of domestic science in the Guelph area. He offered a substantial yearly grant to the Welland Public School Board because he wanted "to have a commencement made in some of our best schools." He expressed annoyance when a Brantford supporter raised the question of cost. "You must not ask me to decide now about the extent of the grant since you know that I am desirous of giving aid to the full extent. If I make a mistake I want it to be on the side of generosity." Pelham Township was promised a special grant if trustees would "seriously take up a good consolidation scheme."[62] It may have seemed strange for a former provincial treasurer to be so lavish with public funds, but Harcourt knew that legislative approval for a formal system of provincial grants would be forthcoming only if local communities led the way. "We will follow the principle which governs our entire system," he told the OEA in 1902, "that of aiding and supplementing local effort. We will commence by offering a small grant to any section which will supplement it by a sum twice as large." Such stimulation was necessary, Harcourt believed, because people usually were slow to demand reforms which involve increased taxation.[63]

During 1903 and 1904 Harcourt moved vigorously to guarantee a future for manual training and domestic science in the province's elementary schools. When initial Macdonald Fund money expired, the new subjects became eligible for fixed annual provincial grants in addition to percentage grants based on teachers' salaries and equipment costs. And in the face of strong teacher opposition, Harcourt mobilized his departmental personnel to champion their retention as optional subjects during a sweeping revision of the elementary school curriculum. Through most of 1903 and into 1904 the province's teachers had an opportunity to discuss the most thorough proposals for curricular reform since Ryerson's retirement. Not surprisingly, the more traditionally oriented university and high school spokesmen within the OEA mounted a strong campaign against the new subjects. They met their match in Harcourt and high school inspector John Seath. "These new subjects have come to stay," warned Seath, "and it would be well for all of you to realize the fact and to use the movement as it may be used, for the proper ends of education."[64] In the end, the advocates of the new subjects carried the day at the 1904 OEA meeting; the revised curriculum regulations announced later in the year retained manual training and domestic science as optional subjects, and added art, nature study, and agriculture. By the end of 1904, Harcourt could take justifiable pride in the progress of school reform; manual training and domestic science classes were spreading throughout urban Ontario, school gardens and school libraries dotted the rural countryside, and the new consolidated school at Guelph seemed a welcome omen of things to come.

Innovations in health care, recreation, child morality, and auxiliary classes — areas where the New Education merged with the broader child-saving movement — had at least as much influence on early twentieth-century Ontario pupils as the various curricular changes. Proposals to link the public school with the growing public health movement fell on receptive ears; the school was an institution that provided a captive audience, since one entire age group was compelled to attend. As early as 1881, education minister Adam Crooks, who usually championed a limited role for the school, saw merit both for the child and the state in "giving familiar information to each child of the rules of health, and in protecting him against bad ventilation, lighting and heating, and other defects of the schoolhouse."[65] Soon the newly formed Ontario Board of Health and its supporters within both the medical and teaching professions embarked on a four-fold crusade: school sanitation, control of infectious and contagious diseases, the inclusion of hygiene in the curriculum, and, finally, medical inspection of schoolchildren.

The provincial board of health launched the campaign by charging in its 1883 report that many Ontario schoolrooms were "in a very unsanitary condition" and that "neglect of precautions to prevent the spread of contagious and infectious diseases" was all too common.[66] It was one thing, however, for a board of health and a department of education to set minimum sanitary standards for schools, but quite another thing to persuade local trustees to apply them. Rural ratepayers in Middlesex County defeated an 1891 motion to ventilate their schoolhouse by a whopping twenty-eight to one vote. Local trustees were reluctant to follow 1886 board of health requirements that called for the exclusion from the school of any children in direct contact with smallpox, cholera, scarlet fever, diphtheria, whooping cough, measles, or mumps; the line of least resistance was to close the schools entirely when faced with a major outbreak. It was even harder to enforce compulsory vaccination laws for all schoolchildren in the face of public hostility to what one Toronto mayor called "a dirty, filthy practice."[67] Meanwhile, public health officials sought to make subjects like physiology and hygiene compulsory for all students, because the "susceptible minds of the young" were "particularly adapted to receive and retain such information."[68] Physical education was also important because, as James Hughes argued, it would "make men healthful and less liable to disease" and "remove hereditary diseases and counteract hereditary tendencies."[69]

By the turn of the century it was evident that neither poorly enforced sanitary regulations, poorly trained teachers, nor hastily prepared hygiene curricula could by themselves win the battle against the childhood disease. What was needed, declared the Ontario Board of Health in its 1899 and 1901 reports, was to have "physicians visit the schools to examine for suspects . . . and to follow up the absentees to their homes."[70] Toronto's chief medical officer at first dismissed school medical inspection as "a pure fad, instituted principally by women" who were "apt to give way to sentiment" and listen "to the talk of agitators" who wanted "easy billets for their friends, with good pay and little work."[71] But under pressure from the Local Council of Women and *Telegram* publisher John Ross Robertson, the Toronto public school-board in 1910 agreed to conduct an initial medical survey of pupils and appoint its first school nurse. Brantford began medical inspection that same year, and by the First World War twelve other Ontario school-boards had followed suit. The Women's Institute led the campaign in rural Ontario, and in 1914 its Parkhill branch secured in the North Middlesex school inspectorate the first medical inspection of country pupils. By this time the school nurse had become the front-line worker in the school health movement. She did the routine inspections, examinations, and readmissions, kept medical records on all pupils, and taught health to teachers and pupils through lectures and demonstrations. In Toronto schools there were the celebrated Little Mothers' Leagues, where senior elementary girls learned infant care at first hand as they brought their baby sisters to school to be bathed, dressed, fed, and put to bed.

Led by Toronto dentist Dr J.G. Adams, the campaign for dental inspection was much more flamboyant and emotional than that for medical inspection. Adams gained as many opponents as supporters with his unsubstantiated claims that "there are not less than one million permanent teeth going to destruction in the mouths of the school children of Ontario."[72] The Niagara Falls town council flatly opposed inspection of pupils' mouths, "energetically protest[ing] against this kind of paternal legislation."[73] Other groups could not agree that dental inspection was a matter of special priority; they argued that the state of pupils' eyes and ears was more crucial for school learning. By about 1910, however, with the initial acceptance of medical inspection and statistical information on the poor state of children's teeth before them, school trustees in urban centres were prepared to begin dental inspection. Again, it was the school nurse who undertook most of the preventive dentistry in the class-rooms. She examined teeth, persuaded parents to have cavities treated, demonstrated the proper use of the tooth-brush by conducting "tooth-brushing drills," and provided needy children with free brushes.

Toronto's widely acclaimed "open air" schools illustrate the extension of the school health movement beyond purely medical concerns into the broader area of moral rehabilitation. Beginning in 1910 with an open-air class-room on the grounds of the Hospital for Sick Children, the public school-board opened two summer "Forest Schools" in 1913–14, and in 1916 converted the two upper-storey rooms of Orde Street School into year-round, open-air class-rooms. The Forest Schools were designed for underprivileged tubercular children, and combined education, nutrition, health care, and morality in May-to-October outdoor sessions. Medical workers were heartened when children during the first summer of the program gained an average of five pounds in weight.[74] Yet the "highest aim" was moral rather than physical. Dr W.E. Struthers, the board's chief medical officer, hoped the experience in the open air and the comradeship of morally upstanding teachers would "give these children a new ambition, a desire to make good in life, a desire to be useful." These were the children "who will otherwise be physical weaklings, who will fill the class of the shiftless, fill the reformatories . . . the prisons, penitentiaries, and asylums, who make the loafers and criminals of adult life, who never had the asset of a healthy, vigorous, clean body, or knew the inspiration of a clean mind."[75]

Toronto reformers also championed the supervised playground as a corrective for the debilitating physical and moral environment of underprivileged urban children. Most citizens agreed that people in urban areas needed plenty of fresh air and exercise, but the major concern and dominant motive of the playground leaders was a belief that there was little for the child to do in the city during the summer vacation, and that idleness led to delinquency and crime. Again, the loose coalition of child-savers like J.J. Kelso and schoolmen like James Hughes went to work. During the winter of 1907–8 they organized the Toronto Playgrounds Association to "save many spirited youngsters from the police court and the prison cell."[76] Within three years they could boast two community and seven school playgrounds, all effectively supervised by a teacher who "takes the place of a wise mother." Not only did she minister to her pupils' physical and recreational needs; she also protected them "from all kinds of evils by seeing that their language and character are at all times proper" and told them "appropriate stories to kindle their imagination and store their minds with pure and high ideals."[77] There were also "vacation classes" at Toronto's Hester How School where the one requirement for pupils wishing to attend was that they come with "clean hands and face." Here some 600 children were provided with "useful occupation during the midsummer holidays."[78]

From health and recreation it was a small step into the area of children's morality. Not resting on its laurels after seeing temperance introduced into the school curriculum, the Woman's Christian Temperance Union found new villains to pursue — cigarette smoking, immoral literature, pornographic picture cards, and the motion-picture industry. A storm of protest was created in London during 1911 when the local WCTU president charged that "the vicious tendencies of today start in the Public Schools and Collegiates." London may be no worse than the rest of the province, added May Thornley, "but the conditions are terrible to consider." Thornley demanded a joint clean-up campaign from city council and the school-board. But the mayor refused to be stampeded into a city-wide morality drive. "Let the parents of the boys and girls be taught the responsibility they have for their children," he responded. "They should be taught morality in the home."[79] The WCTU and other provincial reform groups disagreed; in the years before the First World War they were active in scrutinizing textbooks and library books for the slightest hint of impropriety and in agitating for anti-cigarette lectures at school assemblies. The WCTU in 1905 also introduced sex education into Ontario schools through the "advanced purity" lectures of Arthur W. Beall, the WCTU's "Purity Agent." Six years later the department of education took over the work and appointed Beall as a special lecturer. Invited into schools by local officials, Beall continued to lecture Ontario pupils — largely on the dangers of masturbation — through the 1920s and into the 1930s. The department took no official notice of his work in its annual reports, and at least one inspector was "never convinced that public lectures on this subject to young boys will do more good than harm." Yet thousands of Ontario pupils would remember Beall delivering what he came to call his "eugenics" lectures.[80]

Early twentieth-century reform groups also interested themselves in special schooling for mentally deficient pupils, as stricter enforcement of compulsory attendance laws brought more handicapped children into the schools. According to Dr Helen McMurchy, provincial inspector of the feeble-minded, "in the ordinary school class there is little that the best and kindest teacher can do for the mentally defective child, who is simply a drag on the rest of the class, and cannot learn by ordinary methods."[81] Reformers were encouraged by the work done in small, special classes at the hospital school of the Orillia Asylum. If handicapped children in the public and separate schools could also be taught in segregated classes, perhaps they might be prepared for responsible, productive adulthood, and rescued from the feared perils of poverty, delinquency, and crime. Provincial legislation in 1911 and 1914 permitted local boards to establish classes for the physically handicapped, "promotion classes" for slow children, and "training classes" for mental defectives. By the time of the First World War, five Ontario school-boards were operating these various kinds of "auxiliary classes." And Toronto's inspector of public schools was referring to the "education of the feeble-minded" as one of his board's "chief pressing problems."[82]

Thirty-nine years after his initial appointment as inspector of Toronto public schools, and thirty years after his introduction of the kindergarten, James Hughes approached retirement in 1913. The finale for the Grand Old Man of the New Education movement was his presidential address that year to the Ontario Educational Association. "Modern Tendencies in Education" was the carefully chosen title for his remarks. Still as vigorous as ever, still something of a rebel, Hughes delivered a message that praised the many reforms he had championed and initiated during his long career. Unfortunately, his wish to be "Minister of Education for 30 years" never came true.[83] But his dreams and hopes survived in a younger generation of Ontario schoolmen, many of whom heard his valedictory address. One of these was J.H. Putman, appointed inspector of Ottawa public schools in 1910. Putman quickly reorganized the city's kindergartens, extended manual training into the lower grades, abolished external examinations, reoriented physical training away from military drill towards gymnastics, and introduced nature study, school gardens, pottery classes, and field trips. "I may modestly claim," Putman wrote later, "to have had some share in giving this city a system of elementary education the least academic and the most practical of any in Canada."[84] More than anyone else, Putman provided the link between the New Education reforms of the early 1900s and the Progressive Education movement of the 1930s.

The year 1904 had marked the high-water mark for the curricular reforms of the New Education movement. The new Conservative government which took office in 1905 by no means sabotaged the program; indeed the Whitney administration tried to sustain the reform thrust through increased provincial grants and the appointment of supervisory personnel. But the movement gradually fell prey to the twin perils of teacher indifference and public criticism. The New Education made fresh demands on the province's teachers — a better understanding of the nature of the child and a greater familiarity with the life of the community. "We can improve our schools only as we improve our teachers," stated Putman in 1913. "Compared with the teacher every other factor pales into insignificance."[85] Yet the majority of teachers of the day were immature, poorly trained, and inexperienced. Rather than accept the new challenges, most retreated into the security of traditional concerns. Staff meetings in Toronto public schools in 1913 dealt with routine questions of marking registers, width of margins in work books, playground and lunch-room supervision, and end-of-day dismissal procedures.[86] With Hughes's retirement there was no one in the Toronto system to inspire those teachers with the promise of the New Education. Instead, they were admonished "to give the major portion of our time and energies to the essential subjects."[87]

Nor was the public convinced of the social value of the new subjects. The editor of *Saturday Night* complained that the products of Toronto schools could "dress dolls and fry beef steaks," but were unable to "write decent hands [or] add up a column of figures."[88] "We see education sugar-coated to a degree that must make it nauseous to a sensitive palate," wrote young Vincent Massey in 1910. "Froebel's belief in the divinity of the child — whatever that means — results in child worship. This, in turn, often gives rise to adolescent impudence, which is anything but divine."[89] A Galt principal saw the new subjects as "interfering with the teaching of the branches essential to the foundation of an English education" and thus "detrimental to our highest educational interests." Therefore, urged William Linton, "feathers, frills and fads should find no place in our system."[90] Frills were bad enough; worse still they were "Yankee frills" promoted by Hughes and his high-powered American friends. Any American ideas were highly suspect during the decade of the Alaska boundary dispute and Ontario's decisive rejection of the proposed Canadian-American reciprocity agreement. Principal John Henderson of St Catharines Collegiate received nods of approval when he charged at the 1911 OEA meeting that most of the fads in Ontario education could be traced to American sources. His comment that "what may be good for the United States may be very bad for Ontario" needed no further elucidation.[91]

Kindergarten developments are representative of the slowdown in reform in the years prior to the First World War. Statistics for 1911 were superficially impressive — close to 200 kindergarten classes, with over 350 teachers and some 20 000 youngsters. Yet nearly half of these classes were in Hughes's own Toronto system. Throughout the province the movement had faltered since the early enthusiasm of the 1880s. "At first there was quite a rush of the infantile community to the classes," wrote Brantford's inspector as early as 1889, "but the novelty seems to have passed, and there is less enthusiasm manifested now."[92] Poor management and poor public relations left the province's teachers and the general public unconvinced of the value of kindergartens. One kindergartner placed the blame on the failure of the department to appoint a provincial inspector; this left supervision to principals and trustees "not understanding the work."[93] A professor charged that the poorly run kindergarten subverted the true aim of education. "It does not inculcate punctuality; it permits the little ones to come and go as they please," said E.U. Birchard. "It does not teach obedience to authority, but permits them to follow the inclination of their own wills."[94] One Toronto inspector questioned if even the best run kindergarten was "living up to its promises of years ago" since so many youngsters still remained too long in the First Book classes.[95]

Similar problems befell the manual training movement. By 1911 the subject had been introduced in just 26 of 279 urban municipalities and in only one rural school district. "Even in those places where the subject has been introduced, it is a difficult matter to bring it to a point where it is looked upon as an integral part of the course of study," complained provincial supervisor Albert Leake. "The grade teacher has held aloof and the manual training teacher has refused to have any connection with other school subjects."[96] Hughes and other advocates were criticized for "attempting to make intellectual studies or some wonderful science out of what is valuable only as it is made practical."[97] But was it even practical? Vincent Massey believed it "doubtful if the manufacture of hat-racks and towel-rollers has much more bearing on the average man's life than a course in history."[98] The solution seemed to be to stress the industrial and vocational purposes of manual training, rather than the cultural. Led by Albert Leake, this trend was evident even before Hughes's retirement. "The foundation of all technical education is the Manual Training course of the elementary school," wrote Leake in 1903.[99] At first manual training, like the kindergarten, was aimed at the inculcation of community values, not the occupational preparation of the child. But by the time of the First World War manual training had shifted from the principles of work to the introductory teaching of trades.

On all sides the curricular and administrative reforms of the New Education were at a standstill or in hasty retreat. Domestic science was opposed in rural areas because it seemed to threaten rather than bolster the home. "Let them take up the work of the home there," wrote one village trustee. "It will help make the home what it should be — the best place on earth."[100] A teacher dismissed domestic science as "too much fuss and feathers." It was "too great an attempt to exalt into some wonderful science what needs mostly practical experience, coupled with common sense." The girls should be put to work at home, and judged by practical results. Even nature study in rural schools "seems to have bidden us a sad farewell" because "no one seems to have known exactly what she was."[101] The consolidated school movement had also faltered. Three of the five rural sections withdrew from the Guelph consolidation when Macdonald money expired in 1910. By that date only one other consolidation had been formed in the province — in Hudson Township near New Liskeard. Although consolidation was judged a pedagogical success, increased transportation, salary, and maintenance costs drew local opposition. "If we could *guarantee* no increase in taxation, we *might* carry each section," wrote one inspector, "but even then we should have a stubborn fight."[102] Most important for the failure of consolidated schools was the lack of any perceived need for school reform in the countryside. The one-teacher, ungraded rural school was still giving a satisfactory account of itself.

What, then, was the significance of the New Education movement that ruffled the water of Ontario schools in the twenty years preceding the First World War? Certainly the New Education and the larger child-saving crusades were permeated by a high degree of compassion for the child. The reformers suffered for the child labourer, for the mentally and physically disabled child, the undernourished and underprivileged child, the unhappy and the unadjusted child. They turned to the shcools as strategic centres for humanitarian reform. Here they made the first great strides since the mid-nineteenth-century common-school movement in reforming pedagogical practice. They urged greater understanding of the nature of the child, attempted to take into account each child's personality and background, and encouraged natural growth geared to the child's experience. Of course these pedagogical changes were often geared to conservative purposes, as the reformers grappled with the question of what forms of instruction would be most conducive to desired social ends. It has been argued persuasively that much of the motivation for reform grew from "a desire to order, contain, and mitigate the destructive aspects of urban-industrial growth." Reformers regarded the school as the best instrument for the preservation of social order and traditional moral values.[103] Through subjects like manual training and domestic science, through carefully regulated playgrounds and forest schools, it was hoped to produce in children a character suited to the needs of the times: industrious, clean, thrifty, law-abiding, God-fearing, sound in body and pure in mind. Whitney's provincial secretary, W.J. Hanna, after reciting the specific advantages to the boy of the various aspects of the New Education, perhaps best summed up the hope of the school reformers. "If you launch him with this equipment, he is not likely to prove a serious civic problem," he told the Civic Improvement League in 1916. "Launch a generation of him and your civic problems are largely solved."[104]

That social control and social improvement were central to department of education thinking is evident in a 1915 teachers' manual that was required reading for all normal-school students. In a key chapter entitled "Education for Social Control," the anonymous author catalogued the main purposes of education. First came the role of the school in teaching youngsters the means of individual "social control." Second, the school must disseminate knowledge, for upon knowledge depended "intelligence, social progress and happiness." Third, "by free education for all in our public schools," society met the demand for social improvement. Taxpayers cared "little for the advantage of individual pupils"; they were preoccupied mainly with the welfare of society. Finally, through practical subjects, the school met the demand for "industrial efficiency" and thereby responded to the need "to make each individual a productive social unit."[105] If the realities of both school and the larger society had forced the reformers to scale down their hopes of improving society through the school, those same realities continued to support the goal of fitting the schoolchild for his place in that society. In many ways, the difference between the "old" and the "new" education was a difference in means, not in ends.

Notes

1. J.E. Wetherell, "Conservatism and Reform in Education Methods," OEA *Proceedings*, 1886, 86–88. John Dewey credited Francis W. Parker with christening and launching the New Education movement in 1882 (see Timothy L. Smith, "Progressivism in American Education, 1880–1900," *Harvard Educational Review* 31, 2 (Spring 1961): 168–93), although President Charles Eliot of Harvard had first used the term in the title of an *Atlantic Monthly* article as early as 1869. (See Edward A. Krug, *The Shaping of the American High School, 1880–1920* (Madison: University of Wisconsin Press, 1964), 1:121).

2. James L. Hughes and L.R. Klemm, *Progress of Education in the Century* (London and Edinburgh: W. and R. Chambers Ltd., 1900), 1.

3. Nina Vandewalker, *The Kindergarten in American Education* (New York: Arno Press, 1908, 1971), 171.

4. PAO, RG2, Frederick Merchant to George Ross, 4 Oct. 1899.

5. Frederick Tracy, "The Practical Results of Child Study," OEA *Proceedings*, 1897, 338–44.

6. Hughes and Klemm, *Progress of Education in the Century*, 1.

7. Ada Hughes, "Presidential Address," OEA *Proceedings*, 1901, 81–85.

8. Lorne Pierce, *Fifty Years of Public Service: The Life of James L. Hughes* (Toronto: Oxford, 1926), 90, 93.

9. Agnes MacKenzie, "Kindergarten Extension," OEA *Proceedings*, 1894, 176.

10. AR, 1886, 82.

11. Ibid., 1889, 139.

12. PAO, RG2, Ross to Arthur Brown (copy), 5 March 1895.

13. Alexander Jackson, "Importance of Kindergarten Training to the Nation," OEA *Proceedings*, 1896, 402.

14. J.J. Kelso, "Neglected and Friendless Children," *Canadian Magazine*, Jan. 1894, 215.

15. TBE, *Annual Report of the Inspector of Public Schools*, 1893, 30.

16. James L. Hughes, "Influence of the Kindergarten Spirit on Higher Education," OEA *Proceedings*, 1896, 103–8.

17. PAO, RG2, Ross to R.H. Biggar (copy), 13 Oct. 1896.

18. James L. Hughes, "The Future Evolution of the Kindergarten," *Education*, April 1902, 459.

19. James L. Hughes, "The Influence of the Kindergarten Spirit on Higher Education," OEA *Proceedings*, 1896, 98.

20. James L. Hughes, "European Schools," OEA *Proceedings*, 1908, 244.

21. Toronto *Globe*, 14 Jan. 1901.

22. Pierce, *Life of James L. Hughes*, 27.

23. TBE, *Annual Report of the Inspector of Public Schools*, 1886, 29–36.

24. James L. Hughes, "Manual Training," OEA *Proceedings*, 1897, 352–57.

25. TBE, Wellesley Public School, *Minutes of Teachers' Meetings*, 17 June 1895.

26. Trades and Labour Congress of Canada, *Proceedings*, 1888, 25.

27. W.H. Huston, "Manual Training," OTA *Proceedings*, 1890, 86; J.H. Putman, "Country Schools," OEA *Proceedings*, 1895, 310.

28. James Robertson, "The Macdonald College Movement," *Proceedings of the National Education Association of the United States*, 1904, 92.

29. James Robertson, "Manual Training," *Canadian Magazine*, April 1901, 524.

30. Adelaide Hoodless, "The Labour Question and Women's Work and Its Relation to Home Life," NCWC *Proceedings*, 1898, 257–58.

31. Adelaide Hoodless, "Domestic Science," DEA *Proceedings*, 1907, 192.

32. Ruth Howes, *Adelaide Hoodless: Woman With A Vision* (Ottawa: Federated Women's Institutes of Canada, 1965), 17.

33. Adelaide Hoodless, "Domestic Science," NCWC *Proceedings*, 1902, 118.

34. Hoodless, "The Labour Question and Women's Work," 258.

35. Adelaide Hoodless, *Report to the Minister of Education, Ontario, on Trade Schools in Relation to Elementary Education* (Toronto: L.K. Cameron, 1909), 3.

36. Adelaide Hoodless, "Domestic Science," NCWC *Proceedings*, 1894, 117.

37. Adelaide Hoodless, "Domestic Science," NCWC *Proceedings*, 1902, 119.

38. Howes, *Adelaide Hoodless*, 12.

39. Adelaide Hoodless, "Domestic Science," NCWC *Proceedings*, 1894, 118–19.

40. PAO, RG2, Hoodless to Richard Harcourt, 8 June 1903.

41. Adelaide Hoodless, "A New Education for Women," *Farmer's Advocate*, 15 Dec. 1902.

42. Adelaide Hoodless, "Domestic Science," NCWC *Proceedings*, 1905, 38.

43. PAO, RG2, Hoodless to John Millar, 1 Sept. 1900. For a more detailed account of the home economics movement, see Robert M. Stamp, "Teaching Girls Their 'God-Given Place in Life' — the Introduction of Home Economics in the Schools," *Atlantis* 2, 2 (Spring 1977): 18–34.

44. W.R. Parkinson, "The Centralization of Rural Public Schools," OEA *Proceedings*, 1903, 391.

45. Harvey M. Gayman, *Rittenhouse School and Gardens* (Toronto: William Briggs, 1911); see also, AR, 1905, ix.

46. "Unusual System of Classes in Carleton County," Toronto *Daily Star*, 27 Feb. 1906.

47. Robert Stothers, *A Biographical Memorial to Robert Henry Cowley, 1859–1927* (Toronto: Thomas Nelson and Sons, 1935), 29.

48. AR, 1899, xix.

49. PAO, RG3, George W. Ross file, "Memorandum of a Plan Proposed for the Improvement of Education at Rural Schools," 6 Jan. 1902.

50. James Robertson, "The Macdonald College Movement," 92.

51. Ibid.

52. AR, 1903, xxxiii.

53. R.H. Cowley, "The Macdonald School Gardens," *Queen's Quarterly* (April 1905): 415–18.

54. A.J. Madill, *A History of Agricultural Education in Ontario* (Toronto: University of Toronto Press, 1930), 185.

55. "Memorandum of a Plan Proposed for the Improvement of Education at Rural Schools."

56. Toronto *Globe*, 16 Dec. 1902.

57. Parkinson, "The Centralization of Rural Public Schools," 391.

58. PAO, RG2, Harcourt to Macdonald (copy), 7 Jan. 1902.

59. AR, 1899, xxi.

60. Richard Harcourt, "Address," OEA *Proceedings*, 1903, 95.

61. AR, 1899, xviii.

62. PAO, RG2, Harcourt to J.C. Harstone (copy), 17 Oct. 1901; Harcourt to A.O. Beatty (copy), 2 May 1901; Harcourt to T.H. Preston (copy), 15 Oct. 1901; Harcourt to D.Z. Morris (copy), 28 April 1904.

63. Richard Harcourt, "Address," OEA *Proceedings*, 1902, 61.

64. John Seath, "Some Needed Educational Reforms," OEA *Proceedings*, 1903, 85.

65. AR, 1880–81, 247. For a more detailed analysis of the school health movement in Ontario, see Neil Sutherland, " 'To Create a Strong and Healthy Race': School Children in the Public Health Movement, 1880–1914," *History of Education Quarterly* 12, 3 (Fall 1972): 304–33.

66. Ontario Board of Health, *Report*, 1883, xlvi.

67. Charles E. Phillips, *The Development of Education in Canada* (Toronto: Gage, 1957), 366.

68. Ontario Board of Health, *Report*, 1883, 242–43.

69. James L. Hughes, "Address of Welcome," OTA *Proceedings*, 1892, 114.

70. Ontario Board of Health, *Report*, 1899, 72–74 and 1901, 6.

71. Edward Miller Steven, *Medical Supervision in Schools: Being An Account of the Systems at Work in Great Britain, Canada, the United States, Germany, and Switzerland* (London, 1910), 182–83.

72. PAO, RG2, J.G. Adams to George Ross, 1 March 1901.

73. Ibid., John Thomson to Richard Harcourt, 4 April 1900.

74. Neil S. MacDonald, *Open-Air Schools* (Toronto: McClelland, Goodchild and Stewart, 1918), 54.

75. W.E. Struthers, "The Open Air School," OEA *Proceedings*, 1914, 282–87.

76. Toronto Playgrounds Association, *Account of Its Stewardship* (Toronto: TPA, 1910), 3.

77. TBE, *Annual Report*, 1913, 22.

78. Ibid., 1914, 17.

79. J. Castell Hopkins, ed., *The Canadian Annual Review for 1911* (Toronto: Annual Review Publishing Co., 1912), 442.

80. PAO, RG2, J.H. Putman to A.H.U. Colquhoun, 20 Jan. 1914. For an analysis of the work of Arthur Beall and early sex education in Ontario, see Michael Bliss, " 'Pure Books on Avoided Subjects': Pre-Freudian Sexual Ideas in Canada," Canadian Historical Association, *Historical Papers, 1970*: 89–108.

81. Gerald T. Hackett, "The History of Public Education for Mentally Retarded Children in the Province of Ontario, 1867–1964" (Ph.D. thesis, University of Toronto, 1969), 86.

82. Ibid., 88.

83. PAO, George Howard Ferguson papers, Hughes to Ferguson, 28 Sept. 1927.

84. Ottawa *Journal*, 21 Nov. 1939.

85. Ottawa Public School Board, *Inspector's Annual Report*, 1913, 12.

86. TBE, Givens Public School, diary of teachers' meetings, 1890–1913, and Dovercourt Public School, minutes of teachers' meetings, 1890–1941.

87. Ibid., *Annual Report*, 1913, 54.

88. *Saturday Night*, 20 March 1920, 1.

89. Vincent Massey, "Primary Education in Ontario," *University Magazine*, Oct. 1911, 495–96.

90. William Linton, "A Retrospect," OEA *Proceedings*, 1911, 233.

91. John Henderson, "Reminiscences of Education in Ontario," OEA *Proceedings*, 1911, 172.

92. AR, 1889, 108.

93. PAO, RG2, Mary McIntyre to Robert Pyne, 6 Nov. 1905.

94. I.J. Birchard, "Some Educational Fallacies," OEA *Proceedings*, 1902, 252.

95. TBE, *Annual Report*, 1913, 49.

96. Albert Leake, "Manual Training in the School," *The School*, March 1914, 438.

97. Lyman C. Smith, "The Trend of Education in Our High Schools," OEA *Proceedings*, 1910, 163.

98. Vincent Massey, "Primary Education in Ontario," 498.

99. AR, 1903, 155.

100. PAO, RG2, John Laughton to R.A. Pyne, 29 Nov. 1905.

101. Smith, "The Trend of Education," 155–63.

102. PAO, RG2, H. Gibbard to Richard Harcourt, 25 April 1904; R.H. Cowley to Harcourt, 5 Jan. 1903.

103. Terrence Robert Morrison, "The Child and Urban Social Reform in Late Nineteenth Century Ontario, 1875-1900" (Ph.D. thesis, University of Toronto, 1971), 429-30.

104. Civic Improvement League of Canada, *Report of Conference*, 1916, 31-32.

105. Ontario Teachers' Manuals, *History of Education* (Toronto: Copp Clark, 1915), 177-81.

THE RESOLUTION OF THE ONTARIO BILINGUAL SCHOOLS CRISIS, 1919-1929†

PETER OLIVER

In 1912 the Ontario government, for a variety of reasons, promulgated educational regulations designed to govern the use of the French language in the provincial schools system. Regulation 17 limited the use of French as the language of instruction to the first few years of elementary school, except in special cases, and it restricted the amount of time which could be devoted to French as a subject to one hour per day. The controversy which was engendered by Regulation 17 was a national catastrophe. Although Premier Whitney and the officials of the Department of Education argued that the regulation gave scope for an enormous amount of French education, that its purpose was not the suppression of French but the promotion of English, and that the rejection of the regulation would mean that children in French areas would never be provided with the opportunity to acquire a functional bilingualism, many French Canadians regarded such arguments as sophistry.

Their resistance took many forms, including marches, demonstrations, school strikes and virulent denunciations of Anglo-Saxon bigotry. Inevitably, the bilingual question became intermixed with the other tensions of the war years and the always brittle fabric of French-English co-operation all but collapsed under the strain. Many English Canadians believed the French to be shirkers cynically exploiting a domestic problem to avoid doing their duty overseas. Some French Canadians replied by describing the people of the neighbouring province as "the Huns of Ontario" and proclaiming that they would not fight in Europe because the only place in the world where French civilization was threatened was along the banks of the Ottawa River. The schools question, which had thus escalated into one of the most serious cultural clashes in Canadian history, was conducted in somewhat more muted tones after the Pope intervened in late 1916 on behalf of "counsels of moderation" and after the Judicial Committee of the Privy Council

†*Journal of Canadian Studies* 7 (1972): 22–45.

in twin decisions decided that Regulation 17 was *intra vires* but that the Special Commission by which the government had been attempting to enforce its policies was unconstitutional. Neither side, however, was willing to budge from its essential position.[1] The Franco-Ontarians still regarded Regulation 17 as an outrageous attack on their national rights and the Ontario government remained determined to enforce its educational regulations.

This paper, then, directs its attention to this later period when Regulation 17 remained in effect and Ontarians were forced to live with the consequences of what had been said and done at the height of the storm and to seek some workable resolution. By examining the politics of accommodation and the mechanics of the process by which a settlement was achieved, it seeks to throw some light on certain values and attitudes held in the 1920s by the Franco-Ontarians and by the larger community of which they were a part. Although the schools question touched a wide variety of social and economic interests, its ultimate resolution was achieved within a political context. It was the politicians who most directly confronted the realities of conflict and who negotiated the necessary settlement. Ironically, this was accomplished only after the dispute to a considerable extent had been removed from the arena of party politics. That this was necessary, however, in no way lessened the national significance of the successful resolution of the Ontario bilingual schools question. Hailed on all sides and regarded at the time as a turning point in English-French relations, the solution of 1927 did indeed grant French Canadians extensive new rights in the schools of Ontario. National unity itself had been at stake, said the pundits of the period, and 1927 seemed to most Canadians to represent a happy ending to an oft-times unhappy story. From 1916 to 1919 the Conservative government of Sir William Hearst had reacted to French-Canadian cries of persecution by digging in its heels.[2] Hearst and his colleagues believed they were unjustly maligned and that the opposition was being fomented by politically ambitious agitators who were exploiting the dispute in a ruthless fashion which made compromise impossible. In 1916 Hearst's Acting Minister of Education, G. Howard Ferguson, had told Prime Minister Borden that no government would live an hour if it made the slightest concession.[3] Senator Napoleon A. Belcourt, the best known Franco-Ontarian spokesman, later said of the Hearst government that it "did not try at any time to settle the question, that it did not want the question to be settled, that it looked upon the difficulties caused by Regulation 17 as its best ground for retaining power. . . ."[4] Whatever the accuracy of his assertion, the administration's public stance was undeniably rigid. For awhile it even considered appointing a new commission to replace that which had been struck down by the Judicial Committee and in another hard-line move Franco-Ontarians petitioning for land in Northern Ontario were required to submit signed pledges that they would obey the school laws.[5] The Hearst government was sustained in this attitude by its confidence that what it regarded as the unreasonable opposition fomented by a few individuals could not endure. By applying the regulation in a moderate fashion, by a judicious use of Department of Education grants and through the assertion of other pressures, the government believed it could isolate the leaders of the agitation and win acceptance for its policy.

Leadership of the French community in Ontario continued to be provided by the executive of the Ottawa-based French-Canadian Educational Association of Ontario (ACFEO). The Association was determined that the government's campaign of attrition should not succeed. During the war years it had achieved considerable success by presenting the schools question as a great national issue. Mass meetings and heroic invocations in the French-language press had inspired the population while an alliance with Quebec nationalist organizations had provided financial, political and moral support. In these circumstances, the Ottawa French-speaking community, except for the period of the Special Commission, had maintained control of the city's separate school board while in nearby Prescott and Russell counties the resistance had attained similar successes. Elsewhere in the province the situation was less clear. In the Essex-Kent area there was little French used in the schools; in the great expanse of Northern Ontario, Regulation 17 was formally in effect but often ignored in practice; and in other eastern Ontario counties with a French minority, English was the language of instruction in most instances.[6] Nonetheless some progress had been made. In 1916 in the little village of Green Valley in Glengarry County, not far from the Quebec border, the local French-speaking community, after campaigning unsuccessfully for a French-speaking teacher, had finally decided to found its own school. This was done with the support of ACFEO. As a result of fundraising campaigns in the French-Canadian press, the fame of the "free school" in Green Valley was soon spread among the French community. Green Valley became the model for similar efforts in the 1920s.[7]

Of course the cost of running a small rural school was slight compared to that involved in the operation of the Ottawa Separate School system. The cutting off of the provincial grant was only part of the problem the Ottawa Board faced. The MacKell injunction presented a more serious difficulty. In 1914 R. MacKell and other English-speaking trustees of the Ottawa Separate School Board had obtained an injunction from the Ontario Supreme Court which prevented the board from borrowing or from paying the salaries of teachers so long as it refused to obey the regulations of the Department of Education. Board chairman Sam Genest, at the risk of imprisonment, had continued to pay salaries but throughout this whole period his board was crippled by its inability to engage in ordinary financial operations. At the beginning of 1919 the Board faced a $50 000 deficit.[8] In the spring of the same year the Secretary-Treasurer, Albert Carle, reported that no permanent repairs had been made to any of the buildings for five or six years, that more classroom space was desperately needed and that conditions in the schools were becoming intolerable.[9] The Ottawa Board's financial situation was further complicated by a Judicial Committee judgment of 1919 which held it legally responsible for all the acts of the Special Commission, and obligation amounting in 1921 to $71 000 in principal and $89 000 in accumulated interest.[10] Albert Carle's report also revealed that the board had been losing an average of $35 000 a year over a six-year period as a result of the transfer of separate school supporters to the public school system and a desperate Sam Genest even considered trying to exert pressure on defectors by publishing their names in the press.[11]

The ACFEO leaders, then, were well aware of the dimensions of their task. In August of 1918 Senator Landry, the ACFEO president, had written Cardinal Bégin of Quebec to suggest a more effective method by which funds for the Ontario cause could be raised in Quebec, under a 1916 statute permitting local school boards to make contributions. At the time he reminded the Cardinal that "la lutte ne peut se faire ni poursuivre sans les moyens pécuniaires. . . ." Unfortunately, appeals in *Le Droit* and *Le Devoir* and the small amount raised by such local expedients as card parties and bazaars were not an adequate means of financial support.[12] Nor was it reasonable to expect French-Canadian parents to sustain the burden of "double taxation" for many more years. Obviously, an early solution was highly desirable from the Franco-Ontarian point of view.

Nonetheless, the French-Canadian Educational Association was not inclined to seek a compromise. Despite financial hardships and signs of wavering support, despite the repeated assurances given by departmental officials that those schools which had accepted Regulation 17 found it fair and workable, few French-Canadian leaders ever seriously considered such a solution. They demanded total victory. Anything less, they were certain, would represent a defeat which could be fatal to the French cause in Ontario. Convinced that the acceptance even of a mild form of Regulation 17 would legitimize the argument that the French language had no legal rights outside the province of Quebec, the ACFEO executive viewed the schools question as vital to the very survival of French-Canadian culture outside of Quebec.[13] The members of the Association were greatly worried about the anemic state of that culture. With defeatism and indifference already too prevalent, the acceptance of Regulation 17 would constitute the final symbolic victory of the forces of assimilation in such outposts as Windsor, Sudbury and Pembroke. In 1920, for example, the Saint Jean-Baptiste Society of Pembroke lamented that French Canadians in the area had no sense of patriotism and that a great many were ashamed of being French and did everything possible to hide the fact. The Society reported that "ce régime de parcimonie et surtout de total abandon du français à l'école a fait la sorte que la génération qui pousse est perdue pour la race. . . ."[14] The ACFEO executive knew that the cry of persecution raised so frequently since 1912 had been and was being used to considerable effect to organize the Franco-Ontarians, to forge a powerful alliance with Quebec and generally to assume the offensive on the educational front. But with so much remaining to be done, a compromise would only restore the intolerable state of indifference which had existed before the struggle began and which was still prevalent in many communities. It would permit the bilingual teachers colleges run by the Department of Education to continue to develop teachers unacceptable to ACFEO. It would do nothing to solve the major problems which had faced bilingual schools in the days before Regulation 17 had been promulgated and it would do nothing to prevent local boards dominated by hostile majorities from continuing to refuse to permit French teaching. Undoubtedly Bishop Latulippe of Haileybury had some of this in mind when he assured Premier Taschereau of Quebec that even if Regulation 17 were applied "avec une main gantée de velours, il resterait comme une menace formidable que nous ne pouvons pas accepter."[15] No, the blandishments and the threats must equally be resisted. If there was to be a cultural future for Franco-Ontarians, the victory over Regulation 17 had to be complete and unequivocal.

None of this of course meant that the ACFEO executive wanted the struggle to continue for a moment longer than was necessary. Costs were such that the resistance might collapse at any moment and almost annually Association leaders announced that they feared that the Ottawa schools in particular would not be able to reopen their doors come September. As a result the Association bent every effort to convince the Department of Education and the government that a solution should be effected and to prepare the ground by a variety of means for such a resolution.

There were two major strategies followed by the Association in its efforts to achieve this result. The techniques of confrontation used between 1912 and 1916 had achieved considerable success in publicizing the good cause and galvanizing the faithful. But they had also activated the latent francophobia of many Ontarians and made it impossible for any government, even if so inclined, to grant concessions to the French community. By late 1916 Franco-Ontarian leaders seem to have realized the need for a different approach but the apparent rigidity of the Hearst government made overtures in this direction a useless exercise. Hearst's defeat in 1919, however, excited great expectations among the French community and put an entirely new face on the situation. So too did the return of Senator Napoleon A. Belcourt to the ACFEO presidency in 1920. Belcourt, in contrast to Sam Genest and some others, had never become identified in the public mind with the kind of agitation which had characterized the early war years. A courtly figure, a distinguished lawyer who had served as Speaker of the House of Commons, Belcourt was convinced that the Association should undertake a major campaign to win friends in English Canada and he forthwith embarked upon this endeavor. The Senator, entirely at home in English-speaking circles and married to an English Canadian, possessed definite advantages for this work.

Furthermore, he had correctly judged the changing mood of the times. There were many in Ontario who had been horrified by the wartime collapse of national unity and some of these were beginning to publish sympathetic studies of the French-Canadian's role in Canadian society. These included in 1918 and 1919 P. F. Morley's *Bridging the Chasm*, Arthur Hawkes' *The Birthright*, and W. H. Moore's *The Clash* and his novel *Polly Masson*.[16] Moore had been a member of the wartime *Bonne Entente* movement as had Toronto lawyer John Godfrey, and C. B. Sissons, the Victoria College professor who in 1917 authored the sympathetic study, *Bi-lingual Schools in Canada*. It was to Sissons, Moore, and Godfrey that the Senator paid particular attention. Soon he was doing everything in his power to encourage these men and their friends to speak and write widely about the injustice Regulation 17 perpetrated on the Franco-Ontarians.[17]

Belcourt by no means restricted his attentions to this small group. Under his leadership the association abandoned its angry cries of persecution and its loud denunciations of the Ontario government in favour of a vast campaign whose purpose was to establish contact with and sometimes to bring political pressure to bear on just about anyone who might influence either public opinion or the government. Clerics, businessmen, educators, journalists and such political figures as Premier Taschereau and Conservative leader Arthur Sauvé of Quebec, Prime Minister King, Arthur Meighen and T. A. Crerar in Ottawa, and J. J. Morrison, the powerful secretary of the United Farmers of Ontario, all listened sympathetically and pledged assistance. Every possible argument was marshalled against Regulation 17 and no opportunity was missed to bring influence to bear. These efforts did not achieve early success. They gave rise to years of frustrating negotiations. Yet in spite of broken promises and halting progress, the association, with one or two minor exceptions, refused to abandon its new policy of quiet diplomacy and private pressure.

The second major element in the new strategy was a systematization and elaboration of what had been evolving since 1912. The association had always realized that if Regulation 17 was to be resisted, educational alternatives would have to be provided for Franco-Ontarians. This was being done in Ottawa and in such places as Green Valley. Not only would these experiments have to be prolonged but efforts would have to be made to extend the area of resistance to all communities in which Franco-Ontarians were being deprived of a French education. This much, however difficult to achieve in practice, was simple in concept. Its deficiencies were also clear. Even if a comprehensive, extra-legal school system was established, that achievement would not itself rid the land of Regulation 17. It might only create a stand-off with the government. Franco-Ontarians, many of whom represented the poorer sections of Ontario society, would be forced to bear the cost of a private school system. With only that to look forward to, it seemed unlikely that even that degree of success could be attained.

It was at this point that the shift occurred. Possibly the ACFEO executive turned to the new policy in a piecemeal and gradual fashion; possibly the subtle mind of the politician-lawyer Belcourt seized upon it first and gradually directed his colleagues towards it. Whatever its origins, it was a masterstroke. The association decided it would take to heart the criticism of the English-French schools that Dr. Merchant had levelled in 1912. Merchant had said that in too many instances these schools were providing education of a decidedly inferior standard and were also producing students who were not competent in the English language. The association would, therefore, provide schools in which students would be trained not as under the Regulation 17 regimen but by accepted bilingual techniques. By this the association meant that teaching would be carried on primarily through the instrument of the mother tongue. If such schools, handicapped by the absence of government funds, could produce students who were not only fluent in French and English but who also attained a good general level of academic achievement, the whole ground would be undercut from the supporters of Regulation 17. In these circumstances there could be no legitimate complaint from English Canada. If this were achieved, Belcourt's other strategy would also be faciliated. By demonstrating the success of its educational methods, the association expected to win the support of the great body of moderate opinion which Belcourt believed existed in Ontario. The twin strategies were thus complementary and would go forward at the same time.

The part of this programme which could be carried out from within the French community seemed to meet with considerable success. The Ottawa Separate School Board, led by its chairman Sam Genest and its educational director, the talented Aurélien Bélanger, kept its schools functioning and comparable results were attained in Prescott and Russell counties. The most impressive achievement of the early 1920s was not in these centres of Franco-Ontarian influence but in the outposts. The free school in Green Valley proved so popular with the French community that a second such school was opened and in 1922 ACFEO, with the support of Omer Héroux of *Le Devoir*, organized a public subscription which in a few weeks raised over a thousand dollars for the Green Valley schools.[18] The best publicized of the free schools of the 1920s was L'École Jeanne D'Arc of Pembroke. After a long and bitter struggle with the local school board and the English-speaking Roman Catholic hierarchy, the free school was opened in 1923. It soon moved to a permanent dwelling purchased at a cost of $5 000.[19] The Pembroke school became one of the great French-Canadian causes of the 1920s and its teacher, Mlle Lajoie, achieved the status of folk hero. The struggle which was waged in the village of Alexandria, near Cornwall, had a different conclusion. In 1920 the French element in the community placed a majority of members on the Separate School Board but efforts to establish special bilingual classes were blocked by the ecclesiastical authorities. Finally an unhappy compromise was reached by which a minimal amount of French teaching was permitted and the local community resorted to costly evening classes to supplement this.[20]

The Essex-Kent region presented a special problem. In this area, surrounded by major American and English-Canadian population centres and in the ecclesiastical jurisdiction of Bishop Fallon, the French community was far advanced on the road to anglicization. In rural districts the children sometimes received a small amount of teaching in French but in Windsor this was seldom the case. In 1922 local leaders submitted a report to ACFEO which contained a seven-point programme which they deemed essential "pour sauver la race dans cette partie du pays" from the prevailing indifference and defeatism. Convinced that local boards would remain hostile so long as the unfriendly regime of Bishop Fallon of London endured, this group founded "la Ligue des Patriotes" to press for outside financial support for a private school. This was forthcoming both from ACFEO and from the Association Catholique de la Jeunesse canadienne-française in Montreal. A school was opened in 1922 in a private home and in 1923 it attracted 103 students and moved into new quarters which cost $15 000. Typically, the Windsor free school was soon experiencing financial difficulties.[21]

Thus local conditions determined that the pattern of resistance varied considerably across the province. In Ottawa and in Prescott and Russell counties the concentration of numbers led to French control of local boards. In Pembroke, Green Valley and Windsor free schools had to be established. In Northern Ontario the situation was more complicated. In Sudbury, for example, the French group in 1915 won a majority on the school commission and with the tacit approval of the provincial inspector Regulation 17 was effectively ignored. At nearby Sturgeon Falls, however, the French Canadians encountered an unfriendly inspector and little French could be used.[22] But whatever the nature of the local situation, these communities almost without exception leaned heavily for support on the organizing abilities of the association. The establishment of French schools was only the first step in ACFEO's systematic effort to develop a proficient bilingual schools system in Ontario.

Also important was the association's promulgation of a bilingual program incorporating curricular and pedagogical principles developed by leading Franco-Ontarian educators. A modest effort had been prepared in 1911 but a fuller programme started in 1923 was completed in 1925 and distributed across the province.[23] The association also sponsored a series of conferences to explain the programme to teachers and rally local leaders to its support.

In another initiative the association struck out against an old grievance, the high school entrance examination, which was conducted entirely in English and constituted a major barrier to the advancement of Franco-Ontarians into the high school system. It was, of course, simple enough for the association to set its own bilingual examinations but passing these would not qualify the young Franco-Ontarian for admission to the provincial high school system. And if Franco-Ontarians could not pass the entrance examination into high school the source of teachers would ultimately dry up. In any case, ACFEO believed that teachers educated in the Department of Education's bilingual teachers colleges were trained in the methods of Regulation 17 and were therefore unacceptable in many instances to the association. The only way out of this dilemma seemed to be for the association to sponsor not only high schools but also a teachers college of its own. This was a task of almost unthinkable proportions for a group of men who were struggling desperately to keep open a few elementary schools.

ACFEO, however, was not daunted by large undertakings. And in the University of Ottawa it had an ally whose co-operation rendered this particular task less impossible than it seemed. Not only did the university agree to devise a special secondary school programme for a limited number of students who were primarily teacher training prospects, but it also agreed to accept those students who completed this programme into the university proper. The association therefore, instituted its own bilingual entrance examination and in 1925, its first year of operation, 225 Franco-Ontarians from across the province were able to try this examination under the supervision of an examination board composed of thirty-five professors. The following year some 350 students were examined in twenty-five local centres.[24]

The most audacious part of this programme was the establishment in 1923 of a teachers college in association with the University of Ottawa. The university, of course, was running considerable risk by associating itself with a project which so contemptuously flouted provincial authority. Department of Education officials were outraged by the new move and the Deputy Minister later denounced it as "mere impudence."[25] Even such a close friend of the association as C. B. Sissons warned Belcourt that "I do not think that the people of Ontario would for a moment stand for degrees in Pedagogy given by any institution not under the control of the Department."[26] But the association persisted. The bilingual teachers college capped a truly amazing effort. Belcourt himself best expressed the significance of the whole system of extra-legal schools which the association had inspired when he asserted that they represented ". . . un démenti constant à l'assertion que les Canadiens français s'accomodent au régime qu'on veut leur imposer, une protestation efficace contre le système de dénationalisation de déformation et d'ignorance qu'un certain nombre de coreligionnaires de langue anglaise cherchent imposer. . . ."[27] Both their educational efficiency and their political utility, however, remained to be demonstrated.

Senator Belcourt and his associates hoped to use the free school system to influence public opinion. Their first aim, however, was to convince Premier Drury and his Farmers government that Regulation 17 was unjust and that justice could be done without damaging the political fortunes of the new administration. Immediate steps in this direction were taken by J. A. Caron, a former editor of *Le Droit* who had become a county director of the U.F.O. and had run unsuccessfully in Prescott. Caron emphasized to United Farmer Secretary J. J. Morrison that the three French-language newspapers in Ontario, *Le Droit* of Ottawa, *Le Moniteur* of Hawksbury and *La Défence* of Windsor had "put up a magnificent fight for the U.F.O. during the last campaign" and he told Education Minister R. H. Grant that a motion in favour of the U.F.O. introduced at the ACFEO convention held early in 1919 had been "unanimously carried notwithstanding a vigorous opposition by professional and business men."[28] While making these overtures, Caron was very conscious of the fact that the election of only one Franco-Ontarian under the Farmer banner had weakened his bargaining position but he also knew that, with political forces in the Legislature equally balanced between the Farmer-Labour government and the old-line parties, the support of the five Liberal deputies of French origin would assure Drury of a firm lease on power. Soon Caron assured the Premier that "we are trying as strongly as possible to bring you some more support in the Legislature . . ." and that at least four of the five Liberal members were sympathetic.[29] Another compelling political inducement was held before the government's eyes when Caron promised Morrison that a settlement of the schools question would be "for you the surest way to get to the heart of the French Canadians of the whole Dominion."[30] This became a constant refrain and Father Charles Charlebois, high in ACFEO councils, also assured Morrison that if a solution were achieved "the agrarian movement would have a great vogue in Quebec."[31]

Representatives of ACFEO met with Drury in Toronto within weeks of his elevation to the Premiership. The arguments they levelled against Regulation 17 differed little from those in use since 1912. Drury listened sympathetically and seemed well disposed. He pointed out, naturally enough, that his first duty was to ensure the life of the government and this made it essential that he act with prudence on such a delicate issue. But, although the premier promised nothing and indeed asked that there be no agitation on the subject until the administration was safely through its first session, he led the delegates to believe that they had his support and that action would then be taken.[32] Belcourt accepted the proposed truce the more readily because it coincided so exactly with the strategy he was already pursuing. In the meantime, negotiations went forward over the details of the settlement. In January, 1920, at the government's request, the association presented a list of its proposed changes to the school regulations.[33] Before going to the government the proposals had been submitted to the French-Canadian members of the legislature, to several national societies and to a number of important people in Quebec. Belcourt assured Sissons that everything possible had been done "to make the modifications as reasonable and as moderate as possible" and he particularly emphasized that the principle that the French children shall learn English was not only "not interfered with, but it is specifically recognized. . . ."[34] Further progress was made at a series of April meetings with members of the U.F.O. executive and representatives of the Department of Education.[35]

Then, when the time came for the government to act, it did nothing. In the months and years ahead the association held countless meetings with representatives of the administration and time and again they were led to believe that the government would soon make its move. From some of these meetings the association carried away the impression that the government had committed itself to providing temporary financial help for the embattled Ottawa board; at others Drury seemed to reaffirm his own distate for Regulation 17 but to argue that the time was not quite ripe for him to act.[36] The association's disillusionment grew gradually but inexorably. At the end of 1920 ACFEO's secretary Edmond Cloutier complained to J. J. Morrison that "we have had patience, we have waited since the Session for the solution . . . we have been overwhelmed with nice promises."[37] The Franco-Ontarian leaders were also distressed because they believed that the Department of Education was taking advantage of the truce which had been negotiated to bring pressure to bear on schools which were continuing to resist Regulation 17. In May of 1921 Belcourt, expressing his anger at Education Minister Grant, assured Sissons that "in my thirty years of constant dealing with politicians I have never known one who could more readily forget or dexterously wriggle out of a promise or agreement."[38] By this time the association was beginning to question the government's motives and the secretary suggested that "l'attitude d'atermoiement irraisonnable et impolitique de M. Drury ne nous paraît guère explicable que par le fait qu'il practise avec les adversaires des écoles séparées et qu'il essaye de se ménager la chèvre et le chou."[39]

The association leaders found the government's position even harder to understand in that they believed they had already achieved a breakthrough which should have made it relatively simple for Drury to act. One of the major reasons for the original promulgation of Regulation 17 had been the bitter struggle between English- and French-speaking Roman Catholics. In no part of the province had this rivalry caused more trouble than in Ottawa. So long as Irish and French factions battled each other in the Ottawa separate school system, any government which attempted to intervene from above was likely to invoke the wrath of both sides. ACFEO realized this but all efforts to reach a compromise with the Ottawa Irish had long foundered on Irish insistence that the Separate School Board be divided into two sections. The French in 1920 agreed to accept this arrangement, evidently on the understanding that both divisions would remain under the formal chairmanship of Sam Genest and that the Irish would henceforth support the French in their opposition to Regulation 17.[40] Father Cornell,

O.M.I., was the leader of the Irish group which supported this compromise and in the long negotiations which lay ahead his aid was of enormous assistance. Harmony, however, had not been completely restored and a vociferous minority, representing, ACFEO claimed, only 10 percent of the Ottawa Irish, refused to accept the agreement.

Although this body of irreconcilables was a considerable nuisance during ACFEO's delicate negotiations with the politicians, their influence lessened when Archbishop Neil McNeil of Toronto intervened actively on behalf of the Franco-Ontarians. The Archbishop wanted French support in a major campaign he was about to initiate to win tax concessions for separate schools and after an Ottawa meeting Senator Belcourt agreed to co-operate in return for McNeil's public support in the campaign against Regulation 17.[41] The Archbishop, always a moderate in any case, fulfilled this pledge when he joined Belcourt and leading French-speaking members of the Catholic hierarchy in a March 1921 meeting with Drury. As usual the premier gave the delegation the impression that action would follow at the end of the session; as usual these expectations went unrealized.[42]

A variety of reasons may be advanced to explain Drury's behavior. Despite McNeil's support, there remained elements in Ottawa among both the Irish and, surprisingly, the French, which still refused to line up behind the association. The dissident French group was numerically small and was led by Napoleon Champagne, a local politician who, according to ACFEO, was attempting to ingratiate himself with the government by passing himself off as a French spokesman.[43] The Irish faction was a greater worry. Although ACFEO attempted to write it off as an insignificant minority of the Irish community, Education Minister Grant cited the existence of different groups, "all quite diverse in opinion" as one reason for the government's failure to act.[44]

A more serious obstacle was found in the Education Minister himself. Grant once told Drury that he sat for a constituency which had 85 Orange lodges and no high school.[45] Convinced that concessions to the French would entail political disaster, he informed the Premier that he would not act himself but that he would willingly surrender his portfolio. There was, however, no credible alternative available on the Farmer side of the House so Grant remained in Education.[46] As for Drury himself, aware of his government's many weaknesses, he was probably afraid to take a step which might prove controversial. When he raised the question of Regulation 17 at a caucus held on April 28, 1921, many members opposed early action. According to Grant it now emerged that "man after man" had been approached during the 1919 election campaign and had given pledges not to support any modification.[47] Drury remained unmoved even when Belcourt informed him that "the assurance has been given you by leading members of the Liberal opposition . . . that you can count on the support of the Leader of the Opposition and 17 or 18 of his followers. . . ."[48] He was afraid that Tory leader G. Howard Ferguson, who had been one of the earliest supporters of Regulation 17, would seize the opportunity to exploit the issue on the hustings.[49]

By this time Belcourt had lost all patience with Drury. He told him that if action were not taken the Ottawa schools would not reopen in September and intimated that as Premier he would have to shoulder the blame for the fact that some 10 000 children in the Canadian capital would be "indefinitely deprived of any education at all. . . ." He warned too that the French population was rapidly losing all confidence in leaders who counselled moderation. "Unless the matter is promptly settled, these leaders will . . . be totally unable to exercise any kind of control over their people. The result must inevitably be an agitation wider, more determined and dangerous than ever. . . ."[50]

Belcourt's letter accurately reflected the impatience which prevailed at regional meetings the association sponsored over the summer.[51] Then in August a pamphlet written by C. B. Sissons was distributed among the U.F.O. rank and file. Designed to mobilize support for the French cause in rural Ontario, the new move was supported by Secretary Morrison who was acutely embarrassed by Drury's inactivity.[52] In another effort the following month, U.F.O. Educational Secretary M. H. Staples inspected the Ottawa schools and found that, in spite of depressing physical conditions in many of the schools, the English language was for the most part being effectively taught. Although the Staples report was presented to the public as coming from an independent observer, Belcourt insisted on meeting his expenses and asked to see the report before it was finalized.[53] Then, the following January, the association received mounting evidence that the Department of Education was working hard to enforce Regulation 17 and, in Belcourt's words, was using the truce "for the purpose of carrying on this campaign and thus undermining our cause."[54] The association responded to this challenge by issuing a statement denouncing the efforts of school inspectors in Prescott and Russell.[55] In a more dramatic move Belcourt even intervened in a by-election in Russell that the Drury government desperately wanted to win and told the voters that the Premier had done nothing to redeem his many pledges to the French community.[56] Belcourt also worked through Mackenzie King to convince provincial Liberal leader Wellington Hay that settlement of the schools dispute should be a pre-condition of the formal alliance between Grits and Druryites which was then being discussed. This effort came to naught when the Liberal negotiations with Drury collapsed for other reasons.[57] Finally the Senator spent a good deal of time in 1922 preparing an appeal on behalf of the Ontario minority to the League of Nations. In it he presented a well documented case citing natural law, treaty rights and pedagogical principles to prove that League intervention was warranted. Although this document caused some embarrassment in Geneva, the League's Secretary General Sir Eric Drummond soon replied that the League's procedures with regard to minorities' petitions did not apply to Canada.[58]

In all of these moves Belcourt was moving towards a more offensive stance. In none of them, however, not even in his by-election intervention, did he abandon the strategy he had been purusing since he resumed the ACFEO presidency. Although dealing with the Farmer government was a frustrating experience and Belcourt recognized that he had no choice but to push an administration that needed to be pushed, he never forgot that a return to the open warfare of the 1912–1916 period would be self-defeating. Thus at the same time as he was moving towards a more activist role, he was bringing to fruition a plan which was a far better expression of his thinking. He was organizing the Unity League.

The Unity League was the culmination of Belcourt's efforts to mobilize English-speaking opinion on behalf of the French cause in Ontario. Composed by Belcourt's choice entirely of members of the English-speaking elite of Ontario, the League defined its purpose as "the promotion of good will, better understanding, and more cordial co-operation between English and French-speaking Canadians."[59] Never large numerically, by 1925 the League had attracted a membership of some 150 leading professional and businessmen and academics. Many of its supporters had been identified with the earlier Bonne Entente movement. Sissons, Moore and Godfrey were, along with Belcourt, the League's main organizers.

The work of organization was facilitated by the assurances Belcourt was able to give with regard to ACFEO's record under his leadership. In letters to prospective members the Senator emphasized that the association had demonstrated that it had been able to avoid "intemperate speaking" and that "the English language is being efficiently imparted in all the Separate Schools. . . ."[60] Above all he stressed that the work of the League was of great national significance. National unity itself was at stake and he could not "conceive of any greater duty . . . than that one which this question calls for."[61] Perhaps the careful work of the last several years was about to pay dividends.

There was one aspect of the League which ACFEO kept from public view. The basic idea behind the League was that the organized opposition to Regulation 17 of a group of influential English-speaking Ontarians could not help but have a great impact on public opinion. This, of course, made good sense. In reality, however, the league to a very real extent was a front organization for the French-Canadian Educational Association. Belcourt, although not himself a member, was the mastermind behind the League and ACFEO secretary Cloutier confided to several French-Canadian journalists that not only had the association formed the League but it "continue d'être son impératrice et même sa directrice dans tout ce qu'elle entreprend."[62] It was well that this fact did not become public knowledge. ACFEO expected great things from the League. Cloutier informed the Apostolic Delegate that by its very existence it would give the lie to those who had always denounced the bilingual leaders as agitators and extremists.[63]

Even before the League's existence was announced, it embarked upon its first major project. It commissioned J. L. Hughes, an internationally known Toronto educator who was a friend of the French language and also had long been an active Orangeman, to inspect and report upon the progress of the Ottawa schools. John Godfrey, confident that the report would be favourable, suggested to Belcourt that it be made the basis for the League's whole educational campaign. "With a favourable report from the Past Grand Master of the Orange Lodge of Ontario," he concluded, "I think the other side can make no effective answer to our case."[64] This was the strategy adopted. Not surprisingly, the Hughes Report was one long paean of praise for the Ottawa schools. In December of 1922 the League's existence was announced to the public simultaneously with the release of the report. Although the Toronto papers reacted cautiously, the general press reaction was not unfriendly and the association was particularly pleased when the Ottawa *Journal*, hitherto no friend of the French cause, began to argue that in light of the Hughes findings there could no longer be any justification for the Department of

Education to continue to withhold grants from the Ottawa schools.[65]

The Unity League, although satisfied with its initial impact, had no illusions that the Drury government would be moved to act. The year 1923 would see a provincial election and all sides were anxious that the question not be injected into political debate during the last session of the Legislature or into the campaign. Alarmist notes sounded by the traditionally francophobe *Telegram* and Orange *Sentinel* had little effect and two days before the election Belcourt wrote that he was delighted that Ontario had been saved from "miserable and dangerous" appeals to prejudice.[66]

He had less cause to be happy about the electoral result. Although Godfrey, Sissons and others doubted that Ferguson would emerge with a majority, the realistic Belcourt thought otherwise, and even added, "I hope this is only a bad dream."[67] The bad dream became reality and the Premier's chair was assumed by the man who had introduced the notorious "English only" resolution into the legislature in 1911 and who had led the government defence of Regulation 17 during the war. John Godfrey, expressing the sense of pessimism felt by many Unity League members, told Belcourt that the new premier had such a large majority that he would "probably think it good policy to sit back and do nothing."[68] Whatever his real feelings may have been, Belcourt knew it was necessary to offer some encouragement to his English-speaking friends. He informed Moore that Ferguson "must know that the Regulation was a mistake in every sense of the word" and that his big majority at least gave him freedom to "do just what he likes. . . . He must know that he can render Canada the greatest service since Confederation. He practically has it in his own hands to say whether we shall have a national sentiment . . . or the reverse."[69] And he pointed out that with the Orangemen "almost to a man active members of the Conservative Party," Ferguson would be in an excellent position to deal with them when they raised a howl.[70] As a final inducement, the repeal of Regulation 17 would be the best means for the Tories to break the solid bloc of federal Liberals in Quebec and return to power nationally. "If he has vision," the Senator concluded, "he will see that this is the opportunity of his life both for himself and his party."

Although a less sanguine Godfrey reminded Belcourt that "Drury had the same chance and failed miserably," the ACFEO president had judged both the man and the situation with considerable shrewdness.[71] Howard Ferguson, his contemporaries agreed, was one of the most astute politicians the country had produced. If Belcourt's arguments made sense, Ferguson was not one to let such a golden opportunity slip past. Yet as much as anyone the premier was aware of the explosive potentital of the schools issue. Probably this was why he assumed the Education portfolio himself. He knew too that many officials in the Department of Education remained deeply resentful of the various French efforts to establish an extra-legal educational structure. There is little evidence, however, as to Ferguson's intentions with regard to the schools question in the period immediately following the 1923 election. Probably he had none. He would go slowly and see what the future would bring.

ACFEO for its part reacted swiftly. Edmond Cloutier, for example, asked a friend of the association in Windsor to get in touch with the local member at once. "Pressez, pressez . . . ," he emphasized, "il n'y a pas de temps à perdre. . . ."[72] Letters went out across the province to ask influential French Canadians and friendly English Canadians to set to work without delay. One focus of French attention was Arthur Meighen. The federal Tory leader was then engaged in his great campaign to restore his party's shattered fortunes in Quebec. Of course a major cause of Meighen's unpopularity was his record on conscription. Now a concerted effort was made to convince him, as Belcourt put it to Sissons, that "the one thing which won 65 liberal seats in Quebec . . . was not conscription or anything else — it was Regn. XVII."[73] John Godfrey as Unity League president approached Meighen early in 1924. After admitting that there were those who considered the regulation to be a grievance which was more imaginary than real, he insisted that the French regarded it "as an insult to their nationality. The regulation has become a national obsession. . . ."[74] When Meighen, who was anxious to assist, did indeed use his influence with the Ontario premier, prominent French Canadians hastened to express their gratitude and urge him on to still greater efforts.[75]

Another effort to exploit Tory political ambitions in Quebec offered itself when provincial Conservative leader Arthur Sauvé agreed to co-operate by applying constant pressure to Meighen. Sauvé publicized his position by sending a dramatic telegram to a Tory convention in Toronto to which he had been invited, announcing that he could not co-operate with those he regarded as the enemies of his people. Even two years later Sauvé was refusing to have anything to do with Arthur Meighen who complained bitterly that, "No one is more anxious than I to have this question amicably settled, and I do not think any have worked harder to that end." Nonetheless, Meighen pointed out, the matter was a provincial one and it seemed somewhat unfair to make its settlement the precondition of co-operation with federal Conservatives. Sauvé was unmoved. This, he insisted, was the only means of winning the confidence of French Canada. "Ontario must understand. . . . Failing that, nothing doing."[76]

The association also went to considerable lengths to ensure that French Canadians did not forget that the iniquitous Regulation 17 remained in effect in Ontario. Their fear was that once the animosities of the war years faded into the background it would become progressively more difficult to mobilize opinion. They knew that one result of the truce was that most English Canadians probably assumed that the regulation was being enforced. If the people of Quebec were also allowed to forget that the struggle was continuing, they might conclude, as Cloutier put it to Thomas Poulin of *L'Action Catholique*, that the Franco-Ontarians were "les mieux traités du monde."[77] That would never do. With Arthur Meighen scheduled early in 1924 to make a Bonne Entente visit to Quebec, Cloutier told Mgr. L. A. Paquet of the Quebec Seminary that the settlement of the schools question depended very largely on the coldness of the reception Meighen received and asked him to find some way to cancel a reception planned for the federal Conservative with "Son Eminence."[78] That December, with Ferguson himself scheduled to make a Bonne Entente trip, Senator Belcourt asked Premier Taschereau to see to it that Ferguson understood that there could be no peace between French and English Canadians until justice had been done to the Franco-Ontarians. The Premier replied that the Ferguson visit would not be "a love feast"; the united front had been maintained and strengthened.[79]

In the meantime a series of proposals which had been placed before the Premier by Belcourt on behalf of ACFEO and by Louis Coté, a Conservative lawyer from Ottawa who acted at the suggestion of Arthur Meighen, had elicited no response from Ferguson.[80] In spite of this, rumours that Ferguson was about to effect a settlement began to appear from time to time in the press.[81] A more solid piece of information reached ACFEO from two leaders of the Windsor French community who were members of the Conservative party. Ferguson, they told Edmond Cloutier, had assured them that he had every intention of settling the problem but "by degrees, between sessions and without proclaiming the change from the house-tops."[82] They also added that pressure exerted by ACFEO in February to coincide with the publication of Dr. Hughes' second report, this one on the rural schools of Russell county, had only alerted the Orangemen and had all but precluded any early action by the premier. And Ferguson in fact dismissed a long plea made in April by John Godfrey on behalf of the Unity League with the comment that "so long as smouldering fires are periodically stirred up . . . the misunderstanding and the prejudice from both sides will continue. . . ."[83] Senator Belcourt, however, had been disappointed too many times to give much credence to suggestions that Ferguson wanted to act. In December he engaged in a fruitless correspondence with Ferguson in which the premier related a long allegory about a pair of young lovers whose chance for happiness was destroyed by two "interfering, busy-body, old maid aunts."[84] A few days later a gloomy Belcourt told Premier Taschereau that he had every reason to believe that Howard Ferguson had made up his mind to do nothing.[85]

With the truce thus wearing thin, the association early in 1925 moved to break the silence its supporters had maintained for so long in the Ontario legislature. Aurélien Bélanger, the eloquent director of bilingual education in Ottawa who in 1923 had been elected as Liberal member for Russell, introduced a pro-bilingual motion into the House. Howard Ferguson was well briefed in advance by Dr. Merchant and Deputy Minister of Education A. H. U. Colquhoun, both of whom submitted memoranda which seemed to suggest a hard-line response.[86] Ferguson, however, decided to use the occasion to give the public its first real indication that his own thinking on the issue had changed very considerably since his days as a minister in the Hearst government. Regulation 17, he pointed out, had been formulated after a year-long inquiry by Dr. Merchant. The two recent Hughes Reports, based on the briefest of investigations and doubtless conducted in specially selected schools, were "of no special value." Yet his only object was to see the English language adequately taught to every pupil in Ontario; the only point at issue was how this could best be done and he was in no way "wedded to Regulation 17." There would be, he promised, "a careful, comprehensive survey of the whole situation," whose purpose would be to promote better understanding between French and English Canadians and to provide better methods for Franco-Ontarians "to secure their education in English in the province."[87] Although ACFEO would not have phrased the issue in this way, finally, after so many years of fruitless controversy, an agreement had been reached on the floor of the House. Bélanger happily withdrew his resolution.

From this point on events moved if not swiftly at least surely. The commission was appointed in August of 1925. It was headed by Dr. Merchant with Louis Coté representing the French interest and Judge J. H. Scott of Perth, who had recently defended Regulation 17 in Montreal and was one of the most highly respected Orangemen in the province, as the third member. Soon accusations were made that Ferguson had appointed the commission to attempt to influence the 1925 federal election and in fact, E. L. Patenaude, Meighen's Quebec lieutenant, who had had to be given some kind of assurance with regard to Regulation 17 before he agreed to stand as a candidate, did indeed tell his compatriots during the campaign that they should watch for interesting developments in Ontario.[88] But votes were unlikely to be influenced in advance even of the report.

In the meantime ACFEO, with its usual thoroughness, briefed Louis Coté and did everything it could to create the best possible impression for the commission. Finally, on September 21, 1927, the Merchant-Scott-Coté Report was released. To some extent it was a condemnation of the level of achievement in schools in which the French language was a medium of instruction. The commissioners, after visiting 843 classes in 330 schools, found that the state of affairs in these schools was often unsatisfactory and in some respects had deteriorated since the 1912 investigation. In 70 percent of the schools English reading was unsatisfactory; oral English with some exceptions was at a generally low level; in academic subjects, arithmetic for example, adequate work was being done in only 35 percent of the classes.[89] Furthermore the percentage of children leaving the schools before completing the elementary grades was far higher than the provincial average. In schools in which French was the sole language of instruction only one in ten was reaching grade eight.[90]

The association was far happier with the commissioners' recommendations than with their analysis. The report emphasized the diversity of conditions that existed and suggested that "no rule which prescribes the medium of instruction for different forms or grades of a system can be applied impartially to all schools within that system."[91] As a remedy Dr. Merchant and his colleagues recommended that each case be examined on its own merits by inspectors who would then "consult with a departmental committee to determine the course that might be followed." This committee, to consist of two new appointees, a Director of English and a Director of French Instruction, and the province's chief inspector, would then make its recommendations to the Minister of Education whose decision would be final. Under the proposed system the classification of schools as "English-French" would no longer exist as decisions henceforth would be made on an individual basis. Howard Ferguson immediately announced that he was accepting these recommendations.

ACFEO was delighted. Belcourt and his associates did not seem worried about the great power the new system placed in the hands of the proposed committee.

To a correspondent in western Canada, Cloutier pointed out that "nous avons obtenu d'immenses concessions. . . ."[92] Best of all, perhaps, and the surest proof of the Ferguson government's sincerity was its willingness not only to accept the University of Ottawa's teacher training school into the provincial system but to do so without demanding any significant change in that institution's pedagogical methods. In triumph the ACFEO secretary relayed the news to Omer Héroux of *Le Devoir* with the comment that this would put "virtuellement la formation de nos instituteurs entre nos mains. C'est là une concession encore plus grande que toutes celles qui sont contenues dans les recommendations du rapport."[93] In the months ahead as the new system was put into effect, ACFEO remained more than satisfied. On January 18, 1928, Belcourt told Sissons that "we have been able to come to a complete and thoroughly satisfactory agreeement as to the manner of applying these modifications. . . ." In words which struck a note of happy finality he concluded that the settlement afforded "an amicable and we all hope, permanent adjustment of a perilous educational question in this province . . . it will greatly help the creation and establishment of national unity in Canada"[94] Of course the Ferguson-Belcourt accommodation did not solve all the problems facing French education in Ontario. The new regulations offered no encouragement to instruction in French at the secondary school level. They did nothing to improve the general financial problems confronting separate schools, although they did ensure French-Irish cooperation in the great schools struggles of the next decade. But for the Franco-Ontarians the first and most significant battle had been won. The resolution of the Regulation 17 controversy marked the end of an era.

But how had the victory been achieved and what did it signify? Is it possible to assess the relative influence of the political plums which ACFEO had dangled so temptingly before Drury and Ferguson with the more noble considerations of national unity? Probably not. One can only speculate. Howard Ferguson had not acted without gauging the political implications of his decision. Yet to suggest, as many did, that the Merchant-Scott-Coté Report had been released a few weeks before the Tory convention to select a successor to Arthur Meighen because Ferguson wanted the call, is to overlook the fact that the Ontario premier would shortly refuse to accept the position, although it could have been his almost without a battle. This is not to deny that great benefits accrued to the Conservative Party as a result of the Ferguson move. French Canadians were not lacking in political gratitude. The man they once detested was now described by a member of the Liberal opposition as "the biggest and cleverest Prime Minister Ontario was ever honoured with."[95] In the 1929 election Ferguson effected a minor political revolution. Seats which were regarded as impregnable Liberal-French strongholds fell to the Conservatives and the entire Franco-Ontarian contingent of six in the new House were supporters of the premier.[96] There can be little doubt too that the Ontario settlement was a factor in the major inroads the Conservative party made in Quebec in the 1930 federal election.

The political equation, however, presents too narrow a picture. Equally revealing was the reaction of different interests to the process by which the settlement was achieved. However subtly Senator Belcourt made his case, many Ontarians were less than happy about his efforts and those of the Unity League. One would not be hard pressed to document instances in Ontario in the 1920s of antagonism to this program. The Toronto *Telegram* remained as xenophobic as ever as did the Orange *Sentinel*. The *Toronto Star*, directed by Joseph Atkinson, a man Belcourt regarded as hopelessly fanatical on the French question, was also inclined to react with hostility to any suggestion that Regulation 17 was less than perfect.[97] In 1923 Dr. J. W. Edwards, the Grand Master of the Orange Order in British North America, published a book entitled *The Wedge* which voiced the old Ontario fear that French leaders were encouraging "the growth and development of a separate and distinct French nation within the bounds of a Province supposedly English."[98] The press from time to time printed letters and reports commenting on the substantial increase in French numbers in northern Ontario in particular and in 1927 the premier told one of his back-benchers that there seemed to be a general belief among much of the population that there was a well organized French invasion of the province.[99] Such feelings did not, however, give rise in the 1920s to the kind of reaction which had characterized the previous decade. The statistics cited by Dr. Edwards themselves suggest why his book failed to provoke much of a response. Between 1911 and 1921 the proportion of French to total population in Ontario remained almost static.[100] Thus although individuals whose opinions had been formed in the earlier period continued to express concern, their fears, no longer a reflection of demographic realities, did not strike a responsive chord.

The whole past history of the schools dispute, however, suggested that changes which were greeted with such delight by the French Canadians could not help but excite hostility in traditionally unfriendly circles. Yet in this instance few objected and fewer still seemed to want to make an issue of the government's decision. In the Orange *Sentinel* Horatio Hocken announced that Regulation 17 had been unenforceable and that he favoured the new plan as an attempt to achieve the same end through conciliatory means.[101] With the *Sentinel* following such a moderate line, it was not surprising that scores of newspapers across the country also hailed the new arrangements. With few exceptions the press expressed pleasure that an issue so damaging to national unity had finally been resolved. Some papers demonstrated considerable insight into the significance of the language issue for the country's future. The *Ottawa Citizen*, for example, declared that "nothing could be more absurd than to try to force French-speaking people to put the English language before the French."[102] The loudest applause came from the English-language press of Quebec, ever conscious of its own language rights.[103] French-Canadian newspapers, while proclaiming the settlement and sometimes congratulating Ferguson for his political courage, tended to point out that it was long overdue. Many French journals added that much would depend on how the new system was administered and *Le Devoir* noted that French rights in Ontario were still not equal to English rights in Quebec.[104] The most common element in the press reaction was the general concern for national unity and the oft-expressed hope that the Ferguson settlement had removed one of the major barriers dividing French and English in Canada.[105] The Toronto *Telegram* was one of the few papers to strike a different note when it berated Ferguson for his "surrender."[106]

Several papers, however, missed the significance of what was happening. Headlines in the *Toronto Star* announced that the new regulations would DEAL DEATH BLOW TO BILINGUALISM while the St. Thomas *Times Journal*, after pointing out that the old category of French-English schools would no longer exist, told its readers that the public should be prepared to resist the strong opposition to this which would undoubtedly develop in the French districts because "in this English-speaking province there is no place for language or religious distinctions."[107]

That this confusion as to the meaning of the settlement should develop was no accident. It was a natural result of the way in which Howard Ferguson presented his policy to the Ontario public. The premier obviously did not believe the province was ready to accept the full ACFEO programme of bilingualism. In almost every public statement, therefore, and even more strongly in his private correspondence, Ferguson emphasized that Regulation 17 had proven unworkable and the government was merely attempting to achieve the same end by different means.[108] When an Orange leader from his own home town warned that people were muttering that French had been put on a par with English, the premier replied that the reverse was true.[109] This was also the argument he used to deal with the Orange Order when he appeared before its legislation committee in November, 1927 and before its two major conventions in 1928. Some of the press attempted to paint a picture of an embattled Ferguson facing furious Orangemen in a critical turning point in his career and winning support for his programme by a brilliant oratorical display. Nothing could be further from the truth. The Ferguson appearance before the legislation committee was a carefully stage-managed example of that body being exploited to further the ends of government policy.[110] The premier's purpose was less to stave off opposition to his settlement than to win Orange endorsement and the committee obliged him by putting itself on record in favour of a five-year trial period for the new educational policy.

This is not to suggest that Orange opposition could be lightly regarded. Judge Scott warned the premier that Grand Master J. J. Hunter, a Liberal, and the Toronto *Telegram* were proving difficult and that "a demagogue can easily wave the torch and do a lot of harm."[111] Hunter and some others, convinced that Orange principles were taking second place to the interests of the Tory party, determined to challenge their own legislation committee when its recommendations went before the Order's 1928 conventions. Ferguson's enemies did their best to encourage what they hoped was a rising tide of Orange discontent. The *Toronto Star*, for example, on December 7 ran a sensational story headlined, FEAR FRENCH DOMINATION IN ESSEX COUNTY.[112] The report referred to an unsubstantiated story to the effect that Ursuline teaching sisters had claimed that a French-speaking school inspector was attempting to limit the amount of English used in certain schools. Ferguson recognized the danger this kind of propaganda presented to his position. He immediately summoned the offending inspector to Toronto and fired him.[113] Soon local French leaders were denouncing him for treating his own settlement as a mere scrap of paper.[114] This probably did not displease him. A few weeks later he made another move which occasioned some alarm in Quebec. In a well publicized speech to a Toronto ward meeting he announced that Regulation 17 existed more than ever in spirit and that the French language now had fewer rights than before since it had become totally dependent on the good will of the new committee.[115]

ACFEO was not worried by these Ferguson moves. Its only concern was that its Quebec friends might misunderstand and take up the apparent challenge. Belcourt at once informed the editor-in-chief of *La Presse* that French schools in Ontario were making excellent progress and that a diplomatic silence was in order.[116] Father Charlebois for his part assured the editors of *L'Action Catholique* and *Le Devoir* that the association intended to ignore the Ferguson remarks. "Nous acceptons très volontiers les concessions énormes qui nous sont faites et nous laissons M. Ferguson jouer au politicien devant les orangistes."[117]

In fact Ferguson and his lieutenants had been mending their fences carefully and as the date approached for the Orange conventions, the situation was well in hand. Although the *Toronto Star* claimed that the manoeuvring of the Orange leadership could not disguise the fact that Ferguson had lost the confidence of the rank and file, the Premier proved able to win the almost unanimous backing of convention delegates.[118] "Support Ferguson and help win Quebec" was one cry used at the Grand Lodge Ontario West meeting while one disgusted delegate reported that the convention of the Grand Lodge Ontario East had been run as though it were "a political convention with all the Tory heelers from Ontario East packed in an 80 by 80 hall."[119] When Orange dissidents tried to excite a backlash in the 1929 election through the instrument of an "English Language School League," they failed so totally that the Ottawa *Journal* could claim during the campaign that "there is no longer a language issue in Ontario."[120] That this was the case perhaps owed more to the skill with which Howard Ferguson had moved and to the unique relationship which existed between Tories and Orangemen than to some sudden transformation of opinion in a province which a decade earlier had seemed so totally committed to Regulation 17.

This conclusion, however, exaggerates the premier's power and fails to understand his political method. Howard Ferguson, like most successful politicians, was not a man who would recklessly challenge the beliefs of the electorate. He knew that, however much he might try to disguise the fact, many people would from the beginning realize that his government had made enormous concessions to the French community. Indeed Ferguson even told Premier Taschereau that "if . . . you felt you could say that you recognize it as an honest endeavour on the part of Ontario to meet a difficult situation, it would do more than anything else . . . to allay inflammatory agitation."[121] By soliciting a public thank-you from Taschereau, Ferguson was clearly not only unafraid but even anxious to appear in Ontario eyes as the man who had given Quebec what it wanted. By 1927 it suited the politician whose entire career testified to his acute sense of the public mood to pose more as a statesman of national unity than as the defender of the English language in the province's school system.

Senator Belcourt, another astute observer, believed that for a variety of reasons, including the work of the Unity League, substantial changes had been effected in public opinion in Ontario. In a letter to Henri Bourassa, he claimed that ACFEO had "aidé à produire un grand changement dans la mentalité et l'attitude d'un nombre considérable de Canadiens anglais à l'égard de la langue française, de notre situation véritable dans la Confédération" and even with respect to the support French Canadians furnished for the Canadian national structure.[122] In this last remark Belcourt may have been referring to a viewpoint often expressed by such Unity Leaguers as W. H. Moore and George Wrong. Moore, for example, once told a Franco-Ontarian audience that "you hold the key against the invasion of Americanism" while Wrong noted approvingly that his language shut the French Canadian off "from mental contact with the United States." Moore was drawing on another long-lived Canadian belief when he argued that French and English in Canada were descended from the common stock of North European peoples. "What is in the blood will stay there and that is why we should work together."[123] Nor would he have disagreed with Senator Belcourt's view that French-English co-operation was essential because of "the perilous danger involved in the coming to our shores of millions of immigrants from foreign countries . . . without any knowledge of our institutions and of British Government. . . ."[124] Such considerations, deeply embedded in the Canadian tradition, contributed to the mood which facilitated the schools accommodation. Although more characteristic of elitist than of popular patterns of thought, they also found expression in the provincial press. The Ottawa *Journal*, for example, noted that enlightened Canadians saw in French Canada "a bulwark against many of the things that threaten the great Republic to the south. . . . They see there a people close to the soil, devoted to Canada, law-abiding, God-fearing citizens, the peasantry without which a country cannot be truly strong."[125]

Not even Belcourt, however, believed that a new era of harmony had been magically effected by the resolution of the schools crisis. Although there had been much recent progress, he told Bourassa, it would be many years before French Canadians would be assured of equal treatment and before the English majority would realize that the French constituted the most essential element for the maintenance of Confederation. The Senator remained convinced, however, that Ontario's ready acceptance of the schools settlement substantiated his long-held opinion that the English-speaking majority would demand the repeal of Regulation 17 as soon as it "could be made to realize the real significance and inevitable result" of its application.[126] Was this, then, the real meaning of the accommodation? Do the concessions of 1927 and the absence in the province of any significant backlash suggest that there may have been much truth in the earlier protestations of the Ontario government that it was innocent of any desire to eliminate or even unfairly restrict the use of French in Ontario's schools? Although the origins of Regulation 17 remain a matter of some dispute, and although decisions taken in 1927 can prove nothing about the motive for actions embarked upon fifteen years earlier, the undeniably liberal policy of the Ferguson government may well indicate that to some extent at least better communications and less violent rhetoric would have rendered unnecessary much of the sound and fury of the intervening years. Ontario, as Howard Ferguson once said of himself, was not wedded to Regulation 17. When over-heated emotions were allowed to disappear, the province willingly abandoned a policy which was detested by many of its citizens. This at least was the opinion held by *La Patrie* in 1927 when that journal remarked:

C'est faire injure à nos concitoyens anglais d'Ontario que de penser qu'ils auraient institué et perpétué un régime scolaire impliquant une violation manifeste des droits de la minorité. Il est plus raisonnable de présumer que le Règlement 17 a été décrété par suite d'un déplorable malentendu, que des conversations amicales auraient dissipé, tandis qu'il ne pouvait qu'être aggravé par les menaces et la violence, surtout lorsque ces procédés s'exerçaient de dehors.[127]

Doubtless this erred on the side of generosity; in the mood of 1927, however, it seemed an appropriate and not entirely inaccurate assessment. The passage of time and the shrewd restraint shown by Belcourt and the association had permitted the bitterness of the war years to recede into time. In response, more and more English Canadians were willing to return to the live-and-let-live atmosphere which has probably been most characteristic of English-French relations for the greater part of Canadian history. In this sense, what had occurred by the mid-1920s was perhaps less a break-through in understanding than a return to the normal conditions of disinterested tolerance and benevolent ignorance.

The confrontation over Regulation 17 and the search which was conducted in the 1920s for a viable compromise encompassed and illuminated the perennial Canadian question in a number of its many and oft-times strange guises. The issue forced French and English Canadians to ponder the nature of their relationship with each other and to give some thought to such vital concerns as the role of the French language outside Quebec and the often stormy but nonetheless inevitable association of the country's two most powerful provinces. While contemplating and to some extent reassessing their perception of these great issues, Canadians found it necessary to weigh in the scales a wide spectrum of relationships. The Ontario Orangeman, for example, was forced to look again at his tradition of "English-only" in the Ontario schools and at his support of the Conservative party and the position he arrived at perhaps came as a surprise even to himself. The Irish-Catholic community also had an agonizing reappraisal thrust upon it and many English-speaking Catholics concluded that Bishop Fallon's aggressive stance was compatible neither with justice to their co-religionists nor with the long-run interests of the separate school system.

As for the Franco-Ontarians, after years of sacrifice and struggle they faced a more subtle decision and effected a change in style rather than substance. Finally accepting the implications of their minority status and admitting that good tactics made it essential that they abandon ringing declamations in favour of private negotiation, they won more in the 1920s as a pressure group than they had ever gained as an outraged minority. Although this transformation was at the heart of the Belcourt strategy, the Franco-Ontarian campaign never lost completely the character of a national crusade. The combination proved irresistible and in 1927 the victory was theirs.

But the victory was also a Canadian one. The Regulation 17 issue had divided Canadians deeply since its formal origins in 1912 and the problems in the way of a settlement often seemed all but insurmountable. Yet a settlement was reached and although the controversy left a heritage of bitter memories, it also provided an illustration of French and English Canadians grappling with a fundamental

Canadian problem and achieving what can only be regarded as a creative and amicable solution. The Franco-Ontarian campaign had provoked a wide variety of responses from both within and without the Ontario community. It revealed the existence not of two solitudes but of many voices and of many views. The long search for an accommodation had called forth within Canada a new self-awareness, a fuller acceptance of mutual aspirations and a more mature understanding of the Canadian Confederation and its problems.

Notes

1. The letter of 8 Sept. 1916 that Pope Benedict XV addressed to the Canadian bishops acknowledged the right of the Ontario government to insist that all children learn English in the schools, but it also stated that there was no reason "to contest the right of French Canadians, living in the Province, to claim, in a suitable way, however, that French should be taught in schools attended by a certain number of their children." The Judicial Committee decision, handed down on 2 Nov. found that the B.N.A. Act protected religious minorities and not language rights.

2. For a discussion of the viewpoint of the Ontario government during the years 1912–1919, see my unpublished doctoral dissertation, "The Making of a Provincial Premier, Howard Ferguson and Ontario Politics, 1870– 1923" (University of Toronto, 1969). The early years of the dispute have been examined by several historians, most notably by Marilyn Barber, "The Ontario Bilingual Schools Issue: Sources of Conflict," *Canadian Historical Review* (Sept. 1966).

3. *Diary*, Sir Robert Borden, 8 April 1916. I wish to thank Mr. Henry Borden and Professor Craig Brown of the University of Toronto for permission to use the Borden diary.

4. Archbishop Neil McNeil Papers, Toronto Archdiocesan Archives, Senator N.A. Belcourt to W.H. Moore, 27 July 1921. The Hearst administration certainly attempted to exploit the issue in several by-elections.

5. Legislation of doubtful constitutionality passed in 1917 but never invoked provided for the appointment of such a Special Commission. The fact that French Canadians desiring to claim land in Northern Ontario would have to sign an affidavit was announced in January 1918.

6. A fuller discussion of conditions in these areas, based on the papers of the French Canadian Educational Association of Ontario (now the French-Canadian Association of Ontario), is to be found in my unpublished manuscript, "The Resolution of the Ontario Schools Crisis, 1919–1929," 163 pp., 1971. The ACFEO Papers are deposited in the Centre de Recherche en Civilization Canadienne-française, Université d'Ottawa. According to census figures cited by Lionel Groulx in *L'Enseignement Français au Canada*, vol. 2 (1933), there were 52 429 French Canadians in southwestern Ontario (including Toronto and Simcoe County) in 1921, 79 979 in northern Ontario and 104 936 in eastern Ontario. For totals Groulx gives 250 000 in 1921 and 299 732 in 1931.

7. See ACFEO Papers, Green Valley file.

8. Napoleon A. Belcourt Papers, St. Paul's University Archives, Ottawa, Ontario, Belcourt to Rev. Father Burke, Newman Club, Toronto, 7 Feb. 1919.

9. ACFEO Papers, Albert Carle, Secretary Treasurer, to S.M. Genest, Chairman, 24 April 1919.

10. ACFEO Papers, Edmond Cloutier, Secretary to A.R. Halbert, 9 March 1921. See also Belcourt Papers for the 1921 report of ACFEO's executive committee.

11. Belcourt Papers, Belcourt to Sam Genest, 12 March 1919.

12. ACFEO Papers, Senator Landry to Cardinal Begin, 15 Aug. 1918.

13. ACFEO Papers, Bishop Latulippe to Premier Taschereau, 20 May 1921.

14. ACFEO Papers, Rapport, Assemblé de la Saint-Jean-Baptiste Société, Pembroke, Ontario, 1920.

15. ACFEO Papers, Latulippe to Taschereau, 20 May 1921.

16. All these efforts were published in Ontario. Belcourt and his English-speaking friends also published fairly widely in such periodicals as the *Canadian Forum* and the *Queen's Quarterly* and in pamphlets such as the 1924 effort, *A Principle of Education Vindicated*.

17. Belcourt and his associates expressed some concern about the cynicism which had developped in certain French-speaking circles about the wartime *Bonne Entente* movement and they took steps to ensure that their own efforts would not appear to the public as a mere continuation of the *Bonne Entente* group.

18. See ACFEO Papers, Green Valley file.

19. ACFEO Papers, Pembroke file, Cloutier to Omer Héroux, 27 Nov. 1923.

20. ACFEO Papers, Alexandria file. The "free school" movement is described at some length in the unpublished paper written by the ACFEO secretary, Edmond Cloutier, *Quinze Années de Lutte, 1910–1925, Catéchisme de la Question Scolaire Ontarienne* (N.p., n.d.).

21. ACFEO Papers, Essex-Kent file.

22. See André Lalonde, "Le Règlement XVII et ses Répercussions sur le Nouvel Ontario" (unpublished M.A. thesis, Laval University, 1964), 53–56, 65.

23. This effort is described in the 1928 *Rapport du Comité Exécutif de L'ACFEO*, a copy of which is in the Archidiocesan Archives in Ottawa.

24. Ibid.

25. G. Howard Ferguson Papers, Public Archives of Ontario, Memorandum for Honourable G. Howard Ferguson, 24 Feb. 1925.

26. C.B. Sissons Papers, Public Archives of Canada (hereinafter PAC), Sissons to Belcourt, 21 March 1923.

27. ACFEO Papers, Belcourt quoted in Cloutier "Aux Sociétés re Pembroke," n.d.

28. ACFEO Papers, Caron to Morrison, 30 Oct. 1919 and Caron to Grant, 3 Jan. 1920.

29. ACFEO Papers, Caron to Drury, 4 Dec. 1919. Caron told Drury that of the Liberal deputies, two would support the government on any fair question in return for assurances that the school question would be settled, two others seemed ready to support Drury but "I believe will seek personal favours for that," while the fifth would follow his leader Dewart on all issues. This support was not as anxiously sought after by Drury as it might have been because the premier knew that neither opposition party wanted to defeat the government at this stage.

30. ACFEO Papers, Caron to Morrison, 4 Nov. 1919.

31. ACFEO Papers, Charlebois to Morrison, 27 April 1920.

32. The ACFEO papers contain a useful seven-page document labelled *Synopsis of Negotiations with Ontario Government on School Question from October, 1919 to 1st February, 1922*. This document and a host of other letters leave no doubt that the association received definite assurances from the premier.

33. This document was sent to the government with the approval of a wide variety of school commissions and national societies and was supported by over six hundred signatures. See ACFEO Papers, *Synopsis*.

34. Sissons Papers, Belcourt to Sissons, 26 Jan. 1920.

35. For some of these negotiations, see ACFEO Papers, *Synopsis*.

36. The course of negotiations in this period may be followed in considerable detail through the papers of the association and the Sissons-Belcourt correspondence in the PAC.

37. ACFEO Papers, Cloutier to Morrison, 24 Dec. 1920.

38. Sissons Papers, Belcourt to Sissons, 7 June 1921.

39. ACFEO Papers, Cloutier to Hector Lemieux, 11 June 1921. Lemieux was employed by the United Farmers of Ontario as a secretary and translator.

40. ACFEO Papers, P.J. Nolan, Secretary, Ottawa English Separate School Ratepayers' Committee to J. O'Farrell, Secretary of the English Committee of Trustees, Separate School Board of Ottawa, 26 April 1920. This document presents in some detail the position of the dissident Irish group which objected to the agreement on the grounds that the French were in effect holding the schools of the Irish minority in hostage and forcing them to intervene in the schools dispute in opposition to Regulation 17. John J. O'Meara, an Ottawa lawyer, forwarded this correspondence on 10 May 1920 to the Minister of Education. The 1919 efforts of ecclesiastical authorities to reach an agreement on the language issue in separate schools is described in Franklin Walker, *Catholic Education and Politics in Ontario* (1964), 306. The arrangement the bishops agreed upon was the division, where necessary, of Separate School Boards into two financial committees.

41. See ACFEO Papers, Cloutier to Monseigneur Omer Cloutier, Rome, Italy, 23 March 1921. The ACFEO secretary told Mgr. Cloutier that McNeil was undertaking a major campaign to secure broader

financial support for separate schools and that Belcourt promised full French-Canadian support in this effort. In return, "il fut même convenu que Mgr McNeil . . . se ferait notre défenseur auprès du gouvernement d'Ontario et qu'il combattrait ouvertement le Règlement scolaire actuel." McNeil of course had long believed that the dispute was the major barrier in the way of improving the separate school system and he had previously demonstrated his desire to have it resolved amicably.

42. ACFEO Papers, Cloutier to Morrison, 21 March 1921.

43. ACFEO probably does less than justice to this element. There had always been a number of French Canadians who believed that ACFEO had mishandled the whole issue through its early, aggressive policies. Members of the French-speaking hierarchy may also have believed that negotiations could be better carried on by themselves in the traditional manner than by a body composed primarily of laymen who were elected to their positions at great public conventions which attracted widespread publicity. Canon Groulx looks at this aspect of the question in volume 1 of his *Mémoires* (Montreal, 1970), 358–62.

44. Sissons Papers, Memorandum of Interview with Minister of Education, 10 May 1920.

45. Sissons Papers, "Excerpts and Comments from the Diary of C. B. Sissons." This remark was inserted at a later date in a footnote to the 30 July 1920 entry. Sissons and Drury were cousins and good friends.

46. John Godfrey in a letter to Belcourt argued that Drury wanted to move but that "Grant has him hobbled. I do not think Grant can be got rid of as such an act would probably bring about a crisis in the U.F.O. ranks which might cause the defeat of the Government. Grant's present position is a result of his knowledge, that he has behind him practically every member of the Government and a great majority of the rank and file of the Party. . . . I am very much opposed to making any attack, at present, on the Government. Drury is in my judgment absolutely all right, but is helpless through no fault of his own." Godfrey certainly gave the benefit of the doubt to the premier. He failed to point out that the Morrison faction of the U.F.O. strongly desired action and blamed Drury for failing to move. See Sissons Papers, Godfrey to Belcourt, 19 May 1922.

47. ACFEO Papers, Sissons to Belcourt, 29 April 1921. It is unclear who approached these members in 1919.

48. Sissons Papers, Belcourt to Drury, 29 June 1921.

49. See, for example, ACFEO Papers, Sissons to Belcourt, 21 August 1921 and reply, 25 August. The Memoirs of J.J. Morrison, which are deposited in the PAC, also make it clear that the premier was very much afraid of the Tory leader's political skills. One is left to speculate as to whether Ferguson might deliberately have given Drury the impression that he would oppose any action on Regulation 17, all the while intending to act himself after the 1923 election, thereby gaining great political applause from French Canadians, as in fact did happen ultimately.

50. ACFEO Papers, Belcourt to Drury, 29 June 1921.

51. ACFEO Papers, Father Charlebois to Lemieux, 6 July 1921.

52. Any number of letters in the ACFEO Papers make it clear that Secretary Morrison was a consistent and sincere friend of the association.

53. Sissons Papers, Belcourt to Sissons, 11 Nov. 1921.

54. Sissons Papers, Belcourt to Sissons, 25 Jan. 1922.

55. Sissons Papers, Belcourt to Grant, 14 Feb. 1922. In this letter to the Education Minister, Belcourt complained at length about the activities of Inspector Walsh in Prescott and Russell Counties and argued that these represented a flagrant violation of the truce.

56. Sissons Papers, Belcourt to Sissons, 21 Oct. 1922. The ACFEO president did not, however, make a personal attack on the premier and he even declared that he believed Drury sincerely desired to render justice to the French Canadians.

57. W.L.M. King Papers, PAC, King-Belcourt Correspondence, April-October, 1922.

58. ACFEO Papers, Requête à Leurs Excellences les Membres du Conseil Suprême de la Ligue des Nations, 6 Dec. 1922.

59. This was the motto inscribed on the Unity League letterhead. The figure of 150 is cited by Esdras Terrien in "Quinze Années de Lutte Contre le Règlement XVII" (unpublished manuscript, n.d.), 27. Among League members were S. R. Parsons, the president of the B.A. Oil Co., Allen Ballantyne, president of the Canadian Manufacturers Association, J.J. Morrison of the U.F.O. and such well known academics as George Wrong, O.D. Skelton, R.M. Maciver and W.S. Wallace.

60. Sissons Papers, Belcourt to Kirwan Martin, 22 March 1922.

61. Ibid.

62. ACFEO Papers, Cloutier to l'abbé François Pelletier, n.d.

63. ACFEO Papers, Cloutier to M. Pietro Di Maria, 20 April 1922.

64. Sissons Papers, Godfrey to Belcourt, 19 May 1922.

65. Ottawa *Journal*, 2 Dec. 1922, 12 Jan. 1923.

66. Belcourt Papers, Belcourt to Kirwan Martin, 23 June 1923.

67. Belcourt Papers, Belcourt to Godfrey, 23 June 1923.

68. Belcourt Papers, Godfrey to Belcourt 27 June 1923.

69. Belcourt Papers, Belcourt to W. H. Moore, 5 July 1923.

70. Ibid.

71. Belcourt Papers, Godfrey to Belcourt, 3 July 1923.

72. ACFEO Papers, Cloutier to Dr. Damien St. Pierre, 7 Sept. 1923.

73. Sissons Papers, Belcourt to Sissons, 8 Dec. 1923.

74. Arthur Meighen Papers, PAC, Godfrey to Meighen, 12 Jan. 1924.

75. Meighen Papers, C.P. Beaubien to Meighen, 25 Feb. 1924. Beaubien thanked Meighen for his "timely intervention in the matter of the Ontario school question." See too Rev. Elias Roy to Meighen, 5 April 1924.

76. The extensive Meighen-Sauvé correspondence is in the Meighen Papers. These words, written on 11 May 1926, effectively concluded the correspondence.

77. ACFEO Papers, Cloutier to Thomas Poulin, 25 Jan. 1924.

78. ACFEO Papers, Cloutier to Monseigneur L. A. Paquet, 25 Jan. 1924.

79. ACFEO Papers, Belcourt to Taschereau, 27 Dec. 1924; Cloutier to Mgr. L.A. Paquet et al., 3 Jan. 1925. Of course the entire work both of *Bonne Entente* and later of the Unity League was founded on the assumption that, for reasons which were at once social, economic and political, it was unthinkable that the two great central provinces of Ontario and Quebec should remain estranged. An illustration of the economic side of the equation may be seen in Ontario's hydro-electric power shortage of the 1920s and in her desire to buy power from Quebec sources. Laurent Tremblay's 1963 history of *Le Droit, Entre Deux Livraisons, 1913–1963*, contains this suggestive passage: "En ces années-là, l'Ontario, étant à court d'électricité, demande à Québec de lui louer une partie de ses pouvoirs hydrauliques. Taschereau consent et, dans sa réponse à Ferguson, il ajoute: Quel beau rêve si nos pouvoirs hydrauliques devenaient l'usine qui fait la paix et qui ouvriraient grandes aux petits enfants canadiens-français de l'Ontario les portes de leurs écoles françaises." The first contract between Ontario and a Quebec power company was signed in 1926 but it would be a bold historian who would attempt, failing precise documentation, to assess the extent to which such considerations influenced Ferguson's thinking. Some additional evidence appears in the R.B. Bennett Papers, PAC. On 17 June 1929 Aimé Guertin, M.P.P. of Hull, Quebec wrote Bennett's close associate, Major General A.D. McRae to say that "Honourable Mr. Taschereau has made a declaration at a recent visit to this city, which has been interpreted as meaning that it was conditional upon the abolishment of Regulation 17 of the Ontario School Board, that he agreed to allow the Ontario Hydro Electric Commission to use hydro electric power from the Gatineau River, in the Province of Quebec." Guertin asked McRae to secure a statement from Ferguson, and McRae on 20 June replied that "What you ask is very great indeed and I fear I am not equal to it. Such a statement from the Prime Minister of Ontario would doubtless lead to much discussion."

80. Ferguson Papers, Coté to Ferguson, 11 Jan. 1924, ACFEO Papers, Belcourt to Ferguson, 22 Feb. 1924. See also Sissons Papers, Belcourt to Sissons, 6 Feb. 1924.

81. See *La Patrie*, 26 Feb. 1924; ACFEO Papers, Omer Héroux to Father Charlebois, 4 March 1924. For the alarmed Orange response to these rumours see Ferguson Papers, Horatio Hocken to Ferguson, 17 March 1924 and reply 7 April.

82. ACFEO Papers, Morand to Cloutier, 2 April 1924.

83. Ferguson Papers, Ferguson to Godfrey, 24 April 1924.

84. Ferguson Papers, Ferguson to Belcourt, 5 Dec. 1924 and reply, 9 Dec.

85. ACFEO Papers, Belcourt to Taschereau, 27 Dec. 1924. Taschereau made a number of attempts in 1924 to discuss the schools problem with Ferguson but the Ontario premier in at least two letters asked that such a discussion be postponed. See Ferguson Papers, Taschereau to Ferguson, 15 May 1924 and reply, 2 June; Taschereau to Ferguson 7 Oct. 1924 and reply 11 Oct.

86. See Ferguson Papers, Memorandum for the Minister of Education on Resolutions proposed by Mr. Bélanger and Memorandum for Honourable G. Howard Ferguson, 24 Feb. 1925.

87. Ferguson Papers, "Summary of Mr. Ferguson's Speech on the Bélanger Motion."

88. When efforts to recruit Patenaude for the federal campaign came up against the familiar obstacle of Regulation 17, R.J. Manion reported to Meighen that Patenaude seemed friendly but he "has an impression that the Conservative party is not friendly to French Canadians. . . . His main complaint is Regulation 17, and . . . I believe he would come out for us if that regulation could be wiped out" (Meighen Papers, Manion to Meighen, 10 Jan. 1925, as cited in Roger Graham, *Arthur Meighen*, 2: 291).

89. See pp. 11, 15, 17, 19 and 25–29 of the Merchant-Scott-Coté Report of 1927.

90. C.B. Sissons, *Church and State in Canadian Education*, 93.

91. Merchant-Scott-Coté Report, as cited in Ottawa *Citizen*, 22 Sept. 1927.

92. ACFEO Papers, Cloutier to Père U. Langlois, Prince Albert, Sask., 12 Oct. 1927.

93. ACFEO Papers, Cloutier to Omer Héroux, 29 Sept. 1927.

94. Sissons Papers, Belcourt to Sissons, 18 Jan. 1928.

95. Ferguson Papers, Théodore Legault to Ferguson, 6 Oct. 1927.

96. During the campaign *Le Droit* departed from its usual anti-Conservative policy and remained neutral and French-speaking Conservatives extracted all the mileage they could from the settlement. In Russell, where the Tories won their first victory since 1883, the eloquent Aurélien Bélanger was the victim. Prescott, a Liberal stronghold since 1883, with the exception of a four-vote Tory victory in the Whitney election of 1908, also fell to the Conservatives. Louis Coté's win in Ottawa East gave the riding to the Conservatives for only the second time in its twenty-two-year history as a separate constituency. The loss of Franco-Ontarian support was a devastating blow for the Liberals who returned only twelve candidates, as compared to seven for the Farmer groups and ninety-one for the Tories. My judgment with regard to the 1930 federal election is based on strong circumstantial evidence but remains unsubstantiated by electoral analysis.

97. For Belcourt's view of Atkinson see Sissons Papers, Belcourt to Sissons, 24 Sept. 1921.

98. Although Dr. Edwards' book was concerned primarily with the separate school question, it was perhaps typical of Orange opinion that the French issue was seen as an aspect of the controversy over separate schools.

99. Ferguson Papers, Leo Macaulay to Ferguson, 13 Dec. 1927 and reply, 14 Dec. Ferguson also told Charles Gordon of Owen Sound on 8 Dec. 1927 that "there is not any doubt that there is a well organized colonization campaign going on in the eastern and northern sections of Ontario. . . The one and only way the situation can be met is to teach these people the English language." In his correspondence Ferguson argued that the mistake made in formulating Regulation 17 was that it was of the "Thou shalt not" variety and that "the only other method is to approach them in a helpful, sympathetic manner and show them that it is to their advantage" to learn English.

100. The figures cited by Edwards show that between 1911 and 1921 the proportion of French to total population in Ontario increased only from 9.8 to 10.1 percent. According to 1961 census figures, 10.4 percent of the Ontario population was of French origin.

101. Orange *Sentinel*, 29 Sept. 1927.

102. Ottawa *Citizen*, 23 Sept. 1927.

103. Montreal *Gazette* 23 Sept.; Montreal *Star*, 26 Sept.; Quebec *Chronicle-Telegraph*, 26 Sept. 1927.

104. *Le Devoir*, 22 Sept. 1927.

105. The ACFEO clipping file on this subject contains editorials from scores of papers across the country.

106. There is a long discussion of the *Telegram's* attitude in the Ottawa *Journal*, 30 Nov. The Toronto paper was clearly regarded as a pariah by much of the rest of the Tory press.

107. *Toronto Daily Star*, 22 Sept. 1927; St. Thomas *Times-Journal*, 23 Sept. 1927.

108. For an example of this line of argument see Ferguson Papers, Ferguson to Ernie McQuatt, County Secretary, L.O.L., Ottawa, 1 Feb. 1928.

109. Ferguson Papers, F.M. Robinson to Ferguson, 4 Nov. 1927 and reply 15 Nov.

110. See Ferguson Papers, Judge Scott to Ferguson, 25 Nov. 1927. Such papers as the *Toronto Star* and the Orange *Sentinel* gave enormous space to the premier's appearance before the legislation committee.

111. Ferguson Papers, Scott to Ferguson, 25 Nov. 1927.

112. Father Charlebois believed the *Star* was deliberately fishing in troubled waters and he suggested to Belcourt that influence be brought to bear to try to put an end to such activities. See Belcourt Papers, Charlebois to Belcourt, 11 Dec. 1927.

113. *Toronto Daily Star*, 10 Dec. 1927.

114. *Toronto Daily Star*, 10, 12 Dec. 1927.

115. *The Mail and Empire*, 3 Feb. 1928.

116. See ACFEO Papers, Oswald Mayrand to Belcourt, 15 Feb. 1928.

117. ACFEO Papers, Charlebois to Omer Héroux, 15 Feb. 1928.

118. *Toronto Daily Star*, 15 March 1928.

119. *Toronto Daily Star*, 16 March 1928; 23 March 1928.

120. Ottawa *Journal*, 31 Oct. 1929. According to *Le Droit*, 4 Oct. 1929, Ferguson issued a categorical order that no Conservative candidate was to sign any pledges of support allegedly being circulated to candidates by the League.

121. Ferguson Papers, Ferguson to Taschereau, 21 Sept. 1927 and reply, 28 Sept.

122. Belcourt Papers, Belcourt to Bourassa, 10 Dec. 1927.

123. ACFEO Papers, copy of Moore's speech. His remarks were made in Windsor Collegiate, 12 Feb. 1923. Wrong's remarks appear in "The Two Races in Canada," a paper he read to the Canadian Historical Association in 1925.

124. ACFEO Papers, Belcourt statement on the Merchant-Scott-Coté Report, 1927.

125. Ottawa *Journal*, 8 April 1925.

126. ACFEO Papers, Belcourt statement on the Merchant-Scott-Coté Report, 1927.

127. *La Patrie* (Montreal), 22 Sept. 1927.

FROM LAND ASSEMBLY TO SOCIAL MATURITY. THE SUBURBAN LIFE OF WESTDALE (HAMILTON), ONTARIO, 1911–1951†

JOHN C. WEAVER

With insights drawn from American and British scholarship, Canadian historians and historical geographers have been participating in what has become an international study of cities.[1] In Canada, as elsewhere, writing has tended to focus on the mid-nineteenth century, testing hypotheses relating to a shift from the pre-industrial pedestrian city to the industrial city with mass transit.[2] The decades from 1840 to 1880, therefore, emerge as a critical era for urban and social history. After the nineteenth-century watershed, there remain significant issues concerning "the city building process"[3] and major growth periods with waves of immigration between 1905 and 1913, 1925 and 1930, and again after World War II. Certain of the themes to be developed in twentieth-century urban history represent a continuation of earlier processes, but others indicate divergence. One matter of fundamental interest to all who study the city, one where twentieth-century urban history has an opportunity to advance several distinct trends, concerns the dwelling place. In Canada, planned suburbs with racial and social segregation, the evolution of the real estate agent, changes in land development and the building trades, and an expanding government role were initiated in the first half of the twentieth century. A national study of these concerns rests beyond the scope of the current article; rather it is reasonable to adopt an approach recommended by Michael Katz. "Only through analyzing the expression of the general through the particular," Katz reminds us, "can we construct subtle and satisfactory explanations of social development."[4]

Westdale, the Hamilton community selected as a Canadian measure of twentieth-century urban trends, sheltered more than 1700 households when completed.

†*Histoire sociale/Social History* 11 (1978): 411-40. Research was funded by a McMaster University Arts Research Council Grant. The author is indebted to his research assistants Julie Backholm, Ron Elliott, and Martin Lawlor. Lawlor's research on contractors and mortgage brokers was particularly original. Students in the urban history research seminar have provided essential studies on a variety of related issues. Their works have been cited throughout the study. David Gagan gave vital assistance.

As a private enterprise, commercialism governed Westdale's construction, but like the best planned North American suburbs of the era — the exclusive Country Club District of Kansas City or Vancouver's Shaughnessy Heights — it balanced aesthetic and environmental concerns with financial ones. This made it different from the many commuter suburbs, but its history still progressed in step with national urban circumstances. Developers, builders, and residents shared experiences with counterparts across Canada and the United States. The developers and builders of Westdale worked from a body of knowledge and from traditional practices that were by no means limited to their locale. The pitfalls and business practices of development and contracting were not unique to Westdale. The owners and tenants of the suburb sorted themselves out spatially in ways that conformed with attitudes and economic conditions that were continental in scope.

The Developers

"Someone has said there is only one crop of land, but there is an endless crop of natives and every baby on the face of the earth makes every foot of land more valuable."[5] This article of faith, used by Westdale's developer, has been promoted by "the property industry," past and present. Critics of land developers, on the other hand, have maintained for generations that scarcity is a product of speculators controlling supply. Yet, scarcity forms only one dimension of land value.[6] According to a solid body of historical research, particularly in the United Kingdom, successful land developers have affected land value by creative activity.[7] Discerning patterns of urban growth, both spatial and temporal, they have attempted to interpret and influence public taste. Developers have performed as instruments for drawing together political and legal acumen, capital-raising facilities, planning talents and the building trades. Value judgements about land developers, therefore, must be carefully constructed to permit areas of ambiguity. Westdale, for example, was a well-conceived community with a fine array of amenities. It also encompassed racial discrimination and "clever" tactics on the part of the developer. Nonetheless, it is difficult to indict the developer without condemning the prejudices and business practices of an era.

At the turn of the century, the thrust to Hamilton's expansion was being channelled by topography. By 1910, the escarpment to the south, Burlington Bay on the north, and a wide ravine in the west had turned land development eastward.[8] East-end surveys soon stood at considerable distance from downtown Hamilton. For that reason the level plateau which stood on the far side of the western ravine caught the eye of Toronto contractor, J.J. McKittrick, who, in 1911, began to promote a 100-acre plot, "Hamilton Gardens."[9] His venture lacked urban services and he did not have the resources to secure them. Therefore, McKittrick became associated with local partners whose careers had been meshed with the development of Hamilton. Legal talent came from Sir John Gibson, former Lieutenant-Governor of Ontario. Gibson and other members of the McKittrick syndicate were connected with Hamilton's pioneer utility firm, Cataract Power and Light and with the Hamilton Street Railway. The Southam family, publishers of the *Spectator*, acquired a major interest. Soon the new group

MAP 1

Westdale, 1931

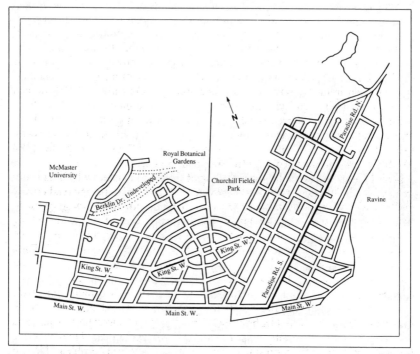

had expanded the original 100 acres to 800 and successfully negotiated an agreement whereby in January 1914 Hamilton annexed the survey.[10] The agreement set down conditions among which was one that forced the syndicate to construct and maintain a bridge. In return, the pre-annexation rural assessments were frozen from 1914 to 1919. Even with entrepreneurial talent and annexation, the endeavour proved unpromising. The 1913–15 recession and the war economy retarded property sales.

The cash flow anticipated by McKittrick Properties dried up for eight years during which time its tax cushion expired and had to be renegotiated for a period extending to 1926. This provided some relief although a further commitment entered into during the balmy days before the war returned to plague that syndicate. To secure a key parcel of 100 acres belonging to the Hamilton Cemetery Board, McKittrick Properties purchased another site, traded in for the desired land and included $40 000 compensation. Financial stringency forced the company to default on a compensation instalment. Eventually, the Board agreed to a settlement, but not before a political move by the syndicate was turned back by the Hamilton electorate. A "McKittrick man" ran for Mayor in 1916 and, despite the backing of the *Spectator*, he was defeated.[11] The early years of the syndicate suggest that even a powerful alliance among the civic elite could experience fiscal and political embarrassment.[12]

Facing difficulties, the developers sought fresh management. One of the investors, John Moodie, president of Eagle Knitwear of Hamilton, invited his son-in-law, F. Kent Hamilton, to guide the company. A Winnipeg lawyer, Hamilton had learned a great deal about the planning and promotion of a suburb from his western experience. Upon his arrival in 1918, Hamilton established a sales staff that grew to eight in good times; he also designed the publicity campaigns for the next seven years. Hamilton commissioned New York landscape architect Robert Anderson Pope to prepare a street plan.[13] Pope was one of many urban planners to have been influenced by German civic concepts. As early as 1910, he had recommended German-style urban decentralization, urging a shift away from urban systems which concentrated lines of transportation on the core city. Pope argued that this led to overcrowding and high residential land costs. New suburbs, more or less self-contained, promised a remedy.[14] When Pope designed Westdale, his plan included a central shopping district.

Kent Hamilton had a full understanding of the housing issues which had concerned North American reformers between 1900 and 1920, having read articles and attended lectures on most of the era's remedies for the housing crisis. In 1919 Hamilton was aware of English garden cities, limited dividend housing companies, tax incentives for builders and home-buyers, company housing, and even the wartime housing constructed by the United States government.[15] For a while, Hamilton considered supporting public housing. For example, he supported the creation of a Hamilton Town Planning Commission, apparently recognizing that studies by such a public body would necessarily benefit McKittrick Properties whose land was the last major tract near the central city and susceptible to an experiment in public housing. In the economic uncertainty of 1919, a sale, even to a public housing corporation, was to be welcomed. There was one further reason why Hamilton supported action on the housing problem. He had been advised that

> failure to take care of the returned soldiers, not only from the stand point of housing, but also from the stand point of opportunity for earning a decent livelihood, may result in a social uprising that in the end would be far more expensive to the city of Hamilton than a theoretical excess cost of providing adequate housing.[16]

The turbulence of 1919 frightened some civic leaders into repression but it moved others toward expedient consideration of reform. However, with the return of social stability, public housing proved a will-o-the-wisp. Indicative of a more conservative approach was a week-long Better Homes Exhibit in the Hamilton Armouries sponsored by Kent Hamilton and the newly created Hamilton Real Estate Board. Their aim was "to educate the average renter into the method and means of ownership."[17] As a tangible move in that direction, the first Westdale surveys came onto the market as workingmen's parcels arranged on a grid layout with thirty-foot frontages. The areas set aside for workingmen had a lower potential land value than elsewhere in Westdale, for along the opposite slope of the ravine the city maintained a garbage dump. As late as 1928, a syndicate official would write that these lands were unattractive: "I do not expect that they ever will be very desirable."[18] One direct incentive hastened the surveying of workingmen's

ILLUSTRATION 1

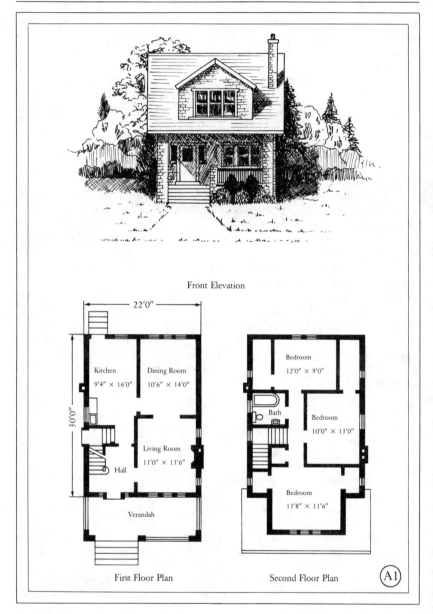

Front Elevation

First Floor Plan   Second Floor Plan   (A1)

lots. The Ontario Housing Act of 1919, applying federal funds, assisted the raising of mortgages for modest six-room homes with minimum standards costing under $4000. In fact, the "Hamilton A-1 Plan" providing a home for $3850

MAP 2

Westdale's Component Surveys & Dates of Registration

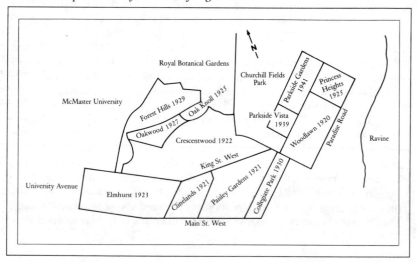

was a government-approved brick dwelling seeing considerable service in Westdale (see illustration 1).[19]

From 1920 to 1926, the syndicate faced lean times. Local conditions formed an element in a national interlude of slow residential construction after the boost provided by the Housing Act. Moderate improvement occurred in 1922, but construction suffered a setback in the next two years. It joined business in a subsequent steady improvement which continued unbroken until 1928, a peak year for residential building.[20] As conditions improved, the syndicate responded, shifting tactics, preparing surveys that would appeal to affluent homebuyers (see table 1). Still, a prosperous clientele brought no sudden windfall. Twenty years after the initial land assembly, ten years after the registration of the first survey only half the residential lots had been built upon. While some of the 830 vacant properties which appeared on the 1931 assessment rolls were held by contractors, the property developers retained 570. Free bus trips for inspection tours, gold certificates buried on a few lots, the opening of a model home, a contest to name Westdale, and the barnstorming of Jack V. Elliott in his *Canuck* aeroplane could not stir sufficient interest. McKittrick Properties went into bankruptcy.

With the prospect of the tax assessment freeze being lifted in 1926 and the suburban bridge, which the syndicate financed, now serving a major highway, the developers requested an amended agreement with the city. In fact, there were serious cash flow problems, while fixed annual charges had to be met. To meet expenses, the syndicate turned to an expedient. Since land had been mortgaged to finance the initial assembly, some additional collateral had to be discovered. The company borrowed against contractor's agreements-to-purchase and loans came from the major shareholders. As contractors repaid the company, the loans were retired.[21] The sticky cash flow became a critical worry, for with time running out on the assessment freeze, the Corporation of the City of Hamilton and the Ontario Municipal Board refused once again to amend the 1913 agreement. Caught in a pinch that required dramatic proof to the city that relief was required, the Board of Directors met in June 1926, refused to pay a minor bill, and precipitated bankruptcy proceedings.[22]

Two major unsecured creditors were affected by the bankruptcy: those shareholders who had loaned funds against the agreements-to-purchase, and the city, which was owed $200 000 in tax arrears and service charges.[23] As real as the financial crisis was, certain features suggest that this bankruptcy had tactical dimensions. Shareholders paid to the full all creditors, except the city.[24] It soon dawned on the Mayor and Board of Control that their obduracy had drastic implications. Future tax revenue, the city's credit rating, and Hamilton's reputation as the "Ambitious City" were jeopardized. The episode had a familiar ring. A major private endeavor had become so closely identified with commitments to expansion that a government hard-line was precluded despite the hard-nosed posturing to convince voters that City Hall was not "soft on" developers. The Public Trustee appointed by syndicate shareholders expressed the situation well enough. "The city asked us to come, as a matter of fact, because they were worried about

TABLE 1

Westdale's Component Surveys, 1920–1941

Plan Name	Registration Date	Approximate Area of Lot	Minimum Building Values
Woodlawn	1920	3000 sq. ft.	$2500
Clinelands	1921	3000 to 4500 sq. ft.	$3000
Paisley Gardens	1921	4000 to 5000 sq. ft.	$3000
Crescentwood	1921	4000 to 5500 sq. ft.	$3000
Elmhurst	1923	4500 sq. ft.	$3000
Princess Heights	1925	3000 to 3500 sq. ft.	none
Oak Knoll	1925	7500 to 10 000 sq. ft.	$7000
Oak Wood	1927	6000 to 15 000 sq. ft.	$8000
Forest Hills	1929	7000 to 10 000 sq. ft.	$8000
Collegiate Park	1930	3000 to 3300 sq. ft.	$3000
Parkside Vista	1939	3000 to 3200 sq. ft.	$2500
Parkside Gardens	1941	3300 to 3600 sq. ft.	$2500

SOURCES: Survey Maps and Sample Property Instruments, Wentworth County Courthouse.

the situation. . . . I told them that there was now no money to pay taxes . . . and out of that arose the suggestion that they might take some of our land for parks, to clear up those arrears of taxes."[25] The city subsequently took 377 acres of ravine land for park purposes and erased the tax debt. That the rugged land was unsuited for development while a park bolstered land values made the agreement a rewarding one for the developer.[26] With the debt lifted and the Ontario Municipal Board approving a relaxed agreement that released the developers from maintenance of the bridge, a newly chartered company composed of shareholders in the old syndicate sprang to life and bought out McKittrick Properties. Except for the sacrificed park land and a legal bill of $7573, the manoeuvre had cost nothing but it had succeeded in forcing the better terms which the syndicate had sought for five years.[27]

Just as the new company took shape, it fell heir to a boon secured by the old syndicate. Commencing late in 1921, Kent Hamilton had begun courting McMaster University which had been considering a move from its Bloor Street location in Toronto.[28] After lengthy negotiations and generous contributory pledges to McMaster from J.R. Moodie, William Southam, G.H. Levy, and Sir John Gibson — all members of the original and new land companies — McMaster located in Westdale.[29] Immediately, property in two of Westdale's surveys was "expected to be more attractive than anything at present on the market as a result of the McMaster University location."[30] The developers also calculated that the University would carry the burden of expense for a major water main, that it would purchase electricity from their power company, and that it would lure "a colony of Professors."[31] For all of the apparent ingenuity and sinister cunning, the syndicate was neither a cohesive nor an instant success. Kent Hamilton sued for payment of commissions owing during the bankruptcy; the Southams found certain legal charges of their syndicate partners, Gibson and Levy, far too high; as for professors, most were too impecunious to buy Westdale land.[32] The Depression ruined whatever expectations had been raised by the new agreement and the enticing of McMaster. Only in the building boom after World War II did vacant fields disappear.

The Builders

The creation of Westdale preceded the era of totally integrated property development. In a sense, Westdale emerged at a mid-point in the evolution of the "property industry." It had the benefit of sophisticated town planning but, unlike recent packaged suburbs, construction was not a branch of the developers' activities. Given this absence of corporate integration, Westdale's completion drew upon an array of traditional crafts and specialists whose relationships tended, for all their diversity, to be intimate and co-ordinated. Mortgage brokers, contractors and subcontractors worked separately, but their ability to deviate from the developer's vision of the community was constrained.

By the early twentieth century it was assumed in real estate circles that unregulated growth, non-conforming buildings (gas stations, tenements, corner stores), and certain ethnic groups offended middle-class home buyers. No longer were building lots sold by auction, a system which minimized the developer's control. Conformity was now deemed important; its implementation with so many individual actors led to the evolution of the real estate agent and to the appearance of planning and restrictive covenants. The latter had wide application in Hamilton. Those enforced in the industrial east-end specified a minimum building value and brick construction,[33] but Westdale's covenants went further and contained two categories: structural and ethnic. The first defined the minimum dwelling value and the building materials. Each of the component surveys in Westdale had a specific set of standards (see table 1). In more exclusive areas, the developer retained the right to approve "the location, plan and specifications, exterior elevation and type of construction." As for the second feature, this was a typical clause: "None of the lands described . . . shall be used, occupied by or let or sold to Negroes, Asiatics, Bulgarians, Austrians, Russians, Serbs, Rumanians, Turks, Armenians, whether British subjects or not, or foreign-born Italians, Greeks or Jews."[34] Developers' brochures emphasized that Westdale was "restricted."[35] Regulation in the early years was enforced. A real estate agent warned a contractor not to sell to an interested Italian green grocer: "Tom, we don't want people like that in here."[36]

Builders, dependent upon credit and a sound reputation with developers, lacked the security to risk breaking covenants. Relying on quick sales, they dared not risk architectural innovations. Most of Westdale's builders operated as family combinations without design facilities. They depended upon standard blueprints of demonstrated popularity. This meant that, for all of Westdale's distinctive planning, the bulk of its housing stock resembled much of contemporary Hamilton. The appeance of large custom-built homes in the 1940s altered styles somewhat, for even smaller homes constructed in these years attempted to incorporate imitations of expensive flourishes: diamond-shaped window panes, stonework, bay windows, and wood and stucco finishing on the second storey.

The builders themselves were a mixed group. For many men anxious to improve themselves, an opportune route out of the labour pool was to become a smallscale builder. Like street peddling or the corner store, contracting provided a few urban labourers with access to an independent occupational ladder. A few, such as the Hamilton-based builder Michael Pigott, carried success beyond their original locality. Some insight into the hustle and flexibility of builders is provided by merely considering the fragments of information conveyed in city directories, advertisements, and assessment rolls. One family, the Theakers, demonstrated a few characteristics of the approximately thirty builders involved in Westdale.[37] The men worked on homes in the east-end and Westdale, using the same plans. Gladys kept the books and worked for a mortgage broker. The family lived within walking distance of Westdale. Occasionally, such family-builders formed transistory partnerships, for the building trades were fluid in their association. J. Vickers and his son held twenty Westdale lots in 1931, but the father also retained several with plasterer Fred Beldham in the east-end. These were small father and son operations, but certain family-builders were virtual dynasties. The Mills family had participated in home construction and property development since the midnineteenth century.[38] The Armstrongs had depth and experience, having constructed by 1930 some 600 dwellings in Hamilton, and with William C. Armstrong as realty and financial agent and William D. Armstrong heading the architectural department, they were the most ambitious domestic contractors in the city.[39] Thomas "Carpenter" Jutter and his son Charles were builders, but Jutter senior, Mayor of Hamilton and later a Member of the Ontario Legislature, was a significant local politician. The father, in his role as Mayor, cut the opening ribbon on a Westdale economy home in 1924; the son was erecting dwellings in Westdale as late as 1948.[40] Whatever their scale of operation, the builders had a local commitment. They depended on local reputation for credit and buyers. They were not working for the large suburban builders with an impersonal corporate name that one finds today. Building techniques have advanced since the 1920s, but there was something of value in having contractors mindful of their community's esteem. One builder, Thomas Casey, could identify the homes that he had constructed fifty years later. Having done so, he proceeded to rhapsodize about the quality and distinctive character of his brickwork.

There was no typical builder in Westdale, but the operations of Thomas Casey, who constructed seventy homes between 1920 and 1932, and between 1945 and 1955, suggest in greater detail the practices used by those with few assets save work and ambition. Raised in Ireland in County Cork, Casey had laboured in Liverpool before emigrating to Canada in 1914. Between 1914 and 1920, he found employment on Toronto construction projects, on a Caledonia, Ontario farm, and in Hamilton and later Pittsburgh steel mills. During the winter and spring of 1919 he built a worker's cottage near Dominion Foundries and Steel, hewing out a basement with pick and shovel. Casey thus illustrated the truth that any man with the ambition and the rudimentary tools could style himself as a contractor. He continued to construct small dwellings in the slow growth of the 1920s, but by his peak year, 1930, Casey employed eight carpenters and was working on fifteen substantial homes in Westdale. Like the land developers who increased the size of their lots in the prosperous late 1920s, builders began to fashion homes for the swelling numbers of middle-class purchasers (see table 1). Reduced to one house a year from 1933 to 1939. Casey left Westdale for Burlington, which had adopted a Depression policy of inducements to attract builders.[41] He returned to Westdale in the mid-1940s when the Central Mortgage and Housing Corporation Act (effective 1 January 1945) once more stimulated construction.

Casey's transient career and his lack of apprenticeship in the building trades present an occasional view of labour history, but it is his building practices which merit attention. Casey normally selected a parcel of adjacent lots in a survey and signed an agreement to purchase. He could not afford clear title. He then put in a number of basements simultaneously and started to erect the frame for one dwelling. Other work he subcontracted to "the seven trades": masons, lathers, plasterers, electricians, plumbers, roofers, and tinsmiths. By staggering construction along a row of basements, Casey provided an even sequence of work. More importantly, the stages in home construction were paced by his line of credit.

The half-dozen major office buildings in downtown Hamilton housed a large and yet almost invisible market. Banks and trust companies provided building loans, but at least thirty non-institutional mortgage brokers advertised in real estate columns during the 1920s. In some instances, barristers functioned as brokers, handling estate funds or working for clients interested in sound investments. During the 1920s mortgage interest varied from 6 to 6½ percent. Casey preferred borrowing through these barristers. Institutional lenders demanded quarterly instalment payments which included principal as well as interest, but private lenders accepted payments of interest and a lump sum for principal when a house was sold. For the builder, loans came in "three draws." When the roof went on, the lender's agent drove out to inspect the dwelling. If he approved, Casey could make his initial draught. When the white finishing plaster dried, he was entitled to a second. With interior trim and fixtures in place, he could make a final draught. Each draught helped to finance subcontracting work on adjacent houses. The chain effect meant that while Casey sensed a declining demand in 1930 and 1931, he could not trim back on building activities. Having signed agreements to purchase lots along one side of a block and having put in basements, he could only continue and hope for the best. He was locked into the completion of what he had begun in a year of incredible optimism, a fact which helps to explain the general over-building in Westdale in 1930 and 1931. What was true for Westdale may well have applied elsewhere, for the national collapse in residential construction did not arrive until 1932.[42] As for Casey, he had to let several of his completed homes. In addition, he exchanged one of the new dwellings for a cheaper east-end dwelling, believing that in hard times it would sell more readily.

Several major property owners had no interest in construction, but instead held lots for future capital gain. In 1931, the largest investor, with twenty-two lots, was a doctor whose brother managed the real estate branch of National Trust and held office as President of the Hamilton Real Estate Board in 1930. The degree of speculation and the background of participants is difficult to establish, in part because of a complex set of "straw companies." Kent Hamilton is a case in point. Besides his connection with McKittrick Properties, he managed several companies which dealt in property: Blackstone Realty Securities Limited and Gorban Land Company Limited. Hamilton and similar property entrepreneurs placed some of their activities (at a remove) in order to limit personal liability, but the numerous corporate labels imply additional motives. They at least suggest the involvement of different combinations of shadow investors and the desire for anonymity.

In many instances, those who dealt in Westdale real estate had assorted interests across the city and engaged in other facets of the housing industry. Kent Hamilton, for example, also functioned as a mortgage broker. Forty Investors, the largest owner of Westdale commercial property was managed by W.C. Thompson, real estate agent and mortgage broker. His other operations included Forty Associates, Hamilton Home Builders Limited, Hamilton Improvement Company, Traders Realty, and Thompson and Thompson Realty. Less diverse agents understandably located their offices close to complimentary services. Realtor Norman Ellis owned three Westdale lots in 1931, and to arrange financing for builders or prospective home owners he had only to go next door to the Hamilton Finance Corporation. Realtor J.W. Hamilton, who held three lots in 1931, sold building lots to contractors. At the same time, he served as secretary of a major wholesale lumber company with offices on the same office-tower floor as his real estate agency. These and a host of comparable connections helped to guarantee Westdale's disciplined development. The realty agents and investors who owned lots were not likely to sell to contractors who might introduce structural or ethnic non-comformity for fear of depressing the value of remaining properties. Moreover, it appears that speculation had few amateurs. Those who owned several lots were involved in real estate or the building industry (see table 3).

Just as Westdale's development preceded the era of integrated development and yet represented a progression from the relatively modest land assembling of the nineteenth century, the financial arrangements illustrate a transition. The home buyer could pay interest in two or four payments annually, repaying the principal at the end of an agreed interval. However, in the mid 1920s, what "Carpenter" Jutter billed as a "modern technique" came into use. After a down payment of $500, the purchaser would pay $42 a month, a blending of principal and interest.

The Community, 1931[43]

Instalment plans notwithstanding, the Westdale of 1931 stood incomplete, frozen midway in its settlement by the economic depression. Of 1734 lots, 48 percent lay vacant, while 46 percent had dwellings with residents and 6 percent had buildings under construction or were unoccupied. There were many signs of the community's raw state. Children raised in Westdale during the 1930s and the war years would recall the opportunities for play in vacant fields and hollows. For several years Anglicans held services in the basement of their unfinished church. Altogether, some 760 families resided in the incomplete suburb, 556 (72 percent) as owner-occupants, and 205 (28 percent) as tenants either in rented homes, over commercial establishments or in the five apartment buildings. The ratio of homeowners to tenant households was quite different from the whole city where 52 percent of households rented, one of many indicators of Westdale's situation as a distinct community within the larger urban setting.

TABLE 2

Urban Canada, Hamilton and Westdale, Homeowners and Tenants, 1931 and 1951

| | 1931 | | | 1951 | |
	Owners %	Tenants %		Owners %	Tenants %
Westdale	72 (556)	28 (217)	Westdale	82.5 (1408)	17.5 (301)
Hamilton	48 (17 876)	52 (19 341)	Hamilton	65.8 (36 090)	34.2 (19 250)
Urban Canada (Cities of over 30 000)	37.6 (226 136)	62.4 (375 445)	Urban Canada (Cities of over 100 000)	46.1 (390 930)	53.9 (457 710)

SOURCE: Westdale file and Census of Canada

TABLE 3

Builders and Speculators: Owners of Two or More Vacant Lots, 1931

No. of Lots		Owner's Occupation	Comments and Names Mentioned in Text
1.	132	Manufacturer	Associated with McKittrick Syndicate
2.	25	Doctor	Brother was President of Real Estate Board
3.	18	Contractor	
4.	16	Contractor	Thomas Casey
5.	15	Contractor	Bryers and Son
6.	12	Contractor	Budd and Son
7.	11	Contractor	Vickers
8.	10	Contractor	
9.	10	Contractor	
10.	10	Real Estate Agent	
11.		Widow	
12.	7	Real Estate Agent	
13.	7	Contractor	
14.	6	Contractor	Theaker Family
15.	6	Contractor	Jutter and Son
16.	4	Contractor	Armstrong Family
17.	3	Contractor	
18.	3	Confectionary	
19.		Manufacturer	
20.	3	Real Estate Agent	Norman Ellis
21.	3	Contractor	
22.	3	Contractor	
23.	3	Contractor	
24.	3	Widow	
25.	3	Contractor	
26.	3	Real Estate Agent	J.W. Hamilton
27.	3	Radio Repairman	
28.	2	Contractor	Most of the owners of two lots appear to have been planning to build homes on a double lot or to build on one and sell the other
29.	2	Locomotive Engineer	
30.	2	Manufacturer	
31.	2	Railway Superintendant	
32.	2	Vice President of Manufacturing Company	
33.	2	Widow	
34.	2	Real Estate Agent	
35.	2	Widow	
36.	2	Merchant	
37.	2	Office Clerk	
38.	2	Widow	
39.	2	Manufacturer	

SOURCE: Westdale files using a COBOL 6 SORT/MERGE Program.

Settled to a large extent between 1925 and 1930, the Westdale of 1931 had a relatively young population, a reflection of the affluent 1920s and the developer's advertising which lauded the suburb as a proper nesting ground. Completion of an elementary school in 1927 and Westdale Collegiate in 1930, touted as the finest institution in the region, reinforced its attraction. With the arrival of McMaster University, a child could progress from kindergarten through university within a mile's radius. The suburb was overwhelmingly Protestant with 95 percent of the households affiliated with Protestant churches (see table 4). Only thirty-three Roman Catholic and five Jewish families resided in Westdale. Restrictive covenants account for part of this resounding Protestant character, but nothing prohibited native-born Catholics or Jews from moving to the suburb. Some further considerations discouraged non-Protestants and attracted Protestants. The developers only encouraged Protestant churches to locate in Westdale. Syndicate partner John Moodie figured prominately in Hamilton's very influential Presbyterian community: "he was . . . behind a movement to build a nice Presbyterian church in Westdale."[44] The campaign to attract McMaster University, a Baptist institution, fitted the Protestant design. Possibly it was coincidental that the winner of the contest to name the suburb was an esteemed Anglican canon, but the *Spectator* made good use of the canon's name and his praise for Westdale's sylvan splendor.[45] It seems plausible to consider these events along with covenants and advertising as signals that Westdale provided an escape from what was regarded as a mounting alien presence elsewhere in the city. The period of heaviest construction, 1925 to 1930, coincided with what would be peak years for eastern and southern European arrivals in Hamilton until after 1945. Hence, in the decision to reside in Westdale, more than simple proximity to work or attractive situation was involved. Conventional nativist and sectarian biases of the 1920s were combined with that powerful determinant of middle-class

TABLE 4

Religious Affiliation of Hamilton and Westdale Residents, 1931 and 1951

	1931		1951	
Denomination	Hamilton	Westdale	Hamilton	Westdale
United Church	20.6	35.4	23.2	35.5
Anglican	29.4	25.6	25.1	21.9
Presbyterian	17.1	18.7	12.4	11.7
Baptist	5.2	6.9	5.1	7.4
Lutheran	1.2	1.1	1.8	0.8
Salvation Army	0.7	0.3	0.5	0.4
Roman Catholic	18.5	4.5	23.0	7.6
Jewish	1.7	0.7	1.5	8.3
Other or Unspecified	5.6	6.8	7.4	6.5
	100.0	100.0	100.0	100.0

1931 Index of dissimilarity = .193
1951 Index of dissimilarity = .211

SOURCE: The percentages for Hamilton were based on Census returns which included all individuals; percentages for Westdale were based on the affiliation of household heads.

behaviour: parental desire to secure decent education and "the right" neighbour-hood influences. Catering to this combination of aspirations and prejudices, the developer added to the land value. Ironically, Westdale Collegiate, designed as part of the suburb's self-contained image, became an instrument of contact between its children and those from quite different backgrounds. Built in advance of the completed community, the collegiate attracted pupils from Hamilton's working-class north end as well as rural Ancaster.[46]

Religious distinction was a consideration in measuring the contrast between Westdale and the city. A common and simple statistical device, the index of dissimilarity yields a rough measure of that contrast. If the index number was 0, then religious affiliations would have been distributed in an identical fashion both in Westdale and the city of Hamilton. If the index number was 1, then the two areas would have been completely distinct in terms of religious affiliation. With the large areas and numerous households involved, a high score close to 1 was unlikely.[47] Even so, the index score of .193 seems low, but it does indicate segregation. Nonetheless, comparable studies of urban segregation treat such a score as marginal.[48] Indeed, another variable in Westdale had a more impressive score. Occupation ranked on a scale devised by Bernard Blishen[49] or classified by economic function (vertical and horizontal classification respectively) showed a contrast between Westdale and Hamilton with index of dissimilarity scores of .383 and .365 (see tables 5 and 6). Professionals on the vertical scale accounted for 40.1 percent of Westdale's household heads while only 14.1 percent of Hamil-ton's male labour force had a corresponding rank. Aside from rank, the employ-ment characteristics expressed in terms of economic sectors reveal other vivid distnctions. If Hamilton was a lunch bucket city, Westdale was a white-collar suburb. Manufacturing and construction provided jobs for 57.1 percent of Hamil-ton's male work force. In Westdale, only 25.3 percent of household heads were

TABLE 5

Vertical Classification of Occupation in Westdale and Hamilton, 1931 and 1951

| | 1931 | | 1951 | |
Rank	Hamilton	Westdale	Hamilton	Westdale
Elite professions	1.6	4.5	1.6	5.1
Professions and management	12.5	35.6	15.3	48.3
White-collar — semi-skilled	2.0	13.6	3.5	8.1
Blue-collar — foreman level	8.2	8.9	6.8	7.2
Skilled labour	33.1	26.4	39.8	24.9
Semi-skilled	17.0	9.1	18.2	4.7
Unskilled	25.6	1.9	14.8	1.7
	100.0	100.0	100.0	100.0

1931 Index of dissimilarity between Westdale and Hamilton = .383
1951 Index of dissimilarity = .429

SOURCE: The percentages for Hamilton were based on census returns for all employed males; percent-ages for Westdale were based on occupation of household heads. Since census data did not combine work force distribution with numbers of widows, widowers and pensioners, the later cases were excluded from the Westdale computation.

so employed, while 57.0 percent worked in trade and commerce, finance, and as clerks and professionals (see table 6). As a further measure of Westdale's social character, comparison can be made with a contemporary land development near Hamilton's industrial district. Completed in the early 1920s, Somerset Park had a 10 percent professional component in 1931; 90 percent of household heads were skilled or unskilled labourers, most working in the metal and electrical industries (see table 7).

Despite Westdale's contrasts with Hamilton proper, it displayed internal variety within its Protestant boundaries. There were identifiable physical and social regions. We have noted how in the year immediately after 1918, the first portions of Westdale to be developed were working-class surveys: Woodlawn and Elmhurst. In addition to a site bordered by a garbage dump, the main survey (Woodlawn) was near the City Isolation Hospital and a brickyard. As Kent Hamilton expressed it: "that brickyard . . . was like a boil on the thumb so far as our property was concerned."[50] House assessments in the area ranged from $1900 to $2500 in 1931 when the mean for the whole Westdale suburb was roughly $2700.

The separate spatial and structural features of workingmen's areas were matched by social distinctions (see table 8). Typical occupations of household heads included railway firemen and brakemen, mechanics, machinists, moulders, truck drivers, printers, bookkeepers, office clerks, and sales and shipping clerks. Though the United Church had the largest following of any denomination in Westdale, in the workingmen's sections the Church of England prevailed. This fact, along with occupational traits, gave these areas a social profile similar to the city. It is

TABLE 6

Horizontal Classification of Employment in Hamilton and Westdale, 1931 and 1951

	1931		1951	
	Hamilton	Westdale	Hamilton	Westdale
Agriculture, forestry and mining	1.4	0.8	0.6	0.1
Manufacturing	47.4	19.9	46.8	20.4
Utilities	2.1	1.0	3.0	0.7
Construction	9.7	5.4	8.7	3.3
Transportation/Communication	11.2	10.2	8.4	5.5
Trade/Commerce	11.3	17.9	6.2	33.5
Finance	1.6	12.0	1.4	6.5
Clerical	5.2	10.1	8.8	8.0
Professional Service	4.8	17.2	6.4	18.0
Personal Service	3.8	2.9	6.9	2.0
Public Service	1.2	2.3	2.4	1.9
Recreational Service	0.3	0.3	0.4	0.1
	100.0	100.0	100.0	100.0

Index of dissimilarity 1931 = .365
Index of dissimilarity 1951 = .376

SOURCE: See the published census of Canada, 1931 and 1951 for the lists of occupations appearing under the classification headings.

TABLE 7

Vertical Classification of Occupation in Westdale and the Workingman's Neighbourhood of Somerset Park, 1931 and 1951

	1931 Westdale	1931 Somerset	1951 Westdale	1951 Somerset
Elite professions	4.2	0.8	4.2	0.0
Professions and management	33.2	6.3	39.8	5.3
White-collar — semi-skilled	12.7	3.1	6.7	4.1
Blue-collar — foreman level	8.3	8.7	6.3	4.1
Skilled labour	24.7	44.2	20.7	33.0
Semi-skilled	8.5	17.3	3.9	14.9
Unskilled	1.8	10.2	1.4	26.4
Widowed, widowers, retired	6.6	9.4	17.0	12.2
	100.0	100.0	100.0	100.0

1931 Index of dissimilarity = .399
1951 Index of dissimilarity = .434

SOURCE: Westdale files and Anna Chiota, "Somerset Part, 1910–1960: A Quantitative Study of an Industrial Suburb" McMaster University, 1977 (Mimeographed).

TABLE 8

Vertical Classification of Occupation in Westdale Subdistricts, 1931 and 1951

	Working-class Area 1931	Working-class Area 1951	Central Core 1931	Central Core 1951	Elite Fringe 1931	Elite Fringe 1951
Elite professions	2.4	1.9	4.2	4.8	5.8	7.0
Professions and management	17.5	30.9	19.0	36.6	54.6	56.7
White-collar — semi-skilled	5.4	6.9	16.9	8.4	14.4	16.5
Blue-collar — foreman level	10.2	8.3	12.0	5.0	7.9	4.9
Skilled labour	41.7	28.9	29.0	18.4	9.4	8.4
Semi-skilled	11.4	5.2	7.0	5.5	4.3	0.7
Unskilled	3.0	1.7	4.2	2.0	0.0	0.0
Widows, widowers, pensioners	8.4	16.2	7.7	19.3	3.6	5.8
	100.0	100.0	100.0	100.0	100.0	100.0

SOURCE: Assessment rolls.

also worth noting that the daily routines of these families remained detached from the more affluent. Located on a grid at the eastern extremity of Westdale, the workingmen's homes were positioned so that residents did not have occasion to travel through abruptly different social areas to shop, reach places of employment, or attend shool. Major thoroughfares, like King and Main, as well as important feeder streets, like Longwood and Stirling, spanned Westdale but did not erode patterns of segregation supported by the location of parks, business districts, and school property (see map 3).

The most isolated and exclusive surveys — Oak Knoll, Oakwood and Forest Hills — clung to a narrow, ravine-indented fringe at the western extremity. Deep lots fronted on secluded curving avenues. Several humble avenues were elevated

MAP 3

Westdale, 1931

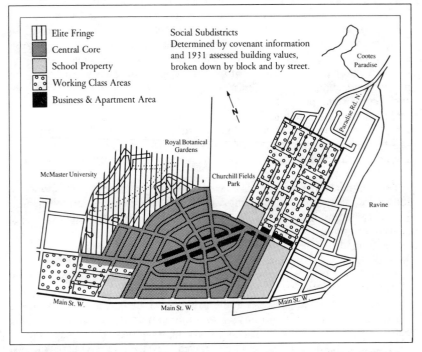

to crescent status as they entered the district. High minimum building values were written into the covenants, many of which inserted specifications for building materials and established broad architectural guidelines. Therefore, like the eastern sector, this neighbourhood evolved an architectural style but with a pronounced difference. Interpretations of English manors, stone as well as stucco and wood, dominated with some sharp variety provided by several examples of the austere international style. A tasteful variety here contrasted with what would become cheap eclecticism a half mile to the east in the workingmen's district. Building assessments reflected the difference, extending from $4000 to $5700 or more than twice that for the workingmen's homes.

Needless to say, the "old" wealthy families of Hamilton did not move into the exclusive portion of Westdale. Hamilton's elite avenues remained settled among the Victorian estates which had backed onto "Hamilton mountain" in the south central part of the city. By a process of "in-filling," spacious homes were constructed within an already prestigious area which had housed two Lieutenant-Governors of Ontario.[51] By contrast, Westdale's unfinished appearance and distinctly middle-class image, established by the developers, meant that the exclusive portion of the suburb attracted not old money, but affluent young professionals. At least 55 percent of household heads had a professional ranking. Merchants, corporate executives, and senior educators were frequently encountered. United

Church affiliation soared to 45 percent as compared with 35 percent for all Westdale and 21 percent for Hamilton. In an industrial centre like Hamilton with its immigrants, labourers, aspiring middle class and old elite, notions of class had recognized boundaries. While the old elite generally shunned even the best sections of Westdale, these same areas must have seemed quite remote to residents of the working-class east-end of Hamilton. What they saw was inaccessibility and the affluence of the elite fringe. One experience, though not conclusive, is suggestive of the outsider's sense of the turf, religion and class which, as an impressionable youth, seemed to threaten his life's goal. At high school he had been considered presumptious for wishing to become a teacher. It was pointed out that he had attended neither Westdale Collegiate nor Westdale United Church. The images of neighbourhood, although they are not perfect assessments of society, have a crude accuracy. Wealthy and poor had carved out, by their feelings and actions, a position for Westdale's exclusive area in a hierarchy of Hamilton neighbourhoods.

The central blocks of Westdale were made up of surveys with moderate convenant restrictions on building values and unpretentious survey names: Crescentwood, Clinelands, and Paisley Gardens. The streets here did not consist of a simple grid pattern like the workingmen's areas, but neither were they protected from the noise and commotion of through traffic like the elite fringe. Geographically and figuratively, the centre was truly mid-way. Contractors responded most frequently to the developer's characterization of the property by constructing the 2½ storey "square-plan" homes which had proven popular across Hamilton. Slight variations in the style of brick, porch, and window details did little to break the monotony or, as some preferred, the continuity. The centre evolved as something of a compromise between the simplicity apparent in workingmen's portions and the elegance arrayed along the fringe, though it inclined toward the former and included a number of the "Hamilton A-1 Plan" houses (see illustration 1). Since Westdale builders responded to the prosperity of 1925–29 with frantic construction of middle-class dwellings, this central portion had a number of blocks completed by 1931. After the 1930s it continued to have more architectural cohesion than any other neighbourhood in the development. For example, while Casey built the whole side of one block, his rival, Vickers, built a row behind him using similar materials, blueprints, and embellishments.

Occupational ranking paralleled the compromise structural features by indicating a middle-class mix of blue and white collar. Households headed by professionals accounted for 23 percent of the total. In the skilled-labour tier, the portion was 29 percent (see table 8). The heart of Westdale housed white collar professionals such as accountants, clergymen, teachers, retail managers, and commercial travellers. It also sheltered manufacturing foremen, railway conductors, station employees, and assorted clerks.

What of the tenants? Some 205 of the Westdale households rented. Approximately fifty resided in five apartment buildings;[52] these had been provided for in Pope's plan and, so as not to jar homeowner tastes, they were located within the business district. A dozen families rented apartments above commercial establishments. The bulk of Westdale's tenants were scattered throughout the suburb, to some extent reflecting the contractors' overbuilding in the early months of the Depression. Four to five years younger than homeowners and with comparatively small families, the heads of tenant households actually had a slightly higher occupational ranking than homeowners. Generally, Westdale's tenants appear to have been upwardly mobile, small, young families who took advantage of the abundant good rental accomodations. Dividing tenants into apartment dwellers and tenants renting homes does not alter this impression of upwardly mobile residents. What did separate those who rented homes from those who rented apartments was their stage in the life cycle. As is shown in table 9, the residents of apartments were considerably younger and had far smaller households than home tenants. Young couples and singles, quite naturally, could accept the limited space and lack of yard inherent in an apartment situation.

TABLE 9

Occupational Rank, Age and Household Size: Homeowners, Home Tenants, Apartment Dwellers, 1931

	All Households	Homeowners	Home Tenants	Apartment Dwellers
(Total cases)	(761)	(556)	(143)	(62)
Elite professions	4.2	4.2	2.8	4.9
Professions and management	33.2	29.1	41.8	36.1
White-collar — semi-skilled	12.7	12.7	14.9	14.8
Blue-collar — foreman level	8.3	9.2	5.7	8.2
Skilled labour	24.7	27.3	20.6	18.0
Semi-skilled	8.5	8.3	7.8	8.2
Unskilled	1.8	2.0	1.4	1.6
Widows, widowers, pensioners	6.6	7.2	5.0	8.2
	100.0	100.0	100.0	100.0
	Age in Years of Household Head			
Mean	40.0	41.0	38.4	31.8
Median	38.7	40.0	37.3	29.8
Mode	32.0	42.0	37.0	28.0
	Household Size by Number			
Mean	3.6	3.7	3.7	2.4
Median	3.4	3.5	3.6	2.2
Mode	3.0	3.0	3.0	2.0

Family and household in Westdale were virtually the same. As a middle-class suburb with certain social attitudes, the practice of taking in boarders appears to have been shunned. What American researchers have observed for the end of the nineteenth century seems applicable in Westdale: "family boarding had lost ... its middle class respectability."[53] Assessment rolls and city directories, despite their limitations as accurate sources for such details, indicate very little boarding and "doubling up" of families. The same sources, however, do indicate that nearly 10 percent of Somerset Park's homes contained two families in 1931. The added income or economy, therefore, do not appear to have been important considerations in Westdale. The records revealed only half a dozen households which contained either in-laws or boarders. A few households headed by a bachelor or spinster included a relative or friend. Though the records did not list or describe all of the household arrangements in suitable detail, it is reasonable to conclude that in household composition, as in occupation and religion, Westdale's deviation from homogeneity and middle-class standards registered in small degrees, if at all.

The Community, 1951

By definition, suburbs stand apart from the city, but eventually lines of distinction fade with land-use transformation and the overlapping of new surveys. However, twenty years after its first period of growth, Westdale retained a separate character. The Chedoke ravine and the McKittrick bridge had preserved the suburb against assimilation by preventing the extension of Hamilton's grid street system. The unique street layout of Westdale itself countered fusion with the new post-war suburbs around Westdale. All the same, the community was not quite what it had been. Age, occupational composition, and denominational features had altered, revealing new social forces at work in Hamilton and across Canada.

The national housing boom that swept Westdale into its second period of construction, eliminating the vacant tracts, came partly through government-stimulated activity. Efforts to encourage residential building began with the Dominion Housing Act of 1935. When revised as the National Housing Act of 1938, fewer than 5000 new units across Canada had benefited from the federal loans. War curtailed operations, but not the involvement of Ottawa in shelter matters. A Wartime Housing Corporation created by Order in Council concentrated on the provision of temporary quarters for immigrants coming into the areas of war industry activity. The affected urban land was not of prime suburban quality. In Hamilton, the areas were scattered. The site nearest to Westdale was over one mile away. In the planning for post-war reconstruction, a revised National Housing Act of 1944 prepared the way for accelerated suburban lending. Frequently reorganized and expanded, the programme joined post-war prosperity in providing a sustained house-building effort that produced 500 000 dwelling units across Canada from the beginning of 1945 to the end of 1951. Abstract books in the Land Registry Office indicate considerable movement in Westdale real estate from 1945 to 1951. During 1951, NHA loans were approved for 800 housing units in Hamilton.[54] Their presence in Westdale was reflected in the fact that many mortgages were held by some of the thirty government-approved institutional lenders and "His Majesty the King, by Minister of Finance." By 1951, home ownership in the nation, Hamilton, and Westdale had risen substantially above 1931 levels (see table 2). The incomplete Westdale of depression and wartime rapidly filled with NHA homeowners.

The 1931 households had had relatively young heads, but in 1951 the average age of household heads tended to be ten years above that of 1931. The initial families had aged and new homeowners had been delayed in their entry into the housing market by depression as well as by the dislocations of life and the construction shortages caused by war. Most striking as a measure of maturation, households headed by pensioners, widowers, and widows increased from 6.6 percent to 16.3 percent. The major component consisted of widows of whom there were 150, or 8.5 percent of household heads. These widows were not impoverished. Of 196 houses rented in Westdale, 72 (36.7 percent) were owned by widows. Seventeen widows owned two dwellings each, living in one while letting the other. Elizabeth Groh illustrated the condition. During the 1920s, her carpenter husband had built and let Westdale homes. In 1951, his widow let two dwellings while residing in a third. Not all of the property-owning widows had been Westdale residents like Mrs. Groh. Twenty appear not to have been former Westdale residents. Some might have purchased homes for rental income and future capital gains. Several appear to have been holding titles to homes in which married sons resided. Widowhood, being more apparent on older streets, was not evenly distributed across the community. Along one of these early streets, South Oval, 24 out of 66 homes were owned by widows.

Unfortunately, cross-sectional analysis prevents a full understanding of widowhood, so it is difficult to estimate how many Westdale wives were widowed between 1931 and 1951. It was probably greater than the 150 found residing there in 1951 since some might have moved away. On the other hand, few widows had moved into Westdale. By tracing through city directories, it was established that all but 14 of the 150 had resided there before the death of their husbands. With an average age of 59.6, it is unlikely that resident widows had lost husbands in the war. Other explanations must be sought for a 5 to 1 ratio of widows to widowers. The answer seems to be the fact that for our time period, across Ontario, male deaths outnumbered female deaths in all age cohorts from birth to 70. The greatest differential appeared in the 50 to 59 age cohort. Significantly, the ratio of male to female heart disease victims in the age group 40 to 59 was 3 to 1.[55] Given the age composition of Westdale household heads in 1931, and of widows in 1951, it seems plausible that the suburb had had a number of male heart-attack victims throughout the 1940s and early 1950s.

In comparison with 1931, there had been a slight upward trend in the occupational ranking of Westdale's household heads by 1951 (see table 5). Very little of this can be attributed to the occupational gains of the older residents. Of the 556 homeowners in 1931, 190 or 34 percent could be located at the same address in 1951. Many had retired. Of the remaining 143 still in the labour force, it can be said that as a group they had realized a few advances in occupational rank with some rising from skilled labour into management (see table 10). More essential to the higher occupational tone of Westdale were 900 new households. Most were beneficiaries of wartime prosperity and the government housing measures. The largest single increase in occupation involved retail merchants. Though there were 33 in 1931, there were nearly 100 more in 1951. As Westdale's occupational profile was enhanced, the measure of its dissimilarity with the city and with the east-end workingman's survey, Somerset Park, broadened moderately (see tables 5 and 7).

The newcomers who effected the shift in occupational distributions also altered denominational traits (see table 4). A Jewish migration into Westdale had begun in 1944, the year in which Ontario passed its Racial Discrimination Act. Although

TABLE 10

Occupational Ranking of Employed Household Heads Who "Persisted" for Twenty Years*

	Persisters in 1931	Persisters in 1951
Elite professions	6.3	6.3
Professions and management	28.7	41.2
White-collar — semi-skilled	9.0	9.1
Blue-collar, foreman level	7.6	9.1
Skilled labour	34.6	24.5
Semi-skilled	10.2	6.3
Unskilled	3.6	3.5
	100.0	100.0

*The address, religion, name and age provided a sure linkage. In no case did the age cited in 1931 vary by more than two years from the twenty year differential anticipated in 1951.

it required considerable litigation by the Canadian Jewish Congress and civil liberties activists, the racial ingredients in restrictive covenants were finally eliminated by 1951.[56] Interestingly, the Jewish population in Westdale concentrated on four of the suburb's thirty streets. Indeed, along one block of Bond Street, sixteen of thirty household heads were Jewish retailers. All four streets had been under-developed prior to the mid-1940s. As lots here had come onto the market, there had been a convergence of events: the challenge to covenants, a housing boom, and the fact that the Jewish community, newly affluent, began to move to the west-end seeking middle-class amenities.[57] Along with United Church adherents, Jews were now over-represented in Westdale when compared with their proportion of the city-wide population. Roman Catholics alone remained under-represented (see table 4) and churchless.

Westdale's completion as a prime and distinctive development was fully realized by 1951, but as a large district whose formative planning in the 1920s had allowed for workers' dwellings, it retained elements of the social mix present in 1931. Overall, however, the proportion of professionals and managers rose while the proportion of skilled and semi-skilled labourers declined. The greatest shifts appeared in the central core and workingmen's surveys where Westdale's image of convenience and prestige dispelled the compunctions of the 1920s about raw and unattractive lots in such surveys as Woodlawn and Princess Heights. Measured against the new suburbs laid out in Stoney Creek, Hamilton mountain, and on land to the west of Westdale, the district had appeal.

In contrast to rising status among homeowners, rental accomodations now housed a population with a lower occupational profile than in 1931. This condition most likely reflected the quite different prospects faced by young families in 1931 and 1951. In the depressed housing market of 1930 and 1931, a few young upwardly mobile families had found abundant rental bargains until financial circumstances brightened. Their 1951 counterparts seeking shelter had the advantages of economic boom and government incentives for home ownership, points conveyed in the rise of city-wide ownership from 48 percent (1931) to 65 percent (1951). The average age of 1951 tenants was still lower than that of home-owning neighbours. However, while small young families continued to rent apartments and homes in Westdale, a group composed of the retired and the widowed accounted for one tenant in five. The ratio was somewhat higher among apartment dwellers (see table 11). In sum, the social attributes of Westdale in 1951 had come to reflect not only the developers' activities of the 1920s, but now they also bore the impression of aging and the significant domestic ramifications of the war.

This cross-sectional analysis of a community has spanned two decades, over depression, recovery, and boom. Conclusions drawn from this admittedly limited process suggest a number of hypotheses pertaining to city-building and to urban society in the twentieth century. Land value was a complex function of natural settings, provision of services, and entrepreneurial activity. These gave tone to the property and that enhanced its value. To create a scarce commodity was not a policy on the part of the developers as demand remained below expectations for nearly thirty years. The creation of a suburban community was neither smooth nor sudden. It required forty years as well as a variety of individual skills and government aid. Moreover, Westdale's history testifies to the importance of examining local events in the light of national and, at times, international forces.[58] The planning and promotional tactics of developers drew on concepts that were not strictly local. Builders followed practices in construction, sub-contracting, and credit that had wide North American appreciation.[59] The local building cycles in Westdale had no independent significance. They coincided precisely with national trends in residential construction. In another important matter, racial discrimination, the Westdale or Hamilton experience did not differ from North American norm.

Peter Goheen has observed that "the element of residential choice which was introduced into the city with the . . . street railway apparently served to rationalize the distribution of families within the city."[60] Westdale supports the generalization. The McKittrick bridge and a streetcar line — at one time operated by some of the same businessmen who had taken up an interest in the land syndicate — made possible this essentially middle-class suburb. And yet, while Westdale demonstrated the "rationalize[d] distribution of families with the city," it embraced a measure of diversity and experienced some modest social transformations. The developers of Westdale originally had attempted to build exclusiveness into their community, but they also had to accede to market forces, government inducements, and legal decisions. The dynamic tension produced when a Protestant, middle-class design was challenged eventually generated a community where managers and truck drivers, and Christian and Jews, resided. Admittedly, they did not dwell in close proximity. Over time, the suburb had matured, progressing from a raw incomplete community with young families and a degree of ethnic isolation into a tree-shaded area familiar with aging and some religious diversity. However unique it might have been in its scale and physical layout, Westdale was so much a part of broad economic and social events that it can serve as one point of departure for comprehending the mundane processes shaping the contemporary Canadian city. Aside from what it demonstrates about the complexity of making a suburb, Westdale offers some reflections on North American social change. More mature than their 1931 counterparts, the post-war newcomers were to

TABLE 11

Occupational Rank, Age and Household Size: Homeowners, Home Tenants, Apartment Dwellers, 1951

	All Households	Homeowners	Home Tenants	Apartment Dwellers
(Total cases)	(1709)	(1408)	(196)	(105)
Elite professions	4.2	4.5	2.6	3.8
Professions and management	39.8	41.6	34.3	26.6
White-collar — semi-skilled	6.7	7.0	6.2	4.8
Blue-collar — foreman level	6.3	6.3	5.1	7.6
Skilled labour	20.7	19.3	25.1	30.5
Semi-skilled	3.9	3.6	6.7	1.9
Unskilled	1.4	1.4	1.5	1.9
Widows, widowers, pensioners	17.0	16.3	18.5	22.9
	100.0	100.0	100.0	100.0
	Age in Years of Household Head			
Mean	50.4	51.4	45.1	47.5
Median	50.4	51.3	42.0	44.4
Mode	52.0	52.0	33.0	40.0
	Household Size by Number			
Mean	3.3	3.4	3.2	2.4
Median	3.2	3.2	3.0	2.2
Mode	2.0	2.0	2.0	2.0

reside in a finished suburb during prosperous years. Thus Westdale became a place where people could aspire to an affluence almost within reach. As well as greater economic security, the arrival of Jews heralded national shifts in which the urban middle class of Canada would become different in outlook and background from its depression counterpart.

Notes

1. See for example Peter Goheen, *Victorian Toronto, 1850 to 1900* (Chicago: University of Chicago, 1970) particularly chs. 1 and 2. Another indicator of international exchange is found in a review of literature on housing in the second footnote of Michael J. Doucet, "Working-Class Housing in a Small Nineteeth-Century Canadian City. Hamilton, Ontario, 1852–1881," *Essays in Canadian Working-Class History,* edited by Gregory S. Kealey and Peter Warrian (Toronto: McClelland and Stewart, 1976). Michael Katz, *The People of Hamilton, Canada West: Family and Class in a Mid-Nineteenth-Century City* (Cambridge: Harvard University Press, 1975) is the most striking attempt to place Canadian social history into an international context.

2. Though Gideon Sjoberg's *The Pre-industry City, Past and Present* (New York: The Free Press, 1960) stimulated a considerable volume of case studies, the concept of a clear shift has been discredited. See for example, Tamara K. Hareven, "The Historical Study of the Family in Urban Society," *Journal of Urban History* I (May 1975): 259–65; Herbert Gutman, "Work Culture and Society in Industrializing America, 1815–1919," *American Historical Review* LXXVII (June 1973): 531–87.

3. For an excellent introduction to the concept of "the city-building process," see Roy Lubove, "The Urbanization Process: An Approach to Historical Research," *Journal of the American Institute of Planners* XXXIII (Jan. 1967): 33–39.

4. Katz, *The People of Hamilton*, 316

5. Hamilton Public Library, Special Collections, F. Kent Hamilton, *Beauty Spots in Westdale* (c. 1928), 7.

6. N.H. Lithwick and Gilles Paquet, "The Economics of Urban Land Use," in *Urban Studies: A Canadian Perspective*, edited by Lithwick and Paquet (Toronto: Methuen, 1968).

7. I am indebted to Jean-Claude Robert of La Groupe de Recherche sur la société montréalise au 19e siècle for calling my attention to a pioneering study of land developers, Maurice Halbwach, *Les expropriations et le prix des terrains à Paris, 1860–1900* (Paris, 1909). Canadian studies of land development include the following: Jean-Claude Robert, "Un seigneur entrepreneur, Barthélemy Joliette, et la fondation du village d'industrie (Joliette), 1822–1850," *Revue d'histoire de l'Amérique française* XXVI (déc. 1972): 375–95; Paul-André Linteau et Jean-Claude Robert, "Propriété foncière et société à Montréal: Une hypothèse," *Revue d'histoire de l'Amérique française* XXVIII (juin 1974): 45–65; Peter Spurr, *Land and Urban Development: A Preliminary Study* (Toronto: James Lorimer, 1976). On the British historiographic trend see Richard Shannon, "The Genius of the Suburbs," *Times Literary Supplement*, 31 Dec. 1976, p. 1626.

8. The clearest indication is established by studying a map prepared by the Ramsay-Thomas Realty Company in 1913. The map presents newly registered and proposed surveys and provides a radius measure indicating distances from the city core. A brief account of the east-end expansion is found in Charles M. Johnston, *The Head of the Lake: A History of Wentworth County* (Hamilton, 1967), 246–48 and Appendix E, "City Growth from the Year of Incorporation to 1914."

9. Hamilton Public Library, Reference Room, Hamilton Collection, Scrapbook on Real Estate, "Action Requested to Promote Old Suburbs," undated clippings.

10. "Copy of Agreement among McKittrick Properties, the City of Hamilton and Ancaster Township presented to the Ontario Railway and Municipal Board, 26 January 1914," *Hamilton City Council Minutes, 1914.*

11. Hamilton *Spectator*, Dec. and Jan. 1916.

12. This is somewhat in conflict with the impression of the Winnipeg business community as analyzed by Alan Artibise, *Winnipeg, A Social History of Urban Growth, 1874–1914* (Montreal: McGill-Queen's University Press, 1975).

13. F. Kent Hamilton Papers, William Lyon Somerville, Robert Anderson Pope and Desmond McDonaugh, *Report of Survey and Recommendations, McKittrick Properties* (1 Feb. 1919); Somerville to Hamilton, n.d.

14. Mel Scott, *American City Planning Since 1890* (Berkeley: University of California Press, 1971) 96–99.

15. F. Kent Hamilton Papers, Somerville et al., *Report on Survey and Recommendations*, passim. Also see Scrapbook 1 for various clippings kept by Hamilton on housing questions.

16. Somerville et al., *Report on Survey and Recommendations*, 16. For similar fears as an impetus to housing reform, see John C. Waver, "Reconstruction of the Richmond District in Halifax: A Canadian Episode in Public Housing and Town Planning, 1918–1921," *Plan Canada* (March 1976): 36–47.

17. Hamilton Real Estate Board, Kent Hamilton Scrapbooks, Scrapbook 2, p. 11, clipping dated June 1922.

18. I am indebted to Mr. St. Clair Balfour and his secretary, Mrs. M. Shano, for providing copies of Southam correspondence relating to Westdale. Southam Papers, J.P. Mills, Secretary, Westdale Properties to F. I. Ker, 19 Nov. 1928.

19. Bureau of Municipal Affairs, *Report re Housing for 1919* (Ontario Sessional Papers, 1920).

20. Canada, Dominion Bureau of Statistics, *Census Monograph No. 8 Housing in Canada (A Study Based on the Census of 1931 and Supplementary Data)*, 104.

21. Supreme Court of Ontario (hereinafter SCO), *in Bankruptcy, Re: McKittrick Properties*, Affidavit of Frank Ernest Roberts, 19 March 1928, 6.

22. SCO, *in Bankruptcy, Re: McKittrick Properties*, Petititon of Charles Delamere Magee, 29 June 1926.

23. SCO, *in Bankruptcy, Re: McKittrick Properties*, Report of the Official Receiver, 28 July 1926.

24. SCO, *in the Matter of the Bankruptcy of McKittrick Properties*, Debtor, filed 6 July 1926.

25. SCO, Depositions of Frank E. Roberts, taken before John Bruce, Special Examiner, 25 Oct. 1927.

26. Hamilton Public Library, Special Collections, Scrapbooks, West-End and Westdale Scrapbook (1926–28), passim.

27. Memorandum on Board of Directors' Meeting, Westdale Properties, 1 Nov. 1928.

28. Charles M. Johnston, *McMaster University*, vol. 1, *The Toronto Years* (Toronto: University of Toronto Press, 1970), 204–36.

29. Baptist Archives, McMaster University, Removal to Hamilton/Hamilton Chamber of Commerce File, F. Kent Hamilton to F.P. Healey, Secretary Chamber of Commerce, 3 Oct. 1921; W.W. McMaster to Chancellor A.L. McCremmon, 21 Feb. 1922. For the contributions, see New McMaster File, W.J. Westaway to Chancellor H.P. Whidden, 13 June 1928. Altogether, those associated with Westdale Properties had pledged $171 000.

30. Southam Papers, J.P. Mills, Secretary, Westdale Properties to F.I. Ker, Hamilton *Spectator*, 19 Nov. 1928.

31. Baptist Archives, New McMaster File, W.J. Westaway to Chancellor H.P. Whidden. Re: Agreement with Westdale Properties, 30 Oct. and 6 Dec. 1928. The power issue was discussed in Westaway to Whidden, 13 June 1928. Westaway destroyed his copy "as I do not want it to appear in our correspondence." The housing of professors was raised in Westaway to Whidden, 12 Oct. 1929; Westaway to Whidden, 7 Apr. 1930.

32. Kent Hamilton's litigation appears in SCO, *in Bankruptcy, In the Matter of the Estate of McKittrick's Limited and In the Matter of the Claim of F. Kent Hamilton*, copy of Depositions of F. Kent Hamilton, 29 Sept. 1927 and 11 Oct. 1927. The conflict among syndicate members is cited in Southam Papers, Memorandum on Board of Directors' Meeting, Westdale Properties, 1 Nov. 1928. The state of the professors' purchasing power is contained in Baptist Archives, New McMaster File, Westaway to Whidden, 7 Apr. 1930.

33. Anna Chiota, "Somerset Park, 1910–1960: A Quantitative Study of an Industrial Suburb," McMaster University, 1977 (mimeographed). Michael Doucet found few covenants between 1847 and 1881 and those examined pertained to building materials. See Michael Doucet, "Building the Victorian City: The Process of Land Development in Hamilton, Ontario, 1847–1881" (Ph.D. dissertation, University of Toronto, 1977). Doucet also provides an excellent discussion of the land auction system.

34. Wentworth County Courthouse, Land Registry Office, property instrument 327114 (Hamilton) is cited, but its racial clause was standard throughout Westdale.

35. Hamilton, *Beauty Spots in Westdale* (c. 1928), 22.

36. Interview with contractor Thomas Casey, 24 Sept. 1976.

37. The information on builders was generated from the 1931 assessment file, the city directories, real estate advertisements between 1920 and 1930, and interviews with a contractor of the era, Thomas Casey. Now 97, Casey had excellent recall and his memory of purchases was cross-checked with the land registry office and found accurate. Although Victorian London was hardly comparable to Hamilton in the 1920s, the latter's family contractors and credit system seems remarkably similar to that outlined in H.S. Dyos and D.A. Reeder, "Slums and Suburbs," in *The Victorian City*, edited by H.S. Dyos and Michael Wolff, vol. 1 (London: Routledge and Kegan Paul, 1973), 378–79.

38. Hamilton *Spectator*, 15 July 1926.

39. Hamilton *Spectator*, real estate section, 30 Apr. 1926.

40. Kent Hamilton Scrapbooks, Scrapbook 2, *Spectator*, 17 Nov. 1924.

41. Interview with Hughes Cleaver, former M.P. and developer cited in Stephen White, "The Business Community in Burlington's Development, 1920–1939," McMaster University, 1977 (mimeographed).

42. Canada, Central Mortgage and Housing Corporation, *Housing in Canada, A Factual Summary* (Oct. 1946), 1:27.

43. Unless otherwise stated, data for this section was derived from the Assessment rolls using S.P.S.S. A COBOL programme was used to sort and list names of occupants and owners alphabetically. This proved useful in establishing the names of owners of more than one property and in linking "persisters" from 1931 to 1951 files. Subjective observations were collected from a number of interviews, including the following: Philip Barrs, Diane Turner, Sheila Scott, Thomas Casey, Mrs. F. Kent Hamilton, and Gordon Hamilton.

44. Baptist Archives, New McMaster File, W.J. Westaway to Chancellor H.P. Whidden, 10 Oct. 1930.

45. Hamilton Real Estate Board, Kent Hamilton Scrapbooks, Scrapbook 2, clippings from *Spectator*, Apr. 1923.

46. Interview with Diane Turner, a former resident raised in Westdale, 20 Nov. 1976.

47. To calculate an index of dissimilarity, the percentages of every category of a variable within a designated area (for example Westdale) are prepared. The process is repeated for another area (Hamilton). The result is a two-column frequency distribution expressed in percentages (see table 4). The difference in percentages in each row is noted and the sum taken of the positive differences is the index of dissimilarity. For more information see Charles M. Dollar and Richard J. Jensen, *Historians' Guide to Statistics: Quantitative*

Analysis and Historical Research (New York: Holt, Rinehart and Winston, 1971), 125; Sam B. Warner, Jr., *The Private City: Philadelphia in Three Periods of its Growth* (Philadelphia: University of Pennsylvania Press, 1968), 13–14.

48. Kenneth L. Kusmer, *A Ghetto Takes Shape: Black Cleveland, 1870–1930* (Urbana: University of Illinois Press, 1976), 44–46.

49. Bernard R. Blishen, "The Construction and Use of an Occupational Class Scale," *Canadian Journal of Economics and Political Science* XXIV (Nov. 1958). Given the valid criticisms against occupation as a surrogate for status, occupations were also coded for horizontal classification. See Katz, *The People of Hamilton, Canada West*, 51–52.

50. SCO, *in Bankruptcy*, Depositions of F. Kent Hamilton, 11.

51. Terry Naylor, "Ravenscliffe: A Hamilton Elite District," McMaster University, 1978 (mimeographed).

52. The apartment dwelling made its most dramatic showing in Hamilton in 1924 when 48 were constructed. Kevin Braybrook, "The First Apartment Dwellers in the City of Hamilton: A Social Profile," McMaster University, 1977 (mimeographed).

53. For a survey of the boarding phenomenon see John Modell and Tamara K. Hareven. "Urbanization and the Malleable Household: An Examination of Boarding and Lodging in American Families," in *Family and Kin in Urban Communities, 1700–1930*, edited by Tamara K. Harevan (New York: New Viewpoint, 1977), 164–83; Dominion Bureau of Statistics, *Census Monograph No. 7, The Canadian Family (A Study Based on the Census of 1931 and Supplementary Data)*, 71–72; Chiota, "Somerset Park," table 24, p. 26.

54. Canada, Central Mortgage and Housing Corporation, *Housing in Canada, A Factual Summary*, (Fourth quarter, 1951), 6:11; Canada, Central Mortgage and Housing Corporation, *Annual Report to Minister for Resources and Development for the Year 1951*, 51.

55. Ontario Department of Health, *Annual Reports*. See "Chief Causes of Death by Age and Sex" for 1948, 1949, 1950, 1951. This observation is supported by Robert D. Rutherford, *The Changing Sex Differential in Mortality* (Westport, Conn.: Greenwood Press, 1975).

56. Alan Burnside Harvey, ed., *The Ontario Reports, Cases Determined in the Supreme Court of Ontario, 1945* (Toronto: Carswell, 1945), 778–80; *Canada Law Reports: The Supreme and Exchequer Courts of Canada*, part 1 (Ottawa: King's Printer, 1951), 64–80.

57. Louis Greenspan, "The Governance of the Jewish Community of Hamilton" (paper prepared for the Center for Jewish Community Studies, 1974), 6.

58. Gilbert A. Stelter, "Sense of Time and Place: The Historian's Approach to Canada's Urban Past." in *The Canadian City: Essays in Urban History*, edited by Stelter and Alan F.J. Artibise (Toronto: McClelland and Stewart, 1977), 435.

59. Sam Bass Warner, Jr., *Streetcar Suburbs, The Process of Growth in Boston, 1870–1900* (Cambridge: Howard University Press and the M.I.T. Press, 1969), 117–52.

60. Goheen, *Victorian Toronto, 1850 to 1900*, 200.

George Drew and the Dominion-Provincial Conference on Reconstruction of 1945–6†

MARC J. GOTLIEB

Federal-provincial conferences have always been a showcase for provincial discontent. Until the early 1950s this was especially true of relations between Ottawa and Toronto, and the Conference on Reconstruction of 1945–6 is a particularly significant example. The quarrel took place under the impact of the massive governmental intervention into nearly all facets of Canadian life brought about by the necessity of fighting a total war. In Ottawa, six years of virtually unlimited emergency powers, combined with the memory of government impotence during the Depression, led politicians and especially civil servants to revise their estimates of the federal government's peacetime capabilities and responsibilities. Only the arbitrary division of powers of an archaic constitution stood in the way. Yet the gospel of the "new economics" had not spread to Queen's Park. Together with his civil servants, Premier George Drew was preparing to carry out his own brand of reconstruction based on a fusion of more traditional economic principles and provincial rights. Queen's Park was unwilling to accede to a process which threatened radically to alter the traditional distribution of power. In addition, the conference exacerbated Drew's personal dislike for Mackenzie King to the point where the premier was scarcely able to restrain it. Not surprisingly, the dawn of the post-war era in Canadian government was marked by a clash of economic principles, political philosophies, and personal relations.

Ottawa had been debating the possibility of a reconstruction conference since 1943. While there were particular political benefits embodied in the idea of such a program, the main impetus for reform came from within Ottawa's vastly enlarged bureaucracy. The task of putting together the federal position at a conference was taken up by Alex Skelton, a leading Bank of Canada economist who had been involved in the preparations for the last conference in 1941.[1] Skelton shared the view typical of the Ottawa planners that the central government possessed exclusive responsibility for national economic development. This attitude was combined with a sophisticated appreciation of the fiscal instruments at the gov-

†*Canadian Historical Review* 66, no. 1 (1985): 27–47. This article could not have been written without the aid of Robert Bothwell, who supervised it in its original form, as well as William R. Young and Hugh D. Reid, who generously helped edit it.

ernment's disposal. But Skelton recognized that the application of the new economics depended on federal possession of taxation and other powers which constitutionally belonged to the provinces; therefore extensive constitutional change was necessary, and "where no satisfactory alternative exists, we cannot afford compromise or delay."[2] Together with other officials, he put together an elaborate package of proposals for presentation to cabinet.

The federal position was revised in the course of 1945. The cabinet was still not united on reconstruction policy and indeed was very gloomy about the prospects of any agreement with the provinces calling for tax transfers and constitutional reform. Mackenzie King himself was uncomfortable with the degree of centralization required by the necessities of the program.[3] Under the direction of W.A. Mackintosh of the Reconstruction Department, officials tried to develop a more rationalized package, eliminating the need for constitutional change. Nevertheless, the core of the new proposals remained the same: an attempt to buy out provincial direct tax fields by offering a per capita subsidy. Such a proposal seemed so favourable to the provinces that "none could refuse it."[4] The final version of the federal brief was completed in the summer of 1945; the "Green Book" was placed in front of the provincial premiers in Ottawa on 6 August.

The war effort had made Ottawa the centre of governmental activity in the country and consultation with the provinces was at a minimum. But at Queen's Park, neither the politicians nor the civil servants were idle. George Drew had been elected premier with a minority mandate in June 1943. He ran on an anti-socialist, red-tory platform known as the "Twenty-two Points" which included an insistence on industrial expansion, social security programs, and the promise of "great public undertakings after the war."[5] However, once in power, Drew's implementation of his program was fitful. Preoccupied with the war effort, Drew concentrated on supervising provincial services as well as fighting the war policies of Ottawa and Quebec City. In the process, Drew developed a profound distrust of Mackenzie King and his administration.[6]

By the end of the war, Drew was in a strong position. He was re-elected with a majority in June 1945, drastically reducing the representation of his provincial enemy, the CCF. With the central issues of the war effort no longer urgent, Drew shifted more of his attention to the task of reconstruction. In the broadest sense, Drew's notion of reconstruction meant the rebuilding of an English-speaking consensus. The central issue for the future, Drew wrote to a fellow imperialist, "is simply whether all the rest of Canada is going to continue appeasing Quebec or whether Quebec is going to march shoulder to shoulder with the rest of Canada."[7] Drew's well-known disgust with French-Canadian isolationism was accompanied by darker fears which had more particular application to the postwar era:

> If we severed our British tie, and if we did not stimulate British immigration in this country, then it would only be a question of a comparatively few years before we had an actual French Canadian majority in Canada . . . we would in effect have lost the war if we won in the struggle against Germany and at the same time destroyed the thing for which so many of us have fought.[8]

While Drew undertook to rebuild the imperial consensus in the years after the war, he also recognized that the Canadian federation was threatened in a more immediate sense. He believed that the next few years would be crucial in determining the long-term future of the province's relationship to the federal government. The postwar era would mark the extension of government-sponsored programs into Canadian life to a degree never experienced in peacetime. This expansion threatened to force fundamental shifts in the operation of the federal system and Drew could not allow this to take place without the consultation and leadership of the nation's most productive province. Indeed, as early as 1944 he was publicly pressing Mackenzie King for a postwar planning conference where the premiers could meet and discuss matters of common concern.[9] Drew believed that family allowances and still newer measures were aimed at French Canada. He was convinced that King was delaying a reconstruction conference because the prime minister knew that the provinces would "not let their money be spent to buy votes in Quebec."[10] Thus, at the outset, Drew's fears about the role of Quebec were themselves linked to his views concerning the centralization of power in Ottawa. Yet the course of the conference would reveal Drew's readiness to distinguish between these two issues and to change his tactics accordingly.

While Drew was worried about Ottawa's plans for reconstruction, he was more confident of the country's economic prospects. The vast fiscal projects of Ottawa's planners were partly motivated by a fear of a postwar depression, such as that of 1919–23. Drew did not share this pessimism. On the contrary, as a result of the productive energies let loose by the war, he believed that the country was on the threshold of "a period of tremendous expansion."[11] Drew took exception to the prevailing outlook concerning Canada's economic prospects, and more significantly, he was worried about the effect new policies based on this outlook might have on the distribution of political power.

If Drew's plans for postwar Ontario were never explicit, it was partly because he preferred to leave the details to his treasurer, Leslie Frost. Like Drew, Frost was worried about the future of federal-provincial relations. Though his political style differed from Drew's, Frost shared his premier's conviction of Ontario's primacy in the maintenance of the nation's economic health. By 1944 Frost also recognized the "extreme danger in the Ottawa sentiment for centralization." He warned Drew that any continuation of this trend would "make us weak and impotent, lower our standard of living, reduce the sums of money which our people should rightly have for the development of our province, and in the end, as far as the dominion Government is concerned, it would kill the goose that lays the golden egg. . . ."[12]

Despite the fanfare surrounding Drew's inauguration of the Department of Planning and Development, Frost's Treasury retained the responsibility for directing Queen's Park's economic policies and for conducting fiscal relations with Ottawa. The ministry was led by Chester Walters, deputy provincial treasurer since 1935. Walters had once worked in Ottawa as dominion tax collector, but he had managed to make himself distinctly unpopular there. Most of the responsibility for the background of the provincial position at the conference was left to Harold J. Chater and his office, the Bureau of Statistics and Research, a division of the Treasury. Provincial statistician since 1943, Chater had worked for the province since 1918. He was assisted in his task by four other relatively senior officials. It was a high-level group, yet not an innovative one. Unlike Ottawa's planners, most of Ontario's officials were trained as accountants and not economic theorists. In general they were sceptical of the idea of total economic planning and would show little sympathy for some of the ideas circulating in the capital. Naturally, they were suspicious of any attempt on the part of Ottawa to assume the province's power in the name of a new economic philosophy.

By the time the conference convened in August 1945, the Treasury had prepared dozens of memoranda on the province's financial and industrial position. Several key documents related to the future of federal-provincial fiscal relations. These were predicated on the belief that Ottawa would automatically give up the extensive emergency taxing powers it had acquired in 1942 and return to the provinces all the lucrative jurisdictions it had invaded. It was taken for granted that the provincial government held most of the responsibility for the province's economic development and that Ontario could provide its own social services better and cheaper than the federal government.[13] Despite these assumptions, the Treasury recognized that the province was faced with some serious financial problems. Departmental estimates for postwar expenditures amounted to nearly double what the province had spent before the war. The increases involved primarily resource development and traditional provincial social responsibilities. Indeed, despite Queen's Park's insistence that it was responsible for social security, there were no plans for any significant new measures in this field.[14] There is certainly no evidence that social security or any other measures were going to be used as fiscal tools to direct economic growth.

Confronted with the prospect of increased expenditures, the Treasury also predicted a decline in its revenues as a result of the anticipated postwar slump. Consequently, it was imperative that the province recover the traditional tax fields which had been taken over by Ottawa during the war. The Treasury realized that the key to postwar financing was the income tax. This tax had been hailed by the Rowell-Sirois Report in 1940 as the tax of the future, and it seemed inconceivable "that the dominion government should abrogate for itself the sole right" to levy this promising source of revenue.[15] As long as governments accepted the principle of federalism, such lucrative sources had to be shared. After evaluating various options, the Treasury proposed to retain the federal government as the central tax gathering agency in combination with separate, though uniform, provincial tax acts. Thus, the province would be allowed to set its own rate. As far as Ottawa's revenue requirements were concerned, the Treasury believed that with the end of the war these would decline drastically. With the lion's share of direct taxes entering provincial treasuries, the idea of a per-capita rental agreement was clearly obsolete.[16] But provincial officials recognized that unless the deal was sweetened there would be little chance of obtaining the other provinces' support. Should they be "unwilling to come into line," certain concessions could be made in the way of grants and subsidies. The difficult part was trying to put such redistribution "on a scientific footing."[17]

The solution adopted eventually became one of the most controversial aspects of the Ontario brief at the conference. It called for the establishment of a system of national adjustment grants based on fiscal need. Provinces might only receive such grants if they had tax rates as high as or higher than those of contributing provinces, and only if genuine fiscal need could be established after a thorough investigation of the claimant province's finances. The latter might then be eligible for a national minimum of public services. That minimum did not imply a standard comparable to that of the wealthier provinces.[18] The grants were to be administered by a provincially appointed commission, the grants and the commission itself being weighed in relation to a province's tax contribution. There was no discussion of any of the constitutional or other difficulties involved.[19]

While both Drew and Frost looked forward to the conference, they had no plans to bring forth the Treasury's proposals at the outset. Drew is unlikely to have read the detailed memoranda and the treasurer preferred to adopt a cautious approach. Indeed, Frost counselled Drew to "let some of the others throw the balls at the outset, enabling us not to offend anyone until such times as we think we can get the maximum good."[20] In the hope of resisting any federal encroachment on the provinces' power, Drew tried to establish a common provincial front before the conference began. In recent years he had held what seemed to be fruitful discussions with Premier Hart of British Columbia, Aberhart of Alberta (replaced by Manning in 1943), and possibly others as well. Leslie Frost had flown to Winnipeg to meet Premier Garson just before the August meeting, and the treasurer also held conversations with Maurice Duplessis in Quebec. Drew had not yet met Quebec's premier.[21] By March 1945, Drew could note that "the other provinces are coming to us to establish a common basis upon which we can meet the Dominion Government when the time for the Conference comes."[22] But when the conference opened on 6 August, it was apparent that no such united front existed. None of the provinces, with the possible exception of Manitoba, knew directly of the Treasury's preparations or wished at that moment to risk an alliance with the Ontario premier.[23] Drew arrived in Ottawa without a general strategy beyond the determination to take up Ottawa's challenge.

Mackenzie King opened the conference with an inoffensive speech calling for co-operation for the greater welfare of Canadians. Each of the premiers responded in turn, with Drew leading off from a prepared text lasting over an hour. He admitted that the entire tax structure of Confederation had to be revised in order to overcome the "new enemies" of "sickness, unemployment, and want." But despite popular approval for the centralization of authority in pursuit of this goal, Drew insisted that "powerful arguments could still be made in favour of the decentralized governmental system."[24] The conference soon adjourned and the provincial representatives returned to their capitals to study the Green Book. A committee of technical experts would gather in the fall, the premiers returning in January.

The proposals were in three parts, and the crucial portion was the last of these on financial arrangements. The dominion offered to buy out provincial income, corporation, and succession duties for an annual indexed per-capita grant of $12. The proposals also outlined additional obligations the dominion would assume in the fields of pensions, health grants, unemployment insurance, and public investment. Clearly the benefits were conditional: the provinces would have to accept the tax transfers as well.[25] It was apparent that Ottawa and Toronto must clash. Explicitly defining its own power in terms of its right to tax, Queen's Park could only understand that by modifying this principle, the provincial government would lose its legitimacy. In his opening speech Premier Drew had stressed the principle that a government which could not tax could not govern. Similarly, the Treasury had confidently expected Ottawa to withdraw from direct tax fields with the termination of hostilities. Now the Green Book was arguing just the opposite.

Although the Treasury would not be able to report on the federal proposals until the fall, on his return from Ottawa Drew was already convinced they were fundamentally flawed. Ideological fears also entered into Drew's campaign against the proposals. His recent visits to the capital had confirmed his fears that wartime centralization had "led to a complete disregard to cost and a form of inefficiency which might prove disastrous in peacetime." Real efficiency was possible only "if we can get government back to the people," which meant back to the provincial governments.[26] The premier also observed that federal cabinet ministers "were so bogged down in detail that they were not getting their work done, and that they were called to rely almost entirely upon their officials." This was a damning weakness. In effect, decisions and power were "being delegated to a hidden form of government in the form of officials."[27] These officials "were extremely dangerous men," for in their pursuit of centralizing policies they would willingly destroy the constitution and set up "An effective dictatorship behind the mask of Responsible Government."[28] Ultimately, the way would be open for a coup by the socialists, and "their dangerous theories" would be brought into practice "almost overnight."[29]

Leslie Frost also reacted negatively to the federal proposals. In assessing them, he instructed his officials to "take a conservative view of what would accrue" to Ontario and "not to underestimate the obligations."[30] Like Drew, Frost believed that the removal of the province's right to gather taxes and to guide its own development was historically wrong and economically unsound.[31] Because the wealthy provinces carried the taxation load of the dominion, the reduction of Ontario's taxing powers would ultimately impede the development of the poorer provinces. Indeed, according to Frost, Ontario was a fairer distributor of wealth than the federal government since "Weakened provincial control with greatly centralized authority might result in the central government developing one section of the country to the disadvantage of another."[32]

Ontario's position took shape by October 1945. In a series of meetings involving the five-man Treasury committee, Drew, and Frost, the official critique was elaborated and the Ontario proposals were developed. The Treasury's final report first objected to the proposals' adverse effect on Ontario's budgetary position. A sudden increase in expenditures had already been forecast, and it was calculated that the proposed federal subsidy would not meet these new requirements. The province would be forced to raise revenues from a radically reduced tax base.[33] The dominion's idea of per-capita subsidies also shocked the Treasury. Only six months earlier the idea had been dismissed as obsolete. The notion of per-capita subsidies seemed to be based on an economically dangerous and unfair principle of geographic distribution. Industrial Ontario would be forced into "subsidizing the people of agricultural and primary industry provinces."[34] Echoing a concern of Drew's, the Treasury also noted that a decline in provincial taxing powers would be even more keenly felt as divergent birth rates in Canada (ie, the higher birth rate in Quebec) shifted the balance of population. A decline in Ontario's relative population might result in a diminution of that province's representation in the federal legislature and therefore Ontario must secure all possible powers within the federal relationship. Officials also noted that Ontario might combat this threatened imbalance by promoting settlement in the Ontario northlands.[35]

Because of the general imprecision, and from the provincial point of view, secondary importance, of the social security proposals, the Treasury restricted itself to a briefer critique. The dominion's suggestion that the cost of old-age pensions be split with the provinces on the basis of the pensioner's age seemed far too complex, verging on "confusion worse confounded."[36] Although not opposed to the principle of social assistance for unemployables, officials feared that the dominion's vague definition of employability would result in the shuffling-off of responsibility for chronic cases to the provinces.[37] In their desire for social security measures, federal economists were moved by a belief that the redistribution of income among classes would increase the circulation of money and foster economic growth. Ontario's officials were sceptical of this aspect of the new Keynesian economics. It was "a hope based entirely upon theory. In order to meet the payments required to be made, money must be taken out of the pockets of other people and taxes must be kept high."[38] But Queen's Park's hostility to the principle of the new economics should not be exaggerated to the point of blanket, ideological rejection. On the contrary, there were aspects of Ottawa's program which found some favour. Perhaps because of the legitimacy public works projects had gained during the Depression, the Treasury expressed sympathy with the dominion's complex public investment proposals. Desirous of managing the economy, federal officials had developed the concept of a "public works shelf" whereby the central government offered to finance 25 percent of approved municipal and provincial works projects in return for control over their time and general supervision. Nevertheless, the Treasury objected to the immense practical difficulties and centralization of power involved.[39] If there were elements of the new economics which attracted Queen's Park, the province balked if these also implied a loss of provincial power.

In light of the inadequacy of the federal brief, Frost instructed the Treasury to formulate its own reconstruction counter-proposals. These had to be "both more favourable to Ontario and at the same time not unattractive to the 'have not' provinces." The Treasury's plans closely resembled some of the memoranda earlier drawn up on the subject.[40] Altogether rejecting per-capita payments to the provinces, officials argued that the province should retain its jurisdiction over direct taxation, including succession duties. In the interests of efficiency, the central government would collect income and corporation taxes for the provinces under uniform though not equal tax acts. Eighty percent of the revenue for these would be distributed to the government where the taxes were generated and 20 percent would be retained by the dominion for redistribution throughout the population on a per-capita basis. Ontario would retain four-fifths of her tax dollars, and of the twenty percent allocated for redistribution the province would also receive an amount according to its population. The scheme was combined with a proposal for the establishment of a National Adjustment Fund along the lines outlined by the Treasury before the conference.[41]

Having set out the financial options, the Treasury then made recommendations concerning other aspects of the dominion's brief. The dominion's position on old-age pensions had already been dismissed as too confused, so matters were simplified by arguing that Ottawa should assume complete financial responsibility. A similar solution was developed with regard to social assistance for unemployables. The Treasury felt, however, that health insurance should remain a provincial responsibility, although it was clear to provincial officials that Ontario would not be ready to introduce this measure for some time.[42] Recognizing the crucial importance of timing for the operation of a public works shelf, the Treasury argued that responsibility should not be left entirely to the federal government. A municipal-provincial-federal tri-level committee might be more complex, but it would provide for more continuity in planning, and relieve the inevitable "political pressures" on federally sponsored public works. The federal government would also have to increase its contribution to 50 percent.[43]

In general the Treasury took a very hard line. From its preferred tax proposals to its recommendations on social security measures, officials sharply criticized the federal brief, and their counter-proposals demonstrated both their unwillingness to give up any autonomy and their scepticism of Ottawa's economic objectives. While the Treasury stressed that the province was responsible for its own development, a certain division of financial responsibility was apparent. Industrial and developmental projects could be financed and administered by the province while social security measures were left to the central government to fund, though not to administer. It added up to a refutation of both the feasibility and desirability of the central economic direction through fiscal means so cherished by the men from Ottawa. Above all, the implications of such a program for the distribution of political power were intolerable. The official version of the Ontario proposals was published by the province and released to the general public in January 1946. Most of the recommended options of the earlier Treasury Committee briefings were adopted outright or slightly revised.[44] Most remarkable was a proposal for a Dominion-Provincial Economic Board, a committee of experts to be administered under the direction of all the premiers or their appointees. The board would administer the National Adjustment Fund, whereby 10 percent of the revenues from each provincial government would be redistributed to the poorer provinces on the basis of "fiscal need." This new tool of economic justice was evidently the same concept which the Treasury had considered confidentially since well before the conference. There appeared to be almost no role for the federal government to play in the redistribution process and still no mention was made of any constitutional or political difficulties this fund might involve.[45]

The Ontario proposals represented George Drew's first foray into the complexities of the federal-provincial relationship. Despite the premier's subsequent reluctance to explain his province's position, Drew, Frost, and several other ministers claimed to be closely attached to the final revision of the January official brief.[46] Drew admitted to having spent "a tremendous time on . . . revision and re-examination." Any suggestion that Queen's Park, in calling for the establishment of a new board and fund, was trying to set up a new government was "sheer nonsense."[47] Indeed, rather than attempting to restrict the role of the federal government, Drew argued that by removing from its purview areas for which it was "not trained and not equipped," Ottawa could better devote itself to truly "national" concerns.[48] Moreover, Confederation was a "partnership" between provinces, and that partnership should be embodied in a more institutionalized form than merely irregular conferences. A special board and National Adjustment Fund, and not centrally allocated subsidies, would best consummate the federal relationship. As Drew pointed out to his correspondents:

> What is also new is the fact that the Fund would be created, not out of the general revenue of the Dominion Government, but would be paid directly from the taxes imposed by the provincial governments. This would give the provincial governments a much more direct feeling of contribution to the other provinces and would tend to develop a spirit of unity through the very fact that it was done that way. . . . As this goes so far beyond the Rowell-Sirois recommendations . . . this will be accepted with surprising warmth from the Maritime and Prairie Provinces. If it is not it will only be because they do not understand it.[49]

Ontario's brief caught the dominion officials off guard. When Alex Skelton, secretary to the cabinet committee in charge of the conference, consulted the premier in November 1945, he had been informed that Ontario was preparing some counter-proposals. Nevertheless, he received the impression that Drew was willing to co-operate and that the two governments could strike a deal on the tax transfers.[50] But Skelton's cautious optimism was shattered by the release of the Ontario brief, for it showed that Premier Drew had quite other plans. Toronto's brief seemed so politically alien and economically unsophisticated that it was difficult to put forward a comprehensive rebuttal. Brooke Claxton, minister of national health and welfare, Skelton, Mackintosh and others circulated various memoranda which tried to pull apart this "masterpiece of ambiguity."[51] The counter-attack began by challenging the assumption that seemed to lie at the core of the Ontario position, that the federal government wished to diminish the power of the provinces, destroy the constitution, and turn Canada into a "unitary state." Officials resented the way in which Ottawa was treated as a "foreign government" while the province was represented as being "closer to the people" and consequently more legitimate. The Ontario case seemed to rest on the "sacred 'compact' or 'Contract' theory of Confederation," a theory which federal officials found hopelessly outmoded. Ontario's own proposals would surely "violate any 'contract' which might have been in the minds of the original framers of the constitution." The proposals were excuses for Ontario's selfishness, and this "dog in the manger" attitude had to be "played up."[52]

Dismissing the claim that the province was primarily responsible for Ontario's past and future prosperity, Ottawa contended that Ontario's wealth depended on the resources and economic contributions of all the provinces as much as its

Dominion-Provincial Conference on Reconstruction, Ottawa, August 1945. From l. to r.: Hon. E.C. Manning, Alberta; Hon. J.W. Jones, Prince Edward Island; Hon. S.S. Garson, Manitoba; Hon. A.S. MacMillan, Nova Scotia; Hon. G.A. Drew, Ontario; Rt. Hon. W.L. Mackenzie King, Prime Minister of Canada; Hon. M.L. Duplessis, Quebec; Hon. J.B. McNair, New Brunswick; Hon. J. Hart, British Columbia; Hon. T.C. Douglas, Saskatchewan.

own. Furthermore, the province's well-being was tied to issues of international trade and finance, a field which was, as yet, still under federal jurisdiction. Thus the federal government must have exclusive jurisdiction over the principal levers of the national economy and this required control over the most important sources of revenue. Of course, centralized control was also essential to the careful management of the economy. Successful economic planning would be impossible if decisions "required the joint action of ten governments rather than one. . . ."[53] The dominion also rejected the provincial claim to control all direct taxes. To return direct taxes to exclusive provincial jurisdiction would simply mean more revenues for Ontario in relation to the provinces which had a smaller tax base. The province's social security proposals appeared equally unfair. Ontario was asking for "an open blank cheque on the Dominion treasury, to be signed not by the Dominion Parliament, but by a committee with nine Provincial Premiers on it, or worse still, nine provincial Legislatures."[54]

Indeed, it was for this board and its accompanying National Adjustment Fund that the Ottawa planners reserved their greatest objections. The fund and the manner of its administration appeared to run contrary to the same constitutional principles which Drew claimed to defend. Provinces simply did not have the right to appropriate sums from their own revenues for the purposes of another province. The political implications were almost comic. "Imagine, for example, the Legislature of Quebec collecting taxes in Quebec to be paid into the Saskatchewan treasury."[55] More fundamentally, the proposed bi-level controlling body contradicted the principles of the parliamentary system. "Totally alien to our political and legal tradition," the body had no real precedent in British, Canadian, or American constitutional law.[56]

To Claxton, Skelton, and the other Ottawa planners, nearly all aspects of the Ontario proposals appeared muddled. They branded its assumptions as fallacious, its principles as selfish, and its proposals both ambiguous and impractical. They would certainly be unacceptable to the other provinces, and indeed, might act as a foil to reveal "how good the Dominion's plan is."[57] For the next meeting of the premiers, Skelton prepared an extensive list of short questions designed to reveal the inadequacy of the province's proposals. In addition, the federal government revised its own brief to make its offer even more attractive to the provinces. Ottawa looked forward to making mincemeat of Drew's proposals.

The Coordinating Committee of Premiers met on 23 January 1946 for three days of talks. Mackenzie King opened the session with another innocuous speech that concluded by asking the committee to turn its attention immediately to the Ontario proposals. If King, the cabinet, and the premiers anticipated a lively discussion of the provincial brief, they were to be disappointed. Despite repeated attempts on the part of the prime minister, Drew blocked any discussion of his province's report; his campaign against the dominion's proposals was not over. When King tried to shift attention to Ontario's brief, Drew interpreted this move as a "transparent" attempt to avoid revealing the inadequacy of the dominion's own proposals. Thus, King could place any responsibility for a breakdown of the conference on Ontario while Drew believed the federal proposals would be the true cause of a rupture.[58]

After threatening to walk out of the conference over a matter of publication procedure, Drew assiduously pressed the federal ministers for details of their own new proposals. Eventually, finance minister J.L. Ilsley was unceremoniously forced to present the revised dominion offers. While not rejecting these outright, Drew then led a provincial attack on the dominion's invasion of the direct tax fields. He insisted that no agreement could be made without an explicit federal guarantee to vacate most of this area immediately and permanently. Drew also objected to the dominion's revised public investment proposals, since these were largely a "back door method of establishing direct contact between the municipalities and the Dominion government."[59] But dominion officials emerged from this session cautiously optimistic. Drew had not explicitly refused to consider the principle of income tax transfers on the basis of a revised per-capita subsidy and it was hoped that his objections over other direct taxes could be negotiated away.[60] They were mistaken. Although Drew had not objected to the principle of some tax transfers, subsequent examination of the revised dominion offer only hardened his position. According to his Treasury's calculations, the dominion had shifted the base year from which the new per-capita subsidy was to be derived, thus diminishing the actual amount that was at first calculated to accrue to Ontario. Drew's suspicions of the underhand methods of Ottawa's bureaucracy were confirmed.[61]

When the premiers' session adjourned until April, George Drew was optimistic, though not for the same reason as the Ottawa planners. He had sabotaged King's attempt to shift the burden of responsibility to Ontario and he had forced the government to revise its proposals. Although disappointed with the ambiguous stance of Premier John Hart of British Columbia, Drew was confident that he had swung several of the provinces to his side on the direct taxes issue. Angus Macdonald of Nova Scotia had remained a firm supporter and Drew had found a valuable new ally in Maurice Duplessis. Drew was impressed with the Quebec premier, finding him "one of the most attractive companions one could ever meet." The formation of the "Drew-Duplessis axis" marked an important transition in Drew's attitudes toward reconstruction and national politics.[62]

At the war's end, Drew was intensely interested in fighting the threat of French-Canadian dominance; however, now he recognized that the peacetime counterpart to Quebec's isolationism was a strong provincial rights philosophy. With the central government as the new and most immediate enemy, Drew found that he and Duplessis could be tactical allies in the campaign to preserve provincial autonomy. The new policy, Drew explained privately, "has established a basis of understanding with Quebec that may be extremely important because they certainly will not agree to centralization any more than we will."[63]

Drew also accomplished another of his most urgent tasks at the conference, "bringing some of the 'Brains Trust' back to reality."[64] Drew's fears concerning the evils of centralization and loss of ministerial responsibility in Ottawa had been confirmed at the January meetings. The sight of Claxton and Ilsley continually consulting their officials had convinced Drew that government had "become little more than a mouthpiece for a group of supposed experts who have never had a day's practical experience, even in a municipal council."[65] However, he was heartened by the fact that Claxton, the "ministerial representative for the Brains Trust," seemed to be losing the support of his fellow ministers at the conference.[66] It surprised Drew how "such a half-baked ninny has been able to impress his colleagues."[67]

The premier returned to Toronto in January confident of ultimate victory. His refusal to discuss his own proposals had saved the conference itself, for by now it was clear to him that the prime minister not only expected the conference to fail "but even wished it."[68] Drew would not fulfil that wish. He would not let Mackenzie King use the Ontario brief as a means of forcing a break-up. For the time being, the Ontario proposals had to be set aside and a new attack made on the revised dominion position. With this objective in view, Drew and his advisers developed another set of proposals more closely related to Ottawa's own brand of planning.

The final session began on 26 April. When the revised Ontario proposals were released on the 29th, it was clear that Ottawa's optimism about the prospects of an agreement had been misguided. While Premier Drew was now willing to rent income and corporation taxes in return for per-capita subsidies, he tied this concession to non-negotiable conditions.[69] Drew was adamant with regard to the problematic issue of other direct taxes such as succession duties or gasoline taxes. The dominion was to vacate and make explicit guarantees not to re-enter these fields. Furthermore, Ottawa must allow provinces and municipalities to meet their debt obligations in the United States at par. Ottawa was to assume the full cost of assistance to unemployables, of old-age pensions, and of pensions for the blind. Also, statutory subsidies under the BNA Act must continue but plans had to be devised to administer fiscal need grants under a National Adjustment Fund, as outlined in the original Ontario brief. Finally, the per-capita subsidies paid by the federal government in exchange for control over direct taxes were to be calculated according to a specific algebraic formula whereby a minimum payment "x" would be set according to both GNP and population. The actual dollar signs for "x" would be arrived at through negotiations.[70] In case the dominion was under the illusion that this could be anything but a temporary arrangement, Premier Drew insisted that another conference be held to re-examine and rewrite federal tax laws. If no new system were devised within the life of the present proposed agreement, the pre-1942 system should be reintroduced.[71]

Drew's new proposals infuriated dominion officials. The Ontario premier had spent most of the April session attacking Ottawa's proposals. Until the eleventh hour, there was no hint that he had revised his own. In light of Drew's own refusal to shift discussion to his earlier January proposals, federal officials understood his new recommendations to be simply "last minute extreme demands" which appeared both "irresponsible" and "hypocritical." Ultimately, they were "calculated to wreck the conference."[72] Ottawa objected to every aspect of the province's proposals. On the succession tax issue particularly, Skelton realized that Ontario's stance jeopardized Ottawa's plans for the centralized management of the economy.[73] For the sake of experiment, federal officials calculated how much the dominion could afford to give if Ontario's own terms were to be met. The figure arrived at was $10 lower than the $15 subsidy offered under the dominion's proposals. When George Drew later identified the "mysterious Mr. 'X' " to be $12, the dominion calculated that it would have to pay five times what it could afford. At this point Ottawa realized how great was the "chasm" between Ontario's minimum demands and the federal government's maximum concessions. There was a limit "beyond which no responsible government could go," officials fumed, and "that limit had been reached."[74] Deliberations were finally adjourned and the Reconstruction Conference never reconvened.

The Government of Ontario was not displeased with the failure to reach an agreement. The Treasury had repeatedly questioned the accuracy of federal statistics and calculations, and it was not disturbed by the prospect of returning to a prewar taxation system. Ontario continued to insist that the dominion was capable of making the necessary income-tax reductions. Indeed, the Treasury suggested that by extending its social services in pursuit of Keynesian economic management the dominion was breaking its own promise to reduce taxes. The Treasury's rejection of the Dominion proposals would permit that promise to be carried out.[75] Nor did the conference's demise upset George Drew. In preserving provincial autonomy and thwarting the plans of the "brains trusters," he had saved the nation's political and economic system. The failure to reach agreement was the "best possible thing that could have happened under the circumstances."[76] Even the willingness of seven of the provinces to strike a deal with the federal government did not irk Drew, for despite Ottawa's tendency to "count the noses of the provincial premiers" he was confident that "any arrangement which excluded [Ontario and Quebec] is unworkable even for a short term."[77]

Drew was anxious for the conference to reconvene and wrote as much to King. Even if only to terminate the conference "officially," Drew looked forward to returning to Ottawa "to expose" the latest "propaganda" of the dominion government and reveal to Canadians the full story.[78] Apparently Drew's fight against Ottawa had reached the point where conflicts of personality and policy were thoroughly intertwined. The actions of Prime Minister King at the conference had fueled Drew's hostility to the point where he told a confidant.

> The more I see of him the more I wonder that no one has yet been tried for some major criminal offence in carrying out their natural instincts in his presence. I should think that justification would be a plea that might almost win with some juries because his complete cynicism in dealing with public affairs imposes the most severe test on restraint that I have ever experienced. Behind the most pious phrases you know he doesn't mean a word of what he says, and yet what he does is actually very effective. In watching through the proceedings in the last two weeks, I became increasingly impressed with his economy of physical effort as well as his economy of honesty. What I marvel at more and more is the measure of support he is able to retain from those who had been associated with him and know exactly what he is.[79]

Unfortunately for Premier Drew, Prime Minister King had no intention of reconvening the conference. But Drew was determined not to let the affair rest. Writing to Leslie Frost soon after the final session, Drew indicated that Ontario must take the aggressive course. "Unless we are to follow a bold course we might just as well admit defeat at the outset. That I think none of us will do. But we must be sure we not only refuse defeat. We must have a plan for ultimate victory. We have no such plan before us. That is our most important task."[80] Eventually Drew would find the new course by fighting in the federal arena, but at the moment his strategy was unclear. Ottawa's intentions after the failure of the conference were uncertain and hard to attack. Within a year all would be clear, and reconstruction in Drew's view, would entail an effort of truly historic magnitude.

By early 1947 the débâcle of the conference had become only a part of a greater struggle. Dominion actions since the end of the conference had convinced Drew that much more was at stake in reconstruction than the power to control taxes and development. Indeed, speaking to Angus Macdonald, Drew confided that even if Ottawa were suddenly to meet all the requirements of Ontario's proposals, "we wouldn't enter into an agreement, temporary or otherwise."[81] Drew was led to this conclusion by a variety of circumstances. The individual agreements Ottawa had signed with the other provinces since the adjournment of the conference appeared irresponsible, for the central government did not explicitly set out how it would spend the revenues. Drew was equally horrified when the

Judicial Committee of the Privy Council of the United Kingdom upheld the 1939 decision that the appeal process could go no farther than the Canadian Supreme Court. Consequently "we have nobody to go outside Canada as an independent referee."[82] As well, careless statements by federal ministers concerning Ottawa's powers, together with the debate over the National Emergency Powers Transition Act in March and April, convinced Drew that the federal democratic system was on the point of extinction.[83]

Ottawa had now created the means for a centralized "Frankinstein" [sic] ripe for a coup by "amoral" socialist leaders who used their creed "simply as a vehicle to attain power."[84] Immediate steps had to be taken to prevent such a crisis and the provinces had to unite for a great new conference:

> Surely we have now reached the point, therefore, that the first consideration is a discussion at a general conference of our constitutional position. It seems that like France a year ago, we first need a Provisional Constitution that will carry us over the period of transition and that we require some deliberative body to examine the whole subject and present for further consideration, a permanent constitution. . . .[85]

By resisting any agreement with Ottawa on taxing powers and simultaneously calling for the resumption of the Reconstruction Conference Drew hoped that Ontario, Quebec and Nova Scotia, three of the founding provinces, might initiate a movement to redraft the constitution. Indeed, "it might even be possible that things could happen that could create something of the situation of 1867 when right across this country people would forget party and get back to simple fundamentals."[86] George Drew, Maurice Duplessis, and Angus Macdonald would forever be remembered as the saviours of Canadian democracy and the architects of her construction.

The story of George Drew and the Conference on Reconstruction is characterized by age-old federal conflicts amid new political and economic conditions. The rejection of Ottawa's proposals had its roots in Ontario's tradition of responsibility for its own development.[87] The legislative integrity of the province was contingent on its historical right to tax. As well, the province's traditional fiscal conservatism was expressed in Queen's Park's hostility to the new economics and the ambitious fiscal goals of the federal government. In 1945, when both provincial authority and fiscal conservatism seemed threatened by the reconstruction process, Ontario responded with a call for the complete restructuring of the federal system. The reaction was natural given the degree of redistribution of power which the federal proposals undoubtedly implied. The shape of the response, however, was startling. In the forefront of this conflict were the politics of George Drew.

In many ways Drew represented the authentic Ontario legacy in Canadian politics. The interests of the nation were felt to be indistinguishable from those of his party and his province. This outlook was molded and given urgency by Drew's personal prejudices. At the outset, beneath many issues lay his fears of French-Canadian dominance. By the time the Dominion-Provincial Conference on Reconstruction had ended, Drew had transformed the problems of tax transfers and social economic policy into a fight for the federal constitution, the nation, and Western democracy. It was an approach to these issues which frustrated their resolution, if indeed any were conceivable.

Notes

1. John English, "Dominion Provincial Relations and Reconstruction Planning 1945–46," *Proceedings* of the Canadian Committee for the History of the Second World War (Ottawa, 1977), 5.

2. Public Archives of Canada [PAC], RG 19, Department of Finance Records, vol. 3448, A. Skelton, "Constitutional Problems of Dominion Post-War Policy," March 1944.

3. English, "Dominion Provincial Relations," 9–11.

4. Queen's University Archives, W.A. Mackintosh Papers, vol. 3, file 76, "Dominion-Provincial Relations Post-War," 19 Feb. 1945, 58.

5. Archives of Ontario [AO], RG 3, George Drew Papers, vol. 454, "George Drew Speaking over a Province-Wide Network, July 8th 1943."

6. J.L. Granatstein, *The Politics of Survival* (Toronto, 1967), 120–22.

7. AO, Drew Papers, "Out," box 7, vol. 13. Drew to H.G. Farthing, 12 March 1945.

8. Ibid.

9. AO, RG 66, Treasury Papers, Series VI-1, vol. 3, Drew to Mackenzie King, 25 March 1944.

10. Ibid., Drew to James Cassidy, telegram 23 July 1944.

11. AO, Drew Papers, "Out," box 7, vol. 13, Drew to J.P. Wyness, 19 March 1945.

12. AO, Leslie Frost Papers, Subject Files, vol. 4, file 11a. "Memorandum of Conversations between M. Duplessis and L. Frost," 4 July 1945.

13. Ibid., vol. 3, file 8a, C.S. Walters to L. Frost, 31 July 1944.

14. Memoranda on this subject may be found in Treasury Papers, Series II-6, vol. 19.

15. Ibid., vol. 19, Ontario Bureau of Statistics and Research [OBSR], Report FP-f-3, "Preliminary Report on the Government of Ontario's Tax System and Possible Ways and Means of Raising Additional Revenue to Finance Ontario's Postwar Expenditures," 23 July 1945, 5.

16. Ibid., 7–8; also vol. 19, OBSR Report FP-f-1a, "A Report on Dominion Unconditional Subsidies with a Proposal for the Establishment of a Dominion-Provincial Fiscal Commission," 22 March 1945, 7.

17. Ibid., 10.

18. Ibid., 10–11.

19. Ibid.

20. Frost Subject Files, vol. 4, "Conversations between Duplessis and Frost," 4 July 1945.

21. J.W. Pickersgill, interview 3 March 1980.

22. AO, Drew Papers, "Out," box 7, vol. 13, Drew to Major Cecil Frost, 12 March 1945.

23. Treasury Papers, Series 1–2, vol. 41, file "Tax Agreement," Garson to Frost, 29 Oct. 1943. It is not clear whether this early exchange of information carried on to 1945.

24. PAC, MG 32 B5, Brooke Claxton Papers, vol. 142, file "Reconstruction 1," Dominion Provincial Conference 1945, *Proceedings*, 9.

25. English "Dominion-Provincial Relations," 18.

26. PAC, MG 32 C3, George Drew Papers, vol. 11, file 82, Drew to John Basset, 31 Oct. 1945.

27. Ibid.

28. AO, Drew Papers, "Out," box 9, vol. 18, Drew to H.A. Bruce, 6 Dec. 1945.

29. Ibid., box 10, vol. 19, Drew to Lord Bennet, 5 Feb. 1946.

30. Frost Subject Files, vol. 3, file 8, Frost to Chater, 14 Aug. 1945.

31. PAC, Drew Papers, vol. 239, file 306, "Memorandum" Frost to Drew, 2 Oct. 1945, 1–3.

32. Ibid., 2.

33. Frost Subject Files, vol. 3, file "Dominion-Provincial 1937–45," "Recommendations and Alternative Proposals of a Committee of the Ontario Department of the Provincial Treasury Resulting from an Examination of the Proposals of the Government of Canada," 25 Oct. 1945, 20.

34. Ibid., 21

35. Ibid., 4.

36. Treasury Papers, Series II-6, vol. 20, OBSR Report FP-g-4, "Preliminary Report re Dominion-Provincial Proposals Public Welfare," Aug. 1945, 4.

37. Ibid., 9.

38. Frost Subject File, "Recommendations and Alternative Proposals," 30.

39. Ibid., 33–34.

40. Ibid., 5–13.

41. Ibid.

42. Ibid., 26.

43. Ibid., 33–34.

44. *Submissions By the Government of Ontario* (Toronto 1945), 5–24.

45. Ibid., 25–39.

46. Frost Subject Files, vol. 3, "Re: Dominion-Provincial Studies," 1.

47. AO, Drew Papers, "Out," box 10, vol. 20, Drew to G. McCullagh, 15 Feb. 1946; and box 10, vol. 19, Drew to L. Frost, 9 Jan. 1946.

48. Ibid., Drew to Frost, 9, Jan. 1946.

49. PAC, Drew Papers, vol. 44, file 365, Drew to Oakley Dalgleish, 5 Jan. 1946.

50. PAC, MG 32 J4, King Papers, vol. 267, file 2665, Alex Skelton, "Notes on Provincial Visits," 26 Nov. 1945, 2.

51. Claxton Papers, vol. 139, file Df-3-2, "The Dominion-Provincial Conference: Refuting the Ontario Case," 1.

52. Ibid., 2–4.

53. PAC, Department of Finance Records, vol. 110, "Reasons for Wishing Exclusive Use of Income and Profit Taxes," 5.

54. Claxton Papers, vol. 139, file DP-3-2, untitled memorandum, 7 Jan. 1946.

55. Ibid.

56. Ibid., "Refuting the Ontario Case," 2.

57. Ibid., untitled memorandum, 7 Jan. 1946.

58. Claxton Papers, vol. 142, "Dominion-Provincial Conference Coordinating Committee Meeting," 3–4; also PAC, Drew Papers, vol. 239, file 306, George Drew, "Re Dominion-Provincial Conference, Ottawa, January 28th to February 1st 1946," 2.

59. Ibid., Drew, "Dominion-Provincial Conference," 8.

60. English, "Dominion-Provincial Relations," 26.

61. PAC, Drew Papers, Drew, "Re Dominion-Provincial Conference," 5.

62. Grant Dexter, *Mr. Drew in Action* (Winnipeg, 1946), 3–39; also AO, Drew Papers, "Out," box 13, vol. 26, Drew to C. Lynch, 27 Dec. 1946.

63. Ibid., box 10, vol. 19, Drew to D.M. Hogarth, 6 Feb. 1946.

64. AO, Drew Papers, Drew to Lord Bennett, 5 Feb. 1946.

65. Ibid., also box 10, vol. 20, Drew to C.L. Burton, 11 Feb. 1946.

66. Ibid., Drew to G. McCullagh, 15 Feb. 1946.

67. Ibid., box 12, vol. 24, Drew to C. Whitton, 7 Aug. 1946.

68. Ibid., Drew to McCullagh, 15 Feb. 1946.

69. Treasury Papers, Series II-6, vol. 20, OBSR Report FP-C-8, "Report on Premier Garson's Remarks on the April-May Conference," 5.

70. King Papers, vol. 267, file 2665, "Statement by Premier George A. Drew to the Dominion-Provincial Conference, April 29th 1946," 7.

71. Ibid., 6.

72. Claxton Papers, vol. 144, file DP 44-46, "Effects of the Ontario Proposals on the Dominion," 1.

73. Ibid., Department of Finance Papers, vol. 110, untitled memorandum, 1–6.

74. Ibid., "Effects of the Ontario Proposals," 1; also Finance Department Papers, vol. 110, "Agreement in 1942 to Return Tax Powers to the Provinces," April 1946, 2–3.

75. Treasury Papers, "Report on Premier Garson's Remarks," 2–5; and PAC, Drew Papers, vol. 56, file 508, George Gathercole, "Comments on Blair Fraser's Article, Confederation, 1946, page 10, *Maclean's*," 15 March 1946, 1; also Treasury Papers, vol. 20, OBSR Report FP-f-7, "Income Tax Reductions and

Savings to the Dominion Treasury Resulting from the Rejection of the Dominion's Proposals," 7 June 1946, 2.

76. AO, Drew Papers, "Out," box 11, vol. 22, Drew to W.W. Saden Irwin, 31 May 1946.

77. Ibid., box 12, vol. 3, Drew to H. Daley, 19 July 1946.

78. Ibid., Drew to C. Whitton, 6 Aug. 1946.

79. PAC, Drew Papers, vol. 11, file 82, Drew to Bassett, 9 May 1946.

80. AO, Drew Papers, "Out," box 12, vol. 23, Drew to L. Frost, 12 July 1946.

81. PAC, Drew Papers, vol. 100, file 256, "Telephone Conversation between George Drew and Premier Angus Macdonald of Nova Scotia," 30 April 1947, 3; the transcript was apparently derived from a recording Drew made using a dictaphone.

82. Ibid., 2.

83. Ibid., vol. 100, file 965, Drew to Vincent Macdonald, 30 April 1947.

84. Ibid.; and AO, Drew Papers "Out," box 7, vol. 13, Drew to H. Farthing, 12 March 1945.

85. PAC, Drew Papers, Drew to V. Macdonald.

86. Ibid., vol. 100, file 956, Drew to Angus Macdonald, 9 May 1947.

87. Christopher Armstrong, *The Politics of Federalism* (Toronto 1982), 233.

INNER-CITY POLITICIAN†

PETER OLIVER

Allan Grossman's political career, from the 1950s to the mid-1970s, provides a perspective on two contrasting approaches to reform politics. Grossman was a progressive Tory, in touch with his working-class and immigrant constituents. Sensitive to their concerns, he fought for social justice and the interests of the downtown neighbourhoods. His efforts, however, were carried out within the traditional party system; he was a consensus politician, generally comfortable with existing social and political structures, desiring only to make them more open and responsive to society's larger needs.

By the mid-sixties Grossman was a battle-hardened veteran, vastly experienced and resilient. He knew hundreds of individuals at the grass-roots and elements of the leadership of almost every ethnic, social, and fraternal group in downtown Toronto; he was an adept constituency politician, proud of his role as protector of his constituents and defender of downtown neighbourhoods.

Enter the urban activists, people like John Sewell, Dan Heap, and James Lorimer. Like Grossman they were ambitious, dedicated, and aggressive. In their view, though, consensus politics perpetuated the control of a powerful and manipulative establishment. For them, significant reforms could not be achieved by someone like Allan Grossman through traditional party politics. Only more radical methods, a tough-minded analysis of Canadian society, and, above all, an utterly different political style, could achieve real reform. There was no place in such a vision for a veteran Tory like Allan Grossman; yet Grossman and his organization were a political reality that radical groups were unable to ignore.

Not surprisingly, given the strength of the Grossman organization and its roots in the downtown areas, the clash between the Grossman forces and the new activists was an epic one. In some ways it was comparable to the battles the eager young Grossman had organized to confront the formidable Communist machine. There was, however, this difference: because Grossman was a more genuine expression of the life of the inner city than the Communists ever had been, he survived where they did not. In fact, notwithstanding the force of the activist challenge, the Grossman organization proved adaptable and sure-footed. Grossman's

---

†From Peter Oliver, *Unlikely Tory: The Life and Politics of Allan Grossman* (Toronto: Lester and Orpen Dennys, 1985), 211–34.

approach to politics possessed a legitimacy and integrity that the reform alternative proved unable to match; the confrontation between his organization and the urban activists was good drama and exciting politics, and offered insights into the contrasting nature of succeeding generations of reform politicians in the inner city.

The late 1960s and early 1970s were unique in Ontario. This was the "Age of Aquarius," of organized protest and dissent, of drugs, the counter-culture, and urban activism. Established values came under attack perhaps more than at any other time in this century, and those who held office and exercised power were excoriated as the instruments of a corrupt and unfeeling establishment. Grossman had always prided himself on his ability to represent not only immigrant and working-class groups but also the more prosperous middle and northern parts of the constituency. He felt personally affronted by suggestions that, because he was a Conservative, he must be controlled by a selfish and reactionary establishment. He knew the city politician must understand the streets and the people:

> I learned from the Communists the need to develop as close to a cell operation as possible. What I attempted was to have key people with their ears to the ground. In Alexandra Park, in the senior citizens' homes, in the Anglican Home for the Aged, in St. Christopher House and in places like that all over the riding, we always had some contact person. Sometimes it would be the president of a social group, sometimes the vice-president of a ratepayers organization, perhaps a Sister in the Anglican Nurses' home or the representative of a tenant group.

In 1967, Grossman's riding was expanded to include part of Kelso Roberts's old constituency, St. Patrick; it now included the University of Toronto, the islands, and other downtown institutions and facilities. Among Grossman's constituents were many of the leading radicals and activists spearheading the anti-establishment protest. The St. Andrew-St. Patrick Association, which resulted from the redistribution, was organized in typical Grossman style; but the work required to maintain a "cell organization" was more massive than ever before. Increasingly Grossman relied on his executive assistant, Evelyn Markle (probably the first woman in Ontario to serve a Cabinet minister in such a post), to respond to constituents who needed assistance, although he continued to believe that grassroots organization and constituency work were as important for a Cabinet minister as for a back-bencher. He believed in keeping in touch with the people and monitoring the pulse of the constituency.

By contrast, Toronto's best-known urban activist has argued that the twenty-five or thirty calls he received each day as an alderman were "a never-ending chore." In John Sewell's opinion, "that type of problem-solving inhibits being a good politician. A good politician gets as many people as possible involved in real decision-making so that most of these problems never happen in the first place."[1] Grossman was never led astray by the elitism and focus on large policy issues that Sewell's remarks suggest were most important to him. As the activist position evolved, and as ratepayer and tenant leaders and other groups demanded power to make "real decisions" (traditionally the responsibility of elected representatives), Grossman became increasingly skeptical about both the activist analysis and the activist solutions. Once he had worked easily and intimately with neighbourhood groups, and had been trusted and accepted by them. By the late 1960s, however, the Grossman organization and the activists jockeyed for position in the streets, in the ratepayer organizations, in the settlement houses, and in practically every social organization in downtown Toronto. Finally, Grossman had to accept that he was involved in a political struggle as basic and as challenging as any he had faced against the Communists.

By the mid 1960s, Grossman's reputation with friend and foe alike was that of someone who fought with total dedication for the interests of his constituents.

> Every politician has to decide whether it is more important to have your colleagues love you, or to do your job and to hell with what they think. If you want them to love you, then you can't keep nagging at them, because they are going to say what Darcy McKeough quite often said to me: "God damn it, Allan, you'd think St. Andrew was the only riding in this province." Eventually your colleagues will think you are a bloody nuisance.
>
> But this is my riding, it's no bloody nuisance, or if it is to you that's too bad but you're just going to have to live with it. Sometimes Cabinet colleagues would complain about a private member bothering them about some local matter and I would say, "Look, he may be a nuisance to us, but that's the way the guy holds his riding and that's the guy who's going to be re-elected." And Bill Davis would nod his head and say, "Of course, you're right."

Yet not even a powerful minister was immune from the political fall-out of the sixties. Suddenly, it seemed, innumerable community organizations and pressure groups were rejecting the traditional processes of government. Instead of urging their MPP to present their point of view to Cabinet and legislature, they demanded direct action, including the delegation of significant decision-making authority to local groups. In the later 1960s there was a remarkable proliferation of resident and ratepayer groups, tenants'-rights movements, student activists, ward councils, and a somewhat motley array of people purporting to speak on behalf of minority groups, the poor, and the disadvantaged.

Ratepayers groups had existed for years, and in the 1950s Grossman had worked closely with such organizations in the Annex and elsewhere. But these new organizations spoke in urgent, often strident tones; they no longer voiced requests but made demands; they employed the rhetoric of class conflict and confrontation; they used marches, demonstrations, and sit-ins to express their engagement in urban warfare.

In downtown Toronto, this new breed of urban activist confronted an entrenched organization whose force and vitality they were hard-pressed to understand. As they fought for control of such existing bodies as the University Settlement, St. Christopher-House, and the ratepayer groups, they inevitably came into conflict with the Grossman organization. The threat to Grossman was immediate and serious. The St. Andrew Tories had contacts, friends, and supporters in many community groups, but they were seldom equipped to fight for control: control had never been an issue. In the University Settlement, for example, where

Grossman was an honorary member of the board, an NDP group took over, and he was no longer welcome. When the redistribution of 1967 made him once again the representative of the Annex, he applied for membership in the Annex Ratepayers. He was told, politely but firmly, that membership was open only to those who owned property in the area. It was foolish, he thought, for the ratepayers to rebuff the local MPP, who could do a great deal for them. This rebuff, he concluded, was part of a strategy to turn community organizations into political stalking horses.

The Grossman organization found itself being ground between the new-style urban activists, who were fighting what they regarded as a reactionary municipal government, and the aggressive New Democratic Party, out to win power by controlling community organizations. The Grossman people fought back at every opportunity. The battle was long and bitter, but ultimately successful for the Grossmans, father and son. In the process Grossman learned a great deal about the new "reformers." Although many of their goals were similar to his own, he detested their narrow self-righteousness and their militant grab for power by setting class against class, neighbourhood against neighbourhood. Their method was not resolution by reasonable compromise, but the perpetuation of conflict to gain power and overthrow the establishment.

The urban citizen movements of the late 1960s and early 1970s took their tactics from the American anti-war movement. Suspicion of authority and of the unprecedented power of the "military-industrial complex" led to angry protest. Thousands of young people adopted the style and rhetoric of the counter-culture. In Toronto, Grossman's constituency was home to substantial numbers of draft-dodgers and political refugees. Student activists, young university lecturers, and Maoists and revolutionaries rejected traditional political methods in favour of the urban-guerrilla tactics preached south of the border.

It took Grossman some time to learn that many of the middle-class ratepayer leaders regarded him as the enemy.

> I was naive enough to think that my years of hard work for the people in the area would be remembered and appreciated and that they would realize that in me they had one of the best members in the House. Finally it dawned on me that they would never trust a man in his sixties with white hair, who publicly described Rochdale College as a "cesspool." They assumed that as a Conservative I could not be sincere in my commitment and therefore that I must be in the pocket of the "big developers" they hated so much. My riding was a good place for people who were power-oriented to walk in and take over. It included a mass of Chinese and Portuguese immigrants who at that time often could not speak English. Unlike the suburbs, where people had good jobs, my area faced almost overwhelming social problems.

Grossman took the rhetoric of the activist groups and the inroads they were making very seriously. His years of effort in the inner city made him one of the few Tories, he believed, able to grasp the significance of these events:

> What was happening was that all these activist groups began to sense that governments weren't too sure of what was going on in the streets and they

felt they could take advantage of the situation. This was when a lot of these programs giving out hundreds of thousands of dollars in youth grants and other hand-outs came into existence. This was a groping attempt on the part of elected representatives to deal with an unprecedented situation. The opportunists had their hands out and found ways of getting grants and developing little organizations for themselves.

They were burning computers, occupying universities. I recall on a number of occasions trying to tell my colleagues that what was going on in Toronto might spread throughout the province. But at least in the earlier stages, this was a "Cry in the Wilderness" except for a few of the members who understood my concern.

It may seem far-fetched that Grossman equated some ratepayer groups, controlled by middle-class elements anxious to protect their properties against the Spadina Expressway or block-busting developers, with Maoists and urban guerrillas. These were young professionals and businessmen, able to engage in the seemingly endless meetings that political organization demanded. Often they were two-income households buying into the downtown areas, and engaging in expensive remodelling, to take advantage of downtown theatres, galleries, and restaurants.

Yet the articulate young professionals seized the radical rhetoric. Assuming the obligatory blue jeans and sandals, they played the game of revolution. An affluent middle class, protecting their renovated neighbourhoods, they were nonetheless performing a service to the community. Although their remodellings often forced the poor to look elsewhere for housing, frequently in the high-rise developments the professionals regarded with such aversion, their efforts helped keep the downtown core alive.

I don't want to give the impression that I felt that no good came from these groups. The efforts of activists in Trefann, Kensington and elsewhere let the establishment know that they had to stop making deals without considering the impact on the people most directly affected. There should have been some militants in Alexandra Park in the early 1950s and that bloody design might have been stopped and the old homes saved.

Grossman's growing hostility to these groups arose in part from their self-deluding rhetoric, radical slogans, and self-righteous arguments to advance ends that were essentially selfish.

Often these new organizations were run by a handful of people, three, four or five people. Any time you took the trouble to go into their membership lists, you would find maybe twelve or fifteen people, three-quarters of whom didn't live in the area. Keep in mind that many of the people living in these areas were Chinese and Portuguese who didn't speak English. There would be attempts made to pretend that the ratepayer groups represented the people. I remember being invited to one so-called community meeting. When I came in, Dan Heap was sitting there with a few others and in another part of the room were perhaps half a dozen Portuguese who, it became evident in a few minutes, understood nothing about what was going on because they didn't speak or understand English. They were a backdrop to create the impression that the community was solidly behind him.

The second element that occasioned and shaped the outburst of urban political energy was rooted in the experience of Ontario cities. Beginning in the mid-fifties, substantial areas of downtown Toronto were designated for urban renewal, which meant razing large numbers of decaying houses and businesses and replacing them with new high-rise towers intended as housing for low-income groups. The first major renewal development in Canada, Regent Park, originated in the late 1940s and was completed in the 1950s. Many in the planning and social-service field regarded Regent Park as a great achievement in slum clearance and social engineering. The City of Toronto Planning Board pinpointed Moss Park, in the Cabbagetown area, close to Regent Park, and Alexandra Park, as priorities for early renewal.[2]

Alexandra Park was in Grossman's constituency. Both Moss Park and Alexandra Park faced uncertainties, as the province was slow to clarify its role in urban renewal. Amendments to the Ontario Housing Development Act of 1948 were passed in 1950 and 1952, to allow the province to co-operate in renewal and other projects with Ottawa, yet Ontario was not inclined to take major initiatives and left the field to a federal-municipal partnership.

In 1957, the City of Toronto provided detailed recommendations for Moss Park and Alexandra Park. For Alexandra Park, the Planning Board recommended an initial clearance of 10.7 acres, comprising the poorer buildings, and the construction of 392 public-housing units to accommodate 1450 people. (This was 15 percent more than were accommodated before clearance.) The Board of Control referred these recommendations to Metro Council, requesting that Metro contribute to the municipal share of the cost of acquisition and clearance, arrange for relocation of dispossessed families, and join the city in an application to the federal and provincial governments for assistance. Metro, however, took the view that rehabilitation and not clearance was called for, and an impasse developed that endured until 1964.

The designation of Alexandra Park as a renewal area undeniably contributed to further deterioration and blight. With Moss Park underway, in March 1959 Grossman complained in the legislature about the hardship caused to Moss Park residents by its designation as a "redevelopment area." Properties had deteriorated, vacancies were not taken up, and the area was worse than ever. The same situation, Grossman pointed out, was likely to occur in Alexandra Park, the next priority. Grossman's remedy was that in any area designated for redevelopment, the municipality issuing the order should be required, within ninety days, to issue an expropriation order that permitted all property owners to dispose of their properties to the municipality. If this was not done within the prescribed time, the designation of "redevelopment area" would be declared null and void. This, he suggested would prevent the deterioration that had occurred in Moss Park. The Minister of Planning and Development, William Nickle, promised to give consideration to Grossman's proposal, but noted that a federal-provincial partnership was involved and doubted that ninety days was long enough. Grossman's concerns were not shared widely enough to lead to any action.[3]

Thus in the early 1960s, Alexandra Park awaited a fate similar to that of Moss Park, while Grossman, as the local member, received appeals from bewildered residents. In a 1961 letter to the Community Planning Branch of the Department of Municipal Affairs, he again objected strenuously to the protracted period between the designation for redevelopment and the beginning of work. Officials, he urged, must get on with it.[4] Although Grossman believed governments were insensitive to individual suffering, like most socially concerned citizens, including professional planners, social workers, and politicians, he still regarded projects like Regent Park and Moss Park as important social improvements. Those in grimy and deteriorating neighbourhoods would be overjoyed, it was assumed, at the opportunity to move into new apartments in subsidized high-rise buildings. Here was the way to prevent the development of large-scale slum areas and the crime and misery that such areas bred. Most of those who were being removed and relocated in the early projects were remarkably docile. Yet in an area like Alexandra Park, for example, many residents were struggling Portuguese labourers, too frightened or too uninformed to protest. Perhaps because they were able to relocate relatively easily in nearby neighbourhoods such as Kenginston, little was heard from them. Social reformers were proud of these early efforts at renewal, and as late as 1968 Albert Rose, a housing expert, lavishly praised Regent Park in the Canada Mortgage and Housing Corporation magazine, *Habitat*. That same year Judy Ramsay, a young community worker associated with St. Christopher House, very tentatively pointed out that some feeling existed that "Alexandra Park is not the successful urban renewal scheme that some say it is."[5]

Although Grossman did not at this time attack the slum-clearance approach to urban renewal, he did express serious reservations. In 1961, for example, he told Robert Macaulay, the minister responsible for housing matters, that he was "not happy with the business of tearing down houses to begin with." Nonetheless, Alexandra Park went ahead, however slowly, and Grossman listened to complaints and tried to effect some redress. In 1964 he told the Alexandra Park Residents Committee that he was "greatly disturbed to hear of a slowdown of the Alexandra Park program."[6] The problem was the unsatisfactory Expropriation Act, which did not give owners fair replacement value for their property.

By 1964 federal and provincial legislation was in place which promised to ensure that the interminable delay between designation of urban renewal and expropriation of property and rebuilding would be largely eliminated. In Ottawa, major amendments to the National Housing Act were passed by the new Pearson government, and federal purse strings were loosened. In July, provincial Municipal Affairs Minister Wilfrid Spooner announced a new program of financial aid and changes to Planning Act. Under the expanded program, Ontario broadened its contribution to cost-sharing and allowed funds to be allocated in new directions, including, for the first time, non-residential projects. It was expected that Hamilton, Kingston, and Toronto, with urban renewal projects in the negotiation stage, would benefit first. The distinguishing feature of urban-renewal projects conceived under the 1964 legislative changes was that they dealt with many concerns: health, education, transportation, and commerce; earlier schemes tended to be single-purpose and to focus exclusively on housing for low-income groups. By 1964, Toronto was poised to begin several major schemes. Provincial and federal programs were in place, the money was there, and municipal politicians seemed anxious that their communities receive their share of it.

Ironically, just as the urban-renewal bulldozer was about to roll, serious doubts were heard from those groups most affected. Growing reservations were now being expressed about Regent Park and Moss Park; some thought the developments were not exciting social experiments, but sterile ghettos for the poor. Repelled by the miles of concrete and disturbed by the pervasive institutional character of Alexandra Park, Grossman no longer doubted that it would have been preferable, and probably less expensive, to rehabilitate the existing houses.

In the later sixties, Grossman was swept into the affairs of several new or refurbished ratepayer groups. The most significant and revealing of these relationships was that with the Kensington Area Ratepayers Association (KARA). Kensington, with its narrow streets and sprawling fruit and vegetable stands, was part of the Spadina planning area. Bounded by College, Dundas, and Bathurst streets, and Spadina Avenue, it had been targeted for urban renewal since the 1956 Planning Board report. When Grossman was a young boy on McCaul Street, "the Jewish Market," as it then was known, was familiar territory, but by the early 1960s, although many Jewish merchants remained, the market was home to diverse nationalities. What had not changed, however, were the sights, sounds, and smells of a busy European-style marketplace, and city police still tended to look the other way at innumerable infractions of traffic bylaws and municipal regulations.

Inevitably, however, city officials, concerned about public health and fire hazards, turned their attention to Kensington. In 1961, the city asked its officials, including the Planning Board, the commissioner of building and development, and the medical officer of health, to prepare a report. The city report, ready late the same year, said the market served an important economic function and embodied unique aspects of the Toronto heritage. Yet congested traffic, lack of parking, blocked access routes, fire hazards, decrepit buildings, substandard housing, illegal encroachments by merchants on public property, outmoded poultry-slaughter houses, the display of perishable foods under conditions that constituted a threat to the public health, all led to the conclusion that "conditions in the Kensington Market area have reached a point in recent years where they are becoming detrimental to the safety of residents."[7]

The report suggested that full-scale redevelopment was not an appropriate solution for Kensington. Moreover, improvements would not likely succeed on a voluntary co-operative basis, because area merchants were highly competitive and individualistic and "there is no association of shopkeepers or businessmen in the area and no recognized leadership in the business community." (In fact, at this time, Grossman began to work with the local merchants to establish such a group, and before long a relatively efficient Kensington Area Businessmen's Association had emerged.) The report recommended limited redevelopment, including the establishment of pedestrian malls, rearrangement of traffic routes, the expansion of rear-lane access, and the provision of off-street parking. These proposals went through several stages; in February 1962 city officials met with merchants at St. Christopher House. By October, preliminary cost estimates were ready, at $1 984 569 for land acquisition and public works. Redevelopment was supported by the merchants and was conceived as a joint public-private enterprise; it would require co-operation between city departments and the merchants.

Despite the enthusiasm of merchants and city officials, the plan floundered. In 1962, provincial and federal support was still directed primarily towards housing redevelopment, and the Kensington scheme did not qualify. Not until federal and provincial policy changed in 1964 did Kensington redevelopment become a realistic option, but even then, other areas had priority. In the meantime, unhappy merchants pressed the city to provide some solution to the chaotic parking situation, which threatened the survival of the market.

As early as 1959, Grossman had urged Education Minister W.J. Dunlop to find a solution, because students and staff of the Provincial Institute of Trades, on Nassau Street, were contributing substantially to the parking morass. The merchants regarded the 1962 Kensington plan as their best opportunity to acquire more parking. But the scheme, under which merchants and city would contribute towards building two parking lots, ran into problems with the Ontario Municipal Board. In 1963, Joe Lottman, president of the Businessmen's Association, appealed to Grossman: "We have been told by people in the know that it is up to you, Allan. If this market does not get parking it will die eventually."[8] Grossman immediately went to work on city politicians and on Municipal Affairs Minister Wilfrid Spooner. Provincial legislation was passed in 1964 and there was another OMB hearing; then the city was able to proceed with the two parking lots.

By this time, however, the Provincial Institute of Trades had expanded into George Brown Community College. Two lots were not enough, and a struggle ensued between the college and the merchants over available spaces. Grossman appealed on several occasions to Education Minister William Davis and the ministers of Public Works and Treasury to find a solution. Joe Lottman wrote to Grossman in 1966 "that the two hundred merchants in the area are being forced out of business by the fact that the Provincial Government has taken no concrete action."[9] More meetings ensued. Finally, after Grossman appeared before the Treasury Board himself, an agreement was reached to provide expanded parking facilities. Mayor Phil Givens assured Grossman that "everyone concerned is delighted with what you have done" and Lottman and the merchants were ecstatic in their praise.[10] Then the whole scheme fell through when doubts were raised as to whether George Brown College would be remaining in Kensington.

By the mid-sixties, Kensington residents were alert to the threat posed by the clearance approach to urban renewal. Renewal had given birth to an epic battle between residents of Trefann Court, Don Mount, Don Vale, and other neighbourhoods, and City Hall planners and politicians. The activist leaders of these struggles, including university lecturer James Lorimer and student lawyer John Sewell, saw pliant city politicians controlled by a ruthless development industry that was indifferent to the feelings of residents. According to Sewell, the decision to raze homes in Trefann Court had been unanimously approved "in five or ten minutes without ever consulting any of the residents."[11] It seemed that City Hall was controlled by the development industry, and that "urban renewal" meant bulldozing entire neighbourhoods.

Late in the summer of 1967, a group calling itself "Concerned Citizens for Kensington" began to organize. Among the "concerned citizens" were several of Grossman's good friends: Dan Martyniuk, an immigrant of Ukrainian background who, in 1964, had been chairman of a "Beautify Our Neighbourhood" campaign; Ed Clarke, a leader of the black community who had worked for Grossman in several campaigns; and friendly, although not a political supporter, Allan Schwam, a part-time university lecturer in town planning. A notice in Portuguese and English asked all residents to attend a meeting at St. Christopher House to discuss the expansion plans of two neighbourhood institutions, George Brown College and Toronto Western Hospital. DO YOU KNOW THAT YOUR HOME MAY BE TAKEN AWAY FROM YOU, said the circular, which urged residents to "unite in a fighting organization."

The result of these efforts, the Kensington Area Ratepayers Association, had some remarkable successes and some revealing failures. The group, which represented an area of mixed population, including a large proportion of poor Portuguese immigrants, became a battleground of ideologies and personalities. Its often tortuous history provides a striking example of ratepayer politics and suggests how one such organization functioned and was finally torn apart by competing interests.

KARA began effectively enough. On 10 October 1967, its executive resolved to work with the city on urban-renewal planning "only on the basis of mutual and prior consideration that our Association is itself involved in commissioning the project and in setting up its terms of reference." The executive would not challenge the right of governments to expropriate properties, but it would demand full replacement value for those whose properties were taken and it would insist that urban renewal not disrupt the life of the community. "If an area cannot be improved for the people who live there, it cannot be improved for anyone else." Above all, government bodies should regard the residents "as the commissioning agent for any study, plan or scheme."[12]

KARA's bold assertions would have turned urban-renewal procedures upside-down. Apart from whatever merit might exist in establishing more democratic procedures and giving more say to residents, there were serious considerations at issue, which perplexed and even frightened some reasonable officials and politicians. Could citizen participation to the degree being proposed prove workable and efficient? Would it lead to insuperable problems and costly delays? Would citizen-participation procedures become a breeding ground for agitators who were less interested in improving neighbourhoods than in overthrowing the system or in gaining personal access to government grants? Would the process of open debate work to the advantage of speculators and add to the cost of some projects? These were all legitimate concerns.

But the realities of politics do not always allow for leisurely consideration. Already, much damage had been done to the inner city by existing procedures, particularly the clearance approach to urban renewal. Allan Grossman had little doubt that even limited acceptance of KARA's proposals would be a vast improvement: the existing situation was breeding genuine distress, uncertainty, and even hatred of government. Yet he did not accept that all developers were greedy exploiters. He had friends in the development industry and had a high regard for their achievements and their integrity. Nor did he believe that City Council was in the hands of the industry. But something had to be done.

In the midst of the 1967 provincial election, a campaign in which local issues were important, the KARA executive, the Merchants Association, and the Alexandra Park Tenants Association organized an all-candidates meeting. The great issue was urban renewal. Each candidate was told that he would be asked how to improve the process and whether he would favour the province refusing to approve proposals "unless the people had participated in making and endorsing the plan." Grossman, as a Cabinet minister, was on the spot, but regarded the meeting as an opportunity to commit the province to major improvements in a process that was not working well. He conferred with Bob Suters, managing director of the Ontario Housing Corporation. Suters pointed out that it was a city responsibility to provide "the counselling and relocation services which are a very necessary part" of urban renewal schemes, and that the province should not interfere. He noted that Alexandra Park was "perhaps a classic example of the delays which in the City of Toronto have become synonymous with urban renewal." He referred Grossman to the North End redevelopment in Hamilton, which had commenced in 1961 and been completed to the satisfaction of all concerned. In Hamilton, the responsibility for urban renewal had been removed from City Council to an urban-renewal committee:

> I believe one or two elected members of Council serve on the Committee, but essentially its members are drawn from interested private individuals. Equally important, the Committee appointed its own commissioner . . . whose specific job is to co-ordinate the activities of City officials.

From the inception of the urban-renewal committee, Suters related, its chairman "encouraged the involvement of the residents through public meetings and by opening offices in the urban renewal area to provide the advice and assistance which is so essential to the success of these schemes."[13]

Although the urban-renewal committee in Hamilton did not give residents the ultimate power KARA wanted, it provided for a substantial degree of citizen participation. Equally important, it had contributed to the enormous success of the process in Hamilton. After further discussions with colleagues, Grossman was ready to make a dramatic announcement at the all-candidates meeting that would upstage his rivals, Adam Fuerstenberg of the NDP and Leonard Shifrin of the Liberals:

> The Ontario Government will not participate in any future urban renewal project unless, in the initial stages, an Urban Renewal Committee is established on which there will be representatives of the residents of that area in which an urban renewal scheme is contemplated.
> This Urban Renewal Committee will provide the vehicle through which the residents will present their plans for conservation, rehabilitation or development which they believe will best suit the needs of the area in which they live.

He also promised the meeting that "you are going to have a great deal to say about how your own district is going to be developed." The Ontario government would not participate in any kind of urban redevelopment unless the people in the area were represented on the committee that made the decisions and unless "they are in agreement with it."[14]

Grossman was not giving local residents an absolute veto, but KARA believed Grossman's pledge represented a step forward. "If the province stands behind this statement," one KARA member commented, "then this is a way to stop the steamroller of urban renewal."[15] The commitment received extensive publicity and raised ratepayer morale considerably. When community groups from across the city met in St. Christopher House on 12 November, they recommended unanimously that "an urban renewal committee be established for each urban renewal area and that residents of the area be represented on such a committee."[16] Responding to fears expressed by some ratepayers that Mayor William Dennison and other city politicians might ignore the pledge, Grossman promised KARA he would keep the provincial commitment before his colleagues and would arrange to have it publicized at a scheduled federal-provincial conference on housing and urban renewal. Speaking for KARA, Allan Schwam told Grossman this was vital because the City Planning Board had already ignored the pledge by approving a zoning change to allow a student-housing project in Kensington without any reference to area residents.

In April 1968, at City Council, Horace Brown, the alderman who represented Kensington, requested on behalf of KARA that a citizens' group be established in fulfilment of "the Grossman commitment." A statement by Joe Lottman on behalf of the Businessmen's Association took the same line. Pointing to their own commitment of time and money the businessmen complained that nothing had yet been achieved for Kensington. There would be no further co-operation with the city, they insisted, "until there is a definite body charged with the responsibility of improving this area."[17] KARA and the businessmen met with the Board of Control. The ratepayers formally asked the board "to initiate the setting up of the Grossman Urban Renewal Committee." They wanted it to consist of representatives of KARA, the two aldermen, and a committee from Council or from the Board of Control with formal responsibility for "all renewal activities in our area."[18]

Grossman had forced City Council's hand. The result was an important experiment in citizen participation in town planning, the Kensington Urban Renewal Committee (KURC), which became responsible for planning and making proposals to the city for the Kensington area. KARA president Allan Schwam gave Mayor Dennison nine names "to comprise the citizens' representation" on KURC, including himself, Dan Martyniuk, Percy Wright, Father Robert Marino, and Ed Clarke.

KARA and KURC were significant beyond the confines of Kensington. In the late 1960s, activist elements mounted a bold challenge to the old-style politicians at City Hall and to the development industry which, they insisted, dominated Toronto politics. The premises of the activist campaign were succinctly stated by the group's leader, John Sewell, who was first elected alderman for Ward Seven in 1969:

> My apprenticeship in the field had only shown me that the City was capable of very little good, that it had no principles, that it enjoyed rationalizing tricks that it pulled, that it was a blockbuster, that it didn't give a fig about people in working-class areas like Trefann, that it wouldn't listen to rational arguments, that it was run by politicians who did everything they could to assure the world that it didn't want to have anything to do with citizens.[19]

From 1969 to 1972, Sewell and Ward Seven's other alderman, Karl Jaffary, fought to force City Hall to call a halt to the slum-clearance approach to urban renewal and to listen to the residents and ratepayer groups. In blue jeans and leather jacket, Sewell preached the politics of polarization. He voiced personal accusations against fellow councillors and did his best to encourage confrontation and to jar what he viewed as a corrupt and reactionary establishment. To a degree, Sewell succeeded. Enormous high-rise developments no longer passed through Council with only cursory scrutiny; aldermen began to think twice about being wined and dined by wealthy builders; and he attracted media attention, not all of it favourable.

For the most part, the leaders of the "reform" effort, who professed to speak for the working class, were articulate members of the middle class. Sewell and Jaffary were lawyers; their ally, William Kilbourn, was a prosperous university professor and writer. The professionals were buying up old houses in Cabbagetown, Kensington, and other newly fashionable working-class neighbourhoods, and engaging in expensive remodelling. They were willing to work hard to preserve the amenities of their addresses.

As befitted their education and status, the young professionals were widely read in the literature of protest, and bolstered their activism with a relatively sophisticated if biased analysis of urban political processes. Perhaps because their analysis was taken primarily from American sources that might be inapplicable to the Canadian experience, it was inconceivable to many of them that an old-time Tory politician like Allan Grossman could share their interest in preserving neighbourhoods. Just as they glibly assumed that City Hall must be in the pocket of the development industry so, too, Grossman, a Tory Cabinet minister, must share the values of "the enemy," rich developers and their political friends.

Much of the testament of the activists is to be found in Sewell's *Up Against City Hall* (1972); James Lorimer's *The Real World of City Politics* (1970); Graham Fraser's *Fighting Back: Urban Renewal in Trefann Court* (1972); and Jon Caulfield's *The Tiny Perfect Mayor* (1974), which argues that the efforts of "reform" politicians like Sewell and Dan Heap were "constantly frustrated by David Crombie, usually working alongside the old guard politicians."[20] Most of these accounts are informed by a profound conviction that society is controlled by conspiracy and shaped by alienation and class conflict. Lorimer, a university lecturer and a publisher, purported to tell the "real" story of city politics, the nasty, behind-the-scenes machinations by which wealthy developers manipulated hapless politicians. In this type of literature, events proceed at two levels: the public debate, where traditional politicians mouth platitudes, half-truths and, sometimes, outright lies; and "the real world" of power relationships where wealthy business interests control policy, and upper-middle-class neighbourhoods are lavished with attention while working-class areas are served up for renewal and exploitation. Working-class communities, Sewell wrote, "didn't get planning help, they didn't get their roads paved as often, or sidewalks fixed as well, or roads ploughed, or garbage picked up properly, or adequate parks, or equal recreation facilities. Working-class communities are second-class communities."[21]

One of the great issues of 1969 was the fight to change the traditional long strip wards, in which wealthy Rosedale residents were represented by the same aldermen as those from Cabbagetown, into block wards which would place people with similar incomes in the same electoral unit. When the Ontario Municipal Board, chaired by J.A. Kennedy, rejected the city's continuing preference for a strip plan in favour of a compact block scheme, City Council appealed to the Ontario Cabinet, where Allan Grossman fought for the traditional strip boundaries. As an alderman, he had found it constructive to represent all income groups and diverse neighbourhoods, and he believed it in the interests of the city to lessen, not emphasize, class differences. According to James Lorimer, City Hall reports had it that in Cabinet the decision was placed in the hands of two city ministers, Grossman and Allan Lawrence, together with Municipal Affairs Minister Darcy McKeough.[22] Although Grossman strongly supported the strip plan, Lorimer maintains, McKeough and Lawrence preferred block wards and Cabinet rejected the city's appeal. Once again Grossman appeared in the eyes of the radicals as an "old guard" politician.

The Marxist-inspired critique of political structures left little room for an alliance with those whose approach to politics was essentially problem-solving and pragmatic. An important part of the "reform" analysis held that the activists spoke for the people and that participatory democracy would restore real power to the people. The elected politicians, James Lorimer argued, could not be trusted. Often they deliberately distanced themselves from the people to better serve the interests of the development industry. Lorimer pointed to KARA, to the Trefann Court residents' association, and to the Don Vale Association of Residents and Homeowners, and insisted that their policies were often "a word-for-word repetition of the virtually unanimous view of the people in their area." In the *Globe*, in August 1969, Lorimer argued that democracy would come to City Hall only when elected representatives were required to follow the directions of citizen groups even to the extent of turning their salaries, or a signed letter of resignation, or both, over to ward councils, to which they would be responsible. Lorimer exalted ratepayer groups as "super-democratic." On two occasions, Sewell attempted to establish ward councils; neither was a success.[23]

Allan Grossman's experience with KARA and other ratepayer groups did not substantiate these arguments. Groups like KARA most often represented very few people and could be manipulated far more readily than popularly elected politicians could be. Often the real working-class elements in the community, the Portuguese and Chinese immigrants, were not represented at meetings. This, Grossman believed, was either because the ratepayers did not reach these groups, or because they did not try to do so, recognizing that the inherent conservatism of many immigrant families would run counter to the politics of middle-class rate-payer leaders. Indeed, Grossman discovered that the KARA executive often was unable to agree among itself. As for the suggestion that political authority be surrendered to such groups, whose elections and subsequent methods and procedures were entirely unsupervised, he believed such a system would lead to petty tyrannies, chaos, and collapse. Only those who were deliberately bent on manipulating the process for their own purpose could, Grossman concluded, even pretend to believe that such groups should receive the power that rightly belonged to democratically elected governments.

Finally, it became the conventional wisdom of activist groups that the politicians of this period, fearful of the people, counter-attacked by challenging the legitimacy of citizen and ratepayer groups, and offered every inducement to business and other organizations to oppose the true spokesmen of the neighbourhoods. As Lorimer put it, "city officials and politicians encouraged the formation of rival groups in urban renewal areas. This policy was aimed at creating an impression of disunity and dissension. . . ." John Sewell makes the same point. One way the city dealt with the Trefann problem, he argues, "was to try to divide the people in the area, show that they couldn't agree on anything."[24]

Yet Grossman found that, far from speaking with a united voice on behalf of all the people, KARA could never seem to agree on what "the people" wanted. The idea that the interest of "the people" was necessarily, or even usually, coterminous with the wishes of the executive of some ratepayer group was a flight of fancy. Grossman, with his contacts with immigrant groups, had at least as much concern for and far more empathy with low-income elements in the downtown neighbourhoods than did the self-proclaimed reformers. Most of all, he was elected by the people to represent their interests. Ultimately, his political legitimacy derived from that irrefutable fact.

Although he was delighted when KURC was established, Grossman was concerned about the motives of some of its leaders. In early July 1968, the Board of Control delayed the formal establishment of KURC because it was not satisfied that members of the Portuguese community were receiving adequate representation. Grossman believed this to be a legitimate concern, and he was dismayed at KARA's angry reaction. KARA drafted a letter to the minister of municipal affairs asking the province to tell the city that funding for a plan for Kensington would be withheld. (Apparently the letter was never sent.) KARA leaders hoped the province would take Kensington's renewal out of the hands of the city.[25] By early September, the Board of Control and City Council had formally approved an urban-renewal committee under the chairmanship of Controller Margaret Campbell, and including aldermen Horace Brown and Monte Harris, as well as citizens. (Allan Schwam was not a member; about this time, he resigned from the presidency of KARA.)

For most of this period, Allan Schwam (before and after his resignation) was a leading figure in KARA's activities; yet Schwam and his associate, Ken Wright, were also in contact with provincial officials in an effort to receive provincial urban-planning contracts for their business, Research Planning Consultants, run from Schwam's home on Oxford Street.[26] Stan Randall, Grossman's Cabinet colleague, became so annoyed at their persistent job-seeking that he lamented: "Allan, I would appreciate it if you would take these guys off my neck and direct their efforts and energies to Ottawa or somewhere else."[27] Grossman noticed that Schwam and Wright became critical of him when it became clear that no provincial employment would be forthcoming.

Furthermore, the concern initially expressed by City Hall persisted, that KARA was not treating members of the Portuguese community fairly. Some of Grossman's information came from Tony Vaz. A Portuguese immigrant, Vaz had received a year's leave from his job with Canadian General Electric to take a position, funded by the city but nominated by KARA, as a bilingual community worker; his task was to educate members of the Portuguese community about urban renewal. Vaz's disillusionment with those in control of KARA began when the mayor asked the KARA executive for a list of area representatives to be appointed to KURC. "In spite of the large majority of residents being Portuguese the list did not have one Portuguese member."[28] Vaz and other Portuguese residents, including Father Cunha, the pastor of St. Mary's (Portuguese) Church, fought to protect the rights of a community that had few leaders and little prestige.

According to Vaz, it was a struggle even to persuade the old KARA executive to hold the 1968 annual meeting; when it was held, it was "organized in an intolerable manner." Many residents received notice only after the meeting had taken place. By March 1969, it was Vaz's view that "the City is doing its level best to treat people fairly. . . . However, it is my honest opinion that some spokesmen from KARA's executive and the URC have taken over the situation and are . . . representing a viewpoint which is not that of the residents in the area." He insisted that KURC should hold all its meetings in public so that "people can observe them in action." Furthermore, members should be "picked by the people, not by a chosen few" and "reappointed by the community on a regular basis." Only in this way could citizen participation "have some true meaning."[29]

Grossman found it difficult to navigate between the competing claims of different factions, particularly during an unseemly squabble between two of the groups which, in the mythology of the sixties, should have been allies in the people's struggle against a reactionary establishment. In early 1968, at the height of student activism at the University of Toronto, the Students' Administrative Council (SAC), led by Steven Langdon, decided to try to find some way to build a student-run residence. When the university board of governors proved unsympathetic, student leaders prevailed on the Minister of University Affairs, William Davis, to provide a special grant of $525 000 to the university for a residence planned and operated by the SAC. On 10 August, the press reported that land for the proposed residence had been acquired near College and Oxford streets, in Kensington. KARA had recently prevented Sinclair Construction from building on the property, and ratepayer leaders were outraged by university plans to erect a high-rise. The SAC incursion seemed designed to bypass comprehensive urban-renewal planning.

The complaints poured in to Grossman, On 14 August he raised the issue in Cabinet, emphasizing the lack of consultation with the residents. Cabinet agreed that the Minister of University Affairs would arrange a meeting with the interested parties. The issue went through various tortuous phases. Grossman urged Robarts to halt all activity until the promised meeting of the residents with William Davis. On 5 September, Premier Robarts again formally asked the minister to convene such a meeting. When nothing was done, Allan Schwam was cited by the *Globe*, on 4 October, as claiming that the province had broken its pledge of citizen participation. In the meantime, KARA's relations with SAC went from bad to worse.

In June or July, the land in question was sold to the Toronto Board of Education for $601 000. This seemed to infuriate Schwam and Wright. Schwam, described in the *Globe* on 22 July as one of KARA's most articulate members, was quoted as saying that "the action of the school board is only a stage in what some people fear is a provincial conspiracy to destroy Kensington."

Undeniably, citizen-participation procedures were not working smoothly. In October, the Liberals raised the issue in the House, arguing that Grossman had let down the people in his own riding. In response, Grossman noted that Allan Schwam had not seen fit to criticize the province's role until it became clear that he was not about to be hired as a consultant. He also put on record a letter he had recently received from KURC member and current KARA president Dan Martyniuk, which objected to charges that the Grossman commitment had been broken. According to Martyniuk:

> None of the authors of the newspaper articles have bothered to seek out the truth from the community as a whole. Rather, they expressed the opinion of a person who has his personal axe to grind with the Provincial Government. . . . The community was deliberately kept in the dark by these self-styled crusaders, and any attempt on my part to inform the people of the Kensington area and solicit their opinion on the subject through the Committee, was always opposed and I was frustrated at every turn.

The efforts of a few demagogues to mislead the Kensington Portuguese were failing, Grossman told the House, "because the Kensington Portuguese and everyone in that area . . . will stick with me and take my word against all of these rabble rousers."[30]

The climax came in 1969. In April KURC presented a fourteen-point program that proposed to strengthen the community, including the market. KURC wanted its recommendations to become part of the official plan; all future development proposals were to conform to its principles and to be submitted to KURC to be "assessed." The power of municipal departments would be strictly limited.[31] It was a sweeping claim for power. KURC was brought down to earth when its budget requests were turned back by City Hall, which requested information.[32]

Ed Clarke, KURC secretary, suspected that the city's goal was not rehabilitation but old-style redevelopment. He asked Grossman to have the province assess KURC's proposals; Grossman asked Darcy McKeough to do so. On 8 August Grossman received an assessment from the Urban Renewal section of Municipal Affairs, which saw no objection in principle to KURC's proposals becoming a part of the official plan. But it was a city matter. Many of the proposals, including a parking garage, were not possible under existing renewal agreements with the senior levels of government. The Urban Renewal Committee, the official concluded, had "misunderstood the existing legislation as the majority of their proposals seem to fall outside the context of not only existing legislation but also the present urban renewal policies of the governments involved."[33]

That summer, the federal government imposed a temporary freeze on all federal contributions to urban renewal. Under these circumstances, Ontario was in no position to make firm policy decisions. City politicians, in turn, although subject to fierce attacks from ratepayer groups for failing to carry through with rehabilitation projects, could do little.

Urban Affairs Minister Robert Andras came to Toronto on 15 October, to meet with City and provincial officials, including Grossman. In an open meeting at City Hall, residents were vocal in their disillusionment. Joe Lottman expressed the feelings of many people when he claimed that "the businessmen of the Market no longer have much faith in government at any level or of any party. . . . We have fulfilled our part of the bargain in urban renewal only to find that some City officials have drawn plans which show market streets converted into feeder lanes for the Spadina Expressway and that the provincial government has permitted the sale of a crucial piece of land to the Board of Education without the promised consultation."[34] The frustration continued. When KURC's term expired on 31 December 1969, the city did not renew its mandate.

Throughout, Allan Grossman retained close ties with a number of KARA leaders, including Ed Clarke, Dan Martyniuk, and Tony Vaz; he continued to believe that the Kensington Urban Renewal Committee offered some hope for citizen participation in urban renewal, and for a system of planning that considered the community. Ed Clarke considers that KURC had important achievements to its credit before its demise. He points particularly to the increased willingness on the part of Toronto Western Hospital and the Board of Education to listen to citizen concerns, to the fact that the City Parks Department supplied more recreation facilities, and to the fact that Cadillac Development worked closely with the community. Yet the process generated distrust and bitterness. All in all, the fate of KURC and the disintegration of KARA represented an unhappy conclusion to the aspirations of those of all political complexions who had supported "citizen participation" and who were active in the exciting ratepayer politics of the late 1960s.

In cities around the world, the approach to urban renewal by which areas could be designated as "blighted" and bulldozed into the ground without reference to existing residents was being replaced by an emphasis on consultation and rehabilitation. Urban renewal in the 1970s generally proceeded along more sensible lines, and the federal government's Neighbourhood Improvement Programme (NIP) of 1973 encouraged such efforts. Yet in the early 1970s, KARA continued to be racked by divisions as Dan Martyniuk was succeeded as president by Dan Heap of the NDP. When a school was finally erected on the much-disputed property near College and Oxford streets, it was a community school based upon open and progressive concepts of education. To Grossman this was further proof that KARA was not greatly interested in the opinions of most Portuguese residents, who preferred a more traditional type of school.

Kensington claimed a disproportionate amount of Grossman's time, but it was only a small part of his riding; he was on call to numerous other ratepayer and tenant groups and to individuals threatened by urban renewal. There were many meetings in 1969, for example, with the members of the Spadina, Queen, Bathurst Businessmen's Improvement Committee, "to consider the desperate conditions . . . caused by a deplorable, delayed, chaotic programme of 'redevelopment' of the north side of Queen Street."[35] This area was part of the Alexandra Park urban-renewal project, and many businessmen and residents were still facing problems; businesses were declining, and property-insurance policies were being cancelled.

Another ratepayer issue was the Huron-Sussex Association's struggle, in 1969 and 1970, with the University of Toronto. Once again the university and Education Minister William Davis were involved, and once again Grossman had doubts about the motives of members of the ratepayers group. However, he believed the university was the aggressor and he gave forceful support to the residents against the unfeeling block-busting tactics of a large institution.

In 1961, the university had published a master plan for expanding its downtown campus, in which houses in the Huron-Sussex area would be left untouched. By 1967, however, the university was quietly buying homes as they came on the market, and by 1969 much of the area was owned by the university. Houses deemed beyond repair were demolished; others were rented, mainly to students. This was a familiar pattern, followed by many large developers, to persuade people who saw their neighbourhood going downhill to sell out. Although university officials denied that the threat of expropriation was being used against area residents, a letter distributed to homeowners demonstrated the hypocrisy of this claim: "The University of Toronto has under law the power to expropriate lands . . . but it is hoped we can reach agreement for a purchase of the lands without recourse to such action."[36]

> Here was the University practically conquering blocks and blocks right in the heart of my district. Aside from the fact that they were taking up part of the area that gave me my best support, the University just forged ahead with its expansion programme. They were completely unfeeling about what happened to the people. They had land lying fallow with nobody using it, yet residents had no place to park their cars. There were vacant buildings being used by winos, the odd fire, everything, right next to where people had their homes, and the University often just wouldn't do anything about it. They were trying to make it difficult for the people who remained, in a word — blockbusting.

The problems were complicated by the fact that the Department of Public Works was assembling land for the expansion of the College of Education, which was under the authority of the Department of Education. It was not clear to residents which institution was in control of specific pieces of property.

As usual, Grossman stirred up trouble. He used his influence to call meetings and to force the university and the provincial departments to face up to the situation. In one indignant letter, he told university president Claude Bissell that about a thousand people faced the threat of being uprooted. What they desired was knowledge of the university's plans "and to date they have been unable to receive any information."

They do object to being evacuated at a time when there is a critical housing shortage if there is no immediate need for the properties. However, they expressed no objection to an orderly expansion under guidance and comprehensive competent planning, which consults with and makes provision for the people being displaced and which clearly explains and justifies the need.

Grossman's impression was that university officials could hardly hide their impatience at having to deal with residents and politicians. He concluded his letter to Bissell sharply:

I am greatly concerned with trends that have developed over the years which in the eyes of the people seem to abrogate the citizens' right to communicate with the institutions which they support, and too often they feel that government and its agencies have become the worst offenders. Democracy simply cannot function without co-operation with the citizens.[37]

At a subsequent meeting attended by ratepayers and university officials, Grossman discovered that he had been misled in his belief that ratepayers had not been contacted by the university.

There's no doubt about it, this was another example of a ratepayer leader more interested in stirring up trouble than in getting something done. These people not only had a Huron-Sussex Ratepayers Organization but they also had a committee on information, so they probably had a grand total of eight ratepayers, four of whom constituted the committee on information.

Such annoyances notwithstanding, Grossman supported the group because they had a good case. When some residents suggested that the university should lose its power of expropriation, Grossman agreed. He believed that only governments elected by the people should have such power — a radical position. Once again Grossman felt strongly enough about a local issue to involve Premier Robarts. He seems to have annoyed the Minister of Education with his persistence. Ultimately, Grossman was able to persuade the university to clean up and sod lots whose buildings had been demolished and which had been left "looking as though a bomb had hit the place." The university finally had its way, but, with Grossman fighting on the side of the ratepayers, it undoubtedly made a substantial effort to consider neighbourhood views.

One expropriation-related case Grossman fought for years was that of Madelene DeFalco. She first contacted the local alderman, Horace Brown, about her problems. "His answer was to get myself a good lawyer. He did nothing for me or anybody else down here. I believe you are more sincere."[38] The work Grossman did for DeFalco, who was a Liberal and lived outside Grossman's constituency, would have earned a lawyer many thousands of dollars.

DeFalco and her father ran a small store just outside the part of Alexandra Park where properties had been expropriated. Surrounding properties were demolished or were deteriorating, and she was unable to buy fire insurance. Her eighty-two-year-old father was ordered by the City Buildings Department to bring the property into conformity with city bylaws. With the orders pending, it was almost impossible to sell the property. Grossman fought the DeFalcos' case with three levels of government. He met with the federal minister responsible for urban renewal. The minister's response was that the building was not in poor enough condition to justify a special expropriation order. "How he could say that when [DeFalco] had a batch of orders from the City of fix this and fix that to the tune of $10 000 in 1969 money, I don't know."

Grossman kept nagging away until officials found a solution. In 1971, an amendment to the original Alexandra Park development plan permitted the acquisition of the DeFalco premises. "The problem was, the longer I was in government, the more of these hassles I got into with other politicians and bureaucrats and they began to get tired of all my pushing and shoving on behalf of my constituents."

The weapons Grossman used to help the DeFalcos — an understanding of urban government in Metro and of urban political processes — also made it inevitable that he should exert a special influence in the Robarts Cabinet on the continuing debate about metropolitan government in Toronto. Almost from the establishment of a federation in 1953, there was pressure to amalgamate city and suburbs; throughout, Grossman was a part of that debate. By 1962, the issue was again being discussed. With the party's first general election under Robarts' leadership approaching, the Liberals argued that the government was remiss in not ensuring that such services as welfare, education, and justice were delivered Metro-wide. The Tories, determined to make a strong showing in Metro constituencies, established a Cabinet committee to consider, once again, the workings of metropolitan government.

Chaired by Grossman, the committee included the other Metro ministers; the Minister of Municipal Affairs, Wilfrid Spooner; and his deputy, Lorne Cumming. With the city's request for amalgamation still pending, the committee debated moving towards a borough system, but agreed that more studies would be required and that "such a plan would stir up too much opposition to the government, which would not be desirable at this time."[39] Most members of the committee favoured a general review by an independent commission, but Cumming feared that it would be impossible to find suitable commissioners for such a complex task. On 18 April, John Robarts announced that a commission would be established; in June, Carl Goldenberg, a distinguished Montreal labour lawyer, was appointed commissioner. According to John Bassett's Toronto *Telegram*, credit for the establishment of the commission belonged to the member for St. Andrew.[40]

Grossman believed that the appointment of a commission was the politically sensible decision. The commissioner could prepare a study and make recommendations; the Cabinet could make the necessary decisions. The Goldenberg report, submitted to the province in June 1965 (after the general election that confirmed the Robarts administration in power), recommended a restructuring of the Metro system, which included the consolidation of the thirteen area municipalities into four cities — Toronto, Etobicoke, North York and Scarborough; Toronto would have thirteen members on Metro Council, and the other three proposed cities would have a total of thirteen members.

The commissioner also recommended that Metro receive greater planning powers and somewhat greater authority in housing, transportation, and waste disposal. The report made no recommendation that public health or fire protection be assumed by Metro; it merely asserted that "it should be the aim of the four cities to make health and welfare services equally available" across Metro. The report suggested that the cities' health officers co-ordinate their work through a Metropolitan Board of Health Officers. The most radical and contoversial recommendation was for the establishment of eleven separate-school districts, with increased powers for the Metropolitan Toronto Board of Education; education would be financed through a uniform tax across Metro. Albert Rose, in his careful study of Metropolitan Toronto, comments that "the Commissioner never satisfactorily explained why he did not recommend four city boards of education," which would have corresponded with his proposed four-city system. Rose argues that opposition to the education proposals "spilled over into other areas," which may have prejudiced the success of the report.[41]

Undoubtedly, there were serious flaws in the Goldenberg report. Rose suggests that some of the flaws may be attributed to Goldenberg's experience as a labour conciliator and his desire to please everyone by compromises. Allan Grossman thought the commissioner was led astray by his unfamiliarity with the Metro system. Grossman recognized that Goldenberg would want to retain his independence by keeping his distance from members of the Cabinet, and he respected that. On the other hand, he felt that his own experience at City Hall and Metro, on the 1957 Commission of Inquiry, and as chairman of the Cabinet committee on Metro, would enable him to offer some informal advice to the commissioner. He told Goldenberg to feel free to call upon him at any time and was surprised not to receive so much as one phone call.

The Goldenberg report had less impact on the form of Metro's restructuring than is commonly assumed. Allan Grossman's critical response to the recommendations was shared by a number of his Cabinet colleagues. In a letter of 23 July 1965, he expressed his preliminary views to Municipal Affairs Minister Wilfrid Spooner, with a copy to John Robarts. He argued that Goldenberg's recommendations would destroy the advantages of a federated system without achieving the advantages of amalgamation. Communities such as Leaside, Forest Hill, East York, Swansea, and Weston, with "the greatest degree of local pride," would be swallowed up by the four big cities.

> I am also deeply concerned about the proposed political structure. Here the Commissioner seems to have been impressed with the necessity of retaining an even balance of votes between the City proper and the other municipalities, and then to have constructed the municipal and electoral boundaries to accomplish such a purpose without regard to the practicability and implications of same. . . . The lack of political electoral experience of the Commissioner may be in evidence here.

Grossman believed that an equal electoral representation for an expanded City of Toronto and the new cities of Etobicoke, North York, and Scarborough would perpetuate city-suburban tensions.

Grossman's next objection related to electoral boundaries. He pointed to

> the overlapping of electoral boundaries, with two aldermen (one local, one metro) from a certain number of wards in some areas, and one Metro councillor from certain combinations of two contiguous wards in others.

Add to this the electing of district "educational councils" from eleven districts, which would again overlap city and Metro Council electoral boundaries, and it is not difficult to envisage the frustration of the electorate in attempting to sort out the various candidates, positions and districts.

Grossman also noted that there was no reference to the local hydro-electric systems, which he viewed as obvious candidates for amalgamation. And he believed it was a mistake "not to provide for the amalgamation of the Fire Fighting Services." So many other recommendations about planning, traffic, housing, waste disposal, and sewer renewals pointed towards amalgamation "that in my view there is not much point in any longer attempting to avoid amalgamation."

But Grossman had not yet become an amalgamationist, as he now made clear to Spooner. Because of his belief in local autonomy, his preference would be to leave the thirteen municipalities in existence (presumably allowing the OMB to continue to hear local amalgamation requests) and to give to Metro only such matters most in need of Metro-wide co-ordination: a uniform education tax levy, amalgamated fire protection, and possibly a Metro Hydro system.

> The political structure and electoral systems he recommended were the things that made me bite my nails. How could he make such recommendations? To me it was evidence of the fact that we were dealing with a person who knew nothing about politics or the political implications of his recommendations. And in fact they weren't carried out. There was no educational council, no educational districts, no change as suggested in the electoral system, no four-city federation.

In the weeks ahead, at meetings of the Metro area Conservative members, including ministers, every detail of the report was scrutinized and debated. By 14 December 1965, Spooner was ready with his recommendations to Robarts; these differed fundamentally from the Goldenberg recommendations. Spooner suggested a six-borough city. East York and York would continue to exist as boroughs; a smaller City of Toronto would have twelve members on Metro; members for the other boroughs would total twenty. The City would receive equal representation with the boroughs on a more powerful Metro Executive Committee.[42] Spooner's position was the basis for John Robarts' 10 January 1966 policy statement to the House, and a few months later found statutory embodiment as Bill 81, the new Metropolitan Toronto Act. So far as Grossman was concerned, the Goldenberg report had served a necessary political purpose, and Bill 81 was a satisfactory stage in the political process.

Notes

1. John Sewell, *Up Against City Hall* (Toronto: James Lewis and Samuel, 1972), xi.

2. For a valuable account of this phase of urban renewal, see Albert Rose, *Regent Park. A Study in Slum Clearance* (Toronto: University of Toronto Press, 1958). In this study Rose, a University of Toronto professor of social work, typically expressed fulsome support for the Regent Park approach to urban renewal.

3. Ontario, House of Commons, *Debates*, 18 March 1959.

4. Grossman Papers (G.P.), Grossman to Colonel Nash, Community Planning Branch, Department of Municipal Affairs, 1961.

5. G.P., J.A. Ramsay, "Community Work Evaluation" (mimeograph, June 1968).

6. G.P., Grossman to Alexandra Park Residents Committee, April 1964.

7. G.P., interim report of city officials, 3 Oct. 1961. Copies of the report were distributed by the City Planning Board to the Committee on Public Works.

8. G.P., Lottman to Grossman, 17 Oct. 1963.

9. G.P., Lottman to Grossman, 9 Feb. 1966.

10. G.P., Givens to Grossman, 7 Oct. 1966.

11. John Sewell, *Up Against City Hall*, 19.

12. G.P., KARA file, 10 Oct. 1967.

13. G.P., H.W. Suters, Managing Director, OHC, to Grossman, 11 Oct. 1967.

14. *The Globe and Mail*, 13 Oct. 1967. Grossman circulated his statement widely within the government. See Grossman to S.J. Randall, 30 Nov. 1967.

15. G.P., KARA file, "Grossman commitment," 1967.

16. G.P., "Memo to Controller Campbell from Alan Schwam — Chairman KARA — Re: meeting of representatives from Toronto Citizens groups, 12 Nov. 1967."

17. *Toronto Daily Star*, 18 April 1968.

18. G.P., "A Brief by KARA to His Worship Mayor William Dennison and the Board of Control," 10 June 1968.

19. John Sewell, *Up Against City Hall*, 39.

20. James Lorimer, *The Real World of City Politics* (Toronto: James Lewis and Samuel, 1970); Graham Fraser, *Fighting Back* (Toronto: Hakkert, 1972); Jon Caulfield, *The Tiny Perfect Mayor* (Toronto: James Lorimer, 1974).

21. Sewell, *City Hall*, 173.

22. Lorimer, *The Real World of City Politics*, 52.

23. Sewell, *Up Against City Hall*, 74.

24. Ibid., 36; Lorimer, *The Real World*, 55.

25. See G.P., W.D. McKeough, Minister of Municipal Affairs to Grossman, 15 July 1968, and attachments, including letter marked "not sent" to McKeough from KARA.

26. See G.P. for evidence of the activities of Wright and Schwam: Kenneth Wright, Research Planning Consultants, to Allan Grossman, 23 Jan. 1968; Allan Schwam to Mrs. Ward Markle, 29 Jan. 1968.

27. G.P., Stanley Randall to Allan Grossman, 24 June 1968.

28. Interview, Tony Vaz. For further confirmation respecting KARA's attitude to the Portuguese community, see the lengthy analysis in the Toronto *Varsity* by Brian Johnson, 28 Nov. 1969.

29. G.P., KARA file, Tony Vaz, March 1969.

30. Ontario, House of Commons, *Debates*, Oct. 1969.

31. G.P., 24 April 1969 meeting, KURC.

32. See interview, Tony Vaz. Vaz believes in effect that KURC was conspiring against the Portuguese community.

33. G.P., 8 Aug. 1969 assessment by Supervisor, Urban Renewal Section, Community Planning Branch.

34. This meeting, reported fully in the press, took place on 15 Oct. 1969.

35. G.P., Representatives of the Spadina, Queen, Bathurst Businessmen's Improvement Committee to Mayor William Denisson [sic], 8 Oct. 1969.

36. See James Lorimer's column in the Toronto *Star*, 15 Sept. 1969.

37. G.P., Grossman to Bissell, 8 July 1969.

38. G.P., Madelene DeFalco to Grossman, 28 Oct. 1967.

39. The Grossman Papers contain a file on the work of the Cabinet committee. See Minutes, 10 Dec. 1962.

40. Toronto *Telegram*, 19 April 1963.

41. Albert Rose, *Governing Metropolitan Toronto*, 113.

42. G.P., Grossman to Wilfrid Spooner, 23 July 1965; memorandum, Spooner to John Robarts, 14 Dec. 1965.

MINORITY GOVERNMENT IN ONTARIO, 1975–1981: AN ASSESSMENT†

VAUGHAN LYON

September 1975 to March 1981 was a period of minority government in Ontario. This experience affords an opportunity to gain understanding of how a legislature and government function when the executive is deprived of its majority control. It is also an opportunity to study the dynamics of legislative reform. With the cabinet not in as firm control, we may well get a clearer indication of the extent and nature of the MPPs' interest in that subject.

This assessment of minority government is based on the view of seventy-one "insiders." During 1982, interviews were conducted with current and former cabinet ministers, deputy ministers, leading members of the opposition parties and representatives of a cross-section of interest groups. In addition, a mailed questionnaire was used to solicit the views of backbench MPPs and of a few people in the above-mentioned categories who were unavailable for interviews.[1] All respondents were assured anonymity.

The Ontario Political Environment: 1975–1981

It is difficult to determine how much of any minority government's performance should be attributed to factors other than its status in the legislature. In the case of Ontario this is especially the case because the Davis governments of the 1975–1981 period drew considerable strength from the Conservative party's position in a three-party system, the province's economic condition, and other factors of less significance.

The Impact of the Three-Party System

J.S. Hodgson has identified two markedly different types of minority governments, and others that fall between.[2] A minority may be new to office and riding a wave of public support likely to carry it to majority status soon. Such a government may confidently challenge the opposition. At the other extreme is a former

†*Canadian Journal of Political Science* 17 (1984): 685–705. The author especially appreciates the help of Jim MacKenzie, executive assistant, Office of the Government House Leader, and Graham White, assistant clerk, Legislature of Ontario, in providing background for this article.

majority government, its popularity ebbing, and obviously doomed. It may gamble recklessly or govern dispiritedly, in either case inviting early defeat. In 1975, after thirty-two years in office, the loss of 8 percent of its popular vote, and the conversion of a thirty-nine-seat surplus into a twenty-three-seat deficit, the Ontario Progressive Conservative administration might have seemed doomed. However, from a low point in 1975, the Conservatives climbed back in the elections of 1977 and 1981 to majority status. In each of the four elections of the decade 1971–81 the percentage turnout of registered voters declined: not the sign of an electorate bent on change.

The basic facts of recent Ontario electoral history are set out in table 1. While the Conservatives experienced an electoral rebuff in 1975, neither opposition party emerged as the clear alternative to them. The Liberals gained in seats and popular vote, but the New Democratic party did even better in terms of seat gain and became the Official Opposition. All parties lost in the 1977 election. The Conservatives again failed to win voting control of the legislature in an election where they tried to make majority government the salient issue. The NDP reverted to its usual third-party role. The Liberals suffered minor losses, but were once again the Official Opposition.

The failure of either of the opposition parties to capture the anti-Tory feeling resulted in each changing its leader. Liberal Robert Nixon resigned after the 1975 election; Stephen Lewis of the NDP left following the 1977 contest. Nixon's replacement, Dr. Stuart Smith, immediately indicated a desire to topple the government, only to be overruled and embarrassed by his caucus. Throughout the minority period, the Liberals waited for support to develop. Michael Cassidy, Lewis' replacement, was faced with the overwhelming task of filling his shoes without the support of the NDP caucus or of the Lewis research team. Like the Liberals, Cassidy and his colleagues felt unready for an election during most of the minority period.

While the opposition parties regrouped under new leaders, Premier Davis' popularity grew.[3] He was the man-in-the-middle; opposition leaders either admired or respected him, while they disliked each other. There was little danger of a combined opposition effort to bring down the government. The cabinet could enlist the support of one or other opposition party on most issues or profit from their inability to agree on an alternative to government proposals, as in the case of Ontario Hydro's uranium purchase.[4]

With one exception, from December 1975 until December 1979, the Liberals supported the government on formal confidence votes. Then, when the Liberal leader declared that he wanted an election and would no longer prop up the government, the NDP provided support. When elections occurred, the government chose the time. The competitive situation required each party to proceed carefully — especially after the 1977 election result which was widely interpreted as a directive to make minority government work. The Conservatives had reason to bless the three-party system and their place in it.

The Economic Situation

From the mid-seventies to the present, "restraint" has been the order of the day at Queen's Park. Commenting on the debt situation, NDP leader Stephen Lewis, from whom the most pressure for increased expenditure might have come, said "Even I say they have gone too far."[5] The general public, too, favoured constraint.[6] As a result, the Conservative government was under less pressure than it might have been in more prosperous times from the two opposition parties to develop and expand programs: to act in an un-Conservative manner. Further, the restraint program enabled the government to refurbish its traditional image as a good manager which had slipped during the relatively free-spending 1960s and early 1970s.

TABLE 1

Ontario Election Results 1971–1981

| General election | Seats | Turnout (percentage) | Seats (percentage of popular vote) | | | (+) Government majority over opposition; (−) Opposition majority over government |
			Conservative	Liberal	New Democratic	
21 Oct. 1971	117	73.5	78(44.5)	20(27.8)	19(27.2)	+39
18 Sept. 1975	125	67.8	51(36.1)	36(34.3)	38(28.9)	−23
9 June 1977	125	65.6	58(39.7)	34(31.5)	33(28)	−9
19 March 1981	125	58.0	70(44.8)	34(33.7)	21(21.1)	+15

SOURCE: Ontario, Chief Electoral Officer, *Election Returns*, 1981.

Performance of the Minority Government/Legislature

Legislative Reform

Our consideration of the record of Ontario's minority governments will start with the matter of legislative reform. This will provide some background on the legislative environment in which the cabinet worked, and it will enable us to identify the kind of changes legislators demanded when it was not as necessary to cater to the cabinet.

After thirty continuous years (1945–75) of majority government by the same party, one might expect the post-1975 legislature to be in a turmoil with the opposition parties struggling to repay past injuries and establish new relationships between legislature and cabinet. Significant changes were instituted in legislative procedures during the minority period. However, this was done quietly, and after the election of a majority government in 1981 it became obvious that basic power relationships had been altered only marginally.

There had not even been a major debate about the fundamentals of legislative reform.[7] There were two basic reasons for this. First, an executive-sponsored reform program, under way prior to 1975, extended into the minority period. Second, despite its new bargainning power, the opposition proved almost as uncritical of the executive-centred model of parliamentary government as the Progressive Conservatives — although it was the source of most of its grievances.[8]

To expand on these two points: in June 1972, the cabinet recognized that the legislature needed modernization and, under opposition pressure, proposed the appointment of the Ontario Commission on the Legislature (the Camp Commission). The Commission was independent in relation to the cabinet, but was firmly committed from the start to the existing system of party/parliamentary government.[9] It submitted its recommendations in five separate reports: the first in 1973 and the last after the 1975 election. Camp provided the cabinet with a ready-made and, in terms of its monopoly over the policy-making process, a safe program for legislative reform, at a time when the opposition no longer had to tolerate being treated as an irrelevant nuisance.

The detailed recommendations of the Commission and the innovations flowing from them have been thoughtfully analysed elsewhere and will only be treated summarily here.[10] The recommendations were intended to enhance the status of the legislature and to shift the orientation of MPPs from constituency case-work to broad policy concerns.[11] They were successful in achieving the first objective. Reform of election financing, an increase in the responsibilities, independence, and support staff of the Speaker, an updating of the standing orders of the legislature, and a very substantial increase in the resources available to MPPs (full-time status with appropriate salaries, funds for travel, increased research help, constituency offices, and so forth) did change the image of the legislature and, especially, the life style of members.

The fact that MPPs had more resources marginally strengthened their position vis-à-vis the executive. It is doubtful, however, whether they were put in a significantly better position to contribute to policy than before Camp, although becoming more involved in the policy-making process was the second major priority of reform-minded MPPs.[12] If their position had improved significantly, or if MPPs were deeply committed to improving it, one might expect this to be reflected in the new procedures governing the introduction of private members' bills: the only direct way in which MPPs can get their policy ideas on the legislature's agenda.

The Legislative Assembly Act states that only the executive can sponsor bills involving public expenditures.[13] Although a literally minded Speaker could find that virtually any private member's bill violates this restriction, there was no suggestion that it be changed. However, Camp and the legislative committees charged with the responsibility for converting the Commission's recommendations into standing orders did review the procedures which the government had used for decades to prevent private members' bills from even coming to a vote.

The procedure agreed on, part of a new set of standing orders, was that private members' bills would come to a vote on second reading unless blocked by twenty members standing in their places or by a petition signed by one-third of the members.[14] The government retained its right to refuse to refer a bill to a committee for clause-by-clause review and then a vote on third reading — a general right stemming from its overall control of the legislative agenda. In other words, even a minority would retain the power to veto private members' bills. All the government conceded was that it would do so somewhat later in the process, and more formally. This was regarded as a great victory by some MPPs and members of the media.[15]

Any illusions which the opposition might have had about the significance of the new rules as they applied to private members' bills were quickly shattered.

Amidst a good deal of mutual congratulation, Bill 89 — "An Act Respecting French Language Services in Ontario" and a private member's bill — was carried on second reading on 1 June 1978, with the vocal support of two cabinet ministers and the votes of the majority of the Conservatives as well as those of opposition members.[16] A significant step in a controversial area was being taken by consensus.

The satisfaction of MPPs was short-lived. As soon as the result of the vote was announced, Premier William Davis issued a press release stating that the government would not allow the bill to proceed further.[17] The media were quick to recognize the direct challenge the premier's manoeuvre posed to the sovereignty of the legislature: "It was the clearest possible repudiation of the polite fiction that basic decisions in our parliaments are made by a majority of the elected representatives of the people. In fact, they are made by individuals who have won a majority of delegate votes at a convention of the governing party: supreme power follows."[18]

Despite the exhibition of the premier's power under existing rules and although there were to be almost three more years of minority, the standing orders were scarcely changed. One attempt to remove the twenty-member block relating to private members' bills (which would have shown spirit and an interest in reform even though it would still have left the government able to prevent a committee stage for amendments and a vote on third reading) was lost because a number of Liberals did not show up for an evening session.[19] In 1980, with the prospect of a majority government looming, MPP Donald MacDonald made a last-minute attempt to shore up the position of the legislature. A resolution carried calling on the premier to consult with leaders of the opposition parties prior to the appointment of the Speaker, and to submit nominations for six other officers of the Assembly to appropriate committees of the legislature prior to confirming appointments.[20] In the case of the NDP, consultation on the appointment of John Turner as Speaker in the majority legislature elected in 1981 amounted to a last-minute telephone call informing the party of the premier's decision. Subsequently, the chairman of the Commission on Electoral Expenses — one of the appointments which was to be referred to committee — was appointed. Again, the "consultation" took the form of telephone calls: the matter of involving a legislative committee in the appointment process was not even discussed.[21]

It seems quite clear from interviews that, had the opposition pressed harder, the government would have conceded it a larger role in the business of the legislature.[22] One senior Conservative (not the house leader) stated:

> Opposition, fortunately for us, tended to focus on rule changes that could be typified as empire-building. Great progress on constituency offices, research. Could have made much more progress on private members' bills. Government would have granted more leeway so that some way to force a matter to a vote on principle. Might have done something on estimates. Process tedious for government and opposition. Maybe all matters on a line-by-line consideration of estimates should not be considered matters of confidence. Room to do something creative there.
>
> Had I been in opposition . . . I would have sought what would have looked to be rather marginal changes but which in minority or majority

period would have given the opposition very significant clout and really had the effect of changing the parliamentary system in the interests of the opposition. But none of that really happened.

The opposition failed to grasp their opportunity. They could have pressed further in a way that to the public would have appeared quite reasonable.

One of the opposition members involved in the whole reform process responded this way when asked if the Liberals and NDP could have demanded more successfully:

It's hard to know. The reality was that they were the government. We had few alternatives short of forcing an election. You could goad and prod but the elephant was not going to move much out of its accustomed path unless you put a landmine under it. That might have been fatal for the rider as well as the elephant. We never seriously considered running an election on the issue. Hardly a grabber in Ontario politics.

The government elephant was not going to move much out of its accustomed path, but neither was the numerically larger opposition elephant lumbering alongside.

The opposition did not insist vigorously on a more significant role in policy-making for several reasons. The increased resources flowing to MPPs as a result of the Camp Commission's recommendations were extremely gratifying to them and, in a minority situation where the government was showing some deference to opposition opinion, it was easy to believe that the reforms underway were more fundamental than was the case. The appointment of NDP member Jack Stokes as Speaker after the 1977 election added to the impression that a new era in executive-legislative relations had dawned. Many of the new members elected in 1975, including Liberal leader Stuart Smith, lacked the experience with minority government which might have made them more aggressive reformers. But, finally, and most important, those involved in negotiating the reforms made a point of mentioning the general lack of interest of their colleagues in procedural questions. Legislative reform was simply a low priority item on most MPPs' personal agendas. However much they may complain about their limited role, most uncritically accept the current norms of the adversarial model of parliamentary government which maintain it.

Eugene Forsey did his best to free up Canadian thinking about parliament in an article on minority government published in 1964.[23] Since then two useful studies have been done of minority government at the national level.[24] In one of these, Linda Geller-Schwartz emphasized how uncomfortable MPs, especially opposition MPs, were in a situation where majority government norms had been weakened.[25] Both remark on the failure of the minority experience to lead to evolutionary change in the system. Geller-Schwartz might have been writing about Ontario when she concluded that during minority periods in Ottawa, "adaptation occurred entirely within the parameter of the Westminster Model and was primarily of a structural pragmatic kind."[26] Clearly it is not the cabinet's determination to protect its powers which is the main barrier to altering roles in the legislature and meeting many of the grievances of MPPs.

The performance of the minority government Assembly in areas other than legislative reform was given a specific rating by the "insider" respondents; these were elaborated on in interviews. Four specific functions were assessed: checking executive-bureaucratic power, articulating interests, educating the public and, finally, legislating. The first three raise the issue of how the minority legislature performed as a representative institution. Under the fourth, legislative performance, it was possible to consider the general issue of the government's ability to govern. Most interviewing time was devoted to this final category because it was the only one on which there was a significant difference in the opinions of government and non-government respondents.

Checking Executive-Bureaucratic Power

In the British parliamentary system as developed in Ontario, policy-making and administration are monopolized by cabinet and bureaucracy: the legislature's role is to prevent those institutions from engaging in conduct which is wasteful, irresponsible, or abusive. It is an enormous challenge with a majority government in place because the subject of scrutiny has the votes to control much of the process. Frequently, the only way the opposition can get some of the leverage it requires vis-à-vis the cabinet is to breach the rules or conventions of the assembly. But this is a double-edged sword: the attention of some members of the public is attracted to the alleged misdeeds of the government, while others get no further than noting what appears to them to be the opposition's irresponsible conduct.

In a minority, on the other hand, the administration is not in control of the scrutinizing process. The fear is that the opposition parties may be too relentless, and obstruct orderly government. However, in the Ontario case there was virtually no suggestion from any of those interviewed that the Liberals and/or NDP passed over the line dividing proper criticism from irresponsible obstructionism. Eighty-two percent of respondents rated the minority legislatures as "better" or "much better" than the preceding majority houses in checking executive-bureaucratic power. The eighty-two percent included eight of the thirteen cabinet ministers interviewed (the rest opted for the "same") and eight of the nine senior bureaucrats.

The primary reason the checking function was performed better was, as already noted, that the opposition could not be outvoted by the government. But, in addition, some of the Camp-inspired reforms, particularly related to the research assistance available to MPPs and to house procedure, gave the opposition more opportunity to review government operations in depth. For example, for the first time any twenty members could refer bills and annual reports of ministries or government agencies to committees.[27] The significance of the latter was not anticipated but MPPs soon found that sending such a report to committee could open up an investigation of any subject falling under the jurisdiction of the reporting agency. Using this provision, the opposition initiated studies of health insurance premiums, acid rain, hospital closings and other timely subjects.[28] And, of course, in a minority the opposition had voting control of committees and some chairmanships. Under these circumstances the notion of cabinet accountability took on real significance.

The investigation of the collapse of the Re-Mor Investment Management Corporation illustrates how vigorous committee investigations can be — if there is a minority. In 1980, provincially licensed and supervised Re-Mor and two related companies went into receivership. Twenty members of the Assembly signed a petition on 18 November 1980, referring the annual report of the ministry administering trust company legislation to the legislature's justice committee, in effect launching the Re-Mor investigation.[29]

The government objected to aspects of the committee's study on the grounds that it might jeopardize certain criminal proceedings.[30] However, the opposition refused to limit the inquiry to accommodate the concerns of the attorney-general and enlisted the support of the legislature in its dispute with the cabinet. Acting on a request from the committee, MPPs instructed the Speaker to issue his warrant requiring the minister of consumer affairs to produce documentation he was withholding.[31] There was talk of contempt charges being laid against the same minister when the Ontario Securities Commission, for which he had responsibility, also resisted providing information.[32] The 19 March 1981 election interrupted the investigation mid-way and returned control of the legislature to the cabinet. The new majority government could now insist that the criminal cases be given priority over the legislative enquiry and, in a wave of bad feeling, the Re-Mor investigation sputtered to a halt.

While the opposition did not demand or get the right to establish select committees or inquiries during the minority period, the government could be pushed into doing so as part of the behind-the-scenes negotiations for support. The Select Committee on Plant Shutdowns and Employee Adjustment was clearly the product of such bargaining as were the commissions on the Northern Environment and Freedom of Information. The Select Committee was itself shut down with a return to majority government as was the much-admired Select Committee on Hydro.

Minority government is, of course, more dramatic and the news media paid more attention to Queen's Park during the minority. As a result of this and of the cabinet's need to avoid antagonizing the opposition unnecessarily, the question period, like the committees, became a more effective check on the government. Government speakers went out of their way to be informative and conciliatory. However, after the 1981 election there was a swift return to high-handedness and secrecy, the norms of majority government.

Articulation of Interests

Minority government weakened the usual monolithic control of policy-making and in the more dynamic political milieu, interest groups stepped up their activity. There was a more forceful and effective articulation of group opinion in the legislature, as distinct from the executive-bureaucratic arena. Respondents overwhelmingly (86 percent) rated minority "better" or "much better" from the perspective of articulating interests.

Opposition "nobodies" became "somebodies" to interest groups now that they had some clout. The much more vigorous lobbying of the opposition meant that opposition critics were better informed about many issues.

Increasingly, lobbying is a two-way street. Governments and politicians reach out to influence and enlist the support of groups, as well as to receive their representations. This dimension of the lobbying process increased as well. One interest group respondent was pleasantly surprised when a previously quite inaccessible bureaucrat phoned occasionally "just to chat." Others noted increased requests for information from all parties, and appeals from the government for help in lining up support.

One aspect of the government's strategy in dealing with the minority situation was to give more advance notice to groups of controversial bills, such as the Family Law Reform Act, in order to mobilize support and explode political landmines harmlessly outside the legislature. This approach, of course, encouraged still higher levels of group activity.

There is no doubt that on a number of issues the lobbyists had considerable impact. Attempts to revise the Pits and Quarries Control Act (the aggregates bill) got bogged down in committee as legislators tried to reconcile the conflicting views of several strong groups. After months of deliberations, the bill was withdrawn. The minority gave a new lease on life to the throw-away pop tin. Efforts at deregulation, especially in trucking, were stymied by interest group resistance, and so on. Interest groups have a substantial impact on majority governments, too, but a minority is, obviously, more vulnerable.

The usual pluralist critique of interest group politicking is that it gives additional advantages to privileged groups. In the Ontario case, however, such groups tend to have solid relationships with the governing party. Most respondents thought the overall impact of the increased lobbying during the minority period was neutral in terms of benefiting particular social classes or categories of interest. However, where a special benefit was noted, it was to the "cause" groups which normally did not have the ear of the government.

Public Education

Ideally, the legislature is the focal point for political discussion. "Tuning in" to its proceedings, the citizenry learns about the issues facing the community, as well as participates vicariously in developing appropriate policy responses. For the legislature to perform this function effectively, the MPPs and the media must both play their parts well. In the minority, the MPPs had a greater incentive to be "parliamentarians" and the uncertainty and novelty of minority guaranteed more press coverage.

Despite these facts, however, the minority legislature's performance was rated less highly in this category than in the two preceeding (56 percent "better" or "much better"; 10 percent "worse"). Those who believed the educational function was performed less effectively thought the public was confused by developments at Queen's Park in the absence of a majority and crystal-clear lines of responsibility.

Legislation

Most respondents thought the legislative function was performed better in the minority situation (see table 2). However, the difference in the assessment of the "government" respondents (cabinet, ex-cabinet and senior bureaucrats) and others is significant. With this division of opinion, interviews and other evidence become crucial.

TABLE 2

Functioning of Legislature: Legislation

Respondents	Much worse	Worse	Same	Better	Much Better	Don't know
Cabinet ministers	1	5	4	3	—	—
Bureaucrats	—	5	1	2	—	2
MPPs						
Conservatives	—	2	2	—	—	—
Liberals	—	—	1	8	3	—
New Democrats	—	1	—	14	3	1
Interest groups	—	1	1	8	2	1
Totals	1	14	9	35	8	4

Commonly held fears are that with a minority there will be a lack of productivity, excessive caution on the part of government, and an absence of ideological coherence in the policies ultimately adopted. Government respondents expressed all these concerns in interviews.

Lack of Productivity

There was a substantial decline in the volume of legislation adopted in the minority period.[33] However, it is difficult to conclude that the minority legislature was sluggish or obstructionist, because there is evidence that this reduction resulted from a government decision. In a 1976 interview the premier and chief legislative "gatekeeper" said: "The one thing we've experienced in this past year is a recognition that we were probably passing too much legislation . . . we've made a calculated effort to reduce the volume of legislation. I think quite frankly that we're over-governed."[34]

The premier's sentiments were echoed in several interviews with ministers. Opposition respondents pointed out that there was no significant increase in the volume of legislation after a return to majority government, in rebutting suggestions that a significant number of bills had been accumulating during the minority.

Excessive Caution

During minority government the cabinet had to be much more aware of the possible reaction of the voters and of the legislature. This had the positive effect of requiring that considerably more care be devoted to preparing bills and that their presentation to the Assembly be better organized. On the other hand, there was even less long-term planning done by administration, according to respondents.

The difficult question, however, is whether the need for caution stalled much needed government action. A significant number of senior policy-makers claimed that new legislation, and housekeeping bills amending existing statutes, were held back because the government wanted to avoid opening up controversial policy areas for legislative debate. But the extent of the government's timidity can be overemphasized easily. A respondent involved in the passage of several highly controversial pieces of legislation found that any hesitation to proceed was more than offset by the desire of the premier to establish an impressive legislative record. The same respondent noted that the impact of the minority may have been exaggerated because it was often used by the premier as a convenient excuse to fend off unwelcome demands for legislation. Another senior policy-maker found financial stringency a much more important "inhibitor" than the government's minority status.

An erratic, irresponsible or super-aggressive opposition might have stalemated the administration. But the opposition was none of these. Almost without exception, government respondents were favourably impressed by its conduct during the minority period and found most opposition legislative amendments constructive. The exceptions were the few occasions when, it was alleged, an opposition member, without caucus consultation and unaware of its far-reaching implications, would scribble an amendment to a complicated piece of legislation on the back of an envelope on the spur of a moment in a committee session and have it adopted. Inevitably, too, there were breakdowns in communications between house leaders which led to some ill-feeling. In general, however, it should be emphasized that one important key to the smooth running of the minority legislatures was the close and constructive working relationship established by these key figures.

The personalities and approaches of ministers sponsoring proposals were of considerable importance. For example, as minister of labour, Bette Stephenson accomplished little. Her successor, a person willing to negotiate with the opposition and interest groups, achieved much.

The strong competitive position of the Conservative party and the government's means of protecting itself must also be considered in weighing the "caution" factor. The government could and did withdraw bills if it appeared that the opposition was going to amend them in ways the ministry found unacceptable. Further, the government gave itself a good deal of latitude by being flexible on "confidence." From the perspective of a legislative outsider, it seems remarkable that the opposition accepted the government's position that any tampering at all with the estimates — say, cutting $100 from total spending of approximately $15 billion — would be a matter of confidence. However, on non-financial issues the government was flexible. When on 15 June 1976, the government's farm income stabilization bill was defeated, the situation was quickly "put right" with the passage of a vote of confidence.[35] The attorney-general let his metropolitan police force complaints project bill proceed to certain defeat to make a point, without causing the government any trauma.[36]

Possibly the best test of a minority administration's willingness to make difficult decisions is found in its financial management. It is sometimes argued that a minority will attempt to spend itself back into public favour. However, the Conservatives consistently used the rhetoric and followed a policy of restraint during virtually the whole of the minority period — election periods excepted. The government held the level of its grants to most groups, and salaries to its own employees, to well below the rate of inflation. The minority status of the government probably helped rather than hindered the restraint programme. One government respondent put it this way:

> It is easier to control spending in a minority situation because one is much less vulnerable to parliamentary sanction if one trims one's own budget by 5 percent than if you let the deficit go up or increase taxes. If the opposition forces an election because you have trimmed your own spending, that is the kind of issue you can face them on in front of the electorate.

Some forms of taxes are, of course, less acceptable than others. The treasurer's attempt to increase revenues by raising fees for the Ontario Health Insurance Plan by 37.5 percent in 1978 illustrated dramatically the political hazards of the minority. McKeough quickly realized the government's vulnerability and, rather than risk an election on the issue, retreated to an 18.75 percent increase which won Liberal support.[37] The reaction to the proposed OHIP increase showed that there were certainly limits to what the opposition would accept in the area of economic management. On the other hand, the very fact that a premium increase of this magnitude would be contemplated by a minority suggests the government's relatively free hand.

While it was claimed that the minority was responsible for discouraging significant policy initiatives, it proved difficult to establish any consensus on what these initiatives were, or how important the alleged phenomenon of "hold back" was. Where one respondent would insist that, for example, market value assessment was a casualty of minority government, the next equally well informed person would ridicule the idea.[38]

Political rhetoric is not where one normally would look for objectivity, but considering that the premier had a vested interest in majority government and no wish to build up the opposition parties, his assessment of how minority government worked may be significant. At the end of the first year of the minority — perhaps the most unstable and menacing from the point of view of the government — the premier told a reporter, "In general, we haven't been inhibited that much." Referring to the defeat of the government's farm income stabilization bill, he commented, "that's the only issue that might have gone differently had we had a majority."[39] And at the end of the minority, as he announced the 1981 election, the premier said:

> For our record during the last Legislature has been, I would contend, sound and progressive. . . . Within our Legislature, we have had to work within the context of minority government which has meant that many factors and decisions were outside the complete control of the government. Yet, as a result of effective leadership, a good deal of common sense, and a certain amount of give and take, we have been able to fulfil our promise to the people of Ontario to serve a full and effective term, and sustain the Legislative process, despite the Opposition majority.[40]

Ideological Coherence and Accountability

The record of the minority government was clearly not a composite of the views of the legislature. Neither of the opposition parties seriously considered insisting that a package of its proposals be adopted by the government. This is not to say that the opposition had no policy impact. Even with a majority, the opposition is not totally without influence and in the minority it was able to affect the pace of government activity in some areas like the introduction of Foodlands Guidelines, and push it further than it intended to go in others, like occupational health and special education.

The one clear exception to the assertion that the legislation passed in the 1975–81 period could be attributed solely to the Conservatives was rent control; a probable exception was severance pay legislation. In the final days of the 1975 election campaign the premier promised some form of assistance to tenants who were victimized by landlords.[41] However, when the election resulted in a minority, the government realized it would have to go further than it desired: the drafting of the rent review legislation became somewhat of a collaborative effort of all parties.[42] In this one case, the government was put in the position feared by opponents of minority government: it had to take most of the responsibility for, and administer a program it found repugnant.

At the end of the minority, the Conservatives again found themselves in difficulty over a particular issue. The Committee on Plant Shutdowns and Employee Adjustment had highlighted the lack of job security in many industries. The government needed NDP support to survive a Liberal nonconfidence motion on the economy, and Minister of Labour Robert Elgie promised to introduce a bill providing severance pay for laid-off workers in partial exchange for this help.[43] The election intervened before action could be taken, but the government was sufficiently committed that it could not avoid bringing in minimal legislation following its return with a majority.

Conclusion

In summary, it is overwhelmingly the opinion of respondents that the increased power the legislature enjoyed during minority government enabled it to perform its "checking," "articulating," and "educating" functions "better" or "much better." Respondents were less united in their assessment of the impact of the minority on the "legislating" function. However, an analysis of the record suggests that to a remarkable degree the Conservative government of Ontario was able to continue to govern as though it had a majority and that the increased impact of the opposition on legislation, while modest, was constructive. The conventional fears of minority government — that it will not get anything done, that it will avoid hard decisions, and that its program will be a mish-mash of values — were unsupported. Instead, the evidence indicates only that a government which had been overly casual in its approach to legislation was now forced to use its power with more discretion.

How the respondents balanced their positive and negative feelings about minority government is revealed in their overall assessment of the minority experience: by more than a three-to-one ratio, respondents reacted positively (see table 3). If we delete opposition MPPs from the sample, the response is still two-to-one. This despite the fact that most insiders worked harder and experienced more tension and insecurity during the 1975–81 period.

TABLE 3

Minority Government: Overall Assessment

Respondents	Positive	Negative	Don't know
Cabinet ministers	6	6	1
Bureaucrats	5	5	—
MPPs			
Conservatives	2	2	—
Liberals	11	1	—
New Democrats	18	1	—
Interest groups	13	—	—
Totals	55	15	1

"Positive" respondents were asked: "Would you favour structural changes in the political system (such as a different electoral system) which would ensure more frequent or continuous minority government?"

Respondents	Yes	No	Don't know
Cabinet ministers	—	6	—
Bureaucrats	1	4	—
MPPs			
Conservatives	—	2	—
Liberals	8	2	1
New Democrats	5	9	4
Interest groups	6	6	1
Totals	20	29	6

The more experience the general public has with minority government, the more its attitude also is affirmative.[44] Clearly many of its attributes are highly valued. However, when those who were positively disposed to minority government were asked whether they would favour its institutionalization, most were opposed. Interviews revealed that the suggestion of a different electoral system was not a significant factor in explaining the opposition to perpetuating minority government. Three other reasons were advanced. First, many government respondents regarded the minorities as a kind of potent tonic: taken occasionally, it could revitalize a long-lived administration. Majority government should, however, remain the norm.

The second explanation was peculiar to NDP respondents. A number took the position that the majority system should be retained for the NDP. With occasional apologies for "smuggery," these MPPs argued that the Conservatives and Liberals, tied to privileged interests, needed the extra pressure which the public and the legislature can mount in a minority period to keep them responsive. However, the NDP would be undesirably inhibited if, as a government, it had to win support for its program from the opposition parties.

Some of the NDP respondents who did not subscribe to this view and wanted minority institutionalized for all parties, stressed the negative effects of majorities on representative government. One stated, "in a majority situation any governing party becomes arrogant and the opposition parties become irresponsible. A system encouraging such behaviour is intolerable."

The third reason advanced for viewing minority government favourably, but opposing its institutionalization, is the most signficant. A number of respondents, in a variety of ways, claimed that minority government, for all its merits, cannot be accommodated in the British model of parliamentary government. Expressed a little differently: minority government is a malfunction of one variant of parliamentary government, not an alternative. There is, indeed, a fundamental tension in minority government that makes it impossible to view it as other than a temporary aberration, however well a particular minority administration may cope. In the British model, it means that one party continues to have almost complete control over the legislative agenda and assumes full responsibility for public administration, while the others have the majority of votes in the legislature. It is obviously an irrational and unstable arrangement.

The situation is this in Ontario: as a means of organizing parliamentary government, a model is used which appears to work best when an election results in a legislature which no party can dominate. However, one cannot just settle for minority government because its successful operation is so tenuous, depending in large part on MPPs continuing to act largely as though a majority were still in place. If the benefits of minority government are to be "captured" and incorporated into the system, perhaps consideration should be given to the adoption of a different model of parliamentary government — one which would legitimate a more significant role for the opposition and for government backbenchers. However, Ontario legislators, even when less subject to cabinet control, showed no interest in even discussing such a model.

Notes

1. Categories of "Insiders"	Interviews	Mailed Questionnaire
Ministers	11	2
Deputy ministers	10	0
MPPs		
Conservative	1	3
Liberal	3	9
New Democratic	5	14
Interest groups	9	4
Total respondents = 71		

Mailed questionnaires were sent to all backbench MPPs who were not interviewed as of 8 December 1980. The percentage return was Conservative, 16; Liberal, 29; NDP, 47. The MPP category is broken down by party to make it clear that the MPPs' reaction is primarily that of opposition members, and disproportionately of the NDP. The relationship of the total number of each party's responses (including cabinet) to its legislative membership is Conservative, 30 percent; Liberal, 35 percent; NDP, 57 percent. The interest group sample's concerns included health and welfare, business and labour, environment, education, municipalities and agriculture. With the exception of the Ministry of Education, those ministries most active in implementing new policies during the minority were included in the sample.

2. J.S. Hodgson, "The Impact of Minority Government on the Senior Civil Servant," *Canadian Public Administration* 19 (1976): 229–31.

3. In an early 1981 poll, William Davis enjoyed the support of 54 percent of the electorate as the man who "would make the best premier" (a record high for his personal popularity) compared to 15 percent for Stuart Smith and 8 percent for Michael Cassidy (*Toronto Star*, 26 Feb. 1981).

4. Ontario, The Legislative Assembly of Ontario, The Select Committee on Hydro Affairs, *Report on Proposed Uranium Contracts*, March 1978, 131–45.

5. *Canadian Annual Review, 1975*, 145.

6. *The Gallup Poll*, 12 Dec. 1979.

7. "The new rules package for the Legislature . . . slipped through almost unnoticed on the last day of the session" ("Great Leap Forward," *Globe and Mail* (Toronto), 31 Dec. 1976.) Also see Graham White, "Teaching the Mongrel Dog New Tricks: Sources and Directions of Reform in the Ontario Legislature," *Journal of Canadian Studies* 14 (1979): 119.

8. White notes that it was difficult to get "more than a handful of members to think seriously about the role of the MPP," and that "the opposition evinced far greater interest in the Report's [Camp Commission's] proposals for improved services to members than in the more fundamental question of attaining an independent legislature" (ibid., 118–19).

9. Ontario, Ontario Commission on the Legislature, *First Report*, 1–2.

10. See Graham White, "The Life and Times of the Camp Commission," *Canadian Journal of Political Science* 13 (1980): 357–75; Donald C. MacDonald, ed., *The Government and Politics of Ontario*, rev. ed. (Toronto: Van Nostrand Reinhold, 1980), 81–101.

11. Formally, the Commission was charged with the responsibility to "study the function of the Legislative Assembly with a view to making such recommendations as the Commission deems advisable with respect thereto, with particular reference to the role of the Private Members and how their participation in the process of Government may be enlarged, including the services, facilities and benefits provided to the Members of the Assembly" (Ontario Commission on the Legislature, *First Report*, preface).

12. White, "Teaching the Mongrel Dog," 18.

13. Ontario, Legislative Assembly Act, R.S.O. 1980, c. 235, s. 57.

14. Ontario, Legislative Assembly of Ontario, *Standing Orders*, approved 14 Dec. 1978, s. 64(e)(i) and (ii).

15. MPP Hugh O'Neil advised constituents: "the MPP . . . will now have the same power as a Cabinet Minister to introduce legislation which may subsequently be passed under his name" (*Belleville Intelligencer*, 24 Feb. 1977). Norman Webster wrote: "This may not sound like much, but in fact it is revolutionary. It breaks the Government's lock on legislation" (*Globe and Mail* (Toronto), 23 Dec. 1976). For a more realistic view, see, "Queen's Park Reform a Snare and Delusion," *Ottawa Citizen*, 3 Jan. 1977.

16. Ontario, Legislature of Ontario, *Debates*, 1 June, 1978, 3030–40.

17. Office of the Premier, "News Release," 1 June 1978.

18. "The Font of Power Displayed," *Globe and Mail* (Toronto), 6 June 1978.

19. See, *Debates*, 13 March 1980; and "Tories Gloat over Liberal Foul-up in Defeat of Procedural Change," *Globe and Mail* (Toronto), 15 March 1980.

20. Ontario, Legislature of Ontario, *Journal*, 3 April 1980, 45.

21. Personal correspondence, David Peterson and Bob Rae with author, 4 May 1983 and 5 May 1983, respectively.

22. The opportunity was publicly advertised but even that did not stir the Legislature to more vigorous action. Harold Greer wrote:

> One of the high hopes out for minority government when it began in Ontario 15 months ago was that it would promote and permit parliamentary reform.
>
> The government, it was thought, would no longer be able by sheer weight of numbers, to refuse long-overdue changes in the system which would reverse the trend to ever-stronger government and ever-weaker Legislatures.
>
> The idea is a snare and a delusion, to judge from the 48 new procedures adopted by the Legislature before its Christmas prorogation.
>
> The new rules are the work of a legislative committee controlled by members of the opposition parties, which would seem to indicate the opposition is no more interested in meaningful parliamentary reform than the government is.

("Queen's Park Reform a Snare and Delusion," *Ottawa Citizen*, 3 Jan. 1977).

23. Eugene Forsey, "The Problems of Minority Government," *The Canadian Journal of Economics and Political Science* 30 (1964): 1–11.

24. Vernon P. Harder, "A House of Minorities" (M.A. thesis, Queen's University, 1977); and Linda Geller-Schawrtz, "The Multi-Party System and Parliament: A Study of the Interrelationship in the Canadian House of Commons" (Ph.D. dissertation, University of Toronto, 1977).

25. Ibid., 242.

26. Ibid., 251. Also see Harder, "A House of Minorities," 93.

27. Standing Orders. s. 56(c) and 33(b).

28. See Graham White, "Special Inquiries—The Ontario Experience,"*Parliamentary Government* 1 (1980): 8.

29. *Journal*, 18 Nov. 1968, 213.

30. *Canadian Annual Review, 1978*, 244–45.

31. *Journal*, 20 Nov. 1980. The Speaker is not bound to issue such a warrant. Having a "non-government" Speaker in place was significant in this case.

32. Significantly, four Conservative committee members joined the opposition members to demand that the minister co-operate. See Rosemary Speirs, "Drea May Face Charge of Contempt," *Globe and Mail* (Toronto), 4 Dec. 1980.

33. The average number of bills passed each year in the three "majority" years 1972, 1973, 1974 was 162; for the "minority" years 1978, 1979, 1980 the comparable figure was 101 (Ontario, Ministry of the Attorney-General, *Annual Report* for relevant years).

34. Douglas Grant, "Ontario's Minority Rule," *Board of Trade Journal* (Fall 1976): 45. Also see *Canadian Annual Review, 1976*, 169.

35. *Canadian Annual Review, 1976*, 170.

36. *Journal*, 1980, xxiv.

37. *Canadian Annual Review, 1978*, 111.

38. The government produced a White Paper on Property Tax Reform on 4 Jan., 1978, which suggested that it intended to proceed with market value assessment, but then, on 8 June 1978, the treasurer "threw in the towel" (*Canadian Annual Review, 1978*, 112). McKeough resigned on 12 Aug. 1978.

39. Grant, "Ontario's Minority Rule," 45.

40. Office of the Premier, "Statement by the Honourable William C. Davis," 2 Feb. 1981, 5.

41. *Canadian Annual Review, 1975*, 139.

42. Ibid., 145.

43. "Tories Broke Promise on Severance, Opposition Says," *Globe and Mail* (Toronto), 22 April 1981. Also see *Canadian Annual Review, 1980*, 245–46.

44. For a comprehensive review of changing public attitudes toward minority government at the federal level see, Lawrence LeDuc, "Political Behaviour and the Issue of Majority Government in Two Federal Elections," *Canadian Journal of Political Science* 10 (1977): 311–39. For the most recent study of strictly Ontario attitudes toward minority government, see F. Fletcher and R. Drummond, "Ontario Provincial Election Study" (Institute of Behavioural Research, York University, June 1977). In this survey respondents were asked: "In this provincial election and the last one, the party forming the government has not had a majority of the seats in the legislature. Some people think that it is better when the government has a majority of seats in the legislature, while others feel that minority government can accomplish more. Which do you feel is better?" Majority government better: 33.8 percent; depends: 8.5 percent; minority government better: 48.1 percent; don't know: 9.0 percent (valid cases: 1197).

WOMEN'S PARTICIPATION IN THE ONTARIO POLITICAL PARTIES, 1971–1981†

SYLVIA B. BASHEVKIN

Writing in 1950, historian Catherine Cleverdon suggested that a brighter future would await Canadian women who sought to become active in partisan politics. Cleverdon believed there existed

> . . . some evidence that political parties are becoming increasingly aware of the need to offer women something more in the way of political activity than to do party chores and to vote for their candidates (male, of course) on election days.[1]

How do Cleverdon's hopeful expectations fare in light of recent changes in Canadian politics and society, including the growth of contemporary feminism? This article examines female participation in the three major provincial political parties in Ontario, using data from the period 1971 through 1981 — or more than two decades since Cleverdon's study first appeared. These data offer the first systematic summary of women's involvement in a provincial party system in Canada.

The discussion has the following objectives: first, to present basic data on riding-level, provincial-level, and campaign participation among women in the three Ontario parties; and second, to evaluate these data in the light of cross-party and, where possible, cross-time comparisons. The data represent the initial results of an ongoing study by the author of women's participation in the Ontario provincial parties. Additional parts of this project, not reported here, will examine the problem of female representation at the two 1982 provincial leadership conventions, as well as the role of women's organizations in the Ontario parties. It is hoped that this first report will provide a useful starting point for readers interested in the Ontario findings, including those who may wish to develop comparisons with other provincial or possibly federal party systems.

†*Journal of Canadian Studies* 17 (1982): 44–54. Research for this article was made possible in part by a Post-Doctoral Fellowship from the Social Sciences and Humanities Research Council of Canada. The author is grateful to the Council, and to Naomi Black, Frederick J. Fletcher, H. Michael Stevenson, and Edward J. Weissman of York University, and Jill McCalla Vickers of Carleton University for their advice and support. The author also wishes to thank the following party officials and activists for their very helpful co-operation: Bari Maxwell of the Ontario Liberal Party; Ed Dale, Marianne Holder, and Marilyn Roycroft of the Ontario New Democratic Party; and Ruth Archibald and Aase Hueglin of the Ontario Progressive Conservative Party.

Research on Women's Participation

Prior to the mid-1970s, little empirical research on women's participation in Canadian politics was available. Studies conducted since that time have considered changes in electoral and campaign involvement resulting from the growth of a women's movement,[2] as well as the relationship between French-English cleavages and broader patterns of mass participation.[3]

While this research on mass-level involvement has generally shown gender differences in political interest and activity to be declining, contemporary studies of elite-level involvement have tended to report only slight changes in older, and very significant, gender differentials. The examination of female recruitment patterns — in Canada by Janine Brodie and Jill McCalla Vickers, in Quebec by Christiane Bacave, and in London, Ontario municipal politics by Kathryn Kopinak — has demonstrated that women remain very much underrepresented in positions of political decision-making, although this situation seems to be improving somewhat at the municipal level.[4] These studies also suggest that female underrepresentation results from two broad sets of factors, namely structural exclusion and discrimination, and established patterns of gender role socialization. Operating in combination, these factors have tended to produce major barriers to female political involvement.[5]

Research on partisan involvement among women in Vancouver and Winnipeg, undertaken as part of a larger Canadian-American project in four metropolitan areas, has also found that women form a disproportionately small segment of urban party elites, particularly in the upper echelons of party leadership.[6] According to Harold Clarke and Allan Kornberg, the few Canadian women who are involved in urban party activities would appear to work harder than their male colleagues and, at the same time, expect fewer tangible rewards for their commitment. Clarke and Kornberg suggest that these females "are in a very real sense 'survivors,' " who seem to have accepted their second-class minority status within party organizations.[7]

Published research on Canadian women elites thus indicates that relatively few females hold public office, especially outside the municipal sphere, and that important structural and cultural factors continue to inhibit their recruitment both to public office and to elite positions within political parties. One question which has not been considered in this literature, however, concerns the basic features of women's participation in a single, well-defined political unit, such as a provincial political party or party system, and the barriers which may affect participation at various levels in this unit. The present study thus begins with the descriptive issue of "where are women?" within Ontario provincial party structures — including the local ridings, provincial executives, and campaign organizations — and then links this descriptive exercise with a number of explanatory issues raised in previous research. In so doing, this discussion goes a step beyond established research on Canadian women as candidates for public office and as participants in urban party elites, to consider participation in the broader context of party life at all levels.

Electoral Behaviour of Women in Ontario

Before considering patterns of local riding participation, it is helpful to review the partisan attitudes of women in Ontario. Surveys conducted since the 1960s have generally found English-Canadian women to be somewhat more supportive of the older Liberal and Conservative parties than men, with men somewhat more favourable toward the CCF/NDP than women.[8] This general tendency has also been cited in Ontario electoral research,[9] and is reflected in the results of a 1979 survey reported in tables 1 and 2. These figures, drawn from a larger nationwide sample for the Social Change in Canada project, indicate that in the spring of 1979, Ontario women were somewhat more likely than men to identify with the provincial Liberals and Conservatives (40.3 versus 34.9 percent; 46.6 versus 39.9 percent), and were significantly less likely than men to identify with the provincial New Democrats (13.1 versus 25.2 percent).

TABLE 1

Provincial Party Identification of Ontario Respondents, 1979*

	Women	Men
Conservative	46.6%	39.9%
Liberal	40.3	34.9
New Democratic	13.1	25.2
Total	100.0%	100.0%
(N)	(472)	(396)

*Data in tables 1 and 2 are derived from the Social Change in Canada Study, directed by Professors T. Atkinson, B. Blishen, M. Ornstein, and H.M. Stevenson of York University.
Respondents were asked: "Thinking of *provincial* politics, do you usually think of yourself as a Liberal, Conservative, NDP, or what?"

TABLE 2

Provincial Party Preference of Ontario Respondents, 1979*

	Women	Men
Conservative	48.0%	38.2%
Liberal	36.9	35.7
New Democratic	15.1	26.1
Total	100.0%	100.0%
(N)	(450)	(387)

*Respondents were asked: "If a provincial election were held today, which party's candidate do you think you would favour?"

In terms of voting preferences were an election held immediately, these same general patterns obtain, although there was a slight shift of women respondents away from the provincial Liberals to the other two parties. If the identification data are employed to establish roughly the composition of each party's electoral base, then it would appear that the NDP base in Ontario was disproportionately male (61.7 percent) in 1979, while those of the Conservatives and Liberals were relatively female (58.2 and 57.9 percent respectively).

It would seem from these figures, as well as from the results of previous research, that women are well represented in the electoral base of the Ontario Liberal and Progressive Conservative parties, and that they are somewhat underrepresented in the Ontario NDP support base. This trend would seem to suggest that while socialist parties such as the CCF/NDP have been historically committed to equal rights for women, their ideological position has not necessarily translated into an equally strong voter base among women and men.

Comparative data from France, Italy, and other European systems also indicate that women have generally been less favourable than men towards parties of the left. This cross-cultural pattern would appear to follow from the predominantly economic, or class-based orientation of leftist parties during the post-war period, which translated organizationally into a preoccupation with the mobilization of (male) working-class, and especially unionized voters. In addition, liberal, conservative, and particularly clerical parties often showed greater interest in the social welfare, including family-related issues of concern to many women during the post-war years and, in most cases, developed more extensive organizational networks within the female electorate than did parties of the left.[10]

Recent data on party support in Canada and Western Europe, however, point toward a systematic decline in gender differences in leftist partisanship. In Ontario and the rest of English Canada, much of this change may be attributed to increasing NDP support among younger women, particularly those who came of age politically since the late 1960s. This pattern tends to suggest that changes in the socio-economic status of women, coinciding with the growth of contemporary feminism, may have contributed to some radicalization in female political attitudes.[11]

We shall now turn to the question of riding participation, in order to consider patterns of male and female representation in the provincial constituencies of Ontario.

Riding-Level Participation

Perhaps the most basic concern to raise in research on Canadian party participation is membership, since it is at this level that one might expect to find base-line evidence of male-female involvement differentials. However, gender breakdowns in party membership are not presently available for any of the three major Ontario parties, in two cases because of the absence of a centralized membership list, and in the third because the existing centralized list is not coded for gender.[12] Therefore, it is not possible at the present time to ascertain the proportion of party members who are male or female in Ontario.

We can thus turn our attention to participation in riding associations in the 125 provincial constituencies, which is summarized in table 3. Figures collected during the fall of 1981, and results of older internal studies in the New Democratic (1973) and Progressive Conservative (1977) organizations, permit us to examine riding presidencies, treasurerships, and secretaryships.[13] They indicate that women in all three provincial parties are far less likely to serve as local riding presidents than men. In 1981, women comprised 14.4 percent of Conservative riding presidents (N = 18), 20.0 percent of Liberal riding presidents (25), and 28.8 percent of NDP riding presidents (36), so that overall, in Ontario, there were 79 female riding presidents out of a possible 375 in the three parties, or 21.1 percent. The level of female representation in riding treasurerships was similar, except in the NDP, where male-female parity was approached (41.6 percent).

TABLE 3

Riding-Level Participation of Women in Ontario, by Party and Year*

Riding Position	Party and Year				
	Liberal	New Democratic		Progressive Conservative	
	1981	1973	1981	1977	1981
President	20.0(25)	8.6(10)	28.8(36)	9.6(12)	14.4(18)
Treasurer/C.F.O.	29.6(37)		41.6(52)	5.6(7)	12.0(15)
Secretary	76.8(96)		67.2(84)	62.4(78)	66.4(83)
Membership Secretary/ Membership Chair			53.6(67)		69.6(87)

*Cell entries represent the percentage of riding positions held by women in the years and parties indicated. Figures in parentheses represent the actual number of women holding these positions. Note that percentages for 1977 and 1981 are calculated on a base N of 125 ridings, while those for 1973 are on a base of 117 ridings.
SOURCE: Cell entries for 1981 are drawn from party records made available to the author, while 1973 and 1977 figures are from internal party studies described in note no. 12.

Comparing riding secretary and membership secretary data with these figures suggests that there may be a "pink collar" sector in local constituency organizations in Ontario. In 1981, riding secretaries in the three parties were between two-thirds and three-quarters female (notably, 76.8 percent in the provincial Liberal organization), and membership secretary positions seemed to be held disproportionately by women as well. Therefore, it would appear that the same types of executive and financial positions which tend to be held by men in the Canadian labour force are also held by them in the Ontario provincial ridings. At the same time, the more clerical and generally less prestigious positions in which women are clustered in the workforce are also those where they seem to be ghettoized in Ontario riding associations. It should be noted, however, that this clustering is least pronounced in the NDP riding associations, where women are better represented as presidents and particularly as financial officers than in the Liberal and Conservative organizations, and are also less likely to be membership secretaries than in the Conservative ridings.[14]

What other conclusions can be drawn from these riding-level data? First, in reference to their decision-making implications, the figures would initially suggest that a few women wield effective power in local party organizations. However, upon closer inspection of internal riding activity in all three cases, we would propose that large numbers of women perform critical human relations, especially communications functions, at the local level. As secretaries and membership chairs, they help to ensure organizational continuity by keeping local riding minutes, recruiting new members, and maintaining older memberships. In cases where the riding president or treasurer is not active, these women would also appear to provide among the only visible evidence of their party's presence in the riding. Therefore, while it is important to recognize the implicit and often indirect nature of "pink collar" power in the Ontario ridings, the importance of women's contributions should not be overlooked.

Second, and parallel with this first point, our research suggests that many Ontario women who have "broken out" of the "pink collar" ghetto have done so in ridings where their party is generally inactive and has little chance of electoral success. That is, a substantial number of female riding presidents in all three parties seem to hold symbolic power only, since they have little opportunity to elect members to their legislative caucus, and thus cannot attract resources from the central provincial organization — which, in turn, helps to propel party activity on the local level.[15] In short, then, the number of women holding formal positions of power on the riding level may be less significant than the electability of party candidates in ridings headed by women, the investment in such ridings made by provincial headquarters, and so on.

Third, the data in table 3 tend to suggest few parallels between partisan attitudes outlined above and the composition of provincial riding executives. Ironically, it is in the Ontario party with the lowest proportion of female electors (the NDP) that female activists would appear to have achieved the greatest direct influence over local decision-making, as reflected in the percentage of local presidencies and treasurerships. Conversely, it is in the Conservative riding associations that women are least numerous as presidents and treasurers, even though the Conservative electoral base is the most female of the three provincial parties. This trend may help to inform contemporary assumptions that a key influence upon women voters in general has been the status of women in party organizations. Rather, such factors as voter age and socio-economic status, the ability of parties to highlight the position of women within their organizations, and the attention paid to women in policy statements, could play a far more significant role in determining voter preferences than either the objective "facts" of female party participation, or official party ideology vis-à-vis women. In addition, regional and rural-urban differences not considered in this initial part of the study may be important in shaping both women's electoral attitudes and the dimensions of their riding involvement.

A fourth conclusion which may be drawn from data in table 3 concerns longitudinal or cross-time change in female riding involvement. While few longitudinal figures are available, those which are suggest a significant increase in women's participation during the past decade, which corresponds with the growth of feminist activism in Ontario.[16] In the provincial NDP, for example, only ten women held riding presidencies in 1973, compared with 36 in 1981. This change represents an increase of more than three-fold over an eight-year period. Data from Conservative ridings suggest increased involvement as well, since 19 women were presidents or treasurers in 1977, and 33 held these positions in 1981. However, during this same four-year period women also became more numerous as Conservative riding secretaries (from 78 to 83), indicating that women continue to fill traditional "pink collar" positions in many Ontario riding associations.

Given that much decision-making in political parties occurs on the provincial, as opposed to the riding level, we now turn our attention to patterns of provincial participation.

Provincial-Level Participation

In considering the participation of women in decision-making bodies on the provincial level in Ontario, it is important to recall that the organization of the three parties differs quite dramatically. Therefore, we will first review briefly the main provincial-level structures in the Ontario Liberal, Progressive Conservative, and New Democratic parties, before discussing patterns of female involvement within each organization.

The Ontario Liberal Party (OLP) is administered by a group of seven table officers who, in conjunction with the past president, party leader, and representatives of the legislative caucus at Queen's Park (one), youth committee (four), and four regions (three per region), form the OLP Executive Committee. Along with 13 other ex-officio members, the members of this Executive Committee are responsible for appointing provincial committees, calling and presiding over annual meetings, overseeing party finances and membership lists, and generally administering party affairs. At both OLP annual meetings and leadership conventions, delegates may include: 1) members of the OLP Executive Committee; 2) riding and youth association presidents; 3) 15 additional delegates per riding, of whom three are designated as youth and three as women; and 4) six delegates "from any District Women's Club recognized by the Executive Committee of the OLP."[17]

The provincial organization of the Ontario Progressive Conservative party is similar to that of the OLP, since the former is governed by officers who comprise the Executive of the Ontario PC Association. This Executive is composed of the party president, 12 vice-presidents (three of whom are designated as men, three as women, three as youth, and three undesignated as to age or sex), a secretary and treasurer, two auditors, the party leader, and the immediate past president of the Association. Ex-officio members of this Executive include the president of the Ontario Progressive Conservative Association of Women (OPCAW), presidents of district women's associations, presidents of the provincial youth and campus associations, and other party officers who, together with the Executive members, form the PC Executive Council. This Council is empowered to call meetings of the provincial Association, to keep track of party monies and records, and "to act for the Association between the [annual general] meetings."[18] Delegates to the PC annual meeting and leadership conventions include 1) officers of the Executive; 2) six officers of OPCAW; 3) five officers of each recognized district women's association; and 4) eight delegates from each provincial riding association (ten at leadership conventions), of whom at least two are women (four at a leadership convention) and two youth (of whom one should be a woman, at a leadership convention).[19]

The provincial organization of the Ontario NDP is perhaps the most complex of the three. The party is formally administered by nine provincial officers who, in conjunction with 15 members-at-large, two delegates to the NDP Federal Council, two youth delegates, and one female delegate to the Participation of Women (POW) Committee on the Federal Council form the provincial executive. However, the party constitution states that "the Provincial Council shall be the governing body between conventions."[20] This Council meets at least three times annually, and its membership includes the provincial Executive, two provincial and two federal caucus members, plus approximately 150 riding delegates, whose numbers are apportioned on the basis of riding membership, with at least one Council delegate from each NDP riding executive in Ontario. The provincial Council and Executive are each empowered to appoint committees to look after administration, fundraising, and various policy areas.

TABLE 4

Provincial-Level Participation of Women in Ontario in 1981, by Party

Party	Liberal		New Democratic			Progressive Conservative
Organization	OLP	Executive Committee	ONDP Provincial Council	ONDP Provincial Executive	ONDP Provincial Committees	Ontario Progressive Conservative Association Executive
Position	Table Officers	Regional Represent	Riding Delegates	Officers and Members	Members, 1981 average*	Table Officers
Percent Women	12.8%	8.3	27.9	39.3	27.6	16.7
(proportion)	(1/8)	(1/12)	(41/147)	(11/28)		(3/18)

*The ONDP Provincial Committees which were included in the calculation of this average were as follows: Administrative, Budget, Campaign Techniques Review, Constitution, Education, Election Planning, Electoral District Agents, Ethnic Liaison, Franco-Ontarian, Fundraising, Media Advisory, Policy and Resolutions, Policy Review, Tripartite, and Youth Steering. The Women's Committee Executive is made up of all women, and was excluded from this calculation as it would tend to distort the results. SOURCE: Data are drawn from party records made available to the author.

At its February 1982 convention, the Ontario NDP approved an affirmative action resolution which urges ridings "to adopt by-laws requiring equal (at least 50%) representation of women in their executives and convention delegations," and which requires equal representation in the provincial Executive and all party committees.[21] It is expected that these requirements will be implemented by the 1984 party convention.

In light of these various constitutional arrangements in the three Ontario parties, what generalizations can be made about provincial-level participation? First, in reference to their official status in the three organizations, women would seem to be best entrenched constitutionally in the New Democratic and Progressive Conservative parties. That is, the formal arrangements for female participation appear to be most conducive to involvement under the NDP affirmative action scheme (sponsored by the provincial Women's Committee) and under the PC constitution (which recognizes officers and delegates of a provincial women's association). The strategies for female participation in the two parties thus differ in that the NDP approach emphasizes the integration of women into existing power structures on the riding and provincial levels, while the PC approach implies development of a parallel support structure through OPCAW. It should be noted that the OLP structure does not include a provincial women's organization, and that formal provisions for female riding representation at OLP party conventions are more modest than in the other two parties (3/15 riding delegates in the OLP, versus 2/8 in the PC Association and 50 percent under NDP affirmative action).

Second, turning to data on the impact of these formal provisions in table 4, we find that it is in the relatively complex and decentralized NDP organization that women are most involved on the provincial level. A comparison of 1981 executive officers in all three parties shows that females comprise 12.8 percent of the Liberal provincial leadership, 16.7 percent of the Conservative, and 39.3 percent of the New Democratic. The composition of NDP Council delegations (27.9 percent female) and provincial committees (27.6 percent female, on average) also indicates relatively high levels of participation by women, while the limited representation of women as regional directors in the OLP (8.3 percent) suggests that their comparatively weak organizational status on the provincial level has produced similarly weak patterns of involvement. However, given that affirmative action is a stated priority of the federal Liberal women's organization in Ontario (the newly constituted Ontario Women's Liberal Commission), it is possible that provincial activists may adopt this strategy toward improving present levels of OLP executive, regional, and perhaps also riding representation.

Since the problem of female participation in Canadian politics is most recognized in the area of candidacy for public office, we shall now turn our attention to features of campaign involvement in Ontario.

Campaign Participation

Much of the existing research on women's participation in Canadian politics has focused on the troubling question of election to public office. Contemporary studies by Janine Brodie, Jill Vickers, and Kathryn Kopinak, as well as older work by such authors as Catherine Cleverdon have considered the dynamics of political nomination, candidacy, and election.[22] Most have concluded that gender role socialization, a lack of time and money among qualified women, discrimination within political organizations, and the more general identification of politics as a public and therefore masculine activity, militate against female involvement in the Canadian campaign process. Furthermore, these same factors have been linked with the proliferation of women candidates in no-win or long-shot constituencies in Canada.

While data presented in tables 5 and 6 do not address the reasons for these trends, they provide the clear evidence that 1) women are less likely than men to contest provincial office in Ontario, although the number of women running has increased substantially over the past decade (from 17 or 4.8 percent of major party candidates in 1971 to 45 or 12.0 percent in 1981); and 2) women candidates in Ontario are heavily clustered in the third-place finish category (notably, 27 out of 45, or 60.0 percent, finished third in 1981, compared with less than 30 percent of male candidates).[23]

TABLE 5

*Campaign Participation of Women in Ontario, by Party and Provincial Election**

Election Party	1971				1975				1977				1981			
	Lib	NDP	PC	T	Lib	NDP	PC	T	Lib	NDP	PC	T	Lib	NDP	PC	T
no. of women candidates	4	7	6	17	18	13	8	39	15	19	10	44	8	24	13	45
no. of women elected	0	0	2	2	1	3	3	7	1	2	3	6	1	1	4	6
no. of women placed 2nd	0	3	2	5	8	2	1	11	8	5	6	19	5	1	6	12
no. of women placed 3rd	4	4	2	10	9	8	4	21	6	12	1	19	2	22	3	27
no. of women campaign managers	–	19	–	–	–	–	–	–	–	–	9	–	28	41	16	85

*Cell entries represent the number of women running for office, etc. Most data on campaign management prior to the 1981 provincial election were not available. Ts represent row totals.
SOURCE: Cell entries for the first four rows are drawn from 1971, 1975, 1977, and 1981 Ontario *Official Election Returns*. Figures on campaign management are from party records.

TABLE 6

*Campaign Participation of Women in Ontario, 1981**

Party	Liberals	New Democrats	Progressive Conservatives
women candidates	6.4(8)	19.2(24)	10.4(13)
women campaign managers	22.4(28)	32.8(41)	12.8(16)
Total (N)	(36)	(65)	(29)

*Cell entries represent percentages, which have been calculated on the basis of the number of women participating (in parentheses), divided by the total number of provincial ridings (125).
SOURCE: Data are drawn from the Ontario *Official Election Returns* for 1981, and from party records.

Using the figures in tables 5 and 6 to compare across parties, we find that in three of the four provincial elections between 1971 and 1981, the NDP has run the largest number of women candidates, falling behind the Liberals once in 1975. In the most recent provincial election, for example, 19.2 percent of NDP candidates were women, compared with 10.4 percent of Conservative and 6.4 percent of Liberal candidates. However, the organization which has elected the largest number of women over the past decade — and here we are speaking in terms of very small numbers of women overall — has been the governing Conservative party. The provincial Tories have elected an average of three women in the four most recent elections, while the NDP has elected an average of 1.5 and the Liberals, 0.75. In proportional terms, however, it should be noted that the four PC women elected in 1981 represent less than 6 percent of the government caucus.

Data on campaign management are somewhat less bleak, since they show that 85 out of 375, or 22.7 percent, of major party campaign managers in the 1981 provincial election were female. Again, the proportion of women managers was highest in the NDP (32.8 percent), with 22.4 percent female managers in the Liberal and 12.8 percent in the Conservative organizations. These data represent some improvement over figures from the 1970s, since only 19 women were NDP managers in the 1971 campaign (versus 41 in 1981), and only 9 were Conservative managers in the 1977 election (versus 16 in 1981).

Our findings suggest that women could potentially become more numerous in the future as provincial candidates, if the campaign management route to political candidacy is exploited successfully by experienced female managers. However, as is the case with riding-level activism and candidacy itself, it is important to consider the viability of party organization in a specific locale in order to determine just how valuable women's campaign management may be to their political mobility.

This conclusion is further strengthened by information in recent official Ontario Election Returns, which shows that the number of women candidates who were employed in political, professional, media, and social service occupations increased between 1971 and 1977. In 1977, for example, sixteen female candidates held political and professional positions, including local government, compared with six in 1971, while ten held positions in education, social work, and nursing, compared with four in 1971. Six women candidates in 1977 were employed as writers or broadcasters, in comparison with only one in 1971. Overall, the 1977 official returns indicate that the proportion of women candidates employed outside the home was highest in the NDP (18/19, 94.7 percent), followed by the Liberal (10/15, 66.7 percent) and PC parties (7/10, 70 percent).[24] In light of the very slight growth in female representation at Queen's Park since 1975, these data tend to suggest that even as the numbers of employed women willing to stand for office increase their involvement as provincial legislators changes little.

One possible alternative for women candidates seeking to hold office at Queen's Park is the "cultivation" of a provincial riding. Rather than waiting for recognition by a party, and risking last-minute nomination in a weak constituency, it has been suggested that individual women work to build up a riding organization on their own. In this manner, they could gain recognition in the provincial party organization through a constituency association base, and then might contest nomination from a position of strength within both the provincial and local bodies. Recent elections in Ontario have provided two examples of such an approach by women, notably by Liberal Sheila Copps in Hamilton Centre, and to a lesser extent by PC candidate Susan Fish in St. George.

This approach to candidacy, however, would appear to be quite costly, particularly in terms of time and effort, and may be best suited to women who have established political credentials prior to "cultivating" their ridings. In other words, this alternative route to nomination and election may offer little as a general alternative, since it seems to require a degree of political experience and confidence which, in light of the preceding sections, may remain disproportionately male resources in the provincial party system.[25]

Conclusion

This discussion of women's participation in the three major provincial parties in Ontario points toward a number of conclusions regarding the dimensions of female underrepresentation in Canadian politics. First, the data presented above indicate that women are less numerous than men in most types of party activity in Ontario, with the prominent exception of "pink collar" riding positions such as local secretary and membership secretary. Riding association presidents and treasurers, as well as members of provincial executives were disproportionately male in all three parties, as were provincial candidates, campaign managers, and elected legislators. These findings are consistent with the results of previous Canadian and comparative research on elite-level participation, although the trend toward a "pink collar" sector in riding organizations has not been noted elsewhere in this literature.

Second, this discussion has offered an important set of cross-party perspectives regarding female participation in Ontario. While indicating that gender parity has not been reached on decision-making levels in any of the three major provincial organizations, the figures reported in this paper do show a substantially greater representation of women on such levels in the New Democratic Party of Ontario. The proportion of women serving as riding presidents, riding treasurers, provincial officers, candidates, and campaign managers is systematically higher in the NDP than in the other two parties. However, the governing Conservative party in Ontario has elected the greatest number of women to the provincial legislature during the past ten years, even though both the Liberals and New Democrats have fielded more female candidates than the Conservatives over this period, and the Liberals became the first to nominate a woman for provincial party leadership — Sheila Copps in 1982.[26]

Third, cross-party comparisons presented above also suggest that formal recognition of female underrepresentation is presently clearest in the Ontario NDP, which passed a comprehensive affirmative action proposal at the 1982 provincial leadership convention. At least two women in the party had conducted internal studies of female participation prior to the passage of this resolution, compared with one PC task force report on women's involvement which was completed in 1977, and apparently no internal studies of this subject in the OLP. Constitutional provisions for women's partisan involvement appeared to be more rigorous in the Conservative, as opposed to the Liberal organization, although the

PC provisions did not establish the "equal (at least 50%)" terms of the NDP resolution on affirmative action. Part of this inter-party difference may be attributable to the absence of a provincial women's organization in the OLP, and to the efforts of NDP women to integrate themselves within existing riding and provincial structures — at the same time as they may attempt to impart a more feminist presence within these structures. By way of contrast, Liberal and Conservative women in Ontario have worked to obtain representation through a separate network of local and area women's associations. As well, in the case of the Conservative women's group (OPCAW), female members have achieved provincial-level representation through their separate, yet supporting organizational network.

Fourth, this discussion has dealt with cross-time changes in female participation. While longitudinal data are not as extensive as might be desired, they do suggest a significant increase in levels of riding and campaign involvement over the past decade. In addition, longitudinal figures show substantial growth in the numbers of employed women contesting provincial office during the 1970s, even though they indicate relatively little change in the actual number of women winning election between 1975 and 1981.

What are the prospects for greater partisan participation by women in the future? Recent public opinion research indicates increasing willingness among Canadians to vote for women candidates at all levels of government.[27] In addition, the Sheila Copps campaign for the OLP leadership suggests that political women are at last receiving serious consideration from the parties, press, and public at large. However, as Thelma McCormack has argued, the cultural stereotypes which may appear to be receding from individual attitudes are deeply imbedded in the structures of Western society.[28] It may therefore be necessary for political parties to adopt structural reforms, including affirmative action, in order to provide individual women with equal opportunities for meaningful political involvement.

By adopting such reforms, political parties could offer women a formal stake in the public agenda, as well as evidence of a practical commitment to democratic representation. These initiatives on the part of political parties may help to redress some of the psychological and structural impediments to female participation in Canadian political life and, at the same time, may influence the partisan attitudes of both men and women for whom equal representation is a significant political issue.

Notes

1. Catherine L. Cleverdon, *The Woman Suffrage Movement in Canada* (Toronto: University of Toronto Press, 1950), 281.

2. Jerome H. Black and Nancy E. McGlen, "Male-Female Political Involvement Differentials in Canada, 1965–1975," *Canadian Journal of Political Science* 12, 3 (1979): 471–98.

3. Carole J. Uhlaner, "Does Sex Matter? Participation by French and English Women in Mass Canadian Politics" (paper presented at Canadian Political Science Association meetings, Montreal, 1980).

4. M. Janine Brodie, "The Recruitment of Canadian Women Provincial Legislators, 1950–1975," *Atlantis* 2, 2 (1977): 6–17; Jill McCalla Vickers, "Where are the Women in Canadian Politics?" *Atlantis* 3, 2 (1978): 40–51; M. Janine Brodie and Jill Vickers, "The More Things Change . . . Women in the 1979 Federal Campaign," in *Canada at the Polls: 1979 and 1980*, edited by Howard R. Penniman (Washington, D.C.: American Enterprise Institute, 1981), 322–36; Christiane Noiseux Bacave, "Le Recrutement politique des femmes au Québec" (paper presented at Canadian Political Science Association meetings, Saskatoon, 1979); Kathryn M. Kopinak, "Women in Canadian Municipal Politics: 'Why so Few?' and 'Why so Many?' " (unpublished manuscript, 1981); and Sandra D. Burt, "The Political Participation of Women in Ontario" (Ph.D. dissertation, York University, 1981).

5. For a concise treatment of constraints upon female participation, see Jeane J. Kirkpatrick, *Political Woman* (New York: Basic Books, 1974), ch. 1.

6. Harold G. Clarke and Allan Kornberg, "Moving up the Political Escalator: Women Party Officials in the United States and Canada," *Journal of Politics* 41, 2 (1979): 442–76; and Allan Kornberg, Joel Smith, and Harold D. Clarke, *Citizen Politicians — Canada* (Durham, N.C.: Carolina Academic Press, 1979), ch. 8.

7. Clarke and Kornberg, "Moving up the Political Escalator," 475.

8. John Meisel, *Working Papers on Canadian Politics* (Montreal and London: McGill-Queen's University Press, 1975); and Jean Laponce, *People vs. Politics* (Toronto: University of Toronto Press, 1969). For a longitudinal analysis of women's partisan attitudes in English Canada, see Sylvia Bashevkin, "Women and Change: A Comparative Study of Political Attitudes in France, Canada, and the United States" (Ph.D. dissertation, York University, 1981), 151–72.

9. Robert J. Drummond, "Voting Behaviour: Casting the Play," in *The Government and Politics of Ontario*, edited by Donald C. MacDonald (Toronto: Van Nostrand Reinhold, 1980), 272–89.

10. See Bashevkin, "Women and Change," for a more thorough discussion of the development of women's political attitudes in North America and Western Europe.

11. On longitudinal change in female partisanship, see ibid.

12. When asked to estimate roughly the proportions of men and women who hold membership in their organizations, officials of all three parties were unwilling to hazard a guess. It should be noted that under the NDP affirmative action resolution passed in February 1982, party membership will be coded for gender. One difficulty in attempting to estimate Ontario party memberships is that in the Ontario Liberal Party, women can be members through provincial ridings as well as through women's Liberal associations or clubs recognized by the party Executive. In addition, Progressive Conservative women may hold membership through ridings, or through riding or district associations of women recognized by the Executive of the Provincial Women's Association.

13. I am indebted to Marilyn Roycroft and Marianne Holder of the Ontario NDP for sharing findings from their 1973 and 1980 studies, and to Ruth Archibald and Aase Hueglin of the Progressive Conservative party for making available the 1977 OPCAW task force results.

14. According to party records, Ontario Liberal riding executives do not include a specific membership position.

15. In the provincial NDP, for example, two of the three London-area constituency organizations were headed by women in 1981, as were those in a number of rural Liberal and suburban government-held seats. Liberal women were elected as constituency presidents in such strong PC ridings as York Mills, Oriole, Scarborough Centre, and Sault Ste. Marie, as well as in the NDP-held seats at Algoma and York South.

16. For a brief review of feminist activism in Canada, see Lynne Teather, "The Feminist Mosaic," in *Women in the Canadian Mosaic*, edited by Gwen Matheson (Toronto: Peter Martin, 1976), 301–46.

17. Constitution of the Ontario Liberal Party (June 1981), article VI, section 3, part c.

18. Constitution of the Ontario Progressive Conservative Association (June 1980), article 9, section f.

19. Ibid., article 4, section a, part xi; and article 14, section 1.

20. Constitution and Resolution of the New Democratic Party of Ontario (June 1980), article 9, section 3.

21. Resolution of 14-33, Affirmative Action Program, to the Eleventh Convention of the Ontario New Democratic Party. This resolution also sets out to: 1) broaden the NDP electoral base by emphasizing policies of particular relevance to women both between and during election campaigns; 2) develop a leadership training programme for women; and 3) recruit female candidates in strong ridings, and to assist with the child care and household management expenses of candidates.

314 SYLVIA B. BASHEVKIN

22. See notes 1 and 4, above.

23. It is important to note that 22 of the 27 female candidates finishing third in 1981 were New Democrats. Since the NDP as a whole fared quite poorly in the most recent provincial elections, and since women candidates were disproportionately New Democrats in 1981 (24 of 45, or 53.3 percent), then at least part of the third-place finish phenomenon would have to be attributed to particular features of partisan competition in 1981.

24. It should be noted that the seven housewives who ran as provincial candidates in 1977 were clustered primarily in rural ridings.

25. It is in this area of electoral mobility that the importance of women's participation in municipal politics becomes clear. See Kopinak, "Women in Canadian Municipal Politics," and Brodie, "The Recruitment of Canadian Women," 12.

26. Between 1971 and 1981, the NDP fielded 63 women candidates, the Liberals ran 45, and the Conservatives fielded 37. On Copps' leadership candidacy, see Sylvia B. Bashevkin, "Women and Party Politics: The 1982 Ontario Leadership Conventions" (unpublished manuscript, 1982).

27. Naomi Black, "Changing European and North American Attitudes Toward Women in Public Life," *Journal of European Integration* 1, 2 (1978): 221–40.

28. Thelma McCormack, "Toward a Non-Sexist Perspective on Social and Political Change," in *Another Voice*, edited by Marcia Millman and Rosabeth Moss Kanter (New York: Anchor, 1975), 1-33.

FURTHER READING

General

Bishop, Olga, B. Barbara, I. Irwin, and Clara G. Miller, eds. *Bibliography of Ontario History, 1867–1976: Cultural, Economic, Political, Social.* 2 vols. Toronto: University of Toronto Press, 1980.

Bothwell, Robert. *A Short History of Ontario.* Edmonton: Hurtig Publishers, 1986.

Bray, Matt, and Ernie Epp, eds. *A Vast and Magnificent Land: An Illustrated History of Northern Ontario.* Thunder Bay: Lakehead University, 1984.

Careless, J.M.S. *Toronto to 1918: An Illustrated History.* Toronto: James Lorimer, 1984.

Forman, Debra, ed. *Legislators and Legislatures of Ontario.* I. *1792–1866.* II. *1867–1929.* III. *1930–1984.* Toronto: Legislative Library, Research and Information Services, 1984.

English, John and Kenneth McLaughlin. *Kitchener: An Illustrated History.* Waterloo: Wilfrid Laurier University Press, 1983.

Fryer, Mary Beacock, and Charles J. Humber, eds. *Loyal She Remains: A Pictorial History of Ontario.* Toronto: United Empire Loyalists' Association of Canada, 1984.

Gentilcore, R. Louis, and C. Grant Head. *Ontario's History in Maps.* Toronto: University of Toronto Press, 1984.

Gilbert, Angus, ed. "Special Issue/Numero special: Historical Essays on Northern Ontario," *Laurentian University Review* XI, 2 (1979): 1–116.

Konrad, Victor A. "Ontario: A Bicentennial Retrospective," *American Review of Canadian Studies* XIV (1984): 125–36.

Lemon, James. *Toronto Since 1918: An Illustrated History.* Toronto: James Lorimer, 1985.

Macdonald, Donald C. *The Government and Politics of Ontario.* Toronto: Macmillan of Canada, 1975.

——————— . *The Government and Politics of Ontario.* 2nd ed. Toronto: Van Nostrand Reinhold, 1980.

——————— . *The Government and Politics of Ontario.* 3rd ed. Scarborough, Ont.: Nelson Canada, 1985.

Macgillivray, Royce, "Local History as a Form of Popular Culture in Ontario." *New York History* LXV (1984): 367–76.

Osborne, Brian, and Donald Swainson. *Kingston: An Illustrated History.* Toronto: James Lorimer, 1984.

Russell, Victor L. *Forging a Consensus: Historical Essays on Toronto.* Toronto: University of Toronto Press, 1984.

Schull, Joseph. *Ontario Since 1867.* Toronto: McClelland and Stewart, 1978.

Swainson, Donald, ed. *Oliver Mowat's Ontario.* Toronto: Macmillan of Canada, 1972.

Weaver, John C. *Hamilton: An Illustrated History.* Toronto: James Lorimer, 1982.
White, Randall. *Ontario: A Political and Economic History, 1610–1985.* Toronto: Dundurn Press, 1985.

Political History

Armstrong, Christopher, *The Politics of Federalism: Ontario's Relations with the Federal Government. 1867–1942.* Toronto: University of Toronto Press, 1981.
Beaven, Brian P.N. "Partisanship, Patronage, and the Press in Ontario, 1880–1914: Myths and Realities." *Canadian Historical Review* LXIV (1983): 317–51.
Careless, J.M.S., ed. *The Pre-Confederation Premiers: Ontario Government Leaders, 1841–1867.* Toronto: University of Toronto Press, 1980.
Beeby, Dean. "Women in the Ontario C.C.F., 1940–1950." *Ontario History* LXXIV (1982): 258–83.
Bullen, John. "The Ontario Waffle and the Struggle for an Independent Socialist Canada: Conflict within the NDP." *Canadian Historical Review* LXIV (1983): 188–215.
Gillis, Peter. "Big Business and the Origins of the Conservative Reform Movement in Ottawa, 1890–1912." *Journal of Canadian Studies* XV, 1 (1980): 93–109.
Hoy, Claire. *Bill Davis: A Biography.* Toronto: Methuen Publications, 1985.
Humphries, Charles W. *"Honest Enough to Be Bold": The Life and Times of Sir James Pliny Whitney.* Toronto: University of Toronto Press, 1985.
Livermore, J.D. "The Ontario Election of 1871: A Case Study of the Transfer of Political Power." *Ontario History* LXXI (1979): 39–52.
McDougall, Allan K. *John P. Robarts: His Life and Government.* Toronto: University of Toronto Press, 1985.
Manley, John. "Women and the Left in the 1930s: The Case of the Toronto CCF Women's Joint Committee." *Atlantis* V, 2 (1980): 100–19.
Morley, J.T. *Secular Socialists: The CCF/NDP in Ontario — A Biography.* Montreal and Kingston: McGill-Queen's University Press, 1984.
Morton, Desmond. "The *Globe* and the Labour Question: Ontario Liberalism in the 'Great Upheaval,' May, 1886," *Ontario History* LXXIII (1981): 19–39.
Neill, Robin. "The Politics and Economics of Development in Ontario," *Ontario History* LXX (1978): 281–90.
Oliver, Peter. *G. Howard Ferguson: Ontario Tory.* Toronto: University of Toronto Press, 1977.
—————————. *Public and Private Persons: The Ontario Political Culture, 1914–1934.* Toronto: Clarke, Irwin and Company, 1975.
Pennefather, R.S. "The Orange Order and the United Farmers of Ontario, 1919–1923." *Ontario History* LXIX (1977): 169–84.
Russell, Victor, *Mayors of Toronto.* I. *1834–1899.* II. *1900–1984.* Erin, Ont.: Boston Mills Press, 1982, 1984.

Economic History

Ankli, Robert E., and Wendy Millar, "Ontario Agriculture in Transition: The Switch from Wheat to Cheese." *Journal of Economic History* XLII (1982): 207–15.

Beach, Noel. "Nickel Capital: Sudbury and the Nickel Industry, 1902–1925." *Laurentian University Review* VI, 3 (1974): 55–74.

Bloomfield, E. "Municipal Bonusing of Industry: The Legislative Framework in Ontario to 1930." *Urban History Review* IX, 3 (1981): 59–76.

de Visser, J., R. Sallows, and J. Carroll. *The Farm: A Celebration of 200 Years of Farming in Ontario.* Toronto: Methuen, 1984.

Lawr, D.A. "The Development of Ontario Farming, 1870–1914: Patterns of Growth and Change." *Ontario History* LXIV (1972): 239–51.

McDowall, Duncan. *Steel at the Sault: Francis H. Clergue, Sir James Dunn, and the Algoma Steel Corporation, 1901–1956.* Toronto: University of Toronto Press, 1984.

Marshall, John U., and W.R. Smith, "The Dynamics of Growth in a Regional Urban System: Southern Ontario, 1851–1971." *Canadian Geographer* XXII (1978): 22–40.

Nelles, H.V. *The Politics of Development: Forests, Mines and Hydro-electric Power in Ontario, 1849–1941.* Toronto: Macmillan of Canada, 1974.

Rea, K.J. *The Prosperous Years: The Economic History of Ontario, 1939–1975.* Toronto: University of Toronto Press, 1985.

Risk, R.C.B. "The Golden Age: The Law About the Market in Nineteenth-Century Ontario." *University of Toronto Law Journal* XXVI (1976): 307–46.

Social History

Acton, Janice, Penny Goldsmith, and Bonnie Shepard, eds. *Women at Work: Ontario 1850–1920.* Toronto: Canadian Women's Educational Press, 1974.

Akenson, Donald Harman. *The Irish in Ontario: A Study in Rural History.* Kingston and Montreal: McGill-Queen's University Press, 1984.

Archibald, Clinton. "La Pensée politique des Franco-Ontariens au XXe Siècle." *Revue du Nouvel Ontario* II (1979): 13–30.

Arnopoulos, Sheila McLeod. *Voices from French Ontario.* Toronto: University of Toronto Press, 1982.

Axelrod, Paul. *Scholars and Dollars: Politics, Economics, and the Universities of Ontario, 1945–1980.* Toronto: University of Toronto Press, 1982.

Biggs, C. Lesley. "The Case of the Missing Midwives: A History of Midwifery in Ontario from 1795–1900." *Ontario History* LXXV (1983): 21–35.

Bacchi, Carol. "Race Regeneration and Social Purity: A Study of the Social Attitudes of Canada's English-Speaking Suffragists." *Histoire sociale/Soical History* XI (1978): 460–74.

Ball, Rosemary R. " 'A Perfect Farmer's Wife': Women in 19th-Century Rural Ontario." *Canada, An Historical Magazine* III, 2 (1975): 2–21.

Bator, Paul Adolphus. "The Health Reformers versus the Common Canadian: The Controversy Over Compulsory Vaccination against Smallpox in Toronto and Ontario, 1900–1920." *Ontario History* LXXV (1983): 348–73.

Cheal, David J. "Ontario Loyalism: A Socio-Religious Ideology in Decline," *Canadian Ethnic Studies* XIII, 2 (1981): 40–51.

Choquette, Robert. *L'église catholique dans l'Ontario française du dix-neuvième siècle.* Ottawa: Éditions de l'Université d'Ottawa, 1984.

_____ . *Language and Religion: A History of English-French Conflict in Ontario.* Ottawa: University of Ottawa Press, 1975.

_____ . *L'Ontario française historique.* Montreal-Quebec: Éditions Études vivantes, 1980.

Clement, Wallace. "The Subordination of Labour in Canadian Mining." *Labour/Le Travailleur* V (1980): 133–48.

Danylewycz, Marta, Beth Light, and Alison Prentice, "The Evolution of the Sexual Division of Labour in Teaching: A Nineteenth-Century Ontario and Quebec Case Study." *Histoire sociale/Social History* XVI (1983): 81–110.

Dennie, Donald. "Le mouvement syndical en Ontario . . . et les Franco-Ontariens." *Revue du Nouvel Ontario* II (1979): 41–58.

De Villiers-Westfall, William E. "The Dominion of the Lord: An Introduction to the Cultural History of Protestant Ontario in the Victorian Period." *Queen's Quarterly* LXXXIII (1976): 47–70.

D'Iorio, Antonio. "Les idéologies de l'Ontario française: un choix de textes (1912–1980)." *Revue du Nouvel Ontario* III (1981): 1–115.

Dodd, Dianne. "The Hamilton Birth Control Clinic of the 1930s." *Ontario History* LXXV (1983): 71–86.

Doucet, Michael J. "Mass Transit and the Failure of Private Ownership: The Case of Toronto in the Early Twentieth Century." *Urban History Review* (1978): 3–33.

_____ . "Space, Sound, Culture, and Politics: Radio Broadcasting in Southern Ontario." *Canadian Geographer* XXVII (1983): 109–27.

Drummond, Ian M. *Political Economy at the University of Toronto: A History of the Department, 1888–1982.* Toronto: University of Toronto Faculty of Arts and Science, 1983.

Gaffield, Chad. "Boom or Bust: The Demography and Economy of the Lower Ottawa Valley in the Nineteenth Century." Canadian Historical Association, *Historical Papers* (1982): 172–95.

Gagan, David. *Hopeful Travellers: Families, Land and Social Change in Mid-Victorian Peel County, Canada West.* Toronto: University of Toronto Press, 1981.

Gauvreau, Michael. "The Taming of History: Reflections on the Canadian Methodist Encounter with Biblical Criticism, 1830–1900." *Canadian Historical Review* LXV (1984): 315–46.

Graff, Harvey J. *The Literacy Myth: Literacy and Social Structure in the Nineteenth-Century City.* New York: Academic Press, 1979.

_____ . "Crime and Punishment in the Nineteenth Century: A New Look at the Criminal." *Journal of Interdisciplinary History* VII (1977): 477–91.

Harney, Robert F., ed. *Gathering Place: Peoples and Neighbourhoods of Toronto.* Toronto: Multicultural History Society of Ontario, 1985.

Heron, Craig, and Bryan D. Palmer. "Through the Prism of the Strike: Industrial Conflict in Southern Ontario, 1901–1914," *Canadian Historical Review* LVIII (1977): 423–58. Reprinted in David J. Bercuson, ed. *Canadian Labour History: Selected Readings*. Toronto: Copp Clark Pitman, 1987.

Homel, Gene Howard. "Denison's Law: Criminal Justice and the Police Court in Toronto, 1877–1921," *Ontario History* LXXIII (1981): 171–86.

Katz, Michael B. *The People of Hamilton, Canada West: Family and Class in a Mid-Nineteenth-Century City.* Cambridge: Harvard University Press, 1975.

Katz, M.B., M.J. Doucet, and M.J. Stern. *The Social Organization of Early Industrial Capitalism.* Cambridge: Harvard University Press, 1982.

Kealey, Gregory S. *Toronto Workers Respond to Industrial Capitalism, 1867–1892.* Toronto: University of Toronto Press, 1980.

Kealey, Gregory S., and Bryan D. Palmer, *"Dreaming of What Might Be": The Knights of Labor in Ontario, 1880–1902.* New York: Cambridge University Press, 1982.

Jones, Andrew, and Leonard Rutman. *In the Children's Aid: J.J. Kelso and Child Welfare in Ontario.* Toronto: University of Toronto Press, 1981.

Lawr, D.A., and R.D. Gidney, "Who Ran the Schools? Local Influence on Education Policy in Nineteenth Century Ontario." *Ontario History* LXXII (1980): 131–43.

Lewis, Jane. "Motherhood Issues during the Late Nineteenth and Early Twentieth Centuries: Some Recent Viewpoints." *Ontario History* LXXV (1983): 4–20.

Li, Peter S. "The Stratification of Ethnic Immigrants: The Case of Toronto." *Canadian Review of Sociology and Anthropology* XV (1978): 31–40.

McConnachie, Kathleen. "Methodology in the Study of Women in History: A Case Study of Helen MacMurchy, M.D." *Ontario History* LXXV (1983): 61–70.

Millett, David. "The Social Context of Bilingualism in Eastern Ontario." *American Review of Canadian Studies* XIII, 1 (1983): 1–12.

Morrison, Jean. "Ethnicity and Class Consciousness: British, Finnish and South European Workers at the Canadian Lakehead Before World War I." *Lakehead University Review* IX, 1 (1976): 41–54.

Morrison, T.R. " 'Their Proper Sphere': Feminism, the Family, and Child-Centred Social Reform in Ontario, 1875–1900. Part I." *Ontario History* LXVIII (1976): 45–64.

—————— . " 'Their Proper Sphere': Feminism, the Family, and Child-Centred Social Reform in Ontario, 1875–1900. Part II." *Ontario History* LXVIII (1976): 65–74.

Oliver, H., M. Holmes, and I. Winchester, eds. *The House that Ryerson Built: Essays on Education to Mark Ontario's Bicentennial.* Toronto: Ontario Institute for Studies in Education, 1984.

Palmer, Bryan D. *A Culture in Conflict: Skilled Workers and Industrial Capitalism in Hamilton, Ontario, 1860–1914.* Montreal: McGill-Queen's University Press, 1979.

Parr, Joy. "Hired Men: Ontario Agricultural Wage Labour in Historical Perspective." *Labour/Le Travail* XV (1985): 91–103.

—————— . *Labouring Children: British Immigrant Apprentices to Canada,*

1869–1924. London: Croom Helm, 1980.

Piva, Michael J. *The Condition of the Working Class in Toronto, 1900–1921.* Ottawa: University of Ottawa Press, 1979.

_____ . "The Toronto District Labour Council and Independent Political Action: Factionalism and Frustration, 1900–1921," *Labour/Le Travailleur* IV (1979): 115–30.

Prentice, Alison. *The School Promoters: Education and Social Class in Mid-Nineteenth-Century Upper Canada.* Toronto: McClelland and Stewart, 1977.

Radforth, Ian. "Woodworkers and the Mechanization of the Pulpwood Logging Industry in Northern Ontario, 1950–1970." Canadian Historical Association, *Historical Papers* (1982): 71–102.

Roberts, Wayne. "Artisans, Aristocrats and Handymen: Politics and Unionism among Toronto Skilled Building Trades Workers, 1896–1914," *Labour/Le Travailleur* I (1976): 92–121.

_____ . "Toronto Metal Workers and the Second Industrial Revolution, 1889–1914," *Labour/Le Travailleur* VI (1980): 49–73.

Rooke, Patricia J. and R.L. Schnell. " 'An Idiot's Flowerbed': A Study of Charlotte Whitton's Feminist Thought, 1941–50," *International Journal of Women's Studies* V (1982): 29–46. Reprinted in Veronica Strong-Boag and Anita Clair Fellman, eds. *Rethinking Canada: The Promise of Women's History.* Toronto: Copp Clark Pitman, 1986.

_____ . "The Rise and Decline of British North American Protestant Orphan's Homes as Women's Domain, 1850–1930." *Atlantis* VII, 2 (1982): 21–35.

Royce, Marion. "Methodism and the Education of Women in Nineteenth Century Ontario." *Atlantis* III, 2 (1978): 131–43.

Sangster, Joan. "The 1907 Bell Telephone Strike: Organizing Women Workers." *Labour/Le Travailleur* III (1978): 109–30. Reprinted in Veronica Strong-Boag and Anita Clair Fellman, eds. *Rethinking Canada: The Promise of Women's History.* Toronto: Copp Clark Pitman, 1986.

Savard, Pierre. "De la difficulté d'être Franco-Ontarien." *Revue du Nouvel Ontario* I (1978): 11–23.

Stamp, Robert M. *The Schools of Ontario, 1876–1976.* Toronto: University of Toronto Press, 1982.

Trofimenkoff, Susan Mann. "One Hundred and Two Muffled Voices: Canada's Industrial Women in the 1880s," *Atlantis* III, 1 (1977): 66–82. Reprinted in Veronica Strong-Boag and Anita Clair Fellman, eds. *Rethinking Canada: The Promise of Women's History.* Toronto: Copp Clark Pitman, 1986.

Zerker, Sally F. *The Rise and Fall of the Toronto Typographical Union, 1832–1972: A Case Study of Foreign Domination.* Toronto: University of Toronto Press, 1982.

David P. Gagan, "Families and Land: The Mid-Century Crisis." From David P. Gagan, *Hopeful Travellers: Families, Land and Social Change in Mid-Victorian Peel County, Canada West* (Toronto, 1981), 40-60. Reprinted by permission of University of Toronto Press. © Her Majesty the Queen in right of the Province of Ontario 1981.

Paul Craven and Tom Traves, "Canadian Railways as Manufacturers, 1850-1880," Canadian Historical Association, *Historical Papers* (1983): 254-81. Reprinted by permission of the authors and the Canadian Historical Association.

Stephen A. Speisman, "Munificent Parsons and Municipal Parsimony: Voluntary vs. Public Poor Relief in Nineteenth Century Toronto," *Ontario History* 65, no. 1 (1973): 33-49; Marilyn Barber, "The Women Ontario Welcomed: Immigrant Domestics for Ontario Homes, 1870-1930," *Ontario History* 72, no. 3 (1980): 148-73. Reprinted by permission of the Ontario Historical Society.

Gregory S. Kealey, "The Orange Order in Toronto: Religious Riot and the Working Class." From Gregory S. Kealey, *Toronto Workers Respond to Industrial Capitalism 1867-1892* (Toronto, 1980), 98-123. Reprinted by permission of University of Toronto Press. © University of Toronto Press 1980.

Kenneth C. Dewar, "Private Electrical Utilities and Municipal Ownership in Ontario, 1891-1900." This article was first published in the *Urban History Review/Revue d'histoire urbaine* XII (June 1983): 29-38. Reprinted by permission of the journal.

Craig Heron, "The Crisis of the Craftsman: Hamilton's Metal Workers in the Early Twentieth Century." Reprinted from *Labour/Le Travailleur* 6 (1980), pp. 7-48 with the permission of the editor. © Committee on Canadian Labour History.

Robert M. Stamp, "The New Education Movement: Those 'Yankee Frills.'" From Robert M. Stamp, *The Schools of Ontario 1876-1976* (Toronto, 1982), 51-73. Reprinted by permission of University of Toronto Press. © Her Majesty the Queen in right of the Province of Ontario 1982.

Peter Oliver, "The Resolution of the Ontario Bilingual Schools Crisis, 1919-1929," *Journal of Canadian Studies/Revue d'études canadiennes* 7 (1972): 22-45; Sylvia B. Bashevkin, "Women's Participation in the Ontario Political Parties, 1971-1981," *Journal of Canadian Studies/Revue d'études canadiennes* 17 (1982): 44-54. Reprinted by permission of the authors and the journal.

John C. Weaver, "From Land Assembly to Social Maturity: The Suburban Life of Westdale (Hamilton), Ontario, 1911-1951," *Histoire sociale/Social History* 11 (1978): 411-40. Reprinted by permission of the journal.

Marc J. Gotlieb, "George Drew and the Dominion-Provincial Conference on Reconstruction of 1945-6," *Canadian Historical Review* 66, no. 1 (1985): 27-47. Reprinted by permission of the author and the University of Toronto Press.

Peter Oliver, "Inner City Politician." From *Unlikely Tory: The Life and Politics of Alan Grossman*, by Peter Oliver, © Peter Oliver, 1985. Reprinted by permission of Lester & Orpen Dennys Ltd., Toronto.

Vaughan Lyon, "Minority Government in Ontario, 1975-1981: An Assessment," *Canadian Journal of Political Science* 17 (1984): 685-705. Reprinted by permission of the author and the journal.

1   2   3   4   5   135531   92 91 90 89 88
0-7730-4739-5